Skull Wars

"*Skull Wars* holds a mirror up to the archaeological community. By helping us see ourselves as we are, Thomas' book will help us understand the sometimes awkward and contentious, but potentially enriching, relationships that can and must be forged between Native Americans and archaeologists."

—David J. Meltzer
Southern Methodist University

"*Skull Wars* treads on delicate and controversial historical ground avoided by many scientists. With characteristic and refreshing frankness, David Hurst Thomas explores competing visions of the early American past and points the way to a new scholarly world where archaeologists do not necessarily call the intellectual shots. This extraordinary and important book is bound to send shock waves through the halls of academe."

—Brian Fagan
Author of *The Great Journey* and *Floods, Famines, and Emperors*

"An outstanding scholarly study of the root causes of the distrust between archaeologists and Native American groups. . . . [An] important piece of work."

—*Library Journal*

"Thorough, detailed, important and well documented."

—The *Seattle Times*

"The ancient history of America is being rewritten, and David Hurst Thomas has written a report from the front lines."

—*Insight*

DAVID HURST THOMAS

Skull Wars

KENNEWICK MAN, ARCHAEOLOGY, AND THE
BATTLE FOR NATIVE AMERICAN IDENTITY

BASIC
BOOKS

A Member of the Perseus Book Group

Published by Basic Books,
A Member of the Perseus Book Group

FIRST PAPERBACK EDITION

LIBRARY OF CONGRESS CATALOGING-IN-PUBLICATION DATA

Thomas, David Hurst.
The skull wars: Kennewick man, archeology, and the Battle for
Native American identity / David Hurst Thomas.
p.   cm.
ISBN-13 978-0-465-09225-3
ISBN-10 0-465-09225-X
1. Indians of North America—Antiquities—Collection and preservation. 2. Kennewich Man. 3. Anthropology—United States—History. 4. Racism—United States. 5. Indians of North America—Ethnic identity. I. Title.

E77.9.T54   2000   99-087516
970.004976dc21

Designed by Jaye Zimet

ILLUSTRATION CREDITS

Page xviii: The Kennewick Fracas: Copyright © 1999 Matt Wverker; xxiii: Reconstruction of Kennewick Man: Copyright © 1999 Jim Chatters; xxiii: Patrick Stewart: The Kobal Collection; xxiii: Chief Black Hawk: The Thomas Glicrease Institute of American History; 24: a) Tom Torlino before and b) Tom Torlino after: The Cumberland County Historical Society; 54: Self portrait of Charles Willson Peale: Pennsylvania Academy of the Fine Arts; 61: a) Franz Boas and b) Hamatsa life-group: National Museum of Natural Historyñ Smithsonian Institution; 66: Alice Cunningham Fletcher: National Museum of Natural History/Smithsonian Institution; 72: a) Frank H. Cushing and b) Frank H. Cushing in Zuni garb: National Museum of Natural History/ Smithsonian Institution; 80: a) Minik in an Eskimo costume and b) Minik with his bicycle: American Museum of Natural History; 86: a) Ishi and b) Ishi two months later: Phoebe Apperson Hearst Museum of Anthropology; 126: Excavating an Ancient Indian Mound: The Saint Louis Art Museum; 135: Paleolithic Handaxes: American Museum of Natural History; 143: George Gillette: AP/Wide World Photos; 150: Folsom points: American Museum of Natural History; 154: Clovis points: American Museum of Natural History; 256: There are early photographs of me: Copyright © N. Scott Momaday.

A NOTE ABOUT HUMAN REMAINS
This book argues, among other things, that scientists must deal with human bones in a more respectful and sensitive manner. Several Native American elders have requested that I not publish photographs or other depictions of American Indian skeletal remains. In specific response to this request, no such images appear in this book.

A significant portion of the proceeds from this book are being donated to the Arthur Parker/Native American Scholarship Fund of the Society for American Archaeology. I believe strongly in this program, which is specifically designed to assist Indian people wishing to pursue advanced studies in archaeology. I respectfully request that other archaeologists writing books-for-profit about American Indians give some serious thought to donating (at least part of) their royalties to the Parker Fund.

I believe it's a wise investment.

DHT

CONTENTS

Part I NAMES AND IMAGES

1 COLUMBUS, ARAWAKS, AND CARIBS: THE POWER TO NAME | 3

Columbus exercises his colonial prerogative to name his discoveries and defines Indian stereotypes that will survive for centuries.

2 A VANISHING AMERICAN ICON | 11

The American Revolution fosters an image of the Indian as an American icon that helps define the New Republic as distinct from Mother England. But the flesh-and-blood Indian is not welcome in nineteenth-century America and must either assimilate or be exterminated.

Part II NINETEENTH-CENTURY SCIENTISTS

once and for all. American anthropologists convert scientific principle into disastrous federal Indian policy.

Frank Cushing pioneers the "participant observation" method of ethnographic research and draws upon rich Native American oral traditions to help interpret archaeological materials from the American Southwest. Although an effective cultural broker between the Zuni and non-Zuni, Cushing also irritates Indian people by making their most private rituals public.

Six Polar Eskimos find themselves stranded on New York's fashionable Central Park West in 1897, an anthropological experiment gone awry. The myth of the Noble Redman comes alive when Ishi—the world's "most uncivilized, uncontaminated man"—wanders out of the California chaparral to become a living museum exhibition in San Francisco. But his death in 1916 triggers a certain regret in mainstream America that the Indian has indeed vanished.

Despite considerable personal risk, a number of Indian people rush to record their vanishing traditions and preserve their disappearing customs. But early twentieth-century anthropology declares that "aboriginal logic" and oral tradition are incompatible with the new objective framework of the "science of mankind." Robert Lowie admits that he "cannot attach to oral traditions any historical value whatsoever under any conditions whatsoever," in the process declaring American Indians to be irrelevant to their own history.

Franz Boas, one of America's most avid skull collectors, initiates a research program that soundly disproves earlier theories of racial determinism. Although mainstream anthropology eventually rejects the concept of enduring racial types and race, vestiges of such thinking resurface to complicate the Kennewick Man controversy.

Part III DEEP AMERICAN HISTORY

12 ORIGIN MYTHS FROM MAINSTREAM AMERICA | *123*

Seeking national history on an epic scale, mainstream Euroamerica explores a range of creation stories to explain the First Americans. Dreams of lost prehistoric races surface across nineteenth-century America—from ancient white Moundbuilders to the Red Sons of Israel to the Arizona Aztecs—looking to archaeology to define a heroic (non-Indian) past.

13 THE SMITHSONIAN TAKES ON ALL COMERS | *133*

New waves of professionally trained archaeologists demolish the mythical Moundbuilders, protect America from a Paleolithic invasion, and attempt to purge amateurs from the business of American archaeology.

14 WHERE ARE ALL THE NATIVE AMERICAN ARCHAEOLOGISTS? | *139*

Although American Indians had been written out of mainstream American history, a residual Indianness helped make the concept of America actually work. Congress passed the 1906 Antiquities Act to protect America's archaeological heritage and, in the process, establish professional archaeologists as the sole proprietors of the remote Indian past—now defined as part of the greater public trust, like Yellowstone and the American bison.

15 BREAKTHROUGH AT FOLSOM | *145*

A catastrophic flash flood exposes bison bones and artifacts near Folsom, New Mexico, and forces professional archaeology, virtually overnight, to award Indian people Ice-Age tenure in America.

16 BUSTING THE CLOVIS BARRIER | *157*

Despite his "spaghetti budget" at Monte Verde, Chile, Tom Dillehay surmounts a solid wall of skepticism to establish, apparently, the presence of pre-Clovis people in the Americas.

The Kennewick and Monte Verde finds have turned the conservative world of First American archaeology upside down. Archaeologists, physical anthropologists, linguists, and molecular biologists scramble to frame new and largely untested theories to explain the first human presence in the Americas.

Indians in the early twentieth century announce that they have not vanished. They are here to stay and intend to use Indian imagery for their own benefit. Several prominent Indians take on roles as cultural mediators, seeking to span the social and racial gulfs between early-twentieth-century Indians and non-Indians.

During the Great Depression, John Collier brings a different perspective to the Bureau of Indian Affairs. The Indian Reorganization Act of 1934 reverses previous assimilation policies and reaffirms the importance of the tribal concept in restoring Indian sovereignty.

In 1969, Deloria publishes Custer Died for Your Sins: An Indian Manifesto, *heavily criticizing anthropology's mandate to study Indians as "pure research." Scoffing at their self-proclaimed "objectivity," he brands archaeologists as exploiters of Indian people, and asks them to stop digging up the dead.*

Congress passes the NAGPRA bill of 1990 that shifts the national narrative by inviting Native Americans to assign their own spiritual and historical meanings to archaeological sites and their contents. Repatriation and reburial become the law of the land, with predictably mixed results as the bones go home.

Part V BRIDGING THE CHASM

NAGPRA directs America's museums to establish the modern tribal affiliation, if any, of ancient human remains and sacred objects in their collections. But previous federal legislation defines modern American Indian tribes in mostly political terms, and scientists have difficulty in tracing tribal ancestry in the archaeological record. Indians deeply resent the fact that archaeologists still control the dialogue linking modern tribes to their ancestors.

While many archaeologists rethink their role as hardcore, "objective" scientists, anthropology at the millennium is revisiting its humanistic roots. Having rejected oral tradition for decades, a number of archaeologists are now exploring traditional knowledge as another key to learning about America's ancient past. Some Indian people welcome the inquiry, others fear that science is once again trying to pry into sacred territory.

Putting aside stale stereotypes, several tribes are actively working with archaeologists to explore their own past. Within this new spirit of cooperation, an increasing number of Native Americans are deciding to pursue careers in professional archaeology.

FOREWORD

WE HAVE TOO much information today. We are saturated by isolated facts for which we have great difficulty finding any familiar context. Indeed, "publication" no longer means acceptance by a prestigious journal. It can often mean simply posting an item on the Internet or talking with a reporter. We have come to believe that what is new is true, and so almost anyone can represent anything by merely appearing as a public figure in a discussion. How then can we make sense of what we think we know? One pseudo-fact can become the pivotal point in a controversy no one understands. Nowhere is this condition more endemic than the social sciences, but geology and archaeology contribute more than their share of confusion.

The social sciences badly need to take a break, collect their thoughts, begin to produce reliable histories of their respective disciplines, and clearly articulate their fundamental doctrines so that we can see the various trees of thought that represent the forests in which we labor. At present only people trained in the various social sciences have any idea where they began, where they have traveled, and where they are now. Lay people have not the slightest notion where social science doctrines and ideas originate. Nor do they know what are "acceptable" beliefs to which a majority of any discipline would subscribe. Scholars working in other disciplines rarely get a glimpse into the inner working of neighboring sciences, so they accept much of the core scientific doctrine in the belief that others have been as rigorous, informed, and sincere as themselves.

The Law provides a sensible and useful model for the social sciences to consider. Recognizing that doctrines change with the passage of time, the development of new theories, and the admissibility of new kinds of evidence, the legal profession has a practice of appointing a prestigious committee of experienced scholars and practicing lawyers to review the various fields of law and issue what are called "Restatements." These documents summarize the current state of such topics as contracts, torts, procedure, and so forth. Judges, justices, practicing attorneys, legal aids, and interested lay people can turn to the Restatements and find an authoritative interpretation of the state of law without engaging in endless searches or being drawn into internecine battles about the primacy of any particular doctrine.

Such a practice might be immensely useful to the rest of the academic disciplines in ensuring that they remain credible sources of reliable information. The American Anthropological Association sent a statement to the Bureau of the Census in 1998 stating that race could not be determined scientifically. At the same time several prominent scholars were in federal court claiming that they had an overwhelming need to do tests on a skeleton found on the banks of the Columbia River, and many archaeologists encouraged the media to believe that they could determine the race of the remains. How can we have such conflicting views? What is the orthodox and proven here and what is speculation?.

Fortunately, we have before us now a major effort to provide an honest history of American archaeology, at least as it has touched human beings—a topic that has hitherto been avoided or summarized in exotic technical articles inaccessible to most interested people. It is, frankly, refreshing and liberating to read *Skull Wars*, since some of the recommended readings I have encountered have been more in the nature of theological apologetics than starkly honest. Here we have a book that serves as a brilliant companion to Stephen Jay Gould's *The Mismeasure of Man* in educating us about the troubles and triumphs of establishing a body of knowledge about our ancestors. *Skull Wars*, consequently, will draw a certain amount of fire from the profession for its frankness and its invitation to the public to learn more about archaeology—more, perhaps, than "the profession" would like us to know.

When I read the manuscript, my rage was almost incandescent, and brushfires of emotion still break out when I think back to the senseless and racist attitudes that have been acceptable to many archaeologists and anthropologists. Unfortunately, some of these ideas are still promoted by segments of the discipline. It is a sordid history and one that was probably kept from the public for many years. Would prestigious scholars have admitted to the world the robbing of Indian graves for the skulls only hours after an internment ceremony? Upon more reflection, however, I began to realize that part of my anger was at my own appalling ignorance of how archaeology developed in the first place.

Why didn't I know these things? How could I not have been skeptical of apparent truths so easily voiced by archaeologists when it seems plainly evident that many of their cherished doctrines are simply speculations that have become doctrine only because senior professors prefer to believe them? How could Junius Bird go to Monte Verde knowing little about the site's stratigraphy, spend forty-five minutes examining the artifacts, and reject the findings? How could thousands of trees have died to provide reams of paper for speculations on "Clovis Man" when the amount of worthwhile evidence can be mailed with a single postage stamp?

Each page here is a revelation, if you are as uninformed as I was, and teaches the reader to look critically at the current headlines instead of cheering science and moving to the sports section. Do we have Australian Aborigines as first settlers in the Western Hemisphere, exterminated by Mongol hordes who swept over the Bering Strait and immediately headed toward South America? Did Europeans march across some 1,400 miles of ice pack from France to Newfoundland to beat out Indians coming from the west? Did Africans colonize Central America in order to carve massive Olmec heads and bury them in the jungles? Can you compare some verb tenses and a few nouns in some Indian languages with some obscure Chinese dialect and announce that "waves" of Indians came across the Bering Strait? Can we pretend that the Vikings, the premier sailors and explorers of the Christian era, were content to set up a small winter village on the continent and explore no further? Is archaeology now more puffery than science?

Why are all of these speculations now demanding our attention? Well, the Native American Graves Protection and Repatriation Act (NAGPRA), passed some years ago with the consent and cooperation of archaeologists, is now experiencing its first major challenge. Congress, in passing the legislation, accepted without comment the popular interpretation of North American prehistory: Indians came first via the Bering Strait—a myth with little to recommend it. NAGPRA then stated that Indians needed only to prove their "cultural affiliation" to demand that bones be returned to them for reburial.

What is cultural affiliation? If you would take the traditional economic areas sketched out by anthropologists—hunters, fishermen, farmers, eastern woodlands, etc.—it would seem to me that about all a tribe would have to prove is that they occupied an area prior to Columbus. The scales were thus tilted far to the side that favored Indians—for a change. But this interpretation was also unfavorable to Indians, as people would be expected to enter every controversy involving ancient bones within a reasonable distance of their traditional occupancy area—whether they wanted to be involved or not. This is why, in some of the most controversial problems today, scholars have shifted their attack to demanding *genetic* proof of tribal affiliation—again, not difficult, but more complicated for many tribes.

Nevertheless, in most areas, scholars and Indians have worked together to discover as much as possible about newly discovered remains. When scholars have gone directly to the tribes involved, much progress has been made. But archaeology has always been dominated by those who waved "science" in front of us like an inexhaustible credit card, and we have deferred to them—believing that they represent the discipline in an objective and unbiased manner. Yet the discovery of a skeleton in the Columbia River with an arrowhead in his bones led to an excessively confused lawsuit over the treatment of the skeleton and a spate of claims by scholars that this skeleton could rewrite the history of the Western Hemisphere.

It has been an amazing experience to watch this discipline throw all caution to the winds and announce wild speculations as proven advances in science. Can a few archaeologists be so concerned with NAGPRA that they are willing to destroy the intellectual base of their own profession to negate it? Apparently so. The erosion will gnaw at the image of archaeology like a cancer. How, the layperson will ask, does archaeological speculation differ from Erich von Daniken's citation of the Nazca lines as evidence of early spacemen?

David Hurst Thomas now marches into the swamp with the news, honestly stated but hardly welcome to his profession, that we should wash our dirty laundry now before things get completely out of hand, that we should carefully evaluate the present state of the discipline, and that we should build on the positive things now happening and work toward a more cooperative and productive future. Wise thoughts from a courageous thinker. Now, will we heed them?

—Vine Deloria, Jr. (Standing Rock Sioux)
Professor of History, Religious Studies,
and Political Science, University of
Colorado, Boulder

PROLOGUE: A HISTORY
WRITTEN IN BONE

I like the way a man from 9,000 years ago could screw up Jim Chatters' life. He makes a scientific pronouncement like he's done thousands of times before and, in this case, he's opened up a hornet's nest.

—John Hannah (1998), writer for People magazine

IN LATE JULY 1996, the coroner of Benton County, Washington, showed James Chatters a skull that had washed out from a Columbia River cutbank in the town of Kennewick. Chatters runs an archaeological consulting firm that, among things, helps the local coroner's office identify the human skeletons and assorted body parts that occasionally turn up. "Bones are my thing," says Chatters. "I just love puzzles."

Chatters has been doing archaeology in the area for three decades, and he's seen plenty of skulls like this one—long with narrow cheekbones and a protruding upper jaw—a typical middle-aged Caucasoid male, he thought. He accompanied the coroner to where the skull had been found by a couple of college students watching a hydroplane race. Sure enough, more bones were lying about the riverbank, and Chatters collected them all.

Laying out the nearly complete skeleton on a lab table, he took a series of measurements on the skull and long bones, then framed his preliminary

The Kennewick Fracas

forensic conclusion: male, Caucasoid, 40–55 years old at death, height about five feet nine inches. The fellow had lived a rough life. His skull had been fractured, chest crushed, and a chipped elbow reduced the use of his left arm. Some sort of large projectile—maybe a bullet or piece of shrapnel—had penetrated well into the right side of his hip. The man had survived this injury, and the bone had healed over, sealing the object deep inside.

Chatters tried x-raying the pelvis, but nothing showed up—the projectile wasn't metal. A CAT scan showed that it was a stone spear point with a distinctive leaf-shape. Deep inside this man's hip was a "Cascade point" like those used by hunters of the Columbia Plateau between 4,500 and 9,000 years ago. "I've got a white guy with a stone point in him," Chatters later told *The New York Times.* "That's pretty exciting. I thought we had a pioneer."

But Chatters had some doubts. How could a white settler get speared by a stone point perhaps thousands of years old? The badly worn teeth suggested a high-grit diet more typical of ancient Indian populations than Euroamerican pioneers, and the lack of cavities also suggested Native American origins. And the skull just looked, well, old. Dogged by the inconsistencies, Chatters sent a scrap of hand bone to Erv Taylor, whose radiocarbon laboratory at the University of California (Riverside) is one of the world's best.

The lab called back three weeks later with news that would change Chatters' life: the bone sample was 9,200–9,500 years old. That made it one of the half-dozen oldest skeletons in the Americas—perhaps the most complete—and he knew that these results spelled big trouble. Shaken by the implications, Chatters e-mailed several archaeologists across the country asking for advice: "Subject: Need Help ASAP." As he said months later, "I knew then it would get very hot and heavy, which it did within 10 minutes."

So began the furious controversy over Kennewick Man, as Chatters called his find. In an interview with *The New Yorker*, published just months after the Kennewick discovery, Chatters said that he'd been "looking around for someone who matches this Kennewick gentleman, looking for weeks and weeks at people on the street, thinking, 'this one's got a little bit here, that one a little bit there.' And then, one evening, I turned on the TV, and there was Patrick Stewart . . . and I said, 'My God, there he is! Kennewick Man!'"

Patrick Stewart is, of course, the actor best known for his role as the suave Capt. Jean-Luc Picard on the television show *Star Trek: The Next Generation*. Chatters added that "On the physical characteristics alone, [Kennewick Man] could fit on the streets of Stockholm without causing any kind of notice. Or on the streets of Jerusalem or New Delhi, for that matter."

The cover of *The New Yorker* asked, "Was someone here before the Native Americans?" The tabloid-style headline in *Discover* magazine trumpeted "Europeans Invade America: 20,000 BC." A cover story in *U. S. News and World Report* featured Kennewick Man as evidence for an "America Before the Indians." An article in *The Santa Fe New Mexican* began this way: "When Columbus came to the New World in 1492 and set in motion the chain of events that led to the decimation of Native Americans, was he unknowingly getting revenge for what was done to his ancestors thousands of years before?"

Based on the sketchiest of evidence, archaeologists and journalists alike began framing fresh theories. Maybe the earliest Americans crossed the land bridge from Asia to America in distinct waves—white-skinned Caucasoids first, followed by the dusky-skinned Mongoloids of northern Asia. What happened when they met up? Was there an ancient American race war? Did the tawny Mongoloids attack Kennewick Man with a stone-tipped spear? Or are modern American Indians descended from a blend of both races—the multicultural product of an original American melting pot? The issue of Indian arrival is critical to Indian people as well, as Vine Deloria, Jr., pointed out. If Indians had "barely unpacked before Columbus came knocking on the door," won't people question Indian claims to the land and its resources?

"It's been like a gold discovery," said Chatters, "where normal people all of a sudden go goofy." But his problems had barely begun.

As theories began to proliferate, archaeologists seemed to agree on just one thing: Kennewick is a monumental find that must be studied extensively by specialists. The bones must be analyzed in great detail, additional radio-carbon tests should be run, and ancient DNA extracted from the bones. To ensure accuracy and eliminate bias, this testing must be conducted in several independent laboratories, supervised by the country's best research scientists. In a 1997 court decision, the judge compared Kennewick Man to "a book that they can read, a history written in bone instead of on paper, just as the history of a region may be 'read' by observing layers of rock or ice, or the rings of a tree."

As the scientific teams geared up, the already dramatic story of Kennewick Man took an extraordinary turn. Five days after the startling results of the radiocarbon tests were made public, the Army Corps of Engineers announced its intent to repatriate the remains to an alliance of five Northwest tribes: Umatilla, Yakima, Nez Perce, Wanapum, and Colville. The Umatilla tribe of northeastern Oregon took the lead, demanding that Chatters immediately—and without further study—surrender the bones. Armand Minthorn, a Umatilla leader, said simply: "Our oral history goes back 10,000 years. We know how time began and how Indian people were created. They can say whatever they want, the scientists. They are being disrespectful." The Umatilla explained that the scientific probing and destruction of human bones was offensive, sacrilegious, and illegal. Citing a 1990 federal law designed to protect Indian graves, the Umatilla demanded that the skeleton be returned for immediate reburial.

Scientists across the country screamed foul. This is one of the oldest, most complete skeletons in the Americas. If this Kennewick Man indeed has many Caucasoid traits, how can an Indian tribe claim his remains? Considerably more study is required before tribal affinity, if any, can be established. No matter how the study comes out, the scientists argued, because the bones are so ancient they rightfully belong to the American public rather than any special-interest group.

The dilemma landed in the lap of the Army Corps of Engineers, the governmental agency with immediate jurisdiction over the area where the bones were found. According to a report in *The Washington Post*, the White House sided with the Indians and secretly pressured the Corps to lock up the bones and prohibit further scientific study. In September 1996, the Corps confiscated the bones and announced plans to turn them over to the Umatilla within 30 days. Although Washington's congressional delegation urged that qualified scientists be allowed to examine the bones, the Corps refused.

In *Bonnichsen et al. v. United States of America*, eight prominent scientists have sued to obtain access to the Kennewick bones: Robson Bonnichsen (archaeologist, Oregon State University), C. Loring Brace (physical anthropologist, University of Michigan), Dennis J. Stanford (archaeologist, Smithsonian Institution), Richard Jantz (physical anthropologist, University of Tennessee), Douglas Owsley (physical anthropologist, Smithsonian Institution), George Gill (physical anthropologist, University of Wyoming), C. Vance Haynes, Jr. (geoarchaeologist, University of Arizona), and D. Gentry Steele (physical anthropologist, Texas A & M University). The lawsuit questions whether the 1990 federal legislation that protects Indian graves is appropriate to 9,400-year-old remains. Citing a lack of due process, the scientists accused the Army Corps of arbitrary decision-making and raised First Amendment concerns. Not only does the U. S. Constitution protect freedom of expression, the scientists argued, it safeguards the right to gather and receive information. If the Kennewick skeleton is locked away or reburied, the American public is deprived of potentially irreplaceable information about its own past.

The lawsuit also reflects the belief that the Corps had violated the Civil Rights Act of 1866. This law, originally written to guarantee nonwhites the same legal protection as whites, has recently been read as offering reciprocal protection to whites: If scientists were denied access because of race or ethnicity, then their civil rights were being violated.

The Army Corps refused to allow scientific study because the Umatilla said that such analysis would violate their religious beliefs about the dead. Chatters and the other scientists countered that Kennewick Man could not be adequately affiliated with any living tribe and, most likely, not with Indian people at all. To permit one tribe—or perhaps a single faction within a tribe—to veto scientific study, they claimed, would violate the rights of all other Americans. These Indians "proceed from the assumption that anyone who died in this country prior to 1492 is native American," complained Alan Schneider, attorney for the anthropologists, "and of course that's not necessarily true. What about the Viking explorations of the New World?"

In the matter of *Bonnichsen et al. v. United States of America*, two trials took place—one in a Portland courtroom and the other in the court of public opinion. Editorials across the country took various positions, but many newspapers weighed in on the side of science. "The information from ancient Kennewick Man," wrote *The Oregonian*, "is simply too important to all peoples to be buried by one people." On a *60 Minutes* television segment, correspondent Leslie Stahl quoted Chatters as believing that "the tribe's fight against further testing of Kennewick Man is based largely on fear, fear that if someone was here before they were, their status as sovereign nations, and all that goes with it—treaty rights, and lucrative casinos . . . could be at risk."

The Kennewick story took yet another bizarre turn when the Asatru Folk Assembly filed its own lawsuit. The Asatruans, who take their name from an Icelandic term meaning "those true to the Gods," are a northern California–based religious group who trace their pre-Christian ancestry to Scandinavian and Germanic tribes of northern Europe. The Asatruans sued to stop the United States government from repatriating the bones to the Indian claimants. In their publication *The Runestone* they wrote, "Kennewick Man is our kin. . . . Native American groups have strongly contested this idea, perceiving that they have much to lose if their status as the 'First Americans' is overturned. We will not let our heritage be hidden by those who seek to obscure it." Asatruans demanded that the bones be turned over to *them* for reburial.

For the next several years, the Army Corps kept the bones of Kennewick Man locked up as accusations flew. The Corps said Chatters had stolen bones before surrendering the skeleton, but this charge has been effectively refuted. The Asatruans accused the Corps of allowing Indians illegal access to the bones and handing some over for secret reburial. During one court-ordered inventory, the Corps claimed that Kennewick Man had an extra pelvis—suggesting that somebody had smuggled bones *into* the high security vault—but a later inventory showed the identification was incorrect. Judge Jelderks accused the government of stalling and ordered them to wrap up the inquiry.

Although allowing a preliminary geological study of the Kennewick site, the Corps soon announced plans to bury it to halt further erosion (which geologists argued was not a problem). Both houses of Congress quickly passed legislation explicitly ordering the Corps to keep its hands off the Kennewick site. But the Army Corps of Engineers defied the will of Congress and on April 6, 1998, covered the Kennewick Man site with 600 tons of boulders, gravel, logs, and backdirt, planting thousands of closely spaced cottonwood, dogwood, and willow trees on top of the fill. In this $160,000 cover-up, the Army Corps had not only made the site inaccessible to scientists and tourists; they had destroyed any undiscovered evidence beyond recovery. To date, the Corps of Engineers has been ineffective in explaining its motives or the results of this "stabilization" effort.

After working for three months with sculptor Tom McClelland, Chatters released a controversial clay reconstruction of Kennewick Man's head. In a presentation to the Society for American Archaeology, Chatters described how he produced the facial reconstruction—"averaging tissue thicknesses for northern hemisphere populations, using the most typical forms of eye fold and lip thickness, making the eyes of clay in a non-eye color and leaving off hair, all to avoid making *a priori* assumptions about relationship to some modern group." The results are striking—a bald, middle-aged man with a big nose and a drawn look of chronic pain. "When his eyes meet mine, it gives me the willies," Chatters commented. "He looks like he's about to speak. And he has an awful lot to tell us."

But deciphering this message has proved troublesome. Popular publications like the *New York Post* remembered Chatters' earlier comments in *The New Yorker*, and compared the Kennewick Man reconstruction to actor Patrick

The New York Post *compared James Chatters' reconstruction of Kennewick Man (upper right) to actor Patrick Stewart (above). But Vine Deloria, Jr. thinks he looks more like a defiant Chief Black Hawk (right) and his son, as painted by John Jarvis in 1833, when they came East as prisoners of war.*

Stewart—implying an early Caucasoid presence in ancient America. But to Deloria, Kennewick Man looked more like Chief Black Hawk, as painted in 1833 when he came East as a prisoner of war. Jim Thorpe—the legendary Olympian and first president of the National Football League—was a direct descendant of Chief Black Hawk, raising the question of whether Kennewick Man might be an ancestor of modern Indian people after all.

WE HAVE NOT heard the final word on Kennewick Man, but one thing is clear: this middle-aged man, who limped badly from a partly healed spear wound, was a lightening bolt exposing deep divisions in our views of ancient America.

Archaeology draws upon a long-standing, implicit social policy emphasizing a common human heritage. As Douglas Owsley, a physical anthropologist at the Smithsonian Institution (with experience on the Jeffrey Dahmer and Branch Davidian cases under his belt) sees it, "People are free to believe what they want to believe, but I think we're resisting the right for them to force that on others. . . . This is information that the American public has a right to know."

Most Indian people feel otherwise. Marla Big Boy, Oglala Lakota Attorney General for the Colville Confederated Tribes of eastern Washington, puts it this way: "The ever changing scientific theories disturb the Colville Tribe because science is not always benign.... The type of scientific and professional arrogance of the *Bonnichsen et al.* plaintiffs is also present throughout history.... What is happening today is similar to the scientific purposes of yesterday."

The multicultural tug-of-war over Kennewick Man raises deep questions about how we can make the past serve the diverse purposes of the present, Indian as well as white. It also challenges us to define when ancient bones stop being tribal and become simply human.

WHOSE MEMORIES BECOME HISTORY?

What is it about the Kennewick fracas that has kept it front-page news for more than three years? Why are Indians and archaeologists still at odds, fighting skull wars begun centuries earlier?

The Kennewick conflict has been portrayed as yet another face-off between science and religion, a reprise of the famous Scopes trial of the 1920s—except that Red Creationists have now assumed the role of Christian fundamentalists. I believe that this reading is incomplete, if not largely incorrect.

The central thesis of *Skull Wars* can be stated rather simply: although limited parallels do exist between the fight over the Kennewick bones and the evolutionist-creationist struggle, the pivotal issue at Kennewick is not about religion or science. It is about politics. The dispute is about control and power, not philosophy. Who gets to control ancient American history—governmental agencies, the academic community, or modern Indian people?

To expose the deeply political nature of the Kennewick conflict, this book explores the long-term interactions between Euroamerican and Indian populations. Over more than five centuries, several distinct American Indian histories have developed, of which three are especially critical: a larger national narrative that glorifies assimilation into the Great American Melting Pot; an academic discourse written by anthropologists and historians who view Indians as subjects of scholarly inquiry; and an indigenous "insider's" perspective long maintained in the oral traditions of Indian people themselves. Although sometimes overlapping, these distinct histories often paint quite different visions of America, past and present. Proponents of each strongly believe that "their" history is the correct one, the version that should be published in textbooks, protected by law, and defended in the courtroom.

In a nutshell, then, *Skull Wars* explores the curious and often stormy relations between American Indians and the non-Indians bent on studying them.

THE FIRST PART, "Names and Images," shows how early European explorers invented the American Indian and how American colonists incorporated this Indian imagery into mainstream history as part of the nation-building process. The resulting narrative lionizes national heroes and emphasizes the most dramatic events in the exploration, settlement, and development of new territory. Histories that minority people tell about themselves—Irish history, black history, Armenian history, and Indian tribal histories—become invisible and irrelevant to this national American epic. Minority histories are typically reduced to stereotypes and cultural cliches.

The great American narrative began with the first encounter between Christopher Columbus and the native people living on a small Caribbean island they called *Guanahani*. Columbus took possession of the land and its people for the Spanish Crown, renaming the island "San Salvador" and the natives "*los Indios*" (the Indians). This formalized naming ritual was a prerequisite to ensure that the conquest would be played by European rules.

Columbus encountered two kinds of people on Guanahani: the real human beings who lived there and the imaginary Indians who existed only in the explorer's minds. The living people of Guanahani—Columbus' so-called peaceful Arawaks—all perished within a decade of this first encounter, victims of invisible microbes and Spanish cruelty. But the stereotypes that Columbus invented on "San Salvador" would define the flow of Euroamerican history for centuries to come.

Building upon what Columbus believed he saw in the Caribbean, the eighteenth-century French philosopher Jean-Jacques Rousseau later described the Native Americans as "the real Youth of the World." As elaborated through the centuries, this imagery associated the Noble Redman with an independent and unembellished innocence reflecting a pure state of nature. These people were seen as repositories of a lost virtue, an uncorrupted human wholesomeness that existed before the rise of civilization: humanity at its happiest, reflecting a natural simplicity and virtue. Native Americans lived in perpetual peace and harmony; war was irrelevant because power was shared among all nations. The image of the Noble Redman was featured in an endless parade of American stamps and coins, romantic writings by James Fenimore Cooper and Henry Wadsworth Longfellow, and more recently in movies like *Little Big Man* and *Dances With Wolves*. Most Americans still get their impressions of Indians not by first-hand interactions but from television, movies, and the occasional potboiler novel. Media imagery today represents los Indios as the first ecologists and idealizes Indian people as somehow spiritually superior to everyone else.

Late in 1492, the Arawak of Hispañola (modern Haiti and the Dominican Republic) told Columbus of a second kind of native people—their violent Carib neighbors who lived for war and committed unspeakable horrors. Columbus soon translated Arawak oral tradition into a second kind of imaginary Indian—the Bloodthirsty Redskin, the very antithesis of a civilized European. Firmly in the clutches of Satan, they committed appalling acts because God sent periodic scourges to punish and instruct Christians. According to the imagery, these often-naked wildmen commonly had multiple mates and led lives of lewdness, eroticism, and narcissism. A callous killer, the Bloodthirsty Savage showed an extraordinary vindictiveness toward his enemies. Cannibalism and human sacrifice were commonplace. They roamed the land without any concept of property ownership, excelling only in thievery and treachery. Victims of superstition, they were controlled by conjurers and medicine men. The Bloodthirsty Savage was wholly incapable of advancing to civilization, Columbus believed, because his innate Indian culture was almost subhuman and without meaningful history. This Good Indian/Bad Indian imagery would inform the relationship between the Euroamerican and Native American cultures for centuries to come.

Yet another Indian image arose during the American Revolution when the Sons of Liberty dressed up like Mohawks and dumped bales of English tea into Boston harbor. Although Europeans of the day believed that Indians lived outside the bounds of civilization, Samuel Adams and the other American patriots increasingly gravitated toward Indian symbolism in their rejection of English-style civilization. The Indian-as-American-icon played directly into the new national narrative, reinforcing the morality and integrity of the New World and demonstrating that the New Republic possessed a distinctive history—a spirit that defined America as unique and divinely favored.

As Euroamericans established themselves in their new homeland, they wrote stirring histories cementing themselves to the land. Rather than accept Indian people as having a long-term and culturally significant history of their own, white America conjured up Lost Tribes, mythical Welsh sailors, and ancient (non-Indian) Moundbuilders as the real First Americans. These white-skinned American ancestors, the argument went, must have been annihilated by Indian interlopers.

When America annexed the trans-Mississippian West, mainstream historians groped for ways to incorporate the new territory, with its distinctive landscape, natural resources, and aboriginal inhabitants, into the American mindset. Nineteenth-century urban America had come to see Indians as a national mascot. But on the frontier, where Indians still raised real problems with the mainstream vision, Victorian America made some different choices: civilization is better than savagery, cities are better than wilderness, and science is better than superstition. According to the prevailing nineteenth-century stereotypes, the Indian must live a life of independence and freedom, or he would die. Native Americans, seen as fragile and unable to coexist with civilization, became a heroic yet sadly vanishing species, victims of their incompatibility with an advancing, superior form of humanity.

So arose the image of the Vanishing American, celebrated in picture and verse, always with the same bittersweet refrain: the Indian race will soon vanish "as the snow melts before the sunbeam." The myth of the disappearing

American Indian conditioned two centuries of federal Indian policy and helped create a new scientific discipline to record in detail the lives and customs of the Vanishing American.

PART II DOCUMENTS how American anthropology arose when eighteenth- and nineteenth-century intellectual America decided it was important to gather facts and artifacts before Indians vanished completely. Anthropologists tried to transcend narrative history and Indian imagery, emphasizing instead what mainstream historians have commonly regarded as trivial and inconsequential—family structure, economics, technology, religions, political organization, and ideology. Thomas Jefferson, America's first scientific archaeologist, argued that Indians could—and really should—be studied as part of the rest of nature. Jefferson defined American Indians as specimens, like mammoth bones and the fruit trees in his own garden, to be empirically investigated and objectively understood.

Nineteenth-century anthropology, grounded as it was in mainstream American values and imagery, promoted a doctrine of racial determinism. By assuming direct correlation between heredity and behavior, early anthropologists attributed cultural differences to deep-seated inherited drives. Asked why Plains Indians so readily fit European horses into their lifestyle, the nineteenth-century scientific racist might have responded that horsemanship was "in their blood." This was hardly the figurative expression it is today; before anything was known of Mendelian genetics or DNA, blood was literally thought to be the medium through which traits were passed from generation to generation. Theories of racial determinism—what anthropologist Marvin Harris terms a "biologization" of human history—dominated nineteenth-century anthropological thinking. To the physical anthropologist, human skulls provided a means to scientifically define the races, and by conflating cultural differences with disparities in human intelligence, scientific racism created a global cultural hierarchy.

From its inception, American anthropology had a practical side, as pre-Civil War studies of human racial variability provided the scientific evidence necessary to document the inequality of the races. The proto-anthropology of Samuel Morton in the 1830s and 1840s and of Louis Agassiz two decades later generated the scientific biological facts that were used to justify slavery. Scientifically sanctioned racism also informed federal Indian policies that enabled Euroamericans to seize Indian lands and justified the disgraceful Indian

Wars. At a time when the American melting pot seemed unworkable and the eventual "civilization" of Indians unlikely, these theories of race suggested that an innate cultural inferiority of the Native Americans doomed them to extinction.

With the publication of *Darwin's On the Origin of Species* in 1859, American science decided that human institutions must likewise be viewed through a lens of evolution, as developing according to unseen natural laws. Regardless of whether Indians were measured according to their racial or cultural destiny, this new evolutionary yardstick confirmed the conventional frontier wisdom: noble he might be, the American Indian was properly grouped with the inferior races—all afflicted with darker skins, flawed behavior, and second-rate biology.

Like Jefferson, nineteenth-century anthropologists viewed Indians as specimens deserving close scientific study. This is why Indian graves were systematically dug up and Indian corpses beheaded on the battlefield to feed the demand for skulls for America's new natural history museums. This is why live Indians were so popular in "ethnographic zoos" at several World Fairs. And this is why Indians became "living fossils" tucked away in the museums of America. In fact, when Indians died, their bodies were sometimes not buried at all but rendered into bones, numbered and stored away as part of America's greater heritage.

Because Indians belonged to a primal stage in the development of modern civilization, the evolutionary process doomed them to extinction, victims of Victorian progress and Manifest Destiny. In the scientific perspective of the day, Indians represented not a just a separate racial type but a distinctive level of social development—a holdover from an earlier, inferior stage of human evolution. Anthropologists became intensely interested in Indians as living exemplars of a previous stage of humanity, what the world was like before Western civilization came to be. As anthropologists arrayed human societies along a social continuum from most primitive to most civilized, American Indians fell somewhere between savagery and barbarism. Once caught in the web of international geopolitics, they would be hapless victims at the mercy of others. White brutality or largess would decide who survived and who did not; Indian courage and enterprise were irrelevant. The immutable laws of nature held that the Indian must vanish.

The Vanishing American theme dominated museum displays and World Fair exhibitions at the dawn of the twentieth century, and this imagery also informed a federal policy designed to nudge the Indian toward his inevitable extinction. As anthropologists rushed to salvage ethnographic tidbits from the last living members of some tribes, mainstream American historians defined Indians as basically invisible once they ceased to be a military menace.

Nineteenth-century anthropologists were not heartless scientists content to watch passively as Indian culture slipped into oblivion. Far from it. As individuals, most anthropologists cared deeply about Indian people, and many served as cultural mediators, helping "their tribe" deal with Euroamerica. American anthropologists tried desperately to harness cutting-edge social theory to help Indian people. Please, the anthropologists argued, leave your outmoded tribalism behind so that you may evolve toward civilization. But these efforts ultimately backfired, creating in Indian Country a lasting legacy of mistrust toward anthropologists and other white do-gooders who ventured their way.

The racial theories of nineteenth-century skull science are, of course, specious. In the 1910s, anthropologist Franz Boas demonstrated the utter inadequacy of scientific racism. Anthropologists belatedly recognized that a Sioux Indian raised in Beijing could learn to speak flawless Mandarin and that an African American attending a conservatory could write symphonies in the classical European tradition. Boas figured out and clearly demonstrated that skull shape was heavily influenced by environmental factors and could change markedly from one generation to the next: skull measurements thus did not necessarily reflect enduring racial affinities.

But the victory over racial determinism was never complete. Although most modern anthropologists view race as a scientifically flawed way of thinking about biological variability, some diehards still cling to racial typologies and stereotypes. Disagreements over racial categories sparked the ugliest controversies in the Kennewick Man affair. As the late Eric Wolf wrote, "race remains a major source of demonology in this country and in the world and anthropology has a major obligation to speak reason to unreason."

BY 1900, American Indians seemed to be vanishing as surely as the American bison and so too were the archaeological vestiges of Indian history. As museum anthropologists hurried to document and collect the last of Indian culture, pothunters plundered one archaeological site after another. Many Americans worried that foreigners, caught up in their own European-style Noble Redskin imagery, were exporting the best of America's ancient past.

Congress responded to this threat by passing the Antiquities Act of

1906, legislation crafted to preserve America's remote past and to ensure its continued study by a rapidly growing scientific community. The new law made looting of Indian sites on federal land a crime, empowered the President to designate key archaeological sites as national monuments, and established a regulatory framework to restrict research permits to professionally trained archaeologists. Congress asked the Smithsonian Institution to identify America's most important archaeological sites and to issue permits to professional archaeologists properly qualified to work on them.

By criminalizing the unauthorized removal of antiquities from federal lands, the 1906 law effectively quashed amateur access, Indian and non-Indian alike, to much of the remote American past. The archaeological record was seen as a critical part of America's national identity because it documented its progression from savagery to the most civilized place on earth, and in 1906 this heritage was formally entrusted to science.

Part III of this book, "Deep American History," traces the development of scientific thinking about American Indian origins and the rise of academically trained archaeologists as the curators of this national narrative. In consigning the American Indian past to the greater public trust, the Antiquities Act never acknowledged that Indian people might have their own religious, spiritual, or historical connections to it. The conflicting imagery of Indians-as-Vanishing-Americans and Indians-as-untutored-amateurs helped exclude American Indians from the Antiquities Act. Indians were seen as representing an earlier, archaic stratum of ancient America, destined to pass gracefully into oblivion. Whatever Indians had to say about their past was irrelevant to the American narrative.

AMERICAN INDIANS, of course, refused to vanish. Their numbers bottomed out in the 1890s and have dramatically increased ever since. Part IV looks at the twentieth-century Indian people who survived their predicted extinction and began exploring non-Indian America on their own, applying their "ancient ways" to fresh pursuits, including art, politics, medicine and the law, sports, and even anthropology. Indians began creating their own reality, defining pathways distinct from those that had nearly destroyed them.

With the rise of the American civil rights movement, the protests against the Vietnam War, the successes of the United Farm Workers, and the growth of feminism, history became a weapon for redressing the imbalances inherent in the top-dog perspective. Academics in the humanities, arts, and social sciences began including gender, race, ethnicity, and class as justifiable arenas of inquiry. Red Power activism is one facet of this movement. The echoes of underdog history carried far beyond the ivory towers, permeating popular culture and, in the process, threatening archaeology's foothold in mainstream American history. Particularly since the 1960s, Indian people stepped up their fight to reclaim and reinforce their treaty-guaranteed sovereignty, borrowing strategies and guidelines from the world of international law. American Indian activists joined up with the so-called Fourth World—the descendants of a nation's original inhabitants who find themselves marginalized and deprived of their traditional territory and its riches.

The roots of such nativist thinking run deep in Indian America, reflecting the belief that native people and whites have separate histories and that the two peoples were created separately and can never live together. As Gregory Dowd points out in *A Spirited Existence*, Indians of the late eighteenth century saw the "Anglo-American East rise as a spiritual as well as a physical menace to the Indian West." Across the eastern woodlands, prophets and culture heroes expressed the conviction that they could retain an essential Indian power through ritual and concerted resistance to encroaching white ways.

These native beliefs had their richest expression in the early nineteenth-century speeches of the Shawnee orator and warrior Tecumseh, who attempted to unite and reinvigorate the demoralized native people. Tecumseh gained his power by promoting pan-tribal alliances based on an unequivocally political message: American lands belonged to all Indian people, and no single tribe, village, or leader has a right to cede these homelands without the approval of all tribes. Rejecting Jefferson's message of peaceful assimilation, Tecumseh and his supporters shared a vision of a pan-Indian confederacy. Indian independence and freedom would be preserved through common ritual and the explicit rejection of the ways of outsiders. Tecumseh dramatized his convictions by wearing only skins and feathers into battle, disavowing all European-type clothing. Although he was killed at the Battle of the Thames in 1813, Tecumseh's message has been repeated through the years and resonates today among modern indigenous groups around the world who place a priority on establishing the legal status of traditional knowledge.

Courts had long given preference to the testimony of non-Indian historians and anthropologists over the authority of tribal elders. Legal authorities have long discounted tribal perspectives; yet they commonly accept at face value the first-hand written observations of European colonists. Mainstream historical perspectives put the onus on indigenous societies to justify their aboriginal claims according to colonial rules. "If aboriginal practices were not recognized as 'rights' by the Europeans and somehow incorporated into common law," observed the political scientist Fae Korsmo, "they could not survive as aboriginal rights today."

Indian people have long been required to furnish western-style historical proof of their origins and historical continuity on the land: "Did you resist us? Did you keep your culture intact? Did we recognize your power? Did we keep records of your whereabouts and your battles with neighboring tribes? In other words," writes Korsmo, "did your forms of resistance resemble ours? Were you sufficiently like us to gain our recognition, yet different enough to be kept separate?"

Tribal leaders and Indian scholars, attacking what they see as myths maintained by historians and politicians, have attempted to revitalize their indigenous identities demolished by war and trampled by dominant culture politics. Seeking to salvage an Indian past from the distortions of non-Indian historians and anthropologists, Haunani-Kay Trask, a leader in the fight for Hawaiian sovereignty, puts it this way:

> *Burdened by a linear, progressive conception of history and by an assumption that Euroamerican culture flourishes at the upper end of that progression, Westerners have told the history of Hawai'i as an inevitable if occasionally bittersweet triumph of Western ways over 'primitive' Hawai'ian ways.... To know my history, I had to put away my books and return to the land.... I had to feel again the spirits of nature and take gifts of plants and fish to the ancient altars. I had to begin to speak my language with our elders and leave long silences for wisdom to grow. But before anything else, I had to learn the language like a lover so that I could rock with her and lie at night in her dreaming arms.*

Such indigenous ideologies assert an essential native subjectivity, promoting themes of self-worth and cultural preservation and suggesting that Indian culture could help correct some problems of the modern mainstream. At the same time, these once powerless groups were defining ways to navigate a cultural tide that had long run against them. Since the 1960s, the emerging Indian identity—what Deloria calls a "retribalization"—has severely threatened the long-standing balance between mainstream and underdog histories. "Until the majority of Americans have concurred, both formally and informally, that American Indians are equal and autonomous entities, entitled to every freedom and course of redress that pertains to its Christian majority," argues Scott Vickers, "then that majority will have failed itself, its own religion, and its historical trajectory toward 'freedom for all'."

Achieving power over their own history has tangible payoffs in the everyday life of Indian people, which is still subject to long-conflicted federal policies. Neither fully sovereign nor wards of the state, Indian tribes remain subject to federal policy and public perception. Their real-world problems include epidemic levels of poverty, suicide, despair, AIDS, and rampant alcoholism. Nearly 20 percent of Indian deaths today may be alcohol-related, against a national American average of 4.7 percent. Indian people are still trying to tackle these challenges as tribal and community issues, trying to rid themselves of dependence on outsiders. But economic development in Indian Country remains integrally connected to politics—intertwined with issues of sovereignty, tribal identity, access to resources, cultural issues, and ideology. By emphasizing histories absent from white-dominated curricula, native people are attempting to build institutional mechanisms to help their communities and reassert their rights. By taking hold of the imagery that still frames negotiations with state and federal governments, they seek to translate historical and cultural identities into tangible political power.

The bottom line is defining which history gets taught and who gets to teach it. In seeking identities independent of non-Indian historians and anthropologists, many Native Americans have come to resent the appropriation of their ancient artifacts and ancestral bones by "experts" claiming an authority denied to the Indians themselves. As native people across the land try to recapture their own language, culture, and history, they are increasingly concerned with recovering and taking control of tribal heirlooms and human remains. Troy Johnson spoke for many when he suggested that "perhaps no more insulting and insensitive scene can be imagined than the desecration of Native American burial sites by researchers or grave robbers who disregard the law and cultural sensitivities of the Native American Indian people." In 1975, the widely distributed Indian newspaper *Wassaja* defined anthropology as a "vulture culture."

Congress responded to these sensitivities in 1990 by passing the Native American Graves Protection and Repatriation Act (NAGPRA for short). NAGPRA protects newly discovered Indian graves, but it also mandates that America's universities and museums audit their Indian collections and return certain cultural items to tribal representatives. This legislation marked a significant shift in the federal stance toward the rights of Indian people and a sea change in the perception and practice of American archaeology. As in 1906, the federal government asserted its right to legislate access to the American past. But the 1990 law explicitly acknowledged that Indian pasts are relevant to the American present. This public and visible benchmark legislation reflected a deep-seated shift in thinking, emphasizing America's self-perception as a multifaceted, pluralistic society. The American Creed shifted away from the time-honored melting pot to newer perspectives recognizing the merits of a multicultural society.

Such an interpretation of the American character was unimaginable in 1906. The Antiquities Act of 1906, which legally transferred the Indian past to the American public domain, was crafted without Indian involvement and with no suggestion that Indian people might have legitimate affiliations with that past. In 1990, for the first time, native people were empowered to question mainstream American ownership of the Indian past, both literally and metaphorically. No longer were Indian bones found on public lands automatically defined as natural resources, as federal property to be safeguarded in scientific custody. No longer did science have a monopoly on defining the meaning of archaeology; instead, native groups were invited to assign their own spiritual and historical meanings to archaeological sites and their contents.

The NAGPRA legislation also underscored the increasing difficulty of defining just which American public was being served by archaeology. Is it the job of science to preserve and study the material remains of the world's diverse human populations, present and past? Is the archaeological record a nonrenewable resource to be held in trust for future generations? Or does each of the world's cultures and its descendants own the material remains of their own pasts and the exclusive rights to their interpretation? As anthropologist Robert McLaughlin asks, does archaeology serve "the" public—or just "a" public?

These questions remain largely unresolved. Whatever decisions are made in the early twenty-first century will doubtless be scrutinized by generations to come. Tribal voices have hardly displaced the authority of state and science, but those voices are now distinctly audible in the contest over who gets to dig up and possess the Indian past.

NOT SURPRISINGLY, some Americans are alarmed by Indian "retribalization" and the recognition by Congress of indigenous ideologies. Census Bureau numbers suggest a skyrocketing American Indian population, and some question the authenticity of these self-proclaimed Indians. Many mainstream Americans still believe that "real, authentic" Indians did indeed vanish a century ago. Some accuse Indians of learning their "traditions" from old anthropology books, and others see twenty-first-century "Indianness" as just another New Age fad. One critic coined the term "MacIndianism" to describe a marketing of Indian heritage and manipulation of historical evidence. Skeptics suggest that NAGPRA and related legislation smacks of public relations exploiting the Noble Redman imagery at the expense of historical accuracy. Some anthropologists accuse Indians of inventing instant traditions for current political purposes. Some professional historians see a self-serving, second-rate scholarship making shoddy use of historical and ethnographic documents. More than one academic has privately scoffed that modern Indians have all become cowboys—it's only the anthropologists, in the end, who understand what "real" Indian culture is all about.

It is hard to overlook the sense of loss among mainstream scientists and historians who see their power and authority eroding as late twentieth-century America experiments with multicultural alternatives to the traditional melting pot imagery. In *The Closing of the American Mind*, Allan Bloom complains of "hearing the Founders charged with being racists, murderers of Indians, representatives of class interests" and condemns the debunkers as "weakening our convictions of the truth or superiority of American principles and our heroes." Those concerned over revisionist myth-making and a lack of objectivity have accused both Indians and Congress of pandering to a political correctness of the moment.

In *The Disuniting of America*, the historian Arthur Schlesinger writes of a "tribalization of American life [that] . . . reverses the historic theory of America as one people—the theory that has thus far managed to keep American society whole." From Yugoslavia to Canada, from the former Soviet Union to much of Africa, post-Cold War Balkanization has torn apart one nation after another. Is America in danger of being torn apart into ethnic and racial tribes? Is Schlesinger correct in saying that tribal identity has become "the AIDS of international politics—lying dormant for years, then flaring up to destroy countries"? With the metaphor of the Great American Melting Pot under attack, Schlesinger sees an America "giving ground to the celebration of ethnicity.... The multiethnic dogma abandons historic purposes, replacing assimilation by fragmentation, integration by separatism. It belittles *unum* and glorifies *pluribus*."

Some go even further, asserting that American values simply cannot be negotiated and remade at will. For them, the American family—a natural institution blessed by God—carries with it critical core values and social attitudes that have raised America above other countries. President Ronald Reagan spoke for many when he wondered aloud if "we made a mistake in trying to maintain Indian cultures. Maybe we should not have humored them in wanting to stay in that kind of primitive lifestyle."

THE FINAL SECTION of this book, "Bridging the Chasm," examines the impact of these conflicting histories on contemporary America and explores some ways of mediating the conflict. Melding these disparate points of view will never be easy—these conflicts have developed over centuries, and their implications reach far beyond some old bones from the State of Washington.

Having examined the three main species of American Indian history—mainstream narratives, academic theories, and indigenous ideologies—I return to the central conflict this book seeks to explore: the long-standing and deep-seated tensions between Indian people and the scientists who wish to study them. Why are Indians still fighting with anthropologists and archaeologists over issues like the Kennewick skeleton? Why can't they just get along?

Half a millennium of white-Indian interactions suggests several answers:

- ◉ THE POWER OF INDIAN IMAGERY: *Romantic stereotypes have defined and directed mainstream American attitudes toward Indian people. Because anthropologists and historians have always been, by and large, middle class whites, these same stereotypes underlie their supposedly objective academic studies of Indian people.*

- ◉ THE POWER OF INDIAN ORIGINS: *The Bureau of Indian Affairs stands as the indelible bureaucratic reminder that Indians are somehow an American minority different. As the historian Patricia Limerick has pointed out, there is today no Bureau of Italian-American Affairs, no Bureau of Hispanic-American Affairs, no Bureau of African-American Affairs. "A minority by conquest is not the same as a minority by immigration," notes Limerick, "and four centuries of history have not blurred the difference." This finders-keepers premise has positioned American Indians as somehow spiritually superior to America's "immigrant" minorities.*

- ◉ THE POWER OF "PHYSICS ENVY" IN TWENTIETH-CEN-TURY ANTHROPOLOGY: *When early twentieth-century anthropologists abandoned their humanistic roots in the search for an objective "science of mankind," they effectively declared American Indians to be irrelevant to their own history.*

- THE ENDURING POWER OF AMERICAN ANTHROPOLOGY'S NINETEENTH-CENTURY RACIST HERITAGE: *The Kennewick controversy vividly demonstrates how anthropology's lingering hangover from nineteenth-century skull science can still create instant headlines whenever anthropologists are naive enough to make racial statements—even seemingly innocuous ones—in public. Some have even seen Kennewick Man as the "Great White Hope," the last best chance to establish Caucasians as the original landlords of America.*

- THE POWER OF THE MEDIA TO REFOCUS THE RESULTS OF SCIENTIFIC RESEARCH. *For the past decade or so, American archaeologists have undertaken a deliberate campaign of "taking their science to the public." But few scientists are adept at dealing with journalists, who often spice up their stories with attention-grabbers to "give the piece a newsworthy focus." As the Kennewick case illustrates, the story conveyed to the American public can be quite different from that intended by the research scientists.*

Each of these components has contributed to the undercurrents of frustration played out in the Kennewick controversy.

But the single most enduring theme throughout the centuries of Indian-Euroamerican interaction involves the power to name, which ultimately reflects the power to conquer and control. The skull wars began when Columbus renamed the islands and the people of the "New World" in which he had landed. As he invoked his power to name and conquer, Columbus reenacted a well-known Biblical scenario—the very first act of the very first human, Adam, as recounted in Genesis:

> *And out of the ground the Lord God formed every beast of the field, and every fowl of the air; and brought them unto Adam to see what he would call them: and whatsoever Adam called every living creature, that was the name thereof. And Adam gave names to all cattle, and to the fowl of the air, and to every beast of the field....*

More than any other single factor, the power to name, define, and conquer has fueled the skull wars. Naming is central to the writing of history, and history is a primary way we define ourselves. The power to name becomes the power to define one's identity and very existence.

The assigning of names is the beginning of nation building. During the five centuries following the Columbian encounter, as wars were fought and new governments born, the New World would be carved up into dozens of new republics, some of which became world powers. This was a logical consequence of the political power struggles that began in 1492. As David Goldberg says in *Racial Subjects*, minorities throughout the world are now learning "to pry loose the hold over naming. This is the first step toward self-determination, for it enables one to assert power over self-definition."

When a nearly complete 9,400 year-old skeleton washed out of a Washington riverbank near the town of Kennewick, Jim Chatters named him "Kennewick Man." Although scientific protocol says the bones were Chatters' to name, something of a local skirmish broke out when civic boosters of two other nearby cities proposed, apparently with straight faces, that the skeleton be renamed "Kennewick-Pasco-Richland Man." It is hardly surprising that the Umatilla tribe, claiming the skeleton as their own, rejected the scientist's name, preferring to call it *"Oyt.pa.ma.na.tit.tite"* or "The Ancient One." From the Umatilla perspective, the bones were theirs to name.

Time and time again, we will see the power of names reflected in the disparities between histories. In a real sense, it is the power to name that created the skull wars and their modern-day legacy in the Kennewick controversy.

THE BATTLE OVER the Kennewick bones is about control and power over America's ancient past. If Indian people lose the fight to retain and rebury their ancestor's bones, will they also lose other treaty-guaranteed rights that define their unique, sovereign status under United States law? If archaeologists surrender the right to study ancient human bones and artifacts, will the scientific community have to fear continual censure by the religious beliefs of a few? Should this happen, then mainstream archaeology's views on American origins will no longer carry the clout of authority.

From whatever perspective, Kennewick has become a very public fight that no side feels it can afford to lose. This is the five-hundred-year story of its roots.

Part I.

NAMES AND IMAGES

It is little wonder that Indian peoples were perceived not as they were but as they "had" to be—from a European point of view. They were whisked out of the realm of the real and into the land of the make-believe. Indians became invariably super- or subhuman, never ordinary. They dealt in magic, not judgment. They were imagined to be stuck in their pasts, not guided by its precedents.

—Michael Dorris (1993, Modoc)

COLUMBUS, ARAWAKS, AND CARIBS: THE POWER TO NAME

1.

[The natives] have often asked me, why we call them Indians.

—*Roger Williams (Plimouth Colony, 1643)*

ON THE MORNING OF October 12, 1492, Cristóbal Colón (Christopher Columbus) guided his small landing party onto dry land. Unfurling the banner of the Spanish monarchy—a green crowned cross emblazoned on a field of white—the Admiral of the Ocean Sea led his little group in a prayerful thanksgiving. He set up a wooden cross and christened the island *San Salvador*—after the Holy Savior who had protected them during their perilous voyage.

Columbus commanded those present—the brothers Pinzón (Martín Alonso and Vincente Yáñez), fleet secretary Rodrigo de Escobedo, and comptroller Rodrigo Sánchez—"to bear witness that I was taking possession of this island for the King and Queen." This new land and its riches now belonged to Spain. Its inhabitants were henceforth Spanish subjects.

The same scene was repeated five years later when John Cabot stepped onto the northern peninsula of Newfoundland in 1497 and made a short speech claiming possession for Mother England. Two Frenchmen, Cartier and Champlain, did the same in the St. Lawrence Valley, as did Henry Hudson in New York Harbor and Captain Cook in Polynesia. Even the moon is graced with an American flag and a plaque signed by Richard Nixon.

LOS INDIOS

For the three months following his first landfall, Columbus piloted his three ships through a maze of islands, "discovering" and naming each one. After San Salvador came *Santa María de la Concepción* and then, on October 16, *Fernandina*, named after King Ferdinand. As he proceeded southward, still seeking the Asian mainland, Columbus soon encountered the island he named *Isabela*. A Haitian harbor became *San Nicholás* (because he entered it on December 6, the feast day of that saint). The nearby headland was *Cabo del Estrella*, named for the Southern Cross in the sky immediately above. "Thus I named them all," Columbus wrote in his diary.

The names established an agenda under which the rest of the encounter would be played out. After discovering a patch of "unclaimed" land, the conqueror would wade ashore and plant his royal banner. He proclaimed that these newly discovered lands were now his patron's domain and laid claim to the new-found riches, the natural resources, and the things living and inanimate—all of which was simply wilderness before being "discovered" and defined by Europeans. During the Golden Age of Discovery, European colonial powers competed in a high stakes game of finders keepers. The power to name reflected an underlying power to control the land, its indigenous people, and its history.

Discovering and naming were not limited to islands. In the letter announcing his feats to the world, Columbus called the people he found *los Indios*, broadening the geographical *India* to denote all of Asia east of the Indus River. Even after Columbus' navigational error (a pair of intervening continents) was recognized, his term *Indios* was retained and eventually translated into the other languages of conquest—the French *Indien* and the English *Indian*. Thus the invented word "Indian," which began as a navigational misnomer, would carry enduring colonial connotations. It would mask the enormous complexities and variability of Native American people by grouping them together into a vastly oversimplified pan-tribal construct.

The Arawak-speaking people who lived on "San Salvador" did not ask Columbus to rename their island. They had called their home *Guanahani* since first arriving there centuries before. As they watched the three ships make their way toward the shore, they must have wondered about the voyagers' origins. They must have applied their own names to these curious bearded strangers. But these names and musings are forever lost because within a decade after the encounter, the Arawak-speakers on Guanahani had all died. Hardly more than a decade after Columbus arrived, European-borne disease and harsh treatment had decimated the native population of Hispañola. They were slaughtered wholesale by fire and torture, the sword, and ferocious war dogs, worked to death as slaves, and mowed down by smallpox, measles, and diphtheria. The Spanish had to venture ever further south in search of slaves to support their fledgling New World colonies.

The names *Indian* and *San Salvador* persist today because they were made up and retained by the conquerors of this "New World." As usual, the winners got to write the history books.

NOBLE ARAWAKS AND BLOODTHIRSTY CARIBS

The Admiral was touched by the poor but generous Arawaks living on the island he called San Salvador. Columbus wrote in his diary a glowing testimonial to the gracious and amiable people he found there. They brought him food and water and asked if he came from the heavens. Although not exactly sure where he had landed, Columbus saw about him a terrestrial paradise, perhaps even the threshold of the Garden of Eden itself.

After some island hopping, the Spanish explorers were befriended by a local chief named Guacanagari. Not long after they met, on December 25, 1492, the flagship *Santa María* ran aground on a shallow coral reef off what today is Haiti. Guacanagari wept at the plight of the stranded foreigners, and he immediately dispatched his people in long canoes to help offload supplies from the stricken ship. The Admiral and his crew were invited to take refuge in Guacanagari's village. His Arawak hosts, Columbus wrote, were among the world's most generous people, living in peace in their island universe. They were loving parents. They venerated their elders and cared for them in old age. Their language lacked even a word for "war." These sentiments were embellished a few years later by Bartholomé de las Casas: "God created these simple people without evil and without guile. They are most obedient and faithful to their natural lords and to the Christians whom they serve. Nor are they quarrelsome, rancorous, querulous, or vengeful. Moreover they are more delicate than princes and die easily from work or illness. They neither possess nor desire to possess worldly wealth. Surely these people would be the most blessed in the world if they only worshiped the true God."

Thus was invented the Noble Redman.

The image of America as earthly paradise was short-lived. The Noble Redman was soon joined by vicious warriors lurking deep within the tropical forest. The Indians of Hispañola told Columbus of a fierce people they called the "Carib," known for their savage ways—particularly their appetite for human flesh. The gentle Arawak recounted a calamitous migration of warriors coming from the deepest jungles to the south. All-male Carib war parties were said to be advancing island by island, seizing food and weapons, hunting down and eating the Arawak men. They castrated young boys and fattened them up like capons to be consumed later at feasts. Female captives were taken as unwilling brides, to bear the next generation of warriors.

Columbus took careful note of the cannibal menace, which he welcomed as strangely good news. Recalling the cannibals so vividly described by Marco Polo two centuries earlier, Columbus took the Arawaks' stories as a sign that Cathay was not far to the west.

During the very first months of his New World adventure, then, Columbus had invented two classic stereotypes that would condition Euroamerican perceptions of Indians for the next five centuries. The peaceful Arawak continued their idyllic Garden of Eden existence even as they were menaced by the brutal Carib monsters, vivid personifications of the Devil himself. The same Good Indian/Bad Indian imagery is peddled in many bookstores today.

In his Pulitzer Prize-winning *Admiral of the Ocean Sea*, published in 1942, and the subsequent *European Discovery of America* (1971–1974), the Harvard historian Samuel Eliot Morison uncritically employed Bad Indians to lionize Columbus, his lifelong hero. An experienced sailor, Morison retraced under sail every mile of the Admiral's epic first voyage to America. He portrayed Columbus, in typically stirring language, as "an intrepid mariner and practical dreamer" who met the hardships of land and sea "with stoic endurance." Among those hardships were the "dreaded man-eating Caribs," said to live on the island of Dominica, killing and eating all who ventured ashore. One day, Morison relates, the Caribs became so violently ill after eating a Spanish friar that they swore off clerics for good. From that time forth, whenever Spaniards were forced to call at Dominica for water, "they either sent a friar ashore or rigged up the boat's crew with sacking and the like to fool the natives."

The occasional brutality shown by Columbus and his men toward the Caribs was more than justified, Morison argued, because it was directed at club-wielding children of nature who existed halfway between humanity and animality. In Morison's view, Columbus was sent to the New World because the Caribs were the antithesis of civilized Europeans. They deserved what they got and Columbus was just the man to set things straight.

Similar portraits turn up in James Michener's *Caribbean*, a historical novel sold in tourist traps from Miami to Trinidad. Michener is not, to be sure, a card-carrying professional historian, but that hardly mattered to generations of Americans looking to soak up a little history on their Caribbean vacations through the rich prose of a best-selling novelist. Though he fictionalized his Carib and Arawak characters, Michener assures the reader, "there is historical evidence for the life of the two tribes as portrayed."

To Michener "the heritage of the Caribs was brutality, warfare and little else." This evil tribe supplied the world with words "originating in force and terror: *cannibal, hurricane,* the war *canoe,* the manly *cigar,* the *barbecue,* in which they roasted their captives." Even the food habits of Michener's Caribs "were totally primitive and graced with none of the refinements that the Arawaks and other tribes had developed; the Caribs ate by grabbing with dirty fingers scraps of meat from the common platter, the men invariably snatching theirs before the women, who were allowed the leftovers." The macho Carib men mistreated their women, "and even their personal adornment was invariably of a warlike nature, and it was the men, never the women, who decorated themselves with the whitened bones of their victims." But Michener's blissfully civilized Arawaks were no match for marauding Carib war parties. "The impending struggles between these two contrasting groups were bound to be unequal, for in the short run brutality always wins; it takes longer for amity to prevail."

Michener's gripping drama about the Carib and Arawak has helped keep the pathos of the pre-Columbian past alive. His books are known for their meticulous research and grounding in historical scholarship. The back cover of *Caribbean* even suggests that "Michener should be assigned by the nation's educators to pep up those dull, dull history books that students yawn through."

THE PROBLEM IS that the Columbus-Morison-Michener renderings of Caribs and Arawaks are totally and utterly false. There were no man-eating Carib marauders. There were no peaceful Arawak villagers. There was no northward invasion by man-eaters.

Recent historical and archaeological research has shown that the Carib and Arawak imagery is pure myth, a product of overactive fifteenth-century European imaginations. Historian Alvin Josephy has called the Caribs "the most maligned humans on earth." Yet these stereotypes of native Caribbean life have persisted for five centuries, handed down from Columbus to Morison, from Michener to the poolside reader on cruise ships.

What Columbus really saw were differing ways of coping with European invaders. During the earliest encounters, native people often tried simple accommodation and compromise. But as the European strangers became more aggressive, the "peaceful Arawaks" fell victim to the Spanish sword and to the accidental germ warfare that wiped out thousands of native people lacking immunity to European diseases. Their strategies of accommodation made the Arawak villagers prime candidates for conversion to Christianity, but their numbers plunged during the first Columbian years, and their traditional culture soon died out.

As Columbus and subsequent explorers pushed their way southward through the Lesser Antilles, native people took up more aggressive tactics of resistance: From a native perspective, the "Carib" warriors were the first American freedom fighters, defending their families, their land, and their tribal sovereignty from foreign conquest. By the seventeenth century, Caribs were forging temporary alliances with the British, French, and Dutch. If the French outstayed their welcome on a particular island, the local Caribs would ally with the British to eject them. Then, after a few years of British rule, the Caribs might go back to join with the French to depose the British. This strategy fended off the tribes' complete disintegration until treaties had been worked out to divide up the Lesser Antilles. Such forms of resistance lasted well into the eighteenth century, and pockets of Carib people survive today. But to the European mind, they were heathens and savages.

Were the Caribs really cannibals? The best modern evidence suggests that they may indeed have engaged in ritual consumption of enemy body parts. The practice is well documented elsewhere in Native America—a ritual perhaps analogous to the rite of Roman Catholic communion. In the hands of the priest, the holy Eucharist *actually becomes* the blood and body of Jesus Christ. The Caribs were obviously not using other humans as merely a source of protein. But there is no credible evidence or first-hand testimony to establish that Caribs consumed human flesh at all. The only direct "evidence," from Columbus and his contemporaries, is lurid hearsay passed along again and again as fact.

YET THIS CANNIBAL image rationalized the Spanish imperative for a New World slave trade. Even the ardently sympathetic Morison recognized that "there never crossed the mind of Columbus, or his fellow discoverers and conquistadors, any other notion of relations between Spaniard and American Indian save that of master and slave." As his letters and log make clear, Columbus was scouting the islands for potential slaves from the very start. Invading America and enslaving her native people were justified, Columbus believed, because the Indians were so clearly inferior to Europeans; they maintained unconscionable institutions and lived in mortal sin. Given such bestiality, he wondered whether conversion to Christianity was even possible.

Queen Isabela and King Ferdinand, conflicted over the issue of New World slavery, were particularly upset by Columbus' proposed trafficking in humanity. Taken by the image of the peaceful Arawaks, the Queen and King saw American Indians as potential vassals and Christians-to-be, fully deserving of royal protection. After all, if they have souls, are you not obligated to love them as you love yourself?

By early 1500, Columbus was no longer a player in the Caribbean, having been hauled back to Europe in chains and in disgrace; but his invention of the Carib presence continued to fuel the dialogue on slavery. Although Isabela forbade slave taking among Indians friendly to the Crown in 1503, she specifically excluded "barbaric people—enemies of the Christian, those who refuse conversion, and those who eat human flesh." If those bloodthirsty Caribs were really decimating and devouring the Queen's gentle Arawaks, then the Spanish had the necessary justification for taking Indian captives. Thus the Caribs—whom the archaeologist William Keegan calls the "great villains of West Indian prehistory"—became fair game. As cannibals, they were beyond Christian redemption, and by long-standing European practice, anybody captured in a "just war" could be enslaved. This is why Spanish explorers welcomed news of mayhem and rebellion in the Indies. Conquistadors from this point forward carefully distinguished the fierce, cannibalistic Caribs from the peaceful Arawak villagers. The notary public became a key member of every exploring party, ready to record whether or not the Indians encountered in the tropical Caribbean were indeed eaters of human flesh. If so, they were subject to merciless attack and enslavement.

This was all a matter of Euroamerican necessity. Columbus and his successors needed the Noble Arawak/Bloodthirsty Carib fictions to rationalize slave taking to the Spanish Crown. Queen Isabela and King Ferdinand needed to maintain the same fiction to ensure that their missionaries could proceed in good faith, even in the face of hostile pagans. The Carib-Arawak dichotomy served the self-interest of an expanding Spanish empire—making up, to some degree, for Columbus' disappointingly meager discoveries of gold and other precious metals. For Morison, the premier Columbus biographer, detestable Carib cannibals justified the inhuman treatment of native people by his heroic Admiral of the Ocean Sea. For Michener, the division into Good Indians and Bad Indians pitted contaminated against uncontaminated, the pristine against the corrupt, the high-minded against the debased, and thus, provided his novel's dramatic tension. The twin imagery of Noble and Bloodthirsty Savage became a tool by which generations of Euroamericans would define and control Indian people. From the time of Columbus onward, the stereotypes created by newcomers led to a near-universal failure to appreciate the intricacies and textures of actual Native American life.

Rally, Mohawks! Bring out your axes.
Let's tell King George, we'll pay no more taxes.

TO A RAUCOUS chorus of war-whoops, hundreds of men poured from Old South Meeting House to storm the Boston dockyards in 1773. With faces painted like Indian warriors, wrapped in tattered blankets, waving hatchets and axes, they overwhelmed the unresisting guards and relieved three ships of their cargo. They hurled 90,000 pounds of tea—representing a small fortune—into the harbor. Their protest complete, the Boston patriots washed off their tawny face paint and tidied up the mess they'd made. Nobody was injured, and they offered to pay for a damaged lock.

Although technically an act of force, the Boston Tea Party was viewed even at the time as street theater, a symbolic bit of civil disobedience. This overtly defiant act helped convince King George III that it would indeed be necessary to use force against the Massachusetts troublemakers, and before long, the American colonists found themselves in a full-scale civil war with Mother England.

"PLAYED-OUT IDEAS" GO OVERBOARD WITH THE TEA

Thus the American Revolution was sparked by the rebels in Indian getup. But, of all the pre-Revolution protests staged in the 1770s against British authority, why has the Boston Tea Party so captured the American imagination?

The United States of America began as a nation vastly different from its Old World counterparts, defining a new kind of relationship between men and their government. The new republic inaugurated a form of self-government based on egalitarian principles central to the American revolutionary ideology. But the American Revolution also posed inevitable questions of identity: what does it mean to be not-British? What does it mean to be an American?

The "Mohawk" malcontents in a sense defined the terms of American independence by asserting a new symbolism for colonists disillusioned with British rule. By assuming a temporary Indian identity, the Boston protesters could cross the boundaries of European-style civility to attack the specific laws that vexed the colonists. They adopted the Indian as their symbol of daring, strength, individual courage, and defiance against hopeless odds. In 1774 and 1775, Paul Revere produced a patriotic series of popular engravings showing colonists—portrayed as Indians—being oppressed by British authorities. Indian imagery soon became commonplace on late eighteenth-century maps, in sculpture and paintings, even on early American wallpaper. Benjamin Franklin applauded the patriots' boycott of English products, emphasizing that both colonists and Indians could live without England, surviving on "Indian corn" if necessary. The logic of a unique Indian-style Americanism energized the Revolution and helped define a new national character. The Sons of Liberty had carved out an identity distinct from that of Mother England.

An important linguistic change took place as well. Before the Boston Tea Party, the term *American* usually meant *Indian* on both sides of the Atlantic. "Had anyone asked Captain John Smith at Jamestown or Miles Standish at Plymouth how the Americans were faring," suggests the anthropologist Robert Venables, "both would have reported on the local Indian nations. Smith and Standish were, after all, Englishmen." But as they adopted Indian symbolism, the rebel colonists began naming themselves "Americans," both asserting a detachment from England and an emerging common identity with the other Americans—the Indians.

Who was more American than a Mohawk? The Indians and the Sons of

Liberty were both American-born. Both embraced a love of independence and a certain skepticism toward authority. Because they had never experienced the feudal conditions of the Old World, Indians were viewed as somehow pure and uncontaminated—the perfect symbols of American life and liberty. "When our ancestors threw the tea overboard in Boston harbor," wrote Daniel Carter Beard, co-founder of the Boy Scouts of America, "there was a lot of junk, in the way of played-out ideas along with a monarchical form of government, which went overboard with the tea."

PATRIOT CHIEFS OF THE NEW REPUBLIC

Although the American Revolution was sparked by symbolic protest at the Boston Tea Party, things took a nasty turn two years later at Lexington and Concord. In the confusion following the "shot heard 'round the world," seventy-three Redcoats lay dead and another two hundred were wounded. The British command—already annoyed by the Indian symbolism affected by the upstart colonials—equated the crime of rebellion with characteristic Indian savagery, accusing the Colonials of tomahawking and scalping the wounded.

George Washington was in Philadelphia in May of 1775, attending the Second Continental Congress, when the fighting broke out in Concord. He had been mildly irritated by the Boston Tea Party, believing it would only encourage the British into further economic excesses. But with the news of bloodshed near Boston, Washington dutifully accepted an assignment as Commander-in-Chief, making him the first (and for a time the only) member of the Continental Army.

As America's most celebrated veteran of the French and Indian war, he was the obvious choice. But ironically, Washington's military career had begun badly; he had lost six of his nine previous military engagements. The worst had come in July 1755, when the twenty-three-year-old Lieutenant Colonel Washington joined the British expeditionary force as they pursued their undeclared war against France in the upper Ohio Valley. As Major General Edward Braddock and his troops prepared to attack Fort Duquesne, they were overwhelmed in a guerilla-style ambush. Braddock's force was demolished by an enemy they hardly saw. British regulars stood frozen in their formalized parade-ground ranks as French officers and Indian sharpshooters picked off the Redcoats. As the carnage unfolded before him, Washington begged for permission to "fight like Indians," to let his men break ranks, hide behind trees and rocks, conduct their own surprise attacks, then slip away into the woods. Braddock indignantly refused the young Virginian's request and died hours later. It was a complete rout—the single darkest day in Anglo-American military history—and a heartsick Washington made his way back to Mount Vernon.

Washington continued to fight in the French and Indian War (1754–1763), developing a reputation for bravery and an indifference to gunfire. He learned firsthand the futility of transplanting European rules of warfare to the American battlefield. Braddock and the other British generals fought according to a military wisdom accumulated over centuries of European conflict. The British rank and file were drilled in "civilized" warfare—emphasizing discipline and unquestioned obedience, marching in straight ranks, and firing in volleys. British troops arrived in America prepared to fight as road-bound armies, tied to supply depots by vast columns of wagons and carts. European military treatises had little to say about what today is called "guerilla warfare," which violates nearly every rule of "civilized" warfare.

Washington learned a valuable lesson as he marched alongside Seneca and Onondaga warriors during the French and Indian War: "Indians are the only match for Indians." Making little distinction between strategies of hunting and warfare, Indians knew how to conceal themselves in the woods. They understood the principle of orderly and strategic retreats. They also knew how to create and seize the psychological moment—charging from concealment with bloodcurdling war whoops. Rather than firing in generally directed volleys—which provided withering fire on the orderly European battlefields but proved worthless in the American woodland—Indian warriors were trained as sharpshooters from an early age. In short, the eighteenth-century Indian fought more like a modern infantryman than a British Redcoat.

As Commander-in-Chief of the Continental Army, Washington adopted Indian-style tactics whenever possible, even letting his men dress in their homemade buckskins. But when he petitioned the Continental Congress for permission to make buckskins the official uniform of the Revolutionary Army, Congress replied with stony silence. Predictably, the British military leaders denounced Washington's soldiers as "savages."

During the winter of 1777, Washington found himself commanding a demoralized, outnumbered, and outgunned army threatened by two thousand Hessian soldiers garrisoned at Trenton, New Jersey. He led his Continentals in a Christmas Day attack, catching the Hessians—who'd scoffed at reports of the advancing colonial army—completely off guard. This action, memorialized in painting and known to every schoolchild, explicitly broke the rules of civilized warfare with tactics inspired by Washington's experience with the Iroquois. Bleary with sleep and blinded by driving snow, the two thousand Hessians quickly surrendered, and not a single Colonial life was lost at Trenton.

Modeled on a Native American design, the Continental Army assumed an image of warriors fighting for their own liberty, protecting their families on their home turf, traveling light, and doing without. "Being devoid of heavy equipment and able to think for themselves," writes historian James Thomas Flexner, Washington's rebels "could move twice as fast as a professional army. Unless actually cornered, they were as hard to catch as quicksilver." Ultimate victory came at Yorktown.

Thus the American Revolution began and ended with Indian imagery.

IN THE DECADES following the Revolutionary War, Indians were key figures in the wildly popular writings of James Fenimore Cooper—America's first major novelist, whose *Leatherstocking Tales* celebrated the American wilderness and the frontier life. Like many of his countrymen, Cooper had little firsthand experience with Indians. Although motivated by compassion toward the Noble Savage, Cooper knew little about real Indian people—and much of what he thought he knew was distorted or downright false. His writings commonly confused one tribe with another, confounding customs, names, and languages.

The Indian imagery in Cooper's *Last of the Mohicans*, first published in 1826, was especially powerful. Appropriating the name of Uncas—an authentic seventeenth-century chief of the Mohegan (Mohican) people—Cooper sanitized his protagonist into the archetypal Noble Redman, a principled and loyal friend of the Euroamerican frontiersman. In Cooper's nostalgic and romantic portrayals, Indians and their cultures had an innate, natural simplicity and virtue that were being corrupted by European civilization. Young Uncas became the Good Indian incarnate—admirable, yet tragically destined for extinction.

If there ever was a Savage Redskin, it was Cooper's Magua. In one memorable passage, the renegade Huron snatches a screaming baby from the arms of its horrified mother, who then:

> *. . . darted, with distraction of her mien, to reclaim her child. The Indian smiled grimly, and . . . flourished the babe above his head, holding it by the feet, as if to enhance the value of the ransom.*
>
> *"Here—here—there—all—any—everything!" exclaimed the breathless woman, tearing the lighter articles of dress from her person, with ill-directed and trembling fingers—"Take all, but give me my babe!"*
>
> *The savage spurned the worthless rags . . . his bantering, but sullen smile, changing to a gleam of ferocity, he dashed the head of the infant against a rock, and cast its quivering remains to her very feet. . . . excited by the sight of blood, the Huron mercifully drove his tomahawk into her own brain. The mother sunk under the blow, and fell, grasping at her child, in death, with the same engrossing love, that had caused her to cherish it when living.*
>
> *At that dangerous moment Magua placed his hands to his mouth, and raised the fatal and appalling whoop. . . .*
>
> *More than two thousand raging savages broke from the forest at the signal, and threw themselves across the fatal plain with instinctive alacrity. . . . Death was every where, and in his most terrific and disgusting aspects. Resistance only served to inflame the murderers, who inflicted their furious blows long after their victims were beyond the power of their resentment. The flow of blood might be likened to the outbreaking of a torrent; and as the natives became heated and maddened by the sight, many among them even kneeled to the earth, and drank freely, exultingly, hellishly, of the crimson tide.*

This massacre could as easily have taken place on the sandy beaches of Michener's *Caribbean*. Uncas, without much of a stretch, could have been one of Michener's virtuous sixteenth-century Arawak farmers, defending his island paradise against the despicable Magua and his bloodthirsty Carib mates as they raped and despoiled their way through the West Indies.

Like a number of American authors, Cooper transfigured the Savage Redskin—an image then still being vividly played out on the western frontier—into something more noble for his worldwide audience of romantics. Indians, of course, only achieved nobility once they no longer posed a threat to the white settlers. With real Indians on the run, Cooper consecrated his imaginary Indians into a convincing, if fanciful, American past. But by 1850, the American reading public had tired of Cooper's literary shortcomings. Contemporary critics faulted Cooper as much for his far-fetched depictions of Indian reasoning and feelings as for his melodramatic and corny style. The images, however, lived on, reinforced by narratives from released captives, which sold well throughout the nineteenth century even after Cooper's novels fell out of fashion.

THE AMERICAN MELTING POT

The new republic began as an amalgam—*E pluribus unum*—an experiment in nation building that asked its citizens to leave behind former loyalties and band together to share a new life. George Washington warned newcomers against retaining the "language, habits and principles (good or bad) which they bring with them." Let them come as individuals, Washington said, ready to be "assimilated to our customs, measures and laws: in a word, soon become *one people.*" "The point of America," writes Schlesinger, "was not to preserve old cultures, but to forge a new American culture," and the analogy of the melting pot arose to denote the process by which immigrants were to become real Americans.

But what to do with the Indian? Though useful as a symbol, the flesh-and-blood American Indian was not welcome in the New Republic. The Declaration of Independence mentions native Americans only once, as "merciless Indian Savages." The Indian must either whiten himself to join civilized America or be exterminated. As western expansion drove Indians off their lands, President Washington encouraged the country to undertake "rational experiments . . . as may time to time suit their condition" with the aim of preparing the Indian for eventual assimilation—just as so many other groups were being drawn into mainstream American life. To be sure, Indians must give up their traditional hunting grounds—huge forest tracts that would doubtless be overrun by white settlers. But if they were to become farmers, they could retain their most fertile lands forever. Washington's plans never materialized, and at the dawn of the nineteenth century the "Indian problem" was left for others to solve.

Thomas Jefferson also favored assimilation. True to his long-standing belief in the capacity of environment to shape humanity, Jefferson and his supporters hoped to "free" the native from his savage background so that he could partake more fully of the national prosperity. Unlike the Negro, Jefferson asserted, the red man is "in body and mind, equal to the white man." In the view of historian Winthrop Jordan, Jefferson "determinedly turned three into two by transforming the Indian into a degraded noble brand of white man. . . . Amalgamation and identification, welcomed with the Indian, were precisely what Jefferson most abhorred with the Negro. The Indian was a brother, the Negro a leper."

Jeffersonian philanthropy required that the Indian abandon his hunter-warrior culture, his tribal order, his pagan superstitions, and his communal ownership of land. In 1808, President Jefferson invited the Indian people to "unite yourselves with us, and join in our great councils and form one people with us and we shall all be Americans." Throughout his Presidency, Jefferson welcomed numerous delegations of his "brothers" to Washington. Addressing a group of Miami, Potawatomi, and Wea leaders, he said, "Made by the same Great Spirit, and living in the same land with our brothers, the red men, we consider ourselves as of the same family; we wish to live as one people and to cherish their interests as our own." To delegation after delegation of Indians, Jefferson repeated his version of Washington's master plan. Addressing Indian leaders of the Northwestern Territory in 1802, Jefferson said it again, "We shall with great pleasure see your people become disposed to cultivate the earth, to raise herds of useful animals and to spin and weave, for their food and clothing. These resources are certain, and they will never disappoint you, while those of hunting may fail, and expose your women and children to the miseries of hunger and cold."

But Jefferson's policy of easy assimilation quickly ran into problems. Because he viewed Native Americans in the abstract, drawing upon both noble and violent imagery, Jefferson had doomed his Indian policy to failure. "The Indian could not hope to equal the level of virtue attributed to him," argues the historian Bernard Sheehan, "because the primitivist formulations drew on a set of presuppositions wholly different from those within the reach of real men." Toward the end of his presidency, a frustrated Jefferson complained that despite all that his administration had done to help them, Indians still clung to their old ways. If an Indian "chose to remain an Indian, in the face of all paternalistic efforts to the contrary," writes the historian Richard Drinnon, "then he confessed himself a madman or a fool who refused to enter the encompassing world of reason and order. The red child then had to be expelled from the landscape of pastoral tranquility—or be buried under it. . . . Yet from the Indian point of view, the end result was pretty much the same: death, flight, or cultural castration." In their zeal to promote an agrarian way of life, the Jeffersonians had seriously underestimated the Indian devotion to their own lifeways. Although altruistic whites had tried their best to uplift the Indian, the native Americans, by preferring tribalism to progress, proved themselves unworthy of the faith placed in them.

Here, then, is Jefferson's fundamental ambivalence toward Indian people—a compassionate altruism tempered by a desire to maintain absolute control. According to Drinnen, Jefferson believed that "Indians *were* children, red shadows dancing through the trees, naughty boys and girls who combatted him. . . . And if they would not listen to reason, would not bury the dancers in themselves, Jefferson would bury them. . . . Eternal children, they were too immature themselves to launch a campaign of resistance; hence they had to have been manipulated or tampered with by crafty agents, most likely renegade whites or foreign agents." With his memorable words, "We hold these truths to be self-evident . . . ," Jefferson had set the cornerstone of white American liberalism. But with respect to Indians, he cast himself in the role of Great White Father. When native people resisted, they mocked their father, and like spoiled children, perhaps they deserved a good spanking.

Discouraged by the failure of his Indian policy, Jefferson could back a brutal war against recalcitrant Indians and take strong measures to take away their tribal lands. As President, Jefferson even suggested that influential Indian chiefs be encouraged to go into debt to government trading houses, then forced to pay off these debts by ceding their tribal lands.

With the apparent failure of melting pot democracy, the United States stepped up its wars of territorial consolidation against Indian people. Although the Indian wars saw inexcusable acts on both sides, the United States never formally declared a policy to exterminate the Native American. The unspoken premise was that Indians would continue to die out through undeclared warfare, disease, and the "natural" process of one race supplanting another. "Jefferson's philanthropy was as real as Jeffersonian animosity," notes the historian Richard White, "but both in different ways envisioned the disappearance of the Indian."

THE WAR OF 1812 AND REMOVAL

Indian-white relations in America were transformed permanently by the War of 1812. When Congress declared war on Great Britain, many tribes sided with the British, upsetting the neat plans for an American melting pot and further discouraging those who believed in their capacity for assimilation. Tecumseh, the gifted orator and chief of the Shawnee, joined with British forces to unite the western tribes into a mighty coalition to oppose further American expansion. But within six months, Tecumseh was dead, and Andrew Jackson had crushed the Creeks at Horseshoe Bend in Tennessee, effectively ending any further Indian resistance in the South.

The tide had turned. As Speaker of the House Henry Clay noted, the Indians were powerful and the colonists weak when the colonies began. But these "poor children of the forest" were driven westward to the foot of the mighty Rocky Mountains, overwhelmed by American progress which "left no other remains of hundreds of tribes, now extinct, than those which indicate the remote existence of their former companion, the mammoth of the New World!"

The Treaty of Ghent ending the War of 1812 provided that Great Britain and the United States would place their Indian allies in the same political status as before the war began. The United States then signed treaties with tribes along the Missouri, bringing these Indians within the reach of the federal government. This was a critical change. By cutting the Hudson's Bay Company out of the fur trade on U.S. soil, it meant that the United States government could henceforth deal for "open lands" in the American West with the assurance that the Indian owners could no longer trade directly with the British. Once valuable allies of America's enemies, the Indians had become militarily impotent. By aligning themselves with the British, these unappreciative Indians were seen as having waived all claims for sympathy.

The disenchantment of the philanthropists and the settlers' unquenchable thirst for land culminated in a policy of Indian removal. The idea of removing the eastern Indians to western reservations originated with President Jefferson, and the land required for Indian removal materialized with his Louisiana Purchase. In its various incarnations, the removal policy was promoted as pro-Indian—a way of providing native hunters with the territory necessary to sustain them and save them from their predatory white neighbors.

In 1824, James Monroe presented to Congress his own plan for "civilizing the Indians" by sending them voluntarily across the Mississippi. Rejecting forced removal as "revolting to humanity and utterly unjustifiable," Monroe asked Congress to provide protection for Indians and their property west of the Mississippi and to find a way to instruct them in "the arts of civilized life and make them a civilized people."

The plan was doomed from the start. How would officials obtain the voluntary consent of those being expatriated? What if they didn't want to leave? And why would Indian people aspire to the "civilized" life of a society that forced Indians out of their homeland? As Drinnon noted, Monroe "merely asked the Native Americans, officially and still cordially, to become the Vanishing Americans."

When the Indians declined, Andrew Jackson pressed the issue, arguing that their only chance was complete segregation from mainstream America by treaties and enforced removals. Although Indians would then disappear as discrete tribal groups, they could survive forever as individuals. Again this policy was described as a terrific deal for the Indians. After all, white settlers were moving hundreds, sometimes thousands of miles westward at their own expense, paying for their new lands, and supporting themselves even while establishing new homes. "Can it be cruel in the government when, by events which it cannot control, the Indian is made discontented in his own home—to purchase his lands, to give him a new and extensive territory, to pay the expense of his removal, and support him a year in this new abode?" Jackson asked. "How many thousands of our own people would gladly embrace the opportunity of removing to the West on such conditions?"

The Indian Removal Act of 1830—a "voluntary" swap of lands by eastern Indians for territory that the federal government would provide west of the Mississippi—did not authorize the use of force, but neither did it require the federal government to protect those Indians being displaced. Left to the mercy of the southern States, the Cherokees and other tribes had little means of resistance. Most lost their land, their homes, and their livestock. In Georgia alone, the Creeks lost more than 25 million acres of land. Although some native people would remain, landless, in their homeland, most of the Indian "hostiles" in the American South, perhaps 60,000 people, were rounded up and forcibly marched westward to Indian Territory in Oklahoma. In retrospect, the Indian removal of the 1830s remains one of the darkest chapters in American history, a precursor of twentieth-century European strategies of ethnic cleansing.

The removal of the Cherokee people, mandated in the Treaty of 1836, set a deadline of May 23, 1838, for them to leave. Most refused to budge. The federal government then dispatched General Winfield Scott to fulfill the conditions of the treaty. Although he directed his troops to treat the Indians with kindness, many tales of inhumanity have surfaced. Waiting out the hot summer, the Cherokees finally agreed to leave in the fall; but they were delayed again by a drought, and the overland caravans did not depart until October. Totaling 13,000, the emigrants, including black slaves, carried along with them all they possessed. Their delayed start took place during the harshest months of the year, and "this Trail of Tears reaped a heavy harvest of misery and death." Estimates of the human cost of the 1838 removal vary. Although government reports claimed that only about ten percent of the Cherokees died, an 1890 report from the Indian Rights Association declared that one-half the tribe perished on the trail. The most commonly accepted figure seems to be about four thousand people, roughly one-quarter of the Cherokee moving westward. Whatever the actual number, one historian has described the Trail of Tears as a "presidentially ordered death march that, in terms of the mortality directly attributable to it, was almost as destructive as the Bataan Death March of 1942."

THE INDIAN WARS

Jackson's hope that removal would solve the Indian problem was short-lived. The United States acquired vast new territories with the annexation of Texas in 1845, the settlement of the Oregon border dispute in 1846, and the addition of California and New Mexico in the same year. As Euroamericans streamed westward in droves, their trails crisscrossed the Great Plains, nominally ruled by the 75,000 Plains Indians who lived there. Except for the Civil War period, prosecuting the Indian Wars would remain the major occupation of the United States Army for the next half century.

As always, language and imagery reinforced the war effort. Although claiming no prior knowledge of Indian people, William Medill, Commissioner of the Bureau of Indian Affairs from 1845 to 1849, was sufficiently comfortable with the reigning opinion to confidently describe his charges as "ignorant, degraded, lazy, [with] no worthwhile cultural traits." Immediately after Medill's term as Commissioner, California Indians were being hunted down by whites, and the newspapers of the day adopted almost identical terms to justify the butchery of the "ignorant, bestial savages who deserve no rights."

Luke Lea, Commissioner from 1850 to 1853, justified his policy of "civilizing" the Indian this way: "When civilization and barbarism are brought into such relation that they cannot coexist together, it is right that the superiority of the former should be asserted and the latter compelled to give away. It is, therefore, no matter of regret or reproach that so large a portion of our territory has been wrested from its aboriginal inhabitants and made the happy abode of an enlightened and Christian people." The next Commissioner in line, Dennis Nelson Cooley (1865-1866), referred to some of his Pueblo Indian wards as "the miserable lizard-eaters of Arizona," and followed a policy in which he articulated "the elimination of Indian culture as a laudable objective."

Such was federal rhetoric during a period when the strongest of the western tribes continued to resist the Euroamerican invasion of their lands, waging wars of attrition against the U. S. Army across the American West. One after another, the Indian tribes met with disaster as their territory continued to shrink under the unrelenting white invasion. The buffalo all but vanished by the early 1880s, and the Army increasingly pressed large-scale campaigns, forcing the tribes onto reservations where they could not interfere with the settlement and development of the West. In treaty after treaty, Indians ceded most of their land and moved to "Reservations," places where their children were to be educated well away from daily contact with whites. Although the vast reservations of the Plains originated only as temporary expedients—on the assumption that Indians would require less land once they switched from hunting to farming—in fact, they proved to be exchanges for grants of land by Indians. As Indians became increasingly dissatisfied with reservation conditions, particularly the failure of Indian Agents to deliver on the stipulations of the various treaties, the military was increasingly required to round up and return recalcitrant Indians to their reservations.

The Army was also assigned the task of keeping the emigrant and stagecoach routes Indian-free. The United States Army perceived itself as the spearhead of American civilization, brushing aside the primitives and making way for a new generation of hard-working Americans. In truth, the army was but one of many instruments of conquest, joining the miners, ranchers, farmers, traders, railroad men, Indian agents, and others responsible for opening the West.

In the late nineteenth century, the U. S. Army took on the scientific task of collecting the heads and bones of Indians slain on the western battlegrounds and shipping them to the museums of the eastern seaboard. As the image of the Vanishing American took hold, Indians were gradually transformed from enemies standing in the way of Manifest Destiny into specimens to be stockpiled and studied by western science.

A PROGRESSION OF IMAGERY

Historian Robert Berkhofer emphasizes that federal Indian policy was always grounded in "the idea of the Indian." Even today, although the language and imagery have moderated somewhat, mainstream America still reflects strangely contradictory love-hate feelings toward the Indian.

The initial period of contact with the Noble Redman commonly began with goodwill and hospitality, feelings inherent in Columbus' images of the "peaceful Arawaks" and the Mohecan Uncas as virtuous innocents inhabiting an Eden-like land. The downside of this image, the stereotype of Indian-as-likable-child, carried over into issues of land title. Europeans relentlessly claimed Indian land by invoking royal charters to areas inhabited by peoples with only imperfect title to the land.

During the subsequent expansion of white civilization, with its attendant displacement of native people, Savage Redskin images re-emerged to justify the Indian schools designed to whiten the red man and rationalize episodes

During the late nineteenth century federal policy dictated that the Indian must either whiten him- self to join civilized America, or he must be exterminated. These 'before" and "after" photographs of Tom Torlino (Navajo) were taken at Carlisle Indian School in 1882 and 1885.

of outright warfare against the Indians. By fantasizing "bad Indians," like the contemptible Magua, Euroamericans could picture their policy of westward expansion as a clash between savagery and civilization, a struggle between good and evil. Nineteenth-century American Indians were effectively given the choice of jumping into the melting pot or fighting it out on the battle- field.

The progression of Indian imagery also had a geographical component. From the seventeenth through early nineteenth centuries, Euroamerican set- tlement concentrated on the coastlines. White populations did not really penetrate the inland plains and basins in significant numbers until the mid- nineteenth century. Across eastern America, where the Indian menace had largely evaporated in the eighteenth century, imagery was mostly of the noble and romantic variety. Eastern liberals of the nineteenth century, raised on tales about Cooper's Uncas, tended to favor missionization and educa- tional, philanthropic, and welfare programs, and other federal policies de- signed to "save the Indian."

Although the Plains were also hit heavily by European diseases, more In- dians had survived because human settlements were more dispersed than those along the populous coasts. On the western frontier, where Plains Indi- ans were still capable of defending themselves against white incursions, In- dian imagery tended toward the Savage Redskin variety, with an attendant push for military conquest and even outright extermination of the Indian foes. Euroamerican expansion onto the American plains also coincided with the end of the Civil War, when the federal government found itself with a huge standing army with little to do. Veteran generals like Sherman and Sheridan, needing to occupy their troops, saw pacifying the Plains Indian as a perfect task for their peacetime armies.

During the final mopping up operations, after effective elimination of an Indian military menace, there arose a wave of nostalgic Vanishing American imagery. Because mainstream Americans in Theodore Roosevelt's era understood Indians mostly as antitheses to themselves, civilization and Indianness would forever remain opposites. The disappearance of Indians from their land coincides with their nostalgic iconography on the most commonly available United States coins: the Indian-head penny (1859-1909), the celebrated buffalo nickel (1913-1938), the gold quarter, and the half eagle (1908-1929). Although Roosevelt suggested in 1905 that an Indian head also appear on the ten-dollar Gold Eagle, he eventually settled for a feathered Indian headdress placed on the profile of the goddess Liberty. In 1912, a full-faced depiction of Sioux warrior Hollow Horn Bear was placed on the 14-cent postage stamp. Since 1899, Chief One Papa has appeared on the five-dollar certificate.

By contrast, no African American face has ever appeared on a regularly circulated United States coin (and not until 1940 did an American stamp recognize any aspect of black achievement). This is because the Indian was invented in a way completely different from any other American minority.

Part II

NINETEENTH-CENTURY SCIENTISTS

It is important for new generations of scholars to become aware of many of the anthropological dilemmas that earlier generations may wish to forget. It would be unreasonable to assume that all of the racist, classist, and sexist assumptions, once central to physical anthropology, have been discovered and resolved.

—*Michael L. Blakey (1987), Bioarchaeologist*

THE FIRST AMERICAN
ARCHAEOLOGIST

3.

IN THE IMPOSING entrance hall of his Monticello mansion, Thomas Jefferson proudly displayed his prize collection of natural history specimens—mastodon bones and other fossils along one wall, a mix of prized Indian relics against the other. His estate at Poplar Forest continued the theme, displaying a Cree deerskin dress collected by Lewis and Clark at Fort Mandan, painted buffalo robes from the Plains, a Chinook woman's skirt of cedar bark, an Omaha tobacco pouch, and a Crow Indian cradleboard.

When Jefferson died, insolvent, his Indian artifact collection was dispersed. A number of his most valued Indian artifacts were later lost to fire. Some were simply discarded by those who did not share Jefferson's enthusiasm for things Indian. Some today are curated in Harvard's Peabody Museum. A few have found their way back to Virginia, installed in a reconstruction of Jefferson's Monticello entrance hall, which the historian Roger Kennedy calls "the nation's first museum of the American Indian."

Jefferson was always fascinated by American Indians and their relationship to the natural world. A catholic scholar, he actively pursued a program of avocational research in paleontology, geology, botany, and zoology—and archaeology. This devotion to natural history would eventually spill over into his life as a founding American patriot.

JEFFERSON DEFENDS THE AMERICAN VIRTUE

Five years after the Boston Tea Party, an American victory in the revolution against England looked increasingly unlikely. France, still smarting from losses in the Seven Years' War and looking for a way to curtail British political ambitions, began to see the war in America as a significant drain on British manpower and resources. So the French furnished the American rebels with military supplies and equipment, clothing, blankets, and a hefty infusion of cash. As the revolution dragged on, with the sides better balanced, French and American interests became increasingly intertwined.

Eager to learn more about its new ally, the French government circulated a semi-official questionnaire among influential members of the Continental Congress, requesting details about life in America. After some debate, the task of responding was given to thirty-seven-year-old Governor Thomas Jefferson of Virginia. The French inquiry arrived during the British occupation of Virginia, one of the darkest times in Jefferson's life, and he immersed himself in the new assignment. His response was published in 1787 as *Notes on the State of Virginia,* his only book. He was at particular pains to disprove the then-prevalent French thinking in natural history that disparaged the New World in general, and the British colonies in particular, as inferior to the created natural order of Europe.

The renowned French naturalist Georges de Buffon, in his multi-volume and authoritative *Histoire Naturelle* (the first volume published in 1749), had taken the concept of a "New World" to its illogical extreme. Employing a geological perspective, Buffon described America as an immature land, still covered with an unhealthy environment of humid swamps and jungles. In Buffon's view, American flora and fauna were smaller and weaker than comparable species in the rest of the world. Since all had left the Ark approximately equal, the American species must have been degraded by their environment. This "degeneration" applied as well to the continent's native people.

Buffon's theory heavily conditioned European images of American Indians. To be sure, Indians were children of nature, brave innocents able to withstand harsh conditions that would kill a European. But Indians were also seen as crafty and cruel, filthy and unschooled, prone to lascivious behavior, cannibalistic, and capable of inflicting great pain without remorse. Buffon, one of the first to see the Indian body as a source of scientific data, wrote that Indians had small, enfeebled organs of reproduction and that their men were prone to impotence. Because they lacked body hair and beards—time-honored European symbols of masculinity—Native American men were seen as effeminate and lacking in "ardor for the female." They fared no better on the social level. Buffon believed that Indians lacked true families, which rendered them incapable of establishing even the rudiments of society: "their heart is frozen, their society is cold, their empire cruel."

By the time of the American Revolution, Buffon's controversial thesis had sparked a lively debate about the relative merits of the American and European continents. European images of Indians were rooted in the belief that the environment directly influenced the organism: if Indians were inferior, they had been degraded by the American environment. European domesticated animals introduced into the Western Hemisphere would degenerate as well. It was just a matter of time, therefore, before transplanted Europeans also became inferior. This was why, in Buffon's view, America was so miserably lacking in the arts and letters: "America has not yet produced one good poet, one able mathematician, one man of genius in a single art or a single scientist."

Not surprisingly, American scholars took great exception to Buffon's theory. Jefferson used his *Notes on the State of Virginia* to defend America's flora, fauna, climate, geology, social institutions, and especially the American Indian. As an empiricist, he had little patience for armchair arguments from Frenchmen relying on hearsay. "It does not appear that [Buffon and his colleagues] have measured, weighed, or seen those [animals] of America. It is said of some of them, by some travelers, that they are smaller than the European. But who were these travelers? Did they measure or weigh the animals they speak of? ...Were they acquainted with the animals of their own country, with which they undertake to compare them? Have they not been so ignorant as often to mistake the species?" The peppery attack on Buffon reflected both Jefferson's deep-seated belief in scientific research and his unabashed national pride. While accepting the environmental premise, Jefferson shifted the terms of debate from theory to data. Because Americans could readily collect their own data on Indians, they could assume a position of authority.

To prove his point, Jefferson prepared an exhaustive table of animal weights for the Old and New Worlds, drawing upon extensive observations, both his own and those of many others. He then mounted an elegant point-by-point refutation of Buffon's key assertions regarding the First Americans:

BUFFON: *"He has neither hair nor beard."*

TJ: *"With [Indians] it is disgraceful to be hairy on the body. They say it likens them to hogs. They therefore pluck the hair as fast as it appears."*

BUFFON: *"They lack ardor for their females, and consequently have no love for their fellow men."*

TJ: *"In contradiction to this representation, [the Indian] is neither more defective in ardor, nor more impotent with his female, than the white reduced to the same diet and exercise."*

BUFFON: *"He has no vivacity, no activity of mind."*

TJ: *"His vivacity and activity of mind is equal to ours in the same situation . . . to judge the truth of this, to form a just estimate of their genius and mental powers, more facts are wanting, and great allowance to be made for those circumstances of their situation which call for a display of particular talents only. This done, we shall probably find that they are formed in mind as well as in body, on the same module with the 'Homo sapiens Europaeus'. . . . Before we condemn the Indians of this continent as wanting genius, we must consider that letters have not yet been introduced among them."*

BUFFON: *"Nature, by refusing [the Indian] the power of love, has treated him worse and lowered him deeper than any animal."*

TJ: *"An afflicting picture indeed, which, for the honor of human nature, I am glad to believe had no original."*

Jefferson pulverized Buffon's treatise, but he did not stop there. Not content merely to ship Buffon a copy of the finished book. Instead, Jefferson booked passage to France to personally deliver it into Buffon's hands, along with an immense panther skin and the carcass of a huge moose—so much for the enfeebled American wildlife.

DIGGING FOR INDIAN ORIGINS

The *Notes* also set out Jefferson's vision for Virginia and America as a whole. In defending the Indians against their European detractors, Jefferson was also defining an emerging American fabric in which Indian identity was becoming indistinguishably intertwined with that of white Americans, giving the United States of America a unique national identity.

Jefferson's *Notes* was also a serious inquiry into First American origins. If Indians were to be lionized as prototypical Americans, then they must be more than warmed-over Europeans. To Jefferson, solving the problem of Native American origins required a two-pronged strategy: first to learn about contemporary Indian culture, and then to see whether living Indians could be linked up with the evidence of past American inhabitants. Trained in classical linguistics, Jefferson reasoned that Native American languages must hold valuable clues to Indian origins. Through his extensive correspondence, he compiled vocabularies from more than forty tribes and wrote a long treatise on the subject (which mysteriously disappeared when he left the White House and was never published). Jefferson later claimed that this volume would have established an Asiatic origin for American Indians. His comparison of vocabularies strongly suggested "the probability of a common origin between the people of color of the two continents."

This theory was reinforced by the reports of Captain James Cook, whose final expedition of 1778 had mapped the Bering Strait region. Cook's information posthumously reinforced Jefferson's feeling, expressed in *Notes*, that "if the two continents of Asia and America be separated at all, it is only by a narrow streight. So that from this side also, inhabitants may have passed into America; and the resemblance between Indians of America and the Eastern inhabitants of Asia, would induce us to conjecture, that the former are the descendants of the latter."

The main archaeological question addressed in *Notes*, however, was not the origins of Indians as such, but of the thousands of earthen mounds that dotted the eastern American landscape. Many scholars of the time believed that a white race had constructed these impressive monuments before mysteriously vanishing; others believed they had been built by the ancient ancestors of the American Indian. Having found contemporary Native Americans in every way the mental and physical equals of the white races, Jefferson concluded that they were quite capable of having constructed the ancient monuments.

Jefferson then framed his primary hypothesis: The earthen mounds were built by ancient Indians to honor their dead. To demonstrate this, he had his slaves excavate one of the mounds located on his property. Today, such a step might seem obvious, but few of Jefferson's contemporaries would have considered resorting to bones, stones, and dirt to answer an intellectual question. Scholarship was located in libraries and archives, not in the soil.

Jefferson wrote up his dig in *Notes on the State of Virginia*. As a good natural scientist must, he first described his data—location, size, method of excavation, stratigraphy, condition of the bones and artifacts. Noting the absence of traumatic wounds such as those made by bullets or arrows and also the interment of children, he rejected the competing hypothesis that the bones were those of soldiers fallen in battle. Similarly, he concluded that the scattered and disjointed nature of the bones militated against the notion of a "common sepulchre of a town," in which one would have expected to find skeletons arranged in more orderly fashion.

Jefferson ultimately surmised that the human skeletons had accumulated in the mound through repeated mortuary use, and saw little reason to doubt that the earthworks had been constructed by the ancestors of eighteenth-century Indian people. Today, two centuries after these pioneering excavations, few archaeologists question his conclusions.

Unlike his contemporaries, Jefferson did not dig to obtain curios for his mantel (although some artifacts did end up there). By excavating an archaeological site to answer a clearly defined question, Jefferson elevated white America's study of the past from a speculative, armchair pastime to an inquiry built on scientific fieldwork and empirical protocols. As a well-educated gentleman of the Enlightenment and a well-schooled natural scientist, Jefferson clearly understood the importance of exposing speculation to a barrage of facts. Because the facts in this case lay buried beneath the ground, that is where he conducted his inquiry.

In so doing, Jefferson pioneered the basics of modern archaeology: defining his hypotheses beforehand, exposing and recording his finds in meticulous detail, and ultimately publishing all for scrutiny by interested scholars. In theory at least, others could impartially test his conclusions on comparable data collected independently.

NOTES ON THE *State of Virginia* established Jefferson as a world-class scholar. The broad range of issues addressed demonstrated both the flexibility of Jefferson's mind and his self-described "canine appetite" for scholarship and learning.

In truth, Jefferson had little first-hand experience with Indian people. By the mid-eighteenth century, disease and warfare had taken a huge toll on Virginia's native population, which during Jefferson's youth survived mostly as diminished and demoralized refugee groups. Although he had seen the occasional delegation of Indians passing through Williamsburg to negotiate with British governors, Jefferson knew remarkably few real Indians. So when he argued that Indians were fully as human as Frenchmen, Jefferson was speaking of a people he rarely saw. He was defending an imaginary Noble Redmen who lived far beyond the confines of his everyday life.

Perhaps this lack of familiarity is what caused Jefferson to study Indian people from a detached, scientific perspective. This side of Jefferson fully anticipated—and to some degree invented—the natural history mentality that would establish nineteenth-century anthropology's approach to Indians as scientific specimens, as objects for study not terribly unlike mastodons and glaciers. This is why archaeology textbooks, including my own, canonize Thomas Jefferson as America's first scientific archaeologist. It is also why many modern Indians see him as America's first scientific grave robber.

A SHORT HISTORY OF SCIENTIFIC RACISM IN AMERICA

Racial determinism was the form taken by the advancing wave of the science of culture, as it broke upon the shores of industrial capitalism. It was in this guise that anthropology first achieved a positive role alongside of physics, chemistry, and the life sciences, in the support and spread of capitalist society.

—*Marvin Harris (1968), Anthropologist*

WHEN COLUMBUS AND Queen Isabela debated whether to enslave the Indians of the Caribbean Sea, they were rehearsing arguments first articulated in antiquity. Beyond the civilized world of classic Greece and Rome lay the land of the *barbarphonoi* (literally, the speakers of *bar-bar*). The "barbarians" wore only skin clothing, behaved unpredictably, and refused to submit to proper religious and legal guidance. Beyond the known barbarians—whom Aristotle considered natural slaves—was the land of the "monstrous races." According to the Roman Plinius, some sported but a single eye in the middle of the forehead, others had dog faces, and still others walked upside down.

This three-part split into the civilized, the barbarian, and the monstrous was transformed under Christendom into the faithful, the unredeemed, and the unredeemable. A map from Columbus' era echoes this division of races in its depiction of how the sons of Noah repopulated the world after the Flood—Japheth went to Europe to father the Caucasians, Shem's descendants became the Asian Mongolians, and Ham ended up in Africa. Johann F. Blumenbach, an anatomy professor at the University of Göttingen in Germany, formalized these racial divisions in his dissertation *On the Natural History of Mankind*, published in 1775. Working from a sample of 82 skulls, Blumenbach defined the first scientific classification of human races: Mongoloid, Caucasoid, Negroid, plus a couple of intermediate "oids." In his *The Mismeasure of Man*, Stephen Jay Gould calls Blumenbach "the founder of anthropology."

Like Buffon and all other educated Europeans, Blumenbach never questioned the biblical view that humanity was the product of a single divine Creation. What, then, accounted for racial differences? As people spread around the world after the Flood, the differences in their bodies must have resulted from the various environments they encountered. The closest living relatives to the primordial type were the people of the Caucasus Mountains, who had strayed the least from the Ark's landing point. "The Caucasian must, on every physiological principle, be considered as the primary or intermediate of these five principal Races. The two extremes from which it has deviated, are on the one hand the Mongolian, on the other the Ethiopian [African blacks]." According to Blumenbach, the Caucasian skull was the most symmetrical when viewed from the top and from the back. Since the circle was the most perfect shape in nature, Blumenbach concluded that the near-perfection of the Caucasian skull must have been the type created by God. Climate, diet, mode of life, hybridization, and disease had all contributed to its degeneration in the non-Caucasian races. With a liberalism unusual for his time, Blumenbach asserted that environmental damage could be undone—that with proper education, there were no limits to human achievement, irrespective of race.

The Swedish botanist Carl von Linné, better known by his Latinized name Linnaeus, was the originator of modern systematic biology. In his attempt to classify all living things, Linnaeus divided *Homo* into distinct races much like those of Blumenbach: Asians (pallid, dour, and governed by opinion); Africans (black, wily, and ruled by whimsy); American Indians (reddish, single-minded, and guided by tradition); and Caucasian Europeans (white, gracious, and governed by reason). The Linnaean classification embodied the very essence of raciology—the conflation of physical attributes, personality, politics, and ethics—and further reinforced traditional white images of Indian people. This basic scheme was refined *ad nauseam* throughout the centuries, with Caucasians universally considered to be the original ("purest") of the races.

THE AMERICAN SCHOOL OF SKULL SCIENCE

Until the time of Darwin, most nineteenth-century European thinking on racial origins was grounded in Christian theology. The Bible was taken as direct support for the theory of monogenesis (origin from a single source): God created humanity at one time, in one place, and everyone was descended from Adam and Eve. This assumption led Blumenbach and others to theorize that observable racial differences had arisen after the Creation due to racial degeneration.

Between 1830 and his death in 1851, Samuel George Morton, a Philadelphia patrician with two medical degrees, promoted a different line of biblical reasoning. A dedicated scientist, Morton electrified his generation with an empirical demonstration that race could be correlated with skull size and, by extension, with various levels of human intelligence. The "American School" Morgan founded was one of this country's first homegrown scientific theories and the first to capture the serious attention of the European scientific community. Morton's obituary in *The New York Tribune* noted that "no scientific man in America enjoyed a higher reputation among scholars throughout the world, than Dr. Morton." His rigorous approach triggered a new wave of scientific research on human skulls, and also set loose the wholesale looting of Indian graves across America.

Morton argued against the single creation theory, developing a view of

Lithograph of mummi-fied Egyptian skulls published in Samuel Morton's Crania Aegyptiaca (1844).

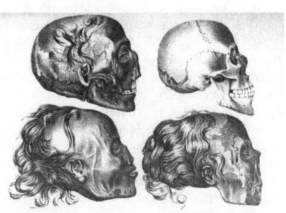

multiple racial creation (polygenesis). Still operating within a biblical frame-work, his theory held that the various races had been created separately and each given specific, irrevocable characteristics. After inspecting several mummies from the ancient Egyptian catacombs, Morton concluded that blacks and Caucasians were already distinct three thousand years ago. Since his Bible indicated that Noah's Ark had washed up on Mount Ararat only a thousand or so years before this, Morton reasoned that Noah's sons could not possibly account for all the modern races. Therefore, the races must have been separate from the start. Thus Morton's theory of polygenesis attracted a loyal and enthusiastic following.

To Morton, the human skull provided a highway back in time, a way to trace racial differences to their beginning. But when it came to demonstrating to his medical students how this worked in 1830, Morton was surprised that he could not find the necessary skulls to make his point. "Strange to say, I could neither buy nor borrow a cranium of each of these races," he later wrote. "Forcibly impressed with this great deficiency in a most important branch of science, I at once resolved to make a collection for myself."

As Morton would soon learn, demand for human anatomical specimens greatly outstripped the legal supply of excavated criminals. Physicians increasingly turned to professional body snatchers, who called themselves "resurrectionists." Understandably, these grave robbers ran into considerable public resistance. New Yorkers rioted for three days in 1788 when some children discovered medical students dissecting human cadavers—including one child's recently deceased mother. A mob numbering in the thousands stormed the hospital and the jail, where the physicians had taken refuge. The militia was called out to quell the so-called "Doctor Riots."

Nineteenth-century physicians had no compunctions about digging up the graves of Euroamericans (in fact, cadavers from the white race were most highly prized for medical purposes). But because it was less dangerous to rob the graves of African Americans and Indians, resurrectionists began concentrating on graveyards of poor people and nonwhites.

Well aware of these difficulties, Morton drew upon his connections with the Philadelphia Academy of Science and the American Philosophical Society as he built up his collection. He readily secured a number of skulls dug up from archaeological sites, but had some difficulty coming up with contemporary Indian crania. Eventually, as smallpox and other epidemics swept across Indian Country, appropriate specimens turned up on the flourishing skull market, and Morton bought them.

Louis Agassiz, at the time perhaps the world's best informed and most capable biologist, was so deeply impressed when he visited Morton's growing skull collection in 1846 that he wrote his mother: "Imagine a series of 600 skulls, most of Indians from all tribes who inhabit or once inhabited all of America. Nothing like it exists anywhere else. This collection, by itself, is worth a trip to America." During his lifetime, Morton's "cranial library" had grown to more than 1,000 specimens and was the world's most comprehensive skull collection. Morton drew upon his collection to establish a new science he called *craniometry*—the scientific analysis of skull size and shape. In his classic *Crania Americana*, published in 1839, he developed his theory of human racial origins, signaling the beginning of physical anthropology in America.

Morton believed not only that the human skull was remarkably resistant to the effects of environment but that it provided an accurate measure of brain size and cognitive powers. Properly analyzed, a large sample of human skulls should simultaneously provide both racial classifications and an index of the mental development of each race.

But the initial problem was what exactly to measure. After considering several possibilities—including exterior dimensions, facial angles, skull shape, suture patterns, and so forth—Morton settled on cranial capacity (brain size) as the single best indicator of race. Cranial capacity was simple to measure—just fill up a skull with something, pour that something out, and then measure the volume. He started with white mustard seeds, but they were too light and tended to compress, producing a variability of perhaps five percent. So he eventually switched to BB-sized lead shot, which provided volume estimates consistent to the nearest cubic inch. Stressing the objectivity of his scientific methods, Morton argued that by using large sample sizes and simple, easily repeatable measurements, he could avoid the aesthetic and subjective judgments that had colored previous cranial studies. His contemporaries were impressed with his scientific rigor, and for decades Morton's cranial statistics provided seemingly unassailable support for scientific doctrines of racial and intellectual inequality.

In *Crania Americana*, Morton demonstrated that Caucasians had big brains (averaging 87 cubic inches), blacks had small ones (78 cu. in.), and Indians fell into the middle (82 cu. in.). But this was not enough: He also wanted to rank the races intellectually and socially. Drawing upon the existing body of phrenological techniques, he correlated cranial size and shape with mental traits as reflected in known customs and behaviors. Morton's colleagues around the world collected skulls for him, and many that arrived in his Philadelphia laboratory were accompanied by specific data about the individual: age, sex, race, occupation, and various personality traits. Morton was thus able to compare specific metric attributes with known behavior traits, generating phrenological correlates that could then be extended to the rest of his skull collection.

But what were these "phrenological techniques" that enabled Morton to move from measurements to racial mentality? The key assumption guiding his work was that brain size was directly linked to intelligence. This "logical principle," which we now know is incorrect, provided Morton a means for mapping the relative intelligence of the races, and an explanation for why one race seemed to act differently from another. In a time when many phrenologists matched specific bumps on the skull with particular personality traits, Morton took the cautious stance that brain size itself was a sufficiently strong predictor of "national traits." Behavior, he argued, could be projected from cranial capacity alone.

Although this logic today seems murky, Morton believed that his skull sample proved that Caucasians were the superior race—with Teutons and Anglo-Saxons at the top, Jews in the middle, and Hindus on the bottom. He found the "Esquimaux" of Greenland to be "crafty, sensual, ungrateful, obstinate and unfeeling. . . . heir mental faculties, from infancy to old age, present a continued childhood." The Chinese were almost as bad, a "monkey race," and the black Hottentots were like "the lower animals." To Morton, these racial differences reflected a divine master plan. The Caucasian type had been and always would be supreme—God's will expressed as natural order and verified by empirical science.

SKULL SCIENCE AND INDIAN POLICY

Morton concluded from his large skull sample that the phrenology of American Indians reflected an unusually uniform mental makeup. The rather small cranial capacity not only betrayed an intellect inferior to other races, but the other cranial indicators necessary for "predilection for the arts or sciences" were entirely absent. The Indian brain was so deficient, said Morton, that the race would be impossible to civilize: "The structure of [the Indian] mind appears to be different from that of the white man, nor can the two harmonise in their social relationships except on the most limited scale."

In a 1842 speech delivered to the Boston Society of Natural History, Morton expanded on the findings in *Crania Americana*. The Indians were "savage people" with a "peculiar and eccentric moral constitution." Their racial stock was decidedly inferior to the Mongolians: "Their minds seize with avidity on simple truths, while they reject whatever requires investigation or analysis." Rejecting any significant environmental effects, Morton reiterated that God, not the environment, had shaped the Indian's skull. He concluded, "He who has seen one tribe of Indians has seen it all."

The American school of anthropology gave pre-Civil War America a way to cope with the Jeffersonian dilemma: whereas the Declaration of Independence proclaimed that all men were created equal, black slaves need be considered equal *only* if they were the product of the very same Creation that gave rise to the Caucasian race. To Morton, the question of monitoring racial equality (and the rights that flowed from it) properly belonged in the hands of objective science. If scientific research could document a single Creation—an essential human unity—then the results must support the abolitionist movement, and slavery must be struck down.

But Morton's craniometry concluded the opposite. The races had resulted from multiple Creations, demonstrating God's intent to deliberately create blacks for the purpose of serving their white betters as slaves. Indians, argued the scientists of the American School, had been created for a rather different reason. As Oliver Wendell Holmes wrote in his 1855 poem "Oration," the Redman was a "sketch in red crayons of a rudimental manhood to keep the continent from being a blank until the true lord of creation should come to claim it." By transferring the study of race from theology to science, Morton mounted an elegant and empirical defense of manifest American destiny: Euroamerican-style civilization was fated to control the Western Hemisphere, but America's indigenous people stood in the way. Although an outright policy of extermination would be decidedly un-Christian, the Indian problem might just resolve itself, since America's native inhabitants were doomed by their own biology.

Science had laid bare God's plan for the red and black races. "It must be borne in mind that the Indian is incapable of servitude, and that his spirit sunk at once in captivity, and with it his physical energy [whereas] the more pliant Negro, yielding to his fate, and accommodating himself to his condition, bore his heavy burden with comparative ease." Shortly after Morton's death in 1851, a leading American medical journal lauded Morton's scientific legacy: "We of the South should consider him as our benefactor, for aiding most materially in giving to the negro his true position as an inferior race."

So there it was—skull science verified what mainstream America already knew from everyday experience: Blacks could live only in slavery, and Indians could survive only in freedom. In the words of Alexis de Tocqueville, "the servility of one dooms him to slavery, the pride of the other to death." There was hope for Negroes only so long as slavery persisted. Freed blacks were destined to perish from their racial inability to cope with the competitive stresses of the capitalist system. Although whites could value blacks as slave labor, they were no longer useful once freed.

The American School held out even less hope for Indians. In *Types of Mankind*, a 1854 memorial tribute to Morton, Josiah Nott and the other contributors confirmed that observable racial differences reflected independent episodes of Creation. It was their racial makeup that led Indian people to reject the government's generous offers to remove them to places of long-term safety. Bad biology led Indians to remain in their now-unsuitable (if traditional) homelands, and clearly the Indians' inferior intellects rendered them forever incapable of becoming civilized. "It is as clear as the sun at noon-day, the last of these Red men will be numbered with the dead," Nott wrote in *Types of Mankind*, "To one who has lived among American Indians, it is in vain to talk of civilizing them. You might as well attempt to change the nature of the buffalo."

Although Morton died eight years before *Origin of Species* was published, Darwin's revolutionary theory of natural selection landed on fertile soil already tilled by the American School. After declaring Darwin "clearly crazy," Nott and the other followers of Morton were quick to applaud his anti-religious overtones. But in the long run, Darwinian evolution spelled the end of the monogenist-polygenist debate because the human races were seen as merely transitory stages of a species. In the larger evolutionary context, the races of humanity had not been created separately and they were hardly fixed and unchanging divisions of the human condition.

Morton's methods and findings were readily transplanted into the new evolutionary theory. Where once skull science had supported polygenism, it was not enlisted to support the ranking of races along an evolutionary gradient. The ranking itself, needless to say, did not change. As biological evolution came to be understood and increasingly accepted, most nineteenth-century investigators believed that cultural evolution worked basically the same way—perhaps it was even a part of organic evolution. To this way of thinking, cultural and social factors were secondary, or perhaps even irrelevant, in molding the individual. "Human beings were what they were," noted the historian Robert Bieder, "because of the tilt of the faces and the shape of their skulls." By conflating culture with biology, Morton and others offered an apparently reasoned and scientific explanation for why some cultures did better than others.

DARWIN AND THE DISAPPEARING AMERICAN INDIAN

5.

It can now be asserted that savagery preceded barbarism in all the
tribes of mankind, as barbarism is known to have preceded civilization.
The history of the human race is one in source, one in experience, one
in progress.

—*Lewis Henry Morgan* (1877), *Anthropologist*

DURING THE LATE nineteenth century, Lewis Henry Morgan, a Rochester lawyer-turned-ethnologist, was America's most influential anthropologist. Raised on a farm in western New York, Morgan encountered his first Indian in the pages of *The Last of the Mohicans*. The powerful imagery of the League of the Iroquois fueled Morgan's life-long fascination with American Indian lore.

As a young lawyer in 1842, Morgan and several upstate New York friends formed a secret literary fraternity called "The Gordian Knot." Their patriotic mission was to pen the great American epic, to distill a fundamentally American national identity. In the process, they would put to rest, once and for all, unfavorable comparisons between the United States and mother Europe. Although members of The Gordian Knot steeped themselves in ancient Greek and Roman imagery, the more they read, the clearer it became that America's elusive character, that essential American ethos, derived not from classical European antiquity but from the First Americans. In 1843, having accepted the importance of the Noble Redman in defining the American identity, Morgan and his friends changed their name to "The Grand Order of the Iroquois" and immersed themselves in Indian imagery. They shifted from meeting halls to campfire sessions in the great outdoors. Through the Grand Order of the Iroquois they hoped to return to an original America, if only through a weekly meeting in Aurora, New York, dressed up in beads and buckskins behind an abandoned Freemason lodge. Reflecting on this toward the end of his life, Morgan admitted, "Whatever interest I have since taken in Indian studies was awakened through my connection with this Indian fraternity." Writing the great American saga was soon forgotten as The Grand Order focused instead on devising its own authentic Indian garb and rituals: "We do not stir a step," wrote Morgan, "until our equipment is right."

"REAL INDIAN PEOPLE BOTH HAD—AND HAD NOT—DISAPPEARED"

As members of The Grand Order learned more about the Indians, they realized that authentic Iroquois culture was disintegrating. Their focus shifted once again, from dressing up as Indians to documenting the real thing before it passed from the American scene. Morgan escaped his law practice whenever possible to attend ceremonies and dances on the Tonawanda, Onondaga, and Tuscarora reservations in western New York State. He took precise notes and interviewed Seneca elders, collecting both artifacts and customs.

In 1845, Morgan happened on a young Seneca man while browsing in an Albany bookstore. Ely Parker was an extraordinary intellect who would later become aide-de-camp to General Ulysses S. Grant during the Civil War and the nation's first Native American Commissioner of Indian Affairs. Anxious to share his first-hand knowledge of Iroquois family and tribal government and, apparently, quite impressed with Morgan, Parker himself enrolled in The Grand Order, providing Morgan even greater access to Iroquois society.

Whenever he was unable to attend ceremonies at the Tonawanda Reservation, Morgan commissioned Parker to record the speeches and events. He impressed upon Parker the importance of accurately recording what happened, fostering a level of ethnographic recording unparalleled for the time. After six years of intensive study, Morgan published his classic *The League of the Ho-dé-no-sau-nee, or Iroquois* (1851), which began with the words: "To encourage a kinder feeling towards the Indian, founded upon a truer knowledge of his civil and domestic institutions, and of his capabilities for future elevation, is the motive in which this work originated." The first modern ethnography of an Indian people, Morgan's *League* set the standards for generations to come. Throughout, Morgan also stressed the urgency of ethnographic research because culturally knowledgeable Indians were fast disappearing.

Morgan saw living Indians as belonging to a cultural stage distinct from that of white America. According to the developing logic of Morgan's social evolution, the only real Indian culture—the only culture relevant to anthropology—belonged to the past. Even though they had survived physically and kept having offspring, Indian people in the present tense were "inauthentic" because their culture differed from that of centuries ago. "Their memories were authentic," writes Philip Deloria, "even if their lives were not."

In the late nineteenth century, as the frontier began to close, the Noble and Bloodthirsty imagery of Indians was gradually overtaken by the Vanishing American. Under Morgan, American ethnography emerged as a vital and influential field of study, a powerful new lens through which mainstream Americans could view Indian people. Anthropology assigned itself the task of recording ancient Indian lifeways, already corrupted by the European presence, before they disappeared. To salvage ethnographic detail on the Vanishing Americans, ethnographers developed a new analytical device for separating living Indian informants from the rest of nineteenth-century America. They invented a synthetic "ethnographic present," by which they began reconstructing "traditional" Indian lifeways by factoring out more recent changes. According to the nineteenth-century historian Herbert Howe Bancroft, they tried to describe Indians "as they were first seen by Europeans . . . along the several paths of discovery . . . in all their native glory, and before the withering hand of civilization was laid upon them." The construct of the "ethnographic present" established Indian people as somehow both alive and archaic. Simultaneously, late-nineteenth-century ethnographers became the world's first time-travelers. Only they, it would seem, could cross the boundaries of time and space, moving at will between the present and the world of traditional authenticity.

Although many white Americans could empathize with the plight of the vanishing Indian, they saw these Indians as also somehow outside social boundaries. Carrying on a tradition begun by Jefferson, anthropologists would express a far greater interest in things "traditionally Indian" than in the modern Indian lives that played out before them. And the Indians being studied would deeply resent them for doing so.

GENERALIZING THE IROQUOIS

As Morgan worked up his Iroquoian data, he increasingly fixed upon kinship relations, which he believed held the key to the inner workings of ancient social organization. He felt that once he fully grasped the nature of Iroquois kinship—the various ways in which people reckoned their relationship to others through marriage and descent—he could reconstruct how the basic Iroquois institutions of government, property, technology, and economy had developed.

To broaden his experience beyond the Iroquois, Morgan started traveling among Indian tribes of the American West and, casting his net still further, sent out questionnaires asking missionaries and Indian agents to record for him the details of Indian kinship across America. When he discovered that similar terminology existed in India, Morgan expanded his mailings abroad, sending hundreds of questionnaires to U. S. consular officials throughout the world.

This was the first systematic attempt to collect ethnographic data on a global scale. Morgan eventually published his results on kinship relations in *Systems of Consanguinity and Affinity of the Human Family*, published in 1870. A few years later in *Ancient Society: Or Researches in the Lines of Human Progress from Savagery Through Barbarism to Civilization* (1877), he refined his kinship data into a whole new theory of social evolution. In *Ancient Society*, Morgan traced the history of the human family, government, private property, and technology through three sequential stages—as the title suggests, from savagery to barbarism to civilization. Morgan's social evolution arranged both contemporary and ancient societies along a kind of developmental ladder. But except for the addition of evolutionary theory, this scheme differed little from the ancient Roman division of humanity into the monstrous, the barbarian, and the civilized.

On the bottom rung of Morgan's ladder—the "lower status of savagery"—were those primeval, rudimentary, and primitive people who subsisted strictly on fruits and nuts. None of these had survived into the historical period. When people discovered how to catch fish and use fire—as exemplified by living Australian aborigines and Polynesians—they were elevated to savagery's "middle status." Morgan's "upper status of savagery," defined by the use of bow and arrow, still survived among the Athapascan tribes of Hudson's Bay Territory.

Higher still were the barbarians, inventors, and manufacturers of ceramics. The Woodland Indians of North America typified barbarians at this "lower status." "Middle status" barbarians domesticated animals, irrigated their crops, and built adobe brick and stone architecture. So viewed, the village people of Mexico and New Mexico were "middle status barbarians." In the "upper stage" of barbarism were the ironworkers, exemplified by Grecian tribes of the Homeric Age and Germanic tribes of the time of Caesar. The top rungs of Morgan's ladder were reserved for various "advanced" societies, civilized society beginning with the onset of phonetic alphabets and production of literary records.

American Indians, in Morgan's view, had "commenced their career on the American continent in savagery; and, although possessed of inferior mental endowments, the body of them had emerged from savagery and attained the Lower Status of barbarism; whilst a portion of them, the Village Indians of North and South America had risen to the Middle Status." Despite having clawed their way up the evolutionary ladder, American Indians ranked well below the Aryans and Semites.

Morgan's theory of social evolution became the backbone of late nineteenth-century anthropology, providing a way for museums and universities to classify the cultures they were studying, and enabling curators to group artifacts from around the world in rows of glass-fronted cases. Morgan saw human history not in the static racial terms of Morton and Agassiz, but as a grand progression from the simple to the complex. This evolutionary sequence was also attractive because it melded an empathetic view of "savage" tribes with a rationalization for the ultimate triumph of "civilization." On both sides of the Atlantic, the conquest of Indian people by Euroamericans could now be seen not as the aggression of one people against another but as part of the inevitable, inexorable expansion of civilized people around the world.

Morgan believed that a group's social, economic, and political institutions—the very essence of the savagery-barbarism-civilization continuum—derived from inherited mental "germs," carried like dormant seeds, ready to sprout under appropriate environmental conditions. He attributed the lack of progress in Indian assimilation to innate Indian biology and saw Indian women as particularly important ingredients in the great American melting pot. Mixed marriages would produce offspring who "will intermarry respectably with our white people and thus the children will become respectable and, if educated, in the second and third generations will become more beautiful and attractive. This is to be the end of the Indian absorption of a small portion, which will improve and toughen our race, and the residue [will be] run out or forced into the regions of the mountains." Such change would take place slowly, however, because Indians retained the "skulls and brains of barbarians, and must grow toward civilization as all mankind have done who attained it by progressive experience." These views on assimilation became central to federal policy when Morgan's protege, John Wesley Powell, created the Smithsonian's Bureau of American Ethnology in 1879.

THE RISING TIDE OF SOCIAL DARWINISM

Ancient Society was published eighteen years after Darwin's *On the Origin of Species*. Darwin had reasoned that since resources are inherently limited, the young of reproductive age struggle to survive. Most do not make it and, in the long run, the survivors persist because they possess traits that give them a competitive advantage of some kind. These physical variations are passed along to the next generation. Thus, with each succeeding generation, the number of individuals with advantageous traits increases, and those with less advantageous traits decline. The evolutionary process, being gradual and continuous, eventually gives rise to new species through what Darwin termed "natural selection." *Origin* introduced the notion that all organisms are descended from a common ancestor and provided evidence that Earth's various life forms are dynamic and ever changing. Darwin thus set out a coherent explanation for Earth's biological diversity. Although he never actually used the term "evolution," the very last word in the first edition of *Origin* is "evolved," and evolutionary theory will forever be associated with his name.

In constructing his theory about the diversity of life, Darwin unwittingly provided a scientific rationale for Morgan's scheme of social evolution. Social Darwinists argued that, like all other organisms, people struggle to survive. The successful ones—the rich and powerful—must therefore be the "fittest" in an evolutionary sense. Social Darwinists confidently ranked human societies according to their "evolutionary" status—from highly evolved groups (mostly upper class Europeans) downward to those only slightly more advanced than apes. The lower socioeconomic classes of Europe—and the "primitive" people throughout the world—were "less fit," less capable intellectually and emotionally, and hence less deserving of survival. Nineteenth-century social Darwinists argued that essentially all human progress depends on competition. Stifle competition and you retard progress. The doctrine of social Darwinism became a handy justification for unfettered global imperialism, racism, and capitalist enterprise.

During the 1860s and 1870s, social Darwinism established a fairly tight linkage between archaeology and ethnology. Archaeologists showed that humanity had a deep past, stretching far beyond previous biblical estimates; ethnologists of the era were developing the explanatory tools necessary to flesh out the specifics of that past (by using what Morgan and others called the "comparative" approach). Ethnology established that there were primitives living among contemporary humanity and social Darwinism explained why they were there: the world's primitive people were living fossils, human leftovers from the Stone Age.

Whereas Thomas Jefferson had idealized the American Indian into an emergent identity for the New American Republic, in the hands of the social Darwinists, Indian people became the prototypes of humanity's earliest condition. Anatomical parallels were quickly drawn between Neanderthal skulls—first found in Germany in 1856—and the skulls of living Australian aborigines; some people suggested cultural parallels as well. Both ancient European cave men and the primitive people of Australia were thought to represent an archaic stage in human social development. The Neanderthals had died out long ago, unable to compete. The nineteenth century's "living fossils," American Indians and Australian aborigines, were likewise destined to fall victim to more evolved forms of humanity.

LUBBOCK'S PRE-HISTORIC TIMES

In 1865, John Lubbock—Darwin's next-door neighbor in Kent, England—published his influential *Pre-historic Times, as Illustrated by Ancient Remains, and the Manners and Customs of Modern Savages*. Widely read throughout Europe and America, it became archaeology's primary textbook.

Lubbock advocated a cross-cultural, comparative method to describe the life of "paleolithic" (Old Stone Age) and "neolithic" (New Stone Age) people by reference to contemporary primitives. That is, now that archaeology had put people into the Pleistocene, it became the task of the evolutionist to show how they got out—a task accomplished easily enough by showing that variation in time corresponded with ethnographic variation across space. Making this case, Lubbock argued that Darwinian-style natural selection had operated on ancient human societies to produce both biological and cultural differences. So viewed, the cultures of the past fell into a neat, linear continuum, with Euroamerican capitalist society being the most advanced. Societies lacking advanced technology, Lubbock argued, were handicapped by inferior intelligence and base emotions.

The message was simple: humanity was improving—biologically, culturally, emotionally, and intellectually—through natural selection. Left to their own devices, capitalist societies would prosper and improve the world. The downside was that the world's primitives were doomed. These backward people had not, in Lubbock's view, evolved sufficiently, and no degree of remedial education could repair the damage done by millennia of natural selection. Although neither Darwin nor Lubbock advocated outright extermination of non-Western people, both seemed to be saying that the modern world was better off without them.

THE GREAT AMERICAN
SKULL WARS

6.

The dead have no rights.

—Thomas Jefferson

BY 1864, the tensions between the white settlers flooding into Colorado and the Cheyenne Indians, whose land it was, had spilled over into the Denver newspapers. A front-page editorial urged "extermination of the red devils" and encouraged the local citizenry to "take a few months off and dedicate the time to wiping out the Indians." Disparaging the ongoing treaty negotiations with the Cheyenne, Major John Chivington, Methodist minister and Civil War hero, proposed to his church deacons that "the Cheyennes will have to be roundly whipped—or completely wiped out—before they will be quiet. If any of them are caught in your vicinity kill them.... It is simply not possible for Indians to obey or even understand any treaty. I am fully satisfied, gentlemen, that to kill them is the only way we will ever have peace and quiet in Colorado."

On an icy November morning, Chivington led a regiment of Colorado Volunteers against the unsuspecting Cheyenne villages of Black Kettle and White Antelope at Sand Creek. "Scalps are what we are after," he exhorted his men. "I long to be wading in gore!" Ignoring the American flag flapping over Black Kettle's lodge—an acknowledged sign of truce for all—Chivington's troops slaughtered hundreds of Cheyenne villagers, mostly women and children. As the wounded moaned unattended, drunken soldiers moved from body to body, scalping, mutilating, and collecting sordid souvenirs. Fleeing children became moving targets for marksmen, and several still-living Cheyennes were scalped. One woman's heart was ripped out and impaled on a stick. Several soldiers galloped around the battleground, sporting bloody vaginas as hatbands.

One trooper cut off White Antelope's testicles, bragging that he needed a new tobacco pouch. Later, nobody could remember whether White Antelope was still wearing the peace medal given to him by President Lincoln. Returning to Denver, the Sand Creek heroes paraded through the streets, to the cheers of throngs. Theatergoers applauded an intermission display of Cheyenne scalps and women's pubic hair, strung triumphantly across the stage.

Several of the Cheyenne dead received special treatment. After the corpses were beheaded, the skulls and bones were defleshed and carefully crated for shipment eastward to the new Army Medical Museum in the nation's capital.

THE GILDED AGE
OF NATURAL HISTORY

It is impossible to comprehend the events at Sand Creek without understanding the power and popularity of scientific racism in mid-nineteenth-century American society.

When Louis Agassiz, famed Swiss naturalist, first visited the United States in the 1840s, he was shocked at the public apathy toward the study of natural history. Like most natural historians of his era, Agassiz believed that the most important scientific task at hand was to collect, describe, and classify the species of the natural world—including man. The small size and poor quality of the natural history collections in the United States appalled him. Although a number of Americans, including Thomas Jefferson, had expressed an interest in classifying the various forms of plants, animals, and minerals, they had either to make their own personal collections or travel to Europe to study the requisite specimens. The few amateur natural history societies that sprang up lacked any public support and members had to store their collections in homes or barns, where they were vulnerable to theft and fire. On ac-

Self-portrait of Charles Willson Peale (1822), opening the curtain to his newly incorporated Museum in Philadelphia, the first natural history museum open to the American public.

cepting a professorship at Harvard in 1847, Agassiz lobbied his adopted country to establish some world class institutions to curate and analyze systematic natural history collections.

Agassiz's extraordinary personality and enthusiasm for science attracted a number of wealthy patrons anxious to see America take its rightful place in the global community. After raising sufficient funds to establish Harvard's Museum of Comparative Zoology in 1856, Agassiz set about building a collection of classifiable specimens for his students. But his was a "teaching" museum, not a museum for the general public. Agassiz also urged the creation of large public museums, along the lines of the fabled British Museum and the Musée National de l'Histoire Naturelle in Paris. The United States government had already in 1840 received a half-million dollar gift (in gold) from an Englishman who never set foot on New World soil. James Smithson's wishes were simple enough—to establish an institution "for the increase and diffusion of knowledge among men." But the bequest touched off a torrid debate over how best to spend the money. After wrestling with several alternatives, including a library, observatory, agricultural experimental station, and university, Congress finally established, in 1846, a new National Museum to be called the Smithsonian Institution. Building the Smithsonian collection began in earnest when zoologist Spencer Baird joined the staff as Assistant Secretary in 1850, and brought his personal collection, part of which had been given to him by John Audubon, with him. Two years after the 1876 Centennial, Baird became Secretary, and the Smithsonian Institution's collecting binge intensified.

Post-Civil War America emerged as the world's first industrial superstate. The transcontinental railroad, the coal and steel complex, and the sophisticated financial markets in New York, Chicago, and San Francisco all came to symbolize America's wealth and power. The new riches generated a wave of homegrown philanthropy and Agassiz's crusade to establish natural history museums soon sparked a response in a culture-hungry America ready to step onto the world stage.

Fearing that the Smithsonian might grab up all the best collections, wealthy private donors founded rival institutions. George Peabody donated part of his huge personal fortune to Yale and Harvard Universities so that each could establish a "Peabody Museum" devoted to the study of natural history, including archaeology and ethnology. He also funded the Peabody Academy of Science in Salem, Massachusetts. Albert Bickmore, an Agassiz student at Harvard, sold his idea of a New York-based natural history museum to that city's social and economic elite, which included J. Pierpont Morgan, Joseph Choate, and Theodore Roosevelt, Sr. The considerable political clout of then-State Senator (later Mayor) William "Boss" Tweed helped establish the American Museum of Natural History in 1869. Located adjacent to Frederick Law Olmsted's Central Park (begun in 1857) and soon joined by the Metropolitan Museum of Art (founded in 1874), the American Museum helped create an urban oasis of culture, education, and amusement. In Philadelphia, the long-standing Academy of Natural Sciences (established in 1812) was joined by the University Museum of Archaeology and Paleontology, established at the University of Pennsylvania in 1887. Chicago's Field Museum was incorporated in 1893, and the Museum of Anthropology at the University of California was founded in 1899. Beyond these major players in the museum world, hundreds of smaller, local museums and historical societies sprang up across America.

Each of these museums began buying up existing natural history collections. The American Museum purchased a huge trove collected by the late

German naturalist Prince Maximilian—more than 4,000 mounted birds, 600 mounted mammals, and 2,000 fish and reptiles preserved in alcohol. In 1874, the same trustees bought, for $64,000, a collection of tens of thousands of fossils representing more than 7,000 species. Agassiz himself had bid unsuccessfully for it arguing that "whoever gets this collection gets the geological museum of America."

But such expensive, ready-made collections severely stretched the museums' limited budgets. The trustees of America's natural history museums were mostly businessmen, and the high cost of purchasing collections went against their best business sense. Wouldn't it be more cost-effective, some asked, if we eliminated the middleman and made our own collections?

Museum curators enthusiastically agreed. As practicing natural scientists, they jumped at the chance to launch their own collecting expeditions; scientifically collected specimens could form the basis of understanding the origin of life and our place in it. Not insignificantly, sensational collecting expeditions could bring prestige and celebrity to the scientists, museums, and benefactors who showed the foresight to grab the lead in America's Golden Age of Natural History.

"LET ME HAVE THE BODIES OF SOME INDIANS"

Skull collecting—long an avocation of the elite natural historian—became in the words of one critic "a cottage industry on the frontier." Collecting human skulls was more dangerous than netting butterflies or digging up dinosaur fossils. One nineteenth-century collector wrote that whereas Indians expressed no particular concern over skulls taken from ancient mounds, they did seem disturbed by the plundering of more recent graves. Another complained, "It is rather a perilous business to procure Indians' skulls in this country—The Natives are so jealous of you that they watch you very closely while you are wandering near their mausoleums & instant & sanguinary vengeance would fall upon the luckless—who would presume to interfere with the sacred relics.... There is an epidemic raging among them which carries them off so fast that the cemeteries will soon lack watchers—I don't rejoice in the prospects of death of the poor creatures certainly, but then you know it will be very convenient for my purposes." Reliable documentation, including the individual's tribe or band, cause of death, level of intelligence, and personality traits, could inflate a skull's market value, sometimes dramatically, because these data helped skull scientists correlate personality and intelligence with cranial attributes.

Faced with the difficulties of financing his new museum at Harvard, Agassiz came up with a novel way to enlarge America's growing natural history collections. In 1865 he wrote to Secretary of War Edwin Stanton with a simple request: "Let me have the bodies of some Indians. All that would be necessary . . . would be to forward the body express in a box. . . . In case the weather was not very cold . . . direct the surgeon in charge to inject through the carotids a solution of arsenate of soda. I should like one or two handsome fellows entire and the heads of two or three more." Soliciting the government for skulls to stock the research collections, Agassiz furthered the trend begun by Thomas Jefferson, who declared Indian skulls and bones to be fair game for scientific inquiry.

U. S. Surgeon General William A. Hammond played along, issuing orders to all medical officers "diligently to collect, and to forward to the office of the Surgeon General, all specimens of morbid anatomy, surgical or medical, which may be regarded as valuable. . . . These objects should be accompanied by short explanatory notes. . . . Each specimen in the collection will have appended the name of the medical officer by whom it was prepared." Hammond's policy succeeded as hoped. As Indian tribes were being confined to reservations or hunted down, the bones of their dead were systematically gathered up and shipped to the newly founded Army Medical Museum. The skulls and skeletons from the Sand Creek Massacre became one of the earliest accessions, and similar specimens were gathered from other western battlegrounds, reservation cemeteries, and deep inside ancient mounds. U.S. Army hospitals became laboratories for processing Indian bones.

Upon the death of a young Yankton Sioux woman—a "squaw having remarkable beauty"—a post surgeon in the Dakotas dug up her grave, severed her head, and dispatched it to Washington as "a fine specimen." Ten days later, the same medical officer dispatched the head of an old man who had "died at this post on the seventh day of Jan. 1869 and was buried in his blankets and furs in the ground about a half mile from the Fort, within a few rods of the tippes [sic] occupied by his friends. I secured the head in the night of the day he was buried. From the fact he was buried near these lodges, I did not know but what I was suspected in this business, and that it was their intention to keep watch over the body. Believing that they would hardly think I would steal his head before he was cold in the grave, I early in the evening with two of my hospital attendants secured this specimen."

Eleven days later in Ellsworth County, Kansas, United States soldiers and local citizens attacked and slaughtered a trading party of Pawnee men as they were peacefully visiting a white farm on Mulberry Creek. Although accounts vary over what started the skirmish, everyone agrees that when the smoke cleared, the post surgeon from Fort Harker, B. E. Fryer, dispatched a civilian to the massacre site to collect the skulls of the dead Pawnee. After he had found and decapitated one corpse, a blizzard set in, and the Pawnee survivors stopped him from collecting the other's skulls. But two weeks later, the weather moderated and Fryer resumed his search, ultimately recovering five additional crania from the Mulberry Creek Massacre. The Pawnee skulls became part of a shipment of 26 sent to Washington, including skulls from the Cheyenne, Caddo, Wichita, and Osage tribes. Fryer was particularly proud of his Pawnee specimens, four of which were recovered in prime condition, but two others, unfortunately, "were injured a good deal by the soldiers, who shot into the bodies and heads several times in the fight in which these Indians were killed."

Between 1868 and 1872, Fryer shipped at least forty-two Indian skeletons to Brevet Lieutenant Colonel George A. Otis, a curator at the Army Medical Museum. By this time, Otis had measured more than eight hundred Indian skulls in his growing collection, concluding that "the American Indians must be assigned a lower position on the human scale than has been believed heretofore."

"IT IS MOST UNPLEASANT WORK TO STEAL BONES...."

Into this bizarre world stepped a thirty-year-old German-born geographer named Franz Boas. Historians of science would one day praise Boas as "the Father of American anthropology," but at the time, he was just another expatriate intellectual coming to 1880s America in search of a good job and a new life.

As a child in Minden, Germany, Boas had learned about the plants found in the woods and the animals of the sea. Over the years, he studied zoology, botany, mathematics, physics, geography, and physiology, and became particularly expert at mapping plant distributions. His doctoral research on the color of seawater reflected Boas' scientific bent toward explicit observation, description, comparison, and classification. He came to America intent upon introducing new canons of empirical research in anthropology, with a distinct emphasis on first-hand fieldwork.

In May 1888, the young Dr. Boas left his editorial assistant's job at *Science* magazine to accept a contract funded by the British Association for the Advancement of Science and the Canadian government. He agreed to undertake a general survey of tribes in British Columbia, concentrating on collecting linguistic and physical anthropological data—mostly measuring skulls of living Indians (many of them locked up in jail). He was also to bring home a collection of Indian skulls and skeletal parts. Discouraged at his inability to become associated with any of the established natural history museums, Boas also used the trip to build up a personal Northwest Coast Indian skull collection as a speculative business venture. He described himself as "just like a merchant," who was hoping that a carefully documented collection, at the going rate of $5 for a skull and $20 for a complete skeleton, might return "a tidy profit"—as well as finally open the door to a permanent curatorship.

While digging in a burial ground near Victoria, British Columbia, Boas used a photographer to distract the Indians while he was doing his grave robbing. On June 6, 1888, he wrote in frustration that "someone had stolen all the skulls, but we found a complete skeleton without head. I hope to get another one either today or tomorrow. . . . It is most unpleasant work to steal bones from a grave, but what is the use, someone has to do it. . . ."

After turning up only a dozen or so skulls on his own, Boas heard of another collection of some 75 skulls in Cowichan, amassed by William and James Sutton for sale on the American phrenological market. Boas spent a day measuring the skulls and, sensing that a market indeed existed for them, he bought the whole collection. He also retained the services of the Suttons to collect still more, promising to buy whatever they could dig up.

Before long, the Suttons complained to Boas that securing the dozens of additional specimens required "a great deal more trouble & expense" than anticipated because the bones were available only from caves and "other out of the way places." Because the Suttons occasionally retained Indian guides to show them to graveyards, word of the skull collecting expedition leaked out and "some half breeds at Fort Rupert started quite a disturbance and tried to incite the Indians to shoot them." Concerned about a possible investigation, Sutton confided to Boas that "I would like to get [the skulls] off my hands as soon as possible."

The situation heated up still further when the Cowichan Indians discovered that their tribal graves had been desecrated. Obtaining a warrant to search the Sutton sawmill, the Indians discovered no bones, but they retained counsel to prosecute the case. Meanwhile, Boas arranged to ship the illicit materials to New York under falsified invoices. Despite some shortages in the Sutton materials—"owing to the rumpus with the Indians"—Boas was looking around for somebody to buy the skeletons. At this point, his collection numbered about two hundred crania, half of which were accompanied by complete skeletons.

The American Museum of Natural History agreed to store his skull collection temporarily, but they ultimately declined purchase, and in 1889 Boas moved the bones to Clark University in Worcester, Massachusetts, where he also signed on as a docent in the Department of Psychology. While there, Boas supervised A. F. Chamberlain, this country's first Ph.D. in Anthropology. Boas added another hundred or so skulls to his collection during this period, but he still had trouble selling the specimens (part of which ultimately went to Berlin's Museum für Völkerkunde, and the rest he sold years later to Chicago's new Field Columbian Museum).

Boas then accepted a short-term assignment to help plan the anthropological exhibits at the upcoming 1893 Chicago World's Fair. His job was to pull together an exhibit on physical anthropology and to create a special exhibit of Northwest Coast materials. He was disappointed that his display of skulls from Vancouver Island, systematically arranged in glass cases, was shoved into a poorly visited building along the southeastern corner of the Fair "likely to be overlooked by nine out of every ten visitors."

More popular in Chicago was the exhibit of living Indians. Boas personally arranged for a dozen Kwakwaka'wakh (Kwalkiutl) Indians to live at the fair, housed in the livestock pavilion until they could move into a traditional beam and plank longhouse. In the fair's "ethnological zoo," the Kwakwaka'wakh (Kwakiut) rubbed elbows with Apache and Navajo families, Iroquois living in bark longhouses, even Arawaks from South America. Down the Midway were Egyptians and Sudanese, Javanese, Chinese, Japanese, Eskimos from Labrador, and bare-breasted Dahomians from West Africa. When the fair finally closed in October 1893, the Kwakwaka'wakh returned home via the Canadian Pacific Railway. Boas' boss, Frederick Ward Putnam, resented having to pay their passage and heatedly insisted to railroad officials that the Kwakwaka'wakh should be granted free passage "just like other exhibits, as they were exhibits in every sense of the term." Boas was happy to see them leave, vowing "never again to play circus impresario."

The question naturally arose about what to do with the huge anthropological collection amassed in Chicago. Some of it went to California's Mid-Winter Exposition, and Washington State took parts for the state museum in Seattle. Boas and others pressed for a new natural history museum in

Franz Boas (above) demonstrating a pose of the Kwakwaka'wakh (Kwakiutl) hamatsa dancer for model makers at the U.S. National Museum (February 1895). The Hamatsa life-group (below) as displayed in the Smithsonian exhibit (ca. 1896).

Chicago, and after considerable prodding the department store magnate Marshall Field—by far the richest man in Chicago—stepped forward with a check for a million dollars. The new Field Columbian Museum opened to the public in June 1894, with Boas appointed as temporary curator. Although fully expecting to be retained as permanent curator, Boas was passed over in favor of William Henry Holmes, who stayed until 1896, to be succeeded by George A. Dorsey.

Having resigned from Clark University in a faculty revolt, an embittered Boas was reduced once again to piecework, acquiring and selling more Indian skulls. At this point, several of the country's new museums—especially Harvard, the Field Museum, the Smithsonian Institution, and the American Museum of Natural History—were vying for control of American archaeology, and Boas landed temporary assignments with the latter two.

The American Museum of Natural History finally hired Boas as a curator in late 1895. Still seething over the "unsurpassed insult" delivered in Chicago, Boas harbored a festering grudge against the upstart Field Museum and its curators—especially Holmes and Dorsey. In a letter written on December 25, 1895, Boas growled that "I'll show Chicago I can go them one better." The intense rivalry that arose between the two institutions reflected not only the personal animosity between ambitious curators (who truly detested each other), but also a deep-seated competition between their host cities. As a railway hub for the north and west, Chicago aspired to national and international status, hoping to equal or even overtake New York.

These "dear enemies" fought for years in a furious and well-financed rivalry over American Indian collectibles. Dorsey's first expedition for the Field Museum, in 1897, was a four-month blitz throughout western North America. His first stop was Browning, Montana, where just seven years earlier nearly a quarter of the local Blackfeet population had starved on Ghost Ridge. Dorsey dug into the shallow graves and shipped three dozen whole skeletons back to Chicago. Flushed with this early success, he moved to the Pacific Northwest, searching out the rich graves, coffins, and caves known to exist there. After exhuming sixteen skeletons and "many objects of ethnological interest" at Skungo Cave, he zipped northward into Tlingit territory in Alaska, where skeletal remains were particularly hard to find because the Tlingit cremated almost everyone except shamans.

In August 1897, while waiting for a steamer at Namu, Boas ran into Dorsey and his guide, Jimmy Deans. Boas wrote his wife that night that "I am mad at myself because there is an element of envy in me which I despise but which I cannot suppress altogether. It does not help that one behaves decently when inside oneself one is as shabby as the next fellow. What makes me so furious is the fact that these Chicago people simply adopt my plans and then try to beat me to it. Well, little Dorsey won't have achieved much with the help of that old ass, Deans. . . . In any event I don't think that Dorsey acted honorably."

At the time, local missionaries were complaining that skull and artifact collectors had destroyed almost every grave in the Virago Sound and North Island area. They were shocked by the men "who however laudable their object, could so mercilessly ride roughshod over the susceptibilities of the Indians." Dorsey was briefly arrested on the Columbia River, but was then released when he promised to return the materials he had taken. Elated at this development, Boas boasted that he had "never come into conflict with the feelings of Indians," conveniently glossing over the hundreds of similar grave-robbing forays he and his agents had conducted through the years. Given the bitter rivalry, it is hardly surprising that ethics and honesty became conditional, at times giving way to deception and theft.

Boas and Dorsey were hardly the first to dig graves in the Pacific Northwest. In his book *The Naturalist in Vancouver Island and British Columbia*, published in 1866, John Keats Lord, recounted his earlier experience at Fort Rupert (British Columbia), where he was told of a Koskimo man, reportedly shot and decapitated in a recent enemy raid. This unfortunate had a distinctive "sugarloaf-shaped" skull, intentionally deformed shortly after birth. The trophy had been hung by a rope from a pole, "fresh, bloody, and ghastly," but Lord was "determined at any risk to have the skull." Under the cover of darkness, he overturned the pole, "*bagged* the skull," and smuggled it out in a pork barrel. Lord later presented his treasure to the British Museum.

Adrian Jacobson, a private artifact and skull collector who worked for several prominent museums, had a similar experience in 1882. He knew that the deformed Koskimo "longhead" skulls were especially valuable, and secured several more. But the supply soon dried up. At Comox, he tried without success to climb up to tree-hung burial boxes, but he did better in nighttime raids on the local cemetery. Knowing that the local Indians were reluctant to sell skeletons or grave carvings, Jacobson decided that "the rule here is: 'Help yourself.'"

THE ANTHROPOLOGY
OF ASSIMILATION

To free the slaves, reformers had to defeat the slaveholders, but to free the Indians, reformers had to defeat—the Indians. Something had been holding blacks back, and that oppressive force was slavery. But what was holding the Indians back, preventing them from taking the opportunity to adopt civilized ways?

—*Patricia Limerick* (1987), *Historian*

ALTHOUGH MAINSTREAM AMERICANS of the late nineteenth century believed Indian cultures and lifeways were destined to disappear, many opposed needless cruelty toward the victims. Activists and reformers pushed for better treatment of Indian people, arguing that under the circumstances, the best way to help the Indians was to elevate them to civilization as rapidly as possible. Beginning in 1883, the so-called "Friends of the Indian" sponsored annual get-togethers at New York's Lake Mohonk, attracting a broad range of supporters. Part of the larger American reformist movement, the Lake Mohonk reformers were dedicated to eradicating Indian poverty and inequality by helping Indians into the melting pot. Participants debated long and hard over why the Indian had failed to assimilate into mainstream American society, many proposing that liberating the American Indian should follow the model of emancipating the American black. But even at the time, some realized how tenuous this analogy was. From what, exactly, was the Indian being freed?

Although the Lake Mohonk reformers assigned blame to failed federal Indian policy, they decided that the main force of oppression in Indian life was tribalism—the ingrained Indianness that kept native people from participating more fully in the American dream. Lewis Henry Morgan's ladder of social evolution had explained the "Indian problem" in scientific terms and, in effect, shifted the blame for the failure of assimilation to the natives themselves. As the final Indian wars played out—as the Lakotas and Comanches, Cheyennes and Apaches fought to retain their lands—cutting-edge anthropological theory affirmed that, unless these Indian diehards could be convinced to give up their tribal ways and join civilized America once and for all, they were doomed by their own cultural and biological inferiority.

The mission of the anthropology-based Bureau of American Ethnology was to turn this scientific perspective into government policy. Of the several voices at the Bureau articulating the new anthropological view, the most forceful came from an unusual source—a soft-spoken Boston blueblood whose impact on federal Indian policy would prove immeasurable.

"A CONVENIENT MARRIAGE OF PUBLIC OUTRAGE AND SCIENTIFIC THEORY"

Alice Fletcher began her long and distinguished career in anthropology during the late 1870s at the age of forty, studying archaeology at Harvard's Peabody Museum under the direct supervision of the eminent Professor Frederic Ward Putnam. She got off to a remarkable start at Harvard's Peabody, digging in the shell mounds of Maine and nearly single-handedly saving Ohio's famous Serpent Mound from destruction. Her archaeological career was short-circuited in 1880, when she met Bright Eyes and Francis La Flesche, two highly acculturated and well-educated Omaha Indians. They had traveled eastward with Ponca Chief Standing Bear, who attempted to arouse public support against federal efforts to remove the Ponca from their tribal lands.

Fletcher was alarmed at their tales of the wretched conditions in Indian Country, and decided that she should record their traditional customs before

Alice Cunningham Fletcher

they disappeared forever. Less than a year after this fateful meeting, the thoroughly citified Fletcher found herself making an arduous trip westward, arriving in Omaha, Nebraska, on September 1, 1881. Bright Eyes La Flesche took her to the Omaha reservation and to several others on the Great Plains—this at a time when memories of the Little Bighorn were less than five years old. Although frail, Fletcher lived with the Omaha under difficult conditions for weeks at a time, listening and learning. She got along well with them, built up a huge collection of recorded songs on her graphophone, and even received permission to study and publish their most private rituals. Fletcher and Francis La Flesche later collaborated on the monumental *The Omaha Tribe*, a highly regarded research monograph containing a wealth of ethnographic detail.

But Fletcher was more than a capable anthropologist. She was part of the large and powerful reform movement that reached across American society toward the end of the nineteenth century. As an ardent pro-Indian reformer, Fletcher remained in close touch with the Lake Mohonk Conferences of the Friends of the Indian; when she could not attend, she sent letters from the field. She brought to the Omaha Reservation an unbending set of beliefs about how to solve the "Indian problem." Armed with glowing letters of support from the Secretaries of War and Interior, the Postmaster General, and various prominent anthropologists, she confronted power-drunk Indian agents and became an outspoken critic of federal Indian policy. In her view, nobody would ever become "civilized" on an Indian reservation.

Fletcher and the Lake Mohonk liberals followed Jefferson in assuming that inside every Indian was trapped a white American, ready to own property, become a farmer, and assume the mantle of United States citizenship. American Indians were being obstructed in their natural evolutionary progression by a corrupt reservation system, which perpetuated a retrograde sense of tribalism by emphasizing communal ties to traditional territories. Fletcher went west brimming with anthropological theory drawn from Morgan's *Ancient Society*, particularly the assurance that private property had historically stimulated the development of civilized behavior and would do so in the future. If tribes like the Omaha were ever to reach the stage of civilization, they must move from reservation life to individually owned self-sufficient farmsteads.

After extensive consultation with the Omaha people, Fletcher went to Washington D.C. in 1882 and presented to Congress her plan for saving the tribe. Every competent adult Omaha tribal member would be allotted an eighty-acre, tax-free plot of reservation land. After a suitable transition period—during which the federal government would continue its financial support—the allottee would receive full title and control of the farmstead. Nonallotted tribal land would be sold off to provide the funds necessary to establish permanent family farms. Fletcher's plan was "a chilling condensation of the social evolutionist blueprint," writes the historian Fred Hoxie, designed to "separate Indians from their homes and their past, divide their land into individual parcels, make them citizens, and draw them into American society."

Fletcher drew upon her considerable political clout to help push this allotment plan through Congress, and in 1883–1884 she was appointed as a special agent of the Indian office, specifically in charge of carrying out the survey and allotment of the Omaha reservation lands. Before long, her vision was extended far beyond Omaha territory. In 1887, Congress passed the Dawes Allotment Act, which was amended to include nearly every tribe in the United States. With the passage of the Dawes Act, surveying parties divided Indian Country into 160-acre parcels (the average for a single Indian family). At the time, the Dawes Act was widely hailed as the "Indians' Magna Carta," reifying total assimilation as an American ideal. Indians were to become farmers, participants in government, and, above all, "civilized." Teddy Roosevelt hailed the Dawes Act as "a mighty pulverizing engine to break up the tribal mass."

In retrospect, the Dawes Act was a monumental disaster for the American Indian. Farming did not work well for many, and the land often was leased immediately to non-Indians who had flocked onto the former reservation lands. Reservations were overrun by land sharks eager to snatch up Indian land by whatever means available. By 1934, Indian people had lost two-thirds of the allotted land to non-Indian outsiders. Anthropologist Peter Nabokov believes that the Dawes Act, passed just two years before the slaughter at Wounded Knee Creek, "probably created more widespread Indian suffering and left a more destructive legacy for Indians in the future than that infamous massacre."

STRONG PAPER TO PROTECT OUR HOME

History has not been kind to Alice Fletcher. Her role in the allotment disaster has largely overshadowed her impressive ethnographic and archaeological achievements. Indians and non-Indians alike have pictured her as the consummate East Coast do-gooder, "dreadfully opinionated" and stubbornly imposing her book learning on Indian Country. Social and political connections enabled Fletcher to help craft the single most disastrous piece of legislation ever perpetrated on Indian people. As one historian put it, "the so-called Friends of the Indian acted in ways that one might more logically expect from enemies."

How could such an intelligent and caring ethnographer so completely misjudge the outcome of her politics—and her anthropology? For one thing, the Dawes Act was tied to the implicit assumption that Indian populations would continue to decline. So viewed, the act was designed to sell off surplus land that would never be needed. Within decades, this assumption would be proved dramatically incorrect, as generations of landless Indians could attest.

Moreover, Fletcher had completely adopted the perspective of the first Indians she met—the well-educated and acculturated La Flesche family, who believed "authentic" Indian life was a thing of the past. Joseph La Flesche went so far as to abolish his own office as chief, believing that the tribal system held his people back from advancing toward civilization. The La Flesches saw allotment as a way of preventing Cherokee-style removal—a real threat in Omaha territory, perhaps, but one not felt by most Omaha people.

Fletcher's misguided reformism must also be viewed against the intense white pressures to assume control of Indian land. She did not see preserving the reservations as an option in the 1880s. The land would soon disappear anyway, victim to the greed of cattlemen, railroad men, and white sodbusters. Faced with this massive white land grab, the Omaha would inevitably lose their land unless it was reserved as individual allotments.

Her views were fully consistent with anthropological theory of the day.

Not a single responsible scientist in the 1880s questioned Lewis Henry Morgan's evolutionary scheme that arrayed human cultural history as a stepwise progression from savagery to barbarism to civilization. If the Indian people of North America were truly trapped in "upper savagery" and "lower/middle barbarism," then a means must be found to elevate them to civilization as rapidly as possible.

Fletcher discussed her plan in great detail with the head of each Omaha family: "Each one had uttered the oft-repeated cry: 'I want a 'strong paper' which will make my home secure.'" These lengthy consultations convinced her that all had agreed to a common plan of action. From a century of hindsight it is clear that the anthropologist and the Omaha attached rather different meanings to the simple term "home."

To Fletcher, "home" conjured up images of prosperous family farms, with tidy Victorian houses and outbuildings surrounded by livestock and plowed fields. Fletcher's allotment scheme reflected deep-seated white American attitudes that saw the ownership of private property as the hallmark of civilized life. Once forced to abandon their primitive ways, with their tribal land divided into single-family plots, reservation Indians would quickly achieve a status comparable to nineteenth-century white rural settlers. Allotment would help the Indian to embrace rather than reject white society.

But the concept of "home" meant something entirely different to the Omaha. When they asked Fletcher to "make my home secure," the Omaha people were seeking her help in hanging onto the shrinking remnants of tribal lands. Their "strong paper" meant concrete legal support for treaty guarantees to secure the tribal homeland necessary to their survival and identity as Omaha people. Fletcher's greatest shortcoming was a tragic misreading of the Omaha cultural landscape. She was neither the first nor the last anthro-American to underestimate the strong connections binding Indian people to their indigenous homeland.

As IT TURNED out, the anthropological theory upon which Fletcher's advocacy was based was fatally flawed. In the early twentieth century, the anthropological tide turned against the ethnocentric (and unmistakably racial) notion of progress. Franz Boas led a successful rebellion against cultural evolutionary theory, and only two decades after the Dawes Act became law, Morgan's theory of social evolution was thoroughly discredited.

Boas argued that cultural development was so complex and had taken so many diverse paths that there could have been no progressive evolution in the human past. The world's most complex forms of social organization were sometimes associated with the very simplest kinds of technology (as among the historic period Australian aborigines). Boas also argued that human institutions, such as slavery, private property, and state-level government, are associated with an amazing array of related sociocultural features. He saw each culture as unique and argued that no sweeping cross-cultural generalizations could be made. This doctrine, commonly known as *cultural relativism*, questions the existence of any universal standards by which to judge either the degree of cultural development or the intrinsic worth of different cultures.

Fletcher's involvement with the allocation fiasco prompted Boas' stern warning to future generations of anthropologists: avoid contemporary politics and abstain from applying their untested theories to actual Indian issues. As Vine Deloria, Jr. would forcefully point out decades later, anthropology's aloof, hands-off policy would create endless tensions between Indian people and the anthropologists who wished to study them.

THE ANTHROPOLOGIST
AS HERO

8.

The past is a foreign country, they do things differently there.

—L. P. Hartley

IN THE FALL of 1879, Frank Cushing, boy genius, stood alone at the entrance to Zuni Pueblo, wondering if he'd made a serious mistake. In the distance, the rest of his Smithsonian field party were riding westward toward Hopi, glad to be rid of their arrogant 22-year-old colleague. One departee, the ethnographer Matilda Cox Stevenson, later called Cushing "the biggest fool and charlatan I ever knew."

When Zuni Governor Palowahtiwa asked his uninvited guest how long he intended to remain, Cushing brashly announced, "Two months." The old chief replied only *"Tuh!"* (Damn!).

Over the months and years to come, Cushing found he was a very long way from home.

THE CUSHING EXPERIMENT AT ZUNI

With this single, unprecedented act—abandoning his mates and moving empty-handed into an Indian pueblo—Cushing established a new way of doing ethnographic fieldwork, and East Coast anthropologists followed the four-year "Cushing experiment" at Zuni with great curiosity.

Born in 1857, in a small Erie County village, Frank Hamilton Cushing was smitten by Indian lore at an early age. He sought out ancient Indian camps and taught himself how to flintknap arrowheads. While still a teenager, he set up his own small-scale archaeological excavations, made some significant finds, and presented his results before a professional audience. Cushing's slight stature and delicate constitution disguised an indomitable spirit and unquenchable thirst to understand the origins of American Indian people. Largely self-taught, he quickly mastered the literature of anthropology, paying particular attention to Lewis Henry Morgan's theory of social evolution.

The Smithsonian Institution hired Cushing, still in his teens, as an assistant curator in 1875. He was directed to assemble the National Museum's exhibit on Indians for the Philadelphia Centennial Exposition of 1876. On the

Frank Hamilton Cushing, as the young genius of the Bureau of American Ethnology, (circa 1879), and dressed in Zuni garb (taken about 1886).

day that George Armstrong Custer fought his last battle, Cushing, resident prodigy at the Bureau of American Ethnology, was patiently arranging pots and arrowheads in preparation for the country's one-hundredth birthday party.

Three years later, the Smithsonian Institution formally established the Bureau of American Ethnology (BAE) to implement a comprehensive research program to record the cultural, linguistic, and physical nuances of the Vanishing American. John Wesley Powell, sparkplug of the BAE, set the agenda: "Rapidly the Indians are being gathered on reservations where their original habits and customs disappear, their languages are being modified or lost and they are abandoning their savagery. If the ethnology of our Indians is ever to receive proper scientific study and treatment the work must be done at once." Lewis Henry Morgan heartily supported Powell's program and used his political connections to help get the BAE off the ground.

Morgan had personally traveled to Colorado and New Mexico in 1878 and was enthusiastic about what he saw. He urged Powell to begin systematic anthropological work in the American Southwest at the earliest possible opportunity. His 1879 Congressional appropriation in hand, Powell moved quickly to field a team of ethnographers to work in the Southwest, including the young curatorial assistant Frank Hamilton Cushing, who jumped at the chance to head west. His specific assignment was to make a detailed archaeological study of various Pueblo ruins and caves in the area, with an eye toward linking up contemporary Southwestern Indians to their remote archaeological past. Although pockets of native resistance remained throughout the American West—Geronimo's surrender and the massacre at Wounded Knee were still years in the future—Cushing relished the chance to work in this "paradise of ethnography."

But the residents of Zuni Pueblo showed little interest in being studied. Sensing this hostility and mistrust, Cushing boldly moved in among the Zuni people. Neither his involuntary hosts nor his Smithsonian colleagues had anticipated this move, nor did he consult either beforehand. In-fighting and personal jealousies had already alienated Cushing from his fellow anthropologists, who welcomed his unexpected departure.

From the start, Cushing's obvious vulnerability encouraged a degree of trust and cooperation from the Zuni people. Governor Palowahtiwa took a liking to the plucky young man, and invited him to move into his house. In return, the Zuni insisted on "hardening his meat," taking away the comfort of his hammock and forcing him to behave like a Zuni.

Although his health deteriorated progressively (and permanently), Cushing stuck with it, doggedly following local Zuni custom whenever possible. He ate Zuni food, dressed in Zuni garb, and worked at learning the Zuni language; it was said that, years later, Cushing delivered harangues in Zuni during a delirious sleep. He even had his ears pierced—signifying his first step toward initiation into the tribe. Cushing wrote of his experience: "Because I will unhesitatingly plunge my hand in common with their dusty ones and dirtier children's into a great kind of hot, miscellaneous food; will sit close to [those] having neither vermin nor disease; will fondle and talk sweet Indian to their bright eyed little babies; will wear the blanket and tie the *pania* around my long hair; will look with unfeigned reverence on their beautiful and ancient ceremonies, never laughing at any absurd observance, they love me, and I learn." Cushing was called *Hets-ithl-to* (Zuni for "the Cricket") "since I was forever whistling and singing, moving and jumping about, running hither and thither over the housetops and up and down ladders, without ever staying myself to behavior seemly or with dignity."

His command of the language improved and so did his relation with the Zuni people. Overstaying one departure date after another, Cushing started pushing his way into secret meetings and initiations. When quietly asked to leave, he pretended not to understand, and the Zuni, too polite to insist, gradually came to accept his presence. By the time Cushing ran into a journalist friend—two years after his arrival—he had been adopted into the Zuni governor's family and had completely entered Pueblo life. The Zuni ultimately initiated Cushing into their prestigious Priesthood of the Bow, an important secret society. In the process, he became a unique human being: Who else could sign his letters as both "Government Ethnologist" and "First War Chief" of the Zuni Indians?

Like many archaeologists of his day, Cushing believed that oral tradition provided the key to the ancient Pueblo past and so tried to relate the "ancient talks" (as he called them) to greater Southwestern archaeology. Mapping specific archaeological sites named in Zuni migration traditions, Cushing explored cemeteries, ruins, caves, and shrines throughout Zuni territory. He firmly believed that he possessed an uncanny talent for penetrating the identities of others—even those long dead. Cushing inspired a generation of American archaeologists who used his method of "conjectural history," employing the rich Native American oral traditions to help reinterpret their rapidly accumulating archaeological materials.

As an ardent advocate for the Zuni, Cushing made powerful enemies in the Senate, including Powell's supporter John Logan from Illinois, who ran unsuccessfully for U. S. Vice President in 1884, the same year that Powell ordered Cushing out of Zuni. But Cushing returned to the Southwest two years later to direct the privately funded Hemenway Southwestern Archaeological Expedition, the first large-scale archaeological program in the Southwest, perhaps in the nation. Cushing attempted to trace the origins of the Zuni people by systematically excavating ruins along the traditional "migration track." Ill health soon forced him to stop digging, but not before his Hemenway Expedition established critical linkages between the nineteenth-century Zuni and the ancient ruins of the Southwest. By the early twentieth century, the alleged Aztec occupation of the American Southwest had faded into myth.

Then, in April 1900—three months short of his forty-third birthday—Cushing swallowed a fishbone and soon died of peritonitis.

NOTHING QUITE LIKE Cushing's adventure at Zuni had occurred before, and nineteenth-century anthropology took notice. Cushing was the first anthropologist to live long-term among the people he was studying, and his biographer calls him "the world's first live-in anthropologist." John Wesley Powell, his boss at the Bureau of American Ethnology, suggested that Cushing single-handedly made the "traveling ethnologist" a thing of the past. Cushing developed an effective relationship with his Zuni hosts and because of his extraordinary access, he recorded an amazingly detailed ethnographic account of Zuni life.

He also worked on behalf of the Zuni people, functioning as the "Chief Councilor" for the tribe by interceding with various missionaries, traders, miners, railroad men, and government officials. Cushing smoothed over difficulties with local ranchers, negotiated with the local sheriff, dealt with local Indian school officials, and helped police the reservation against encroachments from Mormons, Mexicans, and Navajos. When famine loomed, he pulled strings in Washington to get immediate relief. Highly protective of "his" Indians, Cushing called the neighboring Navajos "wandering coyotes"— a decidedly non-anthropological assessment (but one surely reflecting a Zuni perspective). As "First War Chief," he once helped pursue raiding horse thieves. When the guilty parties were caught, two of them were killed. Although Cushing's role in the fatal roundup is unclear, it certainly enhanced his reputation as a war leader who could be counted upon. Rumor has it that Cushing may have once collected an enemy scalp, but the circumstances surrounding this bizarre event remain murky.

Trumpeting his "mastery" over the Indians, Cushing's writings also reflect a certain academic arrogance, reflecting in part his domineering personality and also a flaunting of his Washington connections. While mediating between the Zuni and non-Zuni, Cushing clearly aligned himself with certain tribal factions, and his very presence became a source of friction within the pueblo. Cushing antagonized his hosts by violating local taboos, and some Zuni expressed irritation at his publishing their sacred legends and rituals. They also resented his making a sacred Mudhead mask after his return to the Smithsonian. In his own mind, Cushing breached no Zuni confidences. Arguing that such secrets had meaning only within the context of Zuni society, he saw no betrayal in sharing Zuni secrets with a largely East Coast scientific audience. In his lifetime Cushing never had to confront the possibility of his printed words making their way back to the Zuni, as they surely did after his early death.

The anthropological community was also conflicted over Cushing's Zuni experience. He clearly had defined the "participant observer" format that would become the mainstay of anthropological fieldwork for a century: Establish an intimate relationship with those under study, but simultaneously maintain an objective, scientific perspective. His emphasis on native oral tradition linked the living people with their remote, archaeological past. In an age that both celebrated science and craved romance, Cushing became a legend, the original "anthropologist as hero." But the historian Marc Simmons sees it another way: "The pattern of Cushing's activity—overcoming suspicion, winning acceptance, assisting in the solution of village problems, serving as an agent of acculturation, and eventually betraying this trust—was one repeated often by anthropologists and writers."

Beyond collecting material culture and recording ritual practices, Cushing was also after the underlying Zuni worldview, what one ethnologist would term "that sympathetic projection into alien mentality which anthropology is supposed to foster." These attempts to penetrate the Zuni mind have raised considerable suspicion among later anthropologists. One ethnographer commented that Cushing's observations "were of the keenest, but almost impossible to disentangle from his imaginings," and another noted that Cushing "leaves us wondering how much of his interpretation reflects his own rather than his native hosts' mentality."

The man remains an anthropological enigma. Some dismiss him as a charlatan, while others praise his ability to enter the Indian mind. In 1952, the anthropologist Claude Levi-Strauss suggested that Cushing's refined perception and intuition entitled him "to a seat on Morgan's right, as one of the great forerunners of social-structural studies." But Franz Boas believed that Cushing's genius "was his greatest enemy" and that all his fieldwork would have to be repeated.

COLLECTING YOUR
FOSSILS ALIVE

ON A WINTRY evening in 1898, a curious group huddled against the wind in a garden just off New York's Central Park: The American Museum's renowned curator of anthropology, Dr. Franz Boas, several scientists, some museum employees, and a sad-eyed eight-year-old Polar Eskimo, the newly orphaned Minik. They were gathered to bury young Minik's father, Qisuk, who had died of tuberculosis. Following Eskimo custom, the men carefully mounded stones over the grave. Below lay the lifeless body, shrouded in cloth, with a mask over its face. Minik placed some of his father's favorite possessions near the gravestones. He also made his mark along the north side of the grave, a sign to ward off the spirit of the dead man.

But Boas knew what the boy did not. Qisuk's body was not beneath the stones. Museum workmen had created an imitation corpse from a man-sized log. Qisuk's body had been taken directly to Bellevue Hospital's College of Physicians and Surgeons, where an autopsy was performed. After removing the brain for study, technicians cut up and macerated the body, delivering the bright white bones to the American Museum of Natural History. Qisuk's skull and skeleton, each bone individually numbered, lay in a wooden museum tray among thousands of other anthropological specimens.

"I BEG TO SUGGEST THAT YOU BRING BACK A MIDDLE-AGED ESKIMO"

Beginning in the 1870s, archaeologists like Charles Abbott and Boyd Dawkins argued that Eskimo people (today often called *Inuit*) descended directly from ancient hunters of the European Ice Age who had migrated to the Arctic in pursuit of deer and musk ox as the glaciers melted. In Morgan's social evolution, nineteenth-century Eskimos represented "living fossils," physically and culturally frozen in time, forever trapped in a higher status of savagery.

Having spent fifteen months during the years 1883 and 1894 doing ethnographic fieldwork in the Arctic, Boas did not see Eskimos as "arrested" in an early evolutionary stage. He distrusted Morgan's universal stages and the snobbish definition of progress they implied. Boas instead saw Eskimo customs, traditions, and migrations as adaptations to Arctic life. He emphasized the importance of studying individual Eskimo groups separately and looked for ways to get detailed ethnographic information on isolated and relatively unacculturated groups such as the Polar Eskimo.

Boas had previously arranged for a number of Labrador Eskimos to join the living exhibits at the 1893 Chicago World's Fair, and shortly after joining the curatorial staff of New York's American Museum of Natural History in 1895, he wrote the famed Arctic explorer Robert Peary with a similar arrangement in mind: "I beg to suggest to you that if you are certain of revisiting North Greenland next summer, it would be of the very greatest value if you should be able to bring a middle-aged Eskimo to stay there over winter. This would enable us to obtain leisurely certain information which will be of the greatest scientific importance."

Peary had enjoyed considerable support from Morris Jesup, the Museum's president. Earlier, responding to a plea from Peary's wife, Jesup had helped finance an expedition to rescue Peary when he was stranded in Greenland. Jesup subsequently struck a deal with Peary: he would fund the explorer's future explorations if Peary would help build the Museum's Arctic collections. When Boas wrote his letter, Peary was finalizing his fourth voyage to the Arctic, an expedition to secure a colossal meteorite for the museum's collection.

But Peary never wrote back to Boas.

"SO ONE DAY WE ALL SAILED AWAY"

In September 1897, a triumphant Peary sailed his ship *Hope* into the Brooklyn shipyard with 100 tons of meteorites on board, including the monster known as Alnighito. As the largest meteorite ever recovered, it was destined to join the rapidly growing collection of the American Museum of Natural History. Also on board—to the surprise of Dr. Boas and everyone else—were six Polar Eskimos from Smith Sound, Greenland. Peary had complied with Boas' request and then some.

The Peary Eskimos, as they were sometimes called, became instant celebrities. During their first two days in town, some 30,000 New Yorkers paid twenty-five cents each to view them aboard the *Hope*. Qisuk, the group's leader, had worked intermittently for Peary since 1891, and when asked how they got to New York, the Eskimo explained that "Peary asked if some of us wouldn't like to go back with him . . . so one day we all sailed away." Qisuk even brought his six-year old son Minik along for the ride.

Boas arranged for the newcomers to live at the museum. At first the Eskimos lived in makeshift basement accommodations, but they soon moved into a sixth-floor apartment suite, which they shared with the museum's superintendent, William Wallace. Boas stressed that the Eskimos were visiting New York strictly for scientific purposes—not to be exhibited. It was prohibitively expensive, Boas pointed out, to launch an anthropological expedition to the Arctic; but with the Eskimos at hand the necessary ethnographic and linguistic studies could be made quickly and cheaply. They would return home the next summer. When a reporter asked what the Eskimos did all day, Boas replied, "Oh, we try to give them little things to keep them busy. Their work doesn't amount to much, but they have made some carvings, and occupied themselves either indoors or around the place with any employment that suggested itself to them. They do not seem discontented."

FRANZ BOAS WAS a busy man in the late 1890s. When Peary and the Eskimos arrived unannounced in New York harbor, Boas was finalizing his plan for the Jesup North Pacific Expedition, the most ambitious anthropolog-

Minik, the New York Eskimo, dressed in his Polar Eskimo clothing (shortly after his arrival in New York in 1898), and with his bicycle in Lawyersville, New York.

ical expedition ever undertaken. Under Boas' guidance, the Jesup Expedition set out to "investigate and establish the ethnological relations between the races of America and Asia. . . . There are few problems," he argued, "of greater importance to the early history of the American race than its relations to the races of the Old World." Over the next six years, Boas sent teams of anthropologists around the northern Pacific Rim, collecting artifacts, recording customs, and digging archaeological sites from Oregon to Siberia. The Jesup Expedition was a staggering undertaking, resulting in seventeen massive volumes.

Between organizing this expedition and conducting his own ethnographic fieldwork in British Columbia, Boas found little time to work directly with his resident Eskimos. Once he was sure that Qisuk and the others were secure in their museum quarters, Boas delegated the primary ethnographic responsibility for the New York Eskimos to a bright new student named Alfred Kroeber.

Kroeber had been an English instructor at nearby Columbia University in 1897 when, on a lark, he enrolled in a Boas' graduate course on American

Indian linguistics. Boas held the seminar around the dinner table in his 82nd Street home, just up the street from the museum. "We spent about two months each on Chinook, Eskimo, Klamath, and Salish," Kroeber later recalled. "I was enormously stimulated. Grammatical structure was interesting as presented; but to *discover* it was fascinating. Boas' method was very similar to that of the zoologist who starts a student with an etherized frog or worm and a dissecting table."

At one point, Boas introduced his class to Esther, "a Labrador half-breed Eskimo woman" and wife of a mechanic who worked at the museum. As Esther slowly spoke in her native Eskimo dialect, Boas taught Kroeber to record the words phonetically. The process and the professor captivated the young English teacher. Kroeber later described Boas as "strong physically and psychically, dominant, daemonic, a proper culture hero who passed along to his students the peculiarly slanted romantic humanistic-scientific vision which continues . . . to inspire New World anthropologists." Kroeber immediately signed up for a second American Indian Language seminar and also took Boas' seminar in physical anthropology, a course taught in the Museum's laboratory where Boas showed students how to take anthropometric measurements on the extensive skull collection housed there.

Although still teaching English courses at Columbia, the twenty-one-year-old Kroeber took over the primary responsibility for the ethnographic and linguistic research on the "Peary" Eskimos from Smith Sound.

MINIK "VISITS THE (SUPPOSED) GRAVE OF HIS FATHER"

Not long after their celebrated arrival in New York, all six Eskimos contracted pneumonia. Too ill to live at the Museum, they moved between Bellevue Hospital and Museum superintendent Wallace's upstate dairy farm at Lawyersville. They also spent time at Museum President Jesup's house in High Bridge, New York. A *New York Tribune* reporter asked Boas, "When you found they were sick so much, didn't you think of sending them North again?" Boas responded "Yes, but there was no opportunity to send them. There were ships going north as far as Newfoundland and Labrador, but that would not have been anywhere near their home, and we could not land them in a strange country. When Lieutenant Peary starts on his trip this summer he will take them back with him. They are all fond of him, and were delighted at the prospect of coming here last summer." But Peary did not return northward that summer.

Only eight months after their triumphant arrival, four of the New York Eskimos were dead of tuberculosis. One did make it back to Greenland, and the sixth, the orphaned Minik, remained under Wallace's care. As the tragic affair unfolded, Kroeber doggedly pursued his ethnographic inquiries into Eskimo social organization, religion, and cosmology. Most of Kroeber's ethnographic work used Esther as an interpreter, asking the Eskimos to re-member and describe what took place in Greenland. But when it came to mourning customs, Kroeber could make observations first-hand. He later commented that his mortuary accounts "are exceptionally full, though per-haps the customs are somewhat modified by the unusual surroundings."

When Minik's father died, the surviving Eskimos offered to kill the or-phaned boy (infanticide being a common practice back home in Greenland). Although the life of young Minik was spared, an Eskimo elder "insisted that the boy visit the (supposed) grave of his father, and instructed him how to act," Kroeber later reported. "He told [Minik] what to say at the grave, and gave him some of the deceased's property to lay on the pile of stones." Minik did as he was told and he continued to live with Wallace.

Years later, the 15-year-old Minik read in a New York newspaper the ghastly news that his father's remains were not resting in a grave at all: Qisuk's bones had been accessioned into the Museum's collection of Indian bones. The New York press had a field day with the story of pitiful Minik seeking the return of his father's remains. One lurid account claimed that "An upstairs room—at the museum—is his father's last resting place. His coffin is a show-case, his shroud a piece of plate glass. No quiet of the graveyard is there; the noise of shuffling feet and the tap, tap of hammers as the workmen fix up other skeletons, is ever present. And when the sunlight fades they turn on the electrical lights so that Minik's father may not have even the pall of darkness to hide his naked bones." Pressed for a reaction, Minik reportedly said, "I felt as though I must die then and there. I . . . prayed and wept. I went straight to the director and implored him to let me bury my father. He would not. I swore that I would never rest until I had given my father burial." Minik ap-parently asked for the return of his father's bones over the years, without suc-cess.

When confronted by reporters, Boas and Wallace eventually admitted that they had indeed staged a mock funeral for Qisuk. Boas defended their actions, suggesting that the fake burial was conducted "to appease the boy, and keep him from discovering that his father's body had been chopped up and the bones placed in the collection of the institution." Boas saw "nothing particularly deserving severe criticism. The other Eskimos who were still alive were not very well, and then there was Minik, and of course it was only reasonable to spare them any shock or uneasiness. The burial accomplished that purpose I suppose." Pressed as to why the museum could claim Qisuk's body when relatives were still alive, Boas replied, "Oh, that was perfectly legitimate. There was no one to bury the body, and the museum had as good a right to it as any other institution authorized to claim bodies." When an *Evening Mail* reporter wondered if the body didn't actually "belong" to Minik, Boas bristled "Well, Minik was just a little boy, and he did not ask for the body. If he had, he might have got it."

Boas' students and colleagues published a flurry of very high-quality technical papers and scientific monographs on Qisuk and his band. The bulk of the work fell to young Kroeber. Boas hardly participated in the write-up, but he believed that his Eskimo experiment had paid off handsomely. "Many things heretofore unknown have been learned regarding their language, their traditions and their personal characteristics," he later reflected, adding, "casts of their heads have been made for the museum."

Kroeber produced three scientific publications—"The Eskimo of Smith Sound," "Animal Tales of the Eskimo," and "Tales of the Smith Sound Eskimo"—each published in 1899, only a year after Qisuk's death. Reading these reports a century later, one is amazed at the quality of Kroeber's ethnographic reportage, particularly given his age and lack of anthropological experience. Aleš Hrdlička published two accounts on the biology of the Eskimos, including an illustrated article on Qisuk's brain. But except for comments that appeared in newspaper interviews, Boas never published a word on the Peary Eskimos.

Writing in 1997, the anthropologist Edmund Carpenter provided a very positive assessment of the Eskimo experiment: "Boas and Hrdlička rejected the theory, beloved by racists, that various tribal peoples were arrested at different evolutionary stages. Knowledge gained from these six Polar Eskimos challenged that belief. None lived to know the importance of their contribution, but we do and it should not be forgotten."

LAST OF A VANISHING SPECIES

The Peary Eskimos had inadvertently introduced Alfred Kroeber to his life's work. In 1901, Kroeber received the first Ph.D. degree in anthropology ever given by Columbia University, and became one of the twentieth-century's most influential anthropologists. He served as Curator at the California Academy of Sciences, then became the first anthropologist to teach at the University of California. When Phoebe Apperson Hearst (mother of famed publisher William Randolph Hearst) agreed to finance a new Museum of Anthropology in San Francisco, the Regents and University President appointed Kroeber as its first curator.

Like all American anthropologists of the day, Kroeber saw the American Indian as doomed, and he scrambled to record the ancient customs and lifeways before they disappeared. He scoured California for Indians who remembered the old tribal ways and spoke the ancient tongues. Hoping that his new museum would become a Smithsonian-on-the-Bay, Kroeber established an aggressive program of salvage ethnography among California's Indian population. Above all else, he sought the "uncontaminated" Indian, free of Euroamerican influences.

In 1800, perhaps 300,000 Indians had been living in California, but a century later, only 20,000 California Indians survived. Although many Indians lived on rancherias or reservations within their traditional territories, none of them lived the free life of their ancestors. Kroeber had heard rumors about a handful of still-wild Indians near Oroville, a mining town on the Feather River in northern California. But like most Californians, he was skeptical about the possibility.

"THE MOST UNCIVILIZED, UNCONTAMINATED MAN IN THE WORLD TODAY"

Myth came to life on August 9, 1911.

As dogs snarled, a slight brown man, confused and starving, crouched in a slaughterhouse corral near Oroville. The Indian's hair was hacked off and singed, his tribe's sign of mourning. He wore a wooden plug in his nose, and deer sinew hung from holes in his earlobes. A tattered piece of canvas, scavenged from a covered wagon, hid his nakedness. His family had been murdered, or maybe they had starved. Everyone and everything he knew was gone. Although convinced that nobody in the world still spoke his language, he wanted desperately to live. He must have thought that his only chance was to make contact with other human beings, no matter how different they were.

The local sheriff locked the man in a jail cell reserved for the insane, since "wild" Indians could not be allowed to roam about freely. The sheriff soon received a telegram offering to put his prisoner into a carnival. Another telegram, from a woman in St. Louis, contained a marriage proposal; but he believed that "the truth of the matter was she just wanted to put him on exhibition." Several assimilated Indians and even Chinese-speakers were brought in, but none could communicate with the prisoner.

Kroeber, having read newspaper accounts of the event, sent his young colleague Thomas Waterman to Oroville, equipped with lists of local Indian vocabularies. After considerable trial-and-error, Waterman was able to make himself understood. The wild man of Oroville was apparently the last member of a previously unknown northern California tribe. The Noble Savage had come back to life.

The man was transported to Kroeber's new museum in San Francisco. Kroeber decided that he must belong to a previously unknown group of Yana Indians. Since the Yana had already been divided into Northern, Central, and Southern divisions, Kroeber selected the name "Yahi" to label the newly discovered culture. During those first few days, Kroeber also named the man "Ishi," the Yana word for "man" or "one of the people." Newspapers could now write about the wild man by name. More importantly, Ishi was spared the embarrassment of telling his actual private name to a stranger, since many California Indians considered the use of personal names taboo.

At a press conference, Kroeber pronounced Ishi the "most uncivilized, uncontaminated man in the world today." Like the New York Eskimos, the strange man became a celebrity. The local newspapers touted him as "California's Last Wild Indian," an accurate assessment, as far as it went. The lifeway he gave up in 1911 was close to his ancient ways. For years, he had deliberately shied away from white contacts, tools or foods, and had little first-hand knowledge of the newcomers' customs. Kroeber secured quarters for Ishi in the university museum, surrounded by the artifacts and bones of Indians who had died out. "Ishi received all the attention," notes the historian Brian Dippie, that "would be lavished on a dinosaur that happened to stumble into a paleontologists' convention."

A MONTH AFTER Ishi's arrival, Kroeber opened his new Museum of Anthropology to the San Francisco public and it was a great triumph. Kroeber's was the sole museum west of the Mississippi devoted to the study of man, and the only one anywhere with a wildly popular living exhibit. Crowds flocked

Ishi in Two Worlds. The first photograph of Ishi (left), taken on August 29, 1911, wearing a tattered piece of canvas given him to cover his nakedness; and Ishi two months later at the University of California, San Francisco.

to see Ishi, who volunteered to give demonstrations each Sunday afternoon. Although he came down with pneumonia soon after the museum opened, Ishi insisted on appearing in public anyway, taking great pleasure in making fire with wooden drills, staging archery demonstrations, and chipping arrowheads by the thousands, which he gave away as souvenirs.

Kroeber and Ishi saw each other frequently. Ishi gradually learned enough English to complement Kroeber's limited Yahi. Ishi also became friendly with Waterman's family, and often visited them for dinner. Over the next five years, as Kroeber and his staff taught the Indian the ways of "civilization," Ishi revealed some of his secrets of survival in backcountry California. He patiently tutored linguists in his difficult language and eventually led

Kroeber back to his rocky Mill Creek homeland to show him where his people had spent their last pathetic days.

Newspapers sometimes criticized Kroeber for keeping Ishi in a museum. Although other Indian informants had stayed in the museum for brief periods, this Ishi business was somehow different. A representative of the Bureau of Indian Affairs came to San Francisco to check on conditions and offered Ishi a chance to live on a midwestern Indian reservation. He politely refused. He preferred to stay among the anthropologists, and wished to grow old and die in his new museum home.

Like the Peary Eskimos, Ishi developed a tubercular cough. Dr. Saxton Pope, a physician working at the nearby University of California medical school, treated him daily. Over the years, Pope and Ishi found considerable common ground. Taking Ishi on his hospital rounds, Pope saw in the "wild Indian" an extraordinary compassion for the ill. Ishi would quietly hold a patient's hand during treatment, sometimes softly adding a healing prayer in his native Yahi tongue.

Pope also came to share Ishi's love of archery. They made an odd combination indeed—Pope, the urbane physician paired with the Yahi Indian, shooting arrows in the parks of downtown San Francisco. Pope was a good student, and his association with Ishi led to a lifelong interest in the almost-lost art of archery. Pope studied bows and arrows preserved in museum collections and often test-shot the ancient specimens. In 1923, he published *Hunting With the Bow and Arrow*, describing his experiments in archery. The book not only provided baseline information for interpreting ancient finds but also became the bible of the bow-hunting fraternity.

Had Ishi read an anthropology textbook, he would have learned that early twentieth-century anthropology had soundly rejected the idea of biologically based hierarchies. Kroeber believed that Ishi was the intellectual and physical equal of any white American and that all that separated him from mainstream America were the innumerable generations of education that Ishi had missed. "Ishi himself is no nearer the 'missing link' or any other antecedent form of human life than we are," Kroeber argued. "But in what his environment, his associates, and his puny native civilization have made him he represents a stage through which our ancestors passed thousands of years ago."

"SAY FOR ME THAT SCIENCE CAN GO TO HELL"

Kroeber took a one-year sabbatical in 1915 and 1916, setting up headquarters in New York, and traveling throughout Europe, where he became acquainted with Freud's school of psychoanalysis in Vienna. Ishi moved in with the Waterman family, where Edward Sapir, one of America's most distinguished linguists, worked with him. Ishi supplied Sapir with a torrent of Yahi language, day after day pouring out his native stories and songs. Perhaps Ishi suspected that he was dying and decided to leave as much of his culture as possible behind so that his people would not be forgotten. As Ishi's tuberculosis worsened, Waterman wrote to Kroeber "the poor old Indian is dying. The work last summer was too much for him. He was the best friend I had in the world and I killed him by letting Sapir ride him too hard, and by letting him sneak out for lunches."

Kroeber directed that Yahi burial customs should be followed as closely as possible after Ishi died. The body should be touched and handled as little as possible, then cremated on an out-of-doors funeral pyre. The ashes were to be buried in a funerary urn, the closest available equivalent to the burial basket and rock cairn used in Yahi burial rites.

Kroeber was still in New York City when Ishi died, on March 25, 1916. No doubt recalling the bizarre faux funeral for the Peary Eskimos, he was worried by what might be done in his absence. From a borrowed office in the American Museum of Natural History, Kroeber instructed his California colleagues to adhere to earlier burial plans: "[I] insist on it as my personal wish." While he would permit the casting of a plaster death mask, he strongly objected to an autopsy, for fear that it "would resolve itself into a general dissection. Please shut it down." In uncharacteristically strong language, Kroeber wrote, "As to disposal of the body, I must ask you as my personal representative to yield nothing at all under any circumstances. If there is any talk about the interests of science, say for me that science can go to hell."

"We propose to stand by our friends," Kroeber continued. "Besides, I cannot believe that any scientific value is materially involved. We have hundreds of Indian skeletons that nobody ever comes near to study."

By return mail, Kroeber learned from a California colleague that his letter had arrived too late: "The only departures from your request were that a simple autopsy was performed and that the brain was preserved. The matter was not entirely in my hands—in short what happened amounts to a compromise between science and sentiment with myself on the side of sentiment."

Ishi's body was taken to a funeral parlor, where it was embalmed, but no funeral services were held. Waterman, Pope, and a few anthropologists visited Ishi's coffin, placing in it his bow and quiver filled with arrows, several pieces of dentalia (shell money), some dried venison and acorn meal, firemaking equipment, and a small quantity of tobacco. They accompanied the body to Laurel Hill cemetery, near San Francisco, where everything was cremated and the ashes placed in a Santa Clara Pueblo pottery jar, with the inscription: "Ishi, the last Yahi Indian, died March 25, 1916."

Ishi's death sent Kroeber into an emotional tailspin. Decades later, he would reflect that the two years following Ishi's death were the worst of his life. Not only had his wife Henrietta just died (also of tuberculosis), but Kroeber had developed a chronic ear infection causing disorientation and permanent hearing loss in one ear. Wracked with pain and guilt, Kroeber second-guessed everything. Had he inadvertently exposed Ishi to tuberculosis by introducing him to Henrietta? Or did Ishi contract the disease while making hospital rounds with Pope? Had he brought Sapir to Berkeley earlier, when Ishi was healthier, how much more information could have been recorded? Had Kroeber sacrificed Ishi's health for the sake of science?

Anthropologists of Kroeber's day rarely developed close ties with their Indian informants because most of them were elderly and would soon die. Kroeber and his coworkers were accustomed to visiting rural reservations, interviewing the key elders for a couple of hours or days, then returning to their university or museum headquarters to write out a description of the culture. Usually, there was little emotional investment since the informants rarely left their home and in most cases the anthropologist never saw them again.

But Kroeber slipped into a paralyzing depression and came to question his career choice. After arranging a one-year job swap with Robert Lowie (another Boas student who was then Curator of Ethnology at the American Museum of Natural History), Kroeber settled in New York City in the fall of 1917—ostensibly to work at the American Museum, but more important, to begin psychoanalysis with a New York-based analyst trained by Anna Freud.

Back in Berkeley a year later, he was somewhat refreshed but still suffering from regrets over Ishi's death that would never leave him. He returned to part-time anthropological teaching and began his own psychoanalytic practice. Although Kroeber published extensively, for the rest of his life he refused to write about his experiences with Ishi and he also denied access to anybody seeking to use Sapir's notebooks, which recorded Ishi's language (they surfaced in the 1980s; Kroeber's heirs donated the Ishi documents to the University of California's Bancroft library). To Kroeber, the loss of Ishi created long-lasting anxieties about the propriety and ethics of anthropological research.

For the nation, Ishi's death meant that the last "free" Indian had died. Despite everything mainstream America had done to hasten that demise, there was a certain sadness when the inevitable finally happened.

IS "REAL HISTORY" EMBEDDED IN ORAL TRADITION?

10.

I've let the Omaha tell their own story, rather than fill my pages with stories told about them. I can wait for the truth to prevail.

—Alice Fletcher (1912)

WHILE LIVING IN his museum home, Ishi recited hundreds of songs and stories describing his Yahi way of life, which Kroeber painstakingly recorded on Edison wax cylinders. One particularly memorable set of cylinders documents the tale of *U-Tut-Ne* (The Wood Duck), who came of age and decided he needed a wife. Early one morning, Wood Duck began singing his love song, and no fewer than nineteen maidens offered themselves in marriage, but in the end, Wood Duck remained a bachelor. At times, Ishi would mimic the voices of different characters in the story—one voice for Wood Duck, another for Coyote, a third for Wood Pecker. Reciting the Wood Duck story took six hours and required nineteen repetitions of Wood Duck's love song; Ishi insisted that he get it correct. But nobody alive at the time could make sense of the nuances he so carefully spelled out.

The tale of *U-Tut-Ne* is a creation story. It describes how Earth was created and how people, plants, animals, and other beings came to be. It addresses the most profound of human questions: Who we are, why we are here, the purpose of life and death, humanity's proper role in the world. *U-Tut-Ne* told how humans became separated from the gods, why men are different from women and when this differentiation took place, and where the key elements for survival—salt and corn, acorns and deer—came from. It gives an account of the origins of different tribes and races, the entry of evil into the world, and the separation of the world of the living from that of the dead. It thus addresses the most central questions of value and meaning.

Some Native American creation tales tell of great migrations. Others say that Indian people have lived in the same place since time began.

"THE RELIGIOUS RITES OF A VANISHING PEOPLE"

Ishi and Kroeber spent countless hours recording and transcribing Yahi oral tradition. As Boas' student, Kroeber appreciated the urgency of scientifically documenting Indian traditions and languages before they disappeared. Like many Indian people, Ishi shared a similar concern that his tribal traditions not be lost forever. As famed Lakota elder Black Elk told John C. Neihardt, "What I know was given to me for men and it is true and it is beautiful. You were sent to save it. . . . I can teach you."

Francis La Flesche was another Native American deeply concerned with preserving his rapidly vanishing Indian past. Born on the Omaha Reservation in 1857, La Flesche grew up speaking the Omaha language and practicing traditional Omaha religion as a child. As a "runner" in the last bison hunt held by the Omaha (in 1873), his job was to locate the main herd and report its whereabouts to the rest of the hunters. He is said to have covered one hundred miles on foot during an eighteen-hour period.

La Flesche attended a Presbyterian mission school and rapidly became accustomed to the new white ways. In 1881, he moved to Washington, D.C., became a copyist in the Office of Indian Affairs, and attended National University. He earned his LL.B. in 1892 and his LL.M. a year later. La Flesche became Alice Fletcher's protege (and later her adopted son); he has also been called the "first professional American Indian anthropologist."

Through her friendship with Francis and the rest of the La Flesche family, Fletcher obtained access to Omaha culture in a way never before granted an outsider. In 1883, when she became extremely ill with inflammatory rheumatism, the Omaha sang tribal songs during her long convalescence. Fletcher transcribed the songs and La Flesche recorded them with a graphophone; together they assembled the largest collection of Indian music then in existence.

Fletcher recovered and, with La Flesche, began recording sacred traditions and legends. The primary Omaha creation story told how the ancestors, originally eastern farmers, had followed the bison herds westward across the Great Plains. Somewhere on this long migration, perhaps in Dakota Territory, the Omaha ancestors acquired their "Sacred Pole" (also called the "Venerable Man"), a portable shrine that came to symbolize Omaha tribal identity. Cut from a magical cottonwood tree, the Venerable Man lived in his own special tent, answering prayers and providing for his people. A "keeper" kept the Sacred Pole visible to all by carrying the shrine on his back during buffalo hunts. It embodied the very spirit of the tribe.

Fletcher and La Flesche reported that Omaha elders in the 1880s believed that their tribe was dying, and after considerable soul-searching, decided that the Sacred Pole and other consecrated objects should be buried with their last keeper. But others, including Eddie Cline (a recent tribal Chairman of the Omaha), claim that because the Sacred Pole was a living thing, no nineteenth-century elder would have considered burying him; Cline believes the pending-burial story was a ploy concocted to take the Pole away. Whichever story is true, it is clear that La Flesche, who had himself worshipped the Venerable Man as a youth, agreed that the Omaha tribe was doomed and believed its sacred objects should be preserved. No doubt in consultation with Fletcher, La Flesche suggested that the Venerable Man and associated ritual items should be transferred to Harvard's Peabody Museum for safekeeping.

In *The Omaha Tribe*, Fletcher and La Flesche recount Francis' conversations with the elderly Yellow Smoke, last keeper of the Venerable Man. As the two smoked in the shade after a full dinner, La Flesche reminded Yellow Smoke, now bowed with age, of better days when the elder had been a great orator, when he signed the treaty between the Omaha and the United States. "As my visit was drawing to a close . . . I suddenly swooped down upon the old chief with the audacious question: "Why don't you send the 'Venerable Man' to some eastern city where he could dwell in a great brick house instead of a ragged tent?" A smile crept over Yellow Smoke's face, La Flesche reports, and as the elder cleaned his pipe, he replied "My son, I have thought about this myself but no one whom I could trust has hitherto approached me upon this subject. I shall think about it, and will give you a definite answer when I see you again."

On their next visit, Yellow Smoke took La Flesche into the Sacred Tent and handed him the Venerable Man and his sacred belongings: "This was the first time that it was purposely touched by anyone outside of its hereditary Keepers," La Flesche solemnly recorded. La Flesche formally transferred the Venerable Man and associated sacred artifacts to the Peabody Museum in 1888.

Fletcher and La Flesche recognized that the ethnographic significance of the Venerable Man greatly diminished without a precise and detailed account of the associated ritual songs and sacred legends. Everyone involved knew of the potential danger would be in writing down legends as powerful as the "Venerable Man." When pressed, Yellow Smoke "consented to speak but not without misgivings" because he believed that such an act was "formerly held to be a profanation and punishable by the supernatural." In September 1888, Yellow Smoke came to Joseph (Iron Eye) La Flesche's house to discuss the legend that his people had treasured with the Sacred Pole. After considerable back-and-forth, the old man reluctantly agreed to have the story recorded— but only after Joseph, Francis' father agreed to "cheerfully accept for himself any penalty that might follow the revealing of these sacred traditions."

To everyone's shock, Joseph took ill before their eyes and suddenly died. Francis later recorded in *The Omaha Tribe*. "The fear inspired by the Pole was strengthened in its passing away, for by a singular coincidence the touch of fatal disease fell upon Joseph La Flesche almost at the close of the interview, which lasted three days, and in a fortnight he lay dead in the very room in which had been revealed the Sacred Legend connected with the Pole." Although devastated by his father's sudden death, Francis La Flesche continued to record the customs of his people. He had to search for years for somebody who knew the ritual songs associated with the Sacred Pole because the priest in charge of the songs had died without leaving a successor. In 1897, Francis found another old priest who knew the songs, but he refused to sing them because they rightfully belonged to others. This elder insisted that the songs were not his to give and "knowing that it would be useless even with bribes to attempt to persuade the priest to become a plagiarist," wrote La Flesche, "I refrained from pushing the matter further."

Another year passed and La Flesche asked again, this time pleading that "our people no longer flock to these sacred houses as in times past . . . [you] are the only man who has a full knowledge of [the songs]. Therefore I have made bold to come to you again." The Omaha elder reluctantly agreed to sing the sacred songs, which La Flesche recorded on wax cylinders. "As I listened to the old priest his voice seemed as full and resonant as when I heard him years ago, in the days when the singing of these very songs in the Holy Tent meant so much . . . to every man, woman, and child in the tribe. Now, the old man sang with his eyes closed and watching him there was like watching the last embers of the religious rites of a vanishing people."

"ACCORDING TO THE CANONS OF ABORIGINAL RATHER THAN A SCIENTIFIC LOGIC"

On August 10, 1911, one day after Ishi wandered into the Oroville slaughterhouse corral, the Bureau of American Ethnology released *The Omaha Tribe*, a well-illustrated, 672-page compendium of Omaha history, ethnography, and material culture. The title page credits the two authors—"Alice C. Fletcher (Holder of the Thaw Fellowship, Peabody Museum, Harvard University) and Francis La Flesche (A Member of the Omaha Tribe)." Years later, in a retrospective history of the Bureau of American Ethnology, archaeologist Neil Judd would call *The Omaha Tribe* "one of the most sought after studies ever published by the BAE." But at the time, the book received a more hostile reception.

Robert Lowie, Boas' student and then a curator at the American Museum of Natural History, published an acerbic review in *Science* chiding the authors for their presentation of the basic ethnographic data. Under "Social Life," for instance, they included not only "legitimate topics" like kinship terms, courtship and marriage practices, and etiquette, but also "Avocations of Women" (including cooking, quill work, and weaving), clothing, and amusements. Lowie scolded Fletcher and La Flesche for classifying their data "according to the canons of aboriginal rather than a scientific logic." He also criticized the authors for failing to cite the earlier ethnographic research of Reverend James Owen Dorsey (who had worked among the Omaha in 1878–1880) and reprimanded them for relying too heavily on tribal oral traditions and attaching historical meaning to Omaha creation stories "in spite of their naively rationalistic psychology."

Fletcher took the criticism in stride, responding that "I did not want to attack Mr. Dorsey, because he is dead. He did not understand the Omaha language and made dreadful mistakes and he . . . had theories which colored his views." As for the approach they took toward the data, Fletcher wrote that "I've let the Omaha tell their own story, rather than fill my pages with stories told about them. I can wait for the truth to prevail."

The impact of Lowie's criticism on La Flesche is more difficult to assess. Lacking formal training in anthropology, La Flesche was motivated mostly by his desire to record his own culture and language before it disappeared. Both a reservation-raised Omaha Indian and a Victorian gentleman with strong ties to the scientific establishment, La Flesche was pulled by both worlds. Although living in Washington, he returned home often and never lost touch with his people. But old restraints still protected the sacred traditions, and many Omaha apparently resented his making their private ceremonies and traditions public.

Ironically, as a youth, La Flesche had shared their resentments. He was an informant for the Reverend Dorsey, whose *Omaha Sociology* was published in 1884 by the Bureau of American Ethnology. Boas raved that Dorsey's record on the Omaha showed "deep insight into the mode of thought of the Indian" and recommended Dorsey as a model ethnographer. La Flesche, however, later complained that Dorsey published "too much of the private affairs of many of the Omahas . . . without their consent."

Less than a decade later, La Flesche was himself prying sacred tales and songs from the elders. Working among his own Omaha people and later among the closely related Osage of Oklahoma, La Flesche was acutely aware of the genuine fears of all involved and must have been conflicted over his own father's death.

In another hostile review of *The Omaha Tribe*, published in 1912, an anonymous critic charged that Joseph La Flesche was not even an Omaha (an accusation recently repeated by two anthropologists, James Clifton and R. H. Barnes), raising doubts about his authenticity as the "last Chief of the Omaha." In the 1960s, one faction within the Omaha tribe tried to have the La Flesche family stricken from tribal rolls, on the grounds that they had never rightfully been Omaha according to traditional principles. Still, in 1986 a new wing of the Omaha clinic was named in honor of Susan La Flesche, M.D., Francis' younger half-sister and the first American Indian woman to practice scientific medicine.

For his part, La Flesche remained committed to preserving his native traditions for the rest of the world: "The misconception of Indian life and character so common among the white people," he wrote "has been due largely to an ignorance of the Indian's language, of his mode of thought, his beliefs, his ideals, and his native institutions." Fletcher and La Flesche prided themselves on interpreting Omaha life from an insider's perspective—telling the world something it did not know.

But it was exactly this "insider's" perspective that drew the wrath of Robert Lowie in 1913.

PHYSICS ENVY: A LARGER BOASIAN AGENDA

Lowie's attack on Fletcher and La Flesche was not a random shot. It was an early round in a carefully orchestrated campaign by Franz Boas and his students to establish a more scientific agenda for American anthropology.

Boas had published a programmatic paper in 1899, outlining the basic structure of anthropological research. Broadly defining American anthropology as "the science of man," Boas identified three specific areas of inquiry: physical anthropology (the study of the variability in human form), linguistics (exploring the range of human languages), and ethnology (discovering the laws governing the activities of the human mind, and reconstructing the history of human culture and civilization). As he noted at the time, "these subjects are not taken up by any other branch of science, and in developing them anthropology fills a vacant place in the system of sciences." Although Boas would modify this definition several times during the next forty years— he later annexed archaeology as a fourth branch of anthropology—the 1899 paper defined the modern structure of the field.

This marked a significant departure from the nineteenth-century anthropology of Morgan, Powell, Fletcher, and Cushing. For the first time, Boas specifically defined the subject matter of anthropology in terms of three key variables—biology, language, and culture. "Race" was no longer the sole determinant of cultural behavior. In fact, in the Boasian scheme, none of anthropology's three variables could be assumed to be primary because each varied independently. Boas insisted that different approaches were required to study each branch of anthropology, and that each involved quite separate kinds of historical processes.

Boas published his basic vision of anthropology while a curator at the American Museum of Natural History. After resigning from the Museum in 1905, he devoted his considerable energies to research and teaching at nearby Columbia University. Beginning with Alfred Kroeber, he trained an extraordinary succession of first-rate professional anthropologists, including Robert Lowie, Ruth Benedict, and Margaret Mead. Each student shared Boas' fundamental assumptions about the field of anthropology, and according to anthropological historian George Stocking, "much of twentieth-century anthropology may be viewed as the working out in time of various implications in Boas' own positions."

Boas instilled in his students a sense of scientific professionalism, attempting to raise anthropological standards to a level that would satisfy even a hard scientist: "From physics Boas brought into anthropology a sense of definiteness of problem, of exact rigor or methods, and of highly critical objectivity," Kroeber wrote. "These qualities have remained with him unimpaired, and his imparting them to anthropology remains his fundamental and unshakable contribution to our discipline." In the view of Ruth Benedict, "Boas found anthropology a collection of wild guesses and a happy hunting ground for the romantic lover of primitive things; he left it a discipline in which theories could be tested." Boas placed anthropology firmly within the family of social sciences, his aim being to investigate human culture per se—in all times and in all places, in all its parts and aspects. So defined, the mission of anthropology became to generalize about how culture works, to determine how human beings behave under cultural constraints. As anthropologist Don Fowler sees it, Boas made "a conscious attempt to 'mystify' science as the objective search for Truth, and see scientists as infallible, dispassionate knowledge-makers."

INSIDER VS. OUTSIDER PERSPECTIVES

Boas argued that ethnographic data must be carefully framed into objective and rigorous categories that would eventually lead to the discovery of scientific laws and principles. By these guidelines, ethnographic evidence must be collected objectively and precisely. Hypotheses must be formulated explicitly and tested against independent data. This framework, grounded in Enlightenment science, was designed to ensure that conclusions were objective and true: if two scientifically trained ethnographers observed similar events under similar conditions, they should be able to record, objectively, exactly the same data. Although these goals were grounded in the methods of Samuel Morton and Lewis Henry Morgan, Boas faulted their anthropological techniques and theoretical assumptions. Scientists must observe and describe aspects of a culture that even those participating in that culture do not know. This is why, in his 1913 review of *The Omaha Tribe*, Lowie belittled La Flesche and Fletcher for trying to approximate an "insider's" perspective on Omaha tribal life. Some years earlier, Boas had criticized Frank Cushing on similar grounds.

For his part, Cushing never even considered the value-neutral scientific methods advocated later by Lowie and Boas—he simply immersed himself in Zuni life to see what would happen. La Flesche never pretended to be an objective observer of Omaha life. He was guided strictly by his Omaha belief system. As white outsiders, Cushing and Fletcher prided themselves on gaining extraordinary access to the cultures they studied. Their "insider's view" prompted them to explore what was significant, meaningful, and otherwise "real"—as defined by people being studied. Cushing, in particular, relished the cleverness of the Zuni people—and implicitly, his own shrewdness for being able to discover the inner workings of the Zuni mind.

A number of late nineteenth-century archaeologists shared Cushing's interest in Native American oral tradition. As part of their archaeological research, they collected Indian traditions to help understand chronology, site function, and cultural affiliation of the sites they were studying. Jesse Walter Fewkes noted in 1900 that "this work . . . can best be done under guidance of the Indians by an ethno-archaeologist, who can bring as a preparation for his work an intimate knowledge of the present life of the Hopi villagers." Following a "direct historical approach," these anthropologists saw themselves as operating within an appropriately scientific framework, attempting to begin with an ethnographic "known," and working their way back into an archaeological "unknown."

Boas and his students were advocating a hard-line, physics-based view of science, and this impartial-objective-outsider's perspective won out. The "insider's truth" approach to anthropology was discredited for decades.

LOWIE ON ORAL TRADITION

Nowhere does the Boasian vision for a dispassionate "science of man" emerge more clearly than with respect to native oral tradition. When Lowie criticized Fletcher and La Flesche for attaching historical significance to Omaha creation legends, he was rehearsing an argument that would soon emerge in a much stronger form.

In 1914, two well-respected anthropologists, John R. Swanton, of the Bureau of American Ethnology and Harvard University's Roland B. Dixon, published a widely read paper called "Primitive American History." Swanton and Dixon discussed the distribution of Indian tribes across North America by relying, in part, on the beliefs about origin and migration traditions held by the Indians themselves. They suggested that well-documented tribal traditions could provide a useful starting point for mounting additional linguistic, archaeological, and historical investigations.

In his testy response, Lowie savaged Swanton and Dixon for their uncritical and unscientific use of oral history. "Native 'history' is not history in our sense," argued Lowie, "any more than the fact, even if true, of my neighbor's cat having kittens is history; and as for tribal differences, what criteria have we for estimating them solely on the basis of the traditions? From the traditions themselves nothing can be deduced." Then, in a monumental fit of pique, Lowie threw down the gauntlet: "I cannot attach to oral traditions any historical value whatsoever under any conditions whatsoever."

Stung by the ferocity of Lowie's criticism, Dixon and Swanton admitted that "oral tradition is . . . sometimes grotesquely inaccurate" and "as a matter of fact, the number of cases in which we depend solely on traditional evidence is small." But this lame response only goaded Lowie to intensify his attack. In his address as retiring President of the American Folk-Lore Society, delivered in December 1916, Lowie suggested that any scientists believing that Indian oral traditions had valid "historical value" are like "circle-squarers and inventors of perpetual-motion machines, who are still found besieging the portals of learned institutions."

Lowie "utterly denied" that primitive people possess a historical sense or perspective. "The psychologist does not *ask* his victim for his reaction-time," he argued, "but subjects him to experimental conditions that render the required determination possible. The paleontologist does not interrogate calculating circus-horses to ascertain their phylogeny. How can the historian beguile himself into the belief that he need only question the natives of a tribe to get at its history?" Although "primitive history" might retain some ethnographic interest for study as such, Lowie argued that anthropological evidence obtained "objectively" would always be superior to tribal hearsay.

This assault on Indian oral tradition carried the day and anthropologists across the country chimed in to support Lowie's views. In 1917, Alfred Kroeber wrote, "The habitual attitude of the Zuñi, then, is ahistorical. . . . That now and then he may preserve fragments of a knowledge of the past that approximates what we consider history, is not to be doubted. But it is equally certain that such recollection is casual and contrary to the usual temper of his mind." Archaeologists were swayed by what the cultural anthropologists said. During the summer of 1917, while awaiting assignment to Officer Training

School, Alfred Kidder moved to the First Mesa at Hopi. "I learned a great deal about Hopi archaeology," wrote Kidder, "and among other things discovered that Lowie was quite right. Lowie [said] 'Under no circumstances will I ever believe any historical tradition told me by the Hopi'. . . . When someone like Fewkes began pestering them, and asking them leading questions, they, of course, had to say something, so they just made these things up out of the whole cloth. I don't believe there is any truth to any of that stuff. This history of the development of the Hopi towns has to be worked out archaeologically. . . ." Archaeologist F. W. Hodge, among many others, agreed with Kroeber's earlier assessment: "Zuñi traditional accounts of events which occurred over three centuries ago are not worthy of consideration as historical or scientific evidence."

While admitting that primitive astronomy and natural history might occasionally coincide with "our equivalent branches of learning," Lowie insisted that "in history, as everywhere else, our duty is to determine the facts objectively; if primitive notions tally with ours, so much the better for them, not for ours."

DURING THE EARLY twentieth century, a chasm began to separate American anthropologists from the Indian people they wanted to study. As anthropologists became increasingly concerned with establishing an objective science of mankind, many Indian people expressed their concerns about preserving their own specific tribal histories, customs, and traditions. Mainstream anthropology came to view "insider" anthropologists like Cushing as something of an embarrassing joke—dressed up like an Indian and trying to penetrate the Zuni mind. Although Francis La Flesche was a professional anthropologist—employed for a decade as a Bureau of American Ethnology anthropologist and awarded an honorary doctorate by the University of Nebraska in 1926—his anthropological contributions were marginalized because he too affected an "insider's perspective" rather than the strict empiricism advocated by Boas and his students.

This is why twentieth-century anthropology came to view American Indian perspectives on their own past as basically irrelevant. For their part, Indians became increasingly wary of throwing in their lot with anthropologists. Although plenty of Indian people remained involved in the anthropological enterprise, their non-scientific perspectives commonly reduced their level of involvement from "collaborator" to "informant."

THE PERILOUS IDEA OF
RACE

It is ironic that anthropology and its subfields (physical, cultural, and linguistic anthropology) have been involved in both the creation and the demise of the concept of race.
—Yolanda Moses (1997), President of the City College of New York

IT IS DIFFICULT today to understand the obsession of nineteenth-century anthropologists with simple measurements taken on the human skull. In the 1840s, Samuel Morton relied almost exclusively on cranial capacity as an indication of human intelligence. Pre-Civil War Americans believed that Morton had scientifically proved that Caucasians had bigger brains (and hence were more intelligent) than American Indians. Because the African skulls in Morton's collection had the smallest brains of all, they were judged to be the least intelligent of the human races.

Nineteenth-century skull science also relied on a second measurement, head form, to trace the origins and distribution of peoples. Known more formally as the "cephalic index," head form is simply the ratio of maximum skull breadth to maximum skull length. The cephalic index reflects whether a skull is round-headed (brachycephalic), long-headed (dolichocephalic), or in between (mesocephalic). Negroid skulls are supposed to be long and narrow, Mongoloid crania are traditionally considered to be broader, and so forth. During the late nineteenth-century, the cephalic index gradually came to supplement cranial capacity as the measurement of choice because, after all, head form could be readily calibrated from a living specimen.

As a veteran skull collector, Franz Boas was uneasy with the cephalic index because he knew first-hand that skull shape and size varied markedly, even within the same cultural group. As a natural scientist trained in empirical observation, Boas came to question how any measure as simplistic as "skull shape" could be used to classify the races of humanity. Despite all the glib talk about race during the late nineteenth-century, Boas found that nobody knew what a "race" really was.

Although Morton's belief in separate racial creations was largely forgotten after the Civil War, the almost obsessive urge to classify human skulls into fixed, unchanging races or hereditary "types" continued undiminished. During this period, when mainstream anthropology was still dividing humanity into a fixed number of races, Boas even published a paper defending skull shape as a good indicator of deep-seated racial differences and as a reflection of long-term trends in human heritability.

During the early 1890s, while still teaching at Clark University, Boas began a study on Worcester school children, investigating whether growth changes during adolescence were influenced more by environmental or by hereditary factors. He also took measurements on "Half-Blood Indians" during collecting trips to British Columbia to see how racial characteristics mixed.

After joining the staff of the American Museum of Natural History in 1895, Boas continued to examine these baseline assumptions about race and seek the physical processes that created the racial differences he had been measuring for years. With the ultimate goal of establishing a workable theory of the origins of human "racial types," he developed a research plan to study New York City's swelling immigrant population, looking specifically at the relationship between physical type and physical environment. Boas reasoned that if the theory of distinct racial types had any validity, then immigrant New Yorkers should retain their essential racial characteristics. But if immigrants' "racial characteristics" (such as headform) changed significantly after their arrival in America, then racial differences should be attributed, at least in part, to environment, not simply heredity.

In 1908, Boas began measuring the head shapes of Russian Jewish boys enrolled in New York public school and comparing these data to measurements taken in Europe. Like all anthropologists of the day, he expected to find that head form remained relatively stable. But his preliminary study produced "very striking and wholly unexpected" results: cephalic indices changed significantly in first-generation immigrants. This outcome, if true, would cast serious doubt on the significance of standard racial classifications. Although he grasped its significance, Boas kept a healthy skepticism. Changing head shapes might be restricted to those living in "favorable surroundings." So he branched out to look at immigrant children in less privileged urban areas and a broader spectrum of racial types.

Boas started measuring the heads of immigrants at Ellis Island in 1909, providing himself a baseline sample of "zero degree of American influence." He also supervised a house-to-house canvassing of immigrant neighborhoods, measuring heads of both foreign-born parents and American-born children. A corps of thirteen assistants—many of them his own graduate students at Columbia University—measured 1,200 people a week, eventually collecting body measurements on more than 18,000, including eastern European Jews, Bohemians, Sicilians, Poles, Hungarians, and Scots.

After compiling and analyzing the mountain of statistics entirely by hand, Boas in 1911 confirmed his revolutionary conclusion: "Head form which has always been considered one of the most stable and permanent characteristics of human races, undergoes far-reaching changes coincident with the transfer of the people from European to American soil. . . . These results are so definite that while heretofore we had the right to assume that human types are stable, all the evidence now is in favour of a great plasticity of human types, and the permanence of types in new surroundings appears rather as the exception than as the rule." Boas also noted a trend for human head shape to move toward the intermediate form.

Although a number of New York journalists publicized Boas' research, they missed the point. They took it to support the then-popular notion that a new, uniquely American "race" was emerging from the Great American melting pot of immigrants. Boas quickly disavowed this interpretation and emphasized the true significance of his work. The New York study clearly established that individuals born in the United States had a cephalic index appreciably different from that of their European-born siblings. Headform cannot be a stable indicator of the historical continuity of racial types: "The differences between different types of man are, on the whole, small as compared to the range of variation in each type." Boas had landed a telling blow to the immutability of race.

In this groundbreaking research, Boas showed that the notion of race is grounded in a mistaken assumption that a statistical average somehow approximates a long-standing racial "ideal." He cast serious doubt on "the fixity of human races" by establishing that the most venerable of racial traits, the cephalic index, was significantly influenced by environment. Boas argued, correctly, that broad-headed populations can become long-headed within a single generation. He argued that inborn traits did not determine cultural differences or similarities, and he led physical anthropology away from the taxonomy of race toward the study of human biology and culture. Boas was apparently the first scientist ever to demonstrate through empirical research that Negro and white races, as well as all other races, were biologically equal.

The scientific use of race as a fundamental human category should have disappeared a century ago, when Boas demonstrated that race, language, and culture are independent variables. Boas' conclusion did not, however, spark the anticipated revolution. During the early decades of the twentieth century, physical anthropologists largely ignored Boas' criticisms of racial typing and head measurement. This was not merely an ivory tower issue. As late as the 1920s, anthropologists and government officials at the highest levels still believed that physical and mental differences between races could be arranged in a hierarchy, with European civilization occupying the supreme position. When President Calvin Coolidge signed the 1924 Immigration Act, for instance, he commented that "America must be kept American. Biological laws show that Nordics deteriorate when mixed with other races." Against this tide, Boas and his students continued to stand alone in denouncing anthropology's long-term romance with racial determinism.

By the 1940s, the use of race as scientific shorthand to describe biological variability should finally have vanished with the "new evolutionary synthesis" combining the principles of Mendelian genetics with the process of Darwinian natural selection. Despite the combined influence of Julian Huxley, Theodosius Dobzhansky, Ernst Mayer, and George Gaylord Simpson, physical anthropologists in America still held onto their commitment to doctrines of Nordic superiority and racial determinism. Only in the 1950s did the scientific community begin to support Boas' criticisms of race.

Small wonder that in 1895, Boas complained that he found himself "struggling along—so far practically alone."

THE RACIAL DETERMINISM
OF HRDLIČKA AND HOOTON

This curious delay owes much to the influence of Aleš Hrdlička and Earnest Hooton, the two most influential physical anthropologists in the first half of the twentieth century. Having been recruited by Boas in 1897 to study the Peary Eskimos, Hrdlička, a trained physician, conducted medical examinations of the six while they were alive and subsequently examined four of their skeletons after they died. He also collected Qisuk's brain and described its anatomy in a scientific paper. Hrdlička's involvement with the New York Eskimos, like Kroeber's, sparked a lifelong interest in anthropology. In 1899 and 1900, he accompanied an American Museum expedition to Chaco Canyon, New Mexico, living in a thatched room attached to Pueblo Bonito. He was relentless in seeking out human remains, especially skulls from Chacoan sites; he also measured the heads of several living Navajos and made plaster casts of their faces. Hrdlička believed he could detect a close biological relationship— based mostly on skull measurements—between the earliest Pueblo people (ca. 200 BC) and historic Zuni people. In 1902, he traveled extensively throughout northern Mexico, measuring the heads of the living and collecting the skulls of the dead. Hrdlička ultimately moved on to the Smithsonian's National Museum of Natural History, where he became a dominant figure in the search for the first Americans, bringing a new rigor to the study of human skeletal remains. He firmly believed in the fixity of the human races.

In 1918, Hrdlička founded the *American Journal of Physical Anthropology*, which remains the primary scientific publication in the field. In 1928 he established the American Association of Physical Anthropologists, hoping it would blossom into a grand institution of advanced training and museum research. But he could never attract sufficient funding. Hrdlička remained a museum anthropologist throughout his career, without students to polish his reputation and carry his torch. Although he exerted an enormous influence on the field, the training of anthropologists remained under the control of the university system. This is why Harvard professor Earnest A. Hooton, and not Hrdlička, came to dominate American physical anthropology.

Hooton received his Ph.D. at Oxford University in 1911, the same year Boas published his American immigrant studies. Hooton joined the Harvard faculty two years later and taught there until his death in 1954. He is perhaps best known for *The Indians of Pecos Pueblo: A Study of Their Skeletal Remains*, published in 1930, which carried forward the American School of racial determinism developed by Morton and Agassiz nearly a century before.

Between 1915 and 1929, the Harvard graduate Alfred V. Kidder excavated Pecos Pueblo, several miles southeast of Santa Fe, New Mexico. He found that this important site had been initially occupied sometime after AD 1200. Pecos people were still living there when Coronado rode through in 1540. In 1838, the handful of surviving Pecos Indians moved to Jemez Pueblo, seventy miles to the west. Kidder's Pecos excavations were the most ambitious North American archaeological project of their day. He recovered huge samples of broken potsherds and his meticulous analysis established the ceramic chronology that remains in use throughout the Upper Rio Grande area today. Kidder also found hundreds of human burials at Pecos and nearby sites. Kidder asked Hooton to analyze this huge skeletal sample. Hooton agreed and, in 1920, spent two months digging with the Pecos Expedition and seeing for himself the conditions under which the skeletons were being exhumed.

Kidder kept digging burials at Pecos until 1924, when Hooton decided that the series, by then numbering more than 1800 skeletons, was large enough. This was by far the largest sample ever analyzed from a North American archaeological site, and Hooton's analysis of the Pecos collection took ten years. He determined sex and age at death for each individual and established cause of death whenever possible. He constructed stature estimates, recorded traumatic injuries and ancient diseases, and prepared demographic profiles.

This basic analysis complete, Hooton selected 129 of the best-preserved male skulls for further study, sorting and re-sorting them until a series of eight morphological types emerged. Although most of the Pecos skulls "were merely nondescript specimens of a generalized Southwestern Indian appearance," several unusual skull types emerged. Hooton called one group the "Long-faced Europeans . . . because it seemed to me rather un-Indian, if one may employ such an expression." The "Pseudo-Alpine" type had a very short, broad face with rounded contours. Also present was a "short-slender dolichocephalic . . . [that] bears close craniometric and a less marked morphological resemblance to the brunet or brown skinned group often called the Mediterranean race." The "Pseudo-Australoid" type was, according to Hooton, "certainly a non-Mongoloid . . . it may be an ancient form of brunet white man." A "Pseudo-Negroid" type "manifested . . . metrical and indicial likenesses to all Negro groups . . . [and] I am of the opinion that it is in truth Negroid."

Given this astonishing variability, one might wonder whether the "Long-faced European," the "Pseudo-Alpine," and maybe even the "Pseudo-Negroid" skulls might have come from post-1540 contexts within Pecos Pueblo. Curious about this possibility, Hooton plotted the distribution of morphological types against their archaeological associations (arranged according to Kidder's pottery chronology for the site). Several of the "Long-faced European" and one "Pseudo-Alpine" skull did indeed come from church burials, but sixteenth- and seventeenth-century European contact still did not explain the remarkable variability at Pecos. Arranging the skulls chronologically, Hooton was surprised to find that the eight morphological types spanned the entire occupation of Pecos Pueblo. That is, all eight skull types showed up in the earliest occupations—the so-called "Black-on-white" and "Glaze I" periods (dating from AD 1300–1425)—and all but one racial type carried into the post-1540 period.

Why so many racial types at Pecos? Why were "Pseudo-Negroids," "Long-faced Europeans," and "Pseudo-Alpines," living side-by-side with "generalized Southwestern Indians" in AD 1300? Was Pecos Pueblo the original American melting pot?

This is precisely what Hooton proposed. An inveterate advocate of racial typology, he believed that the human skull contained clues that would allow science to track the origins and migrations of the modern races. To Hooton, the "Pseudo-Australoid" type was the "most primitive" kind of American Indian skull, similar to the modern Ainu of Japan; these people, he believed, represented the "first wave of immigrants" into the New World, bringing with them across the Bering Strait a primitive hunting and fishing culture. The next arrivals were "purely Mongoloid in race," which meant to Hooton that their capacity for cultural development was limited. But other "Mongoloids" were racially mixed (as evidenced by their high-bridged and often convex nose), including Hooton's "Long-faced Europeans." Thinking that these people looked like Armenians or Nordics, Hooton described them as "later invaders . . . capable of higher cultural development than the early pioneers and . . . responsible for the development of agriculture and for the notable achievements of New World civilization."

Working squarely within the tradition of Morton and Agassiz, Hooton saw preserved in the Pecos skulls the racial and cultural history of earliest America—not just biological characteristics but also intellectual ability, creativity, personality, and even economic potential. As a genetically inferior race, the American Indians learned to farm only because the "Long-faced Europeans," with their superior intellect and capacity for "higher cultural development," showed them how.

Hooton's tangled views on race and culture did not stop with ancient America. He was a staunch advocate of Nordic superiority, arguing for the exclusion of immigrants from Asia and less favored parts of Europe. In a 1939 essay entitled "Noses, Knowledge, and Nostalgia—The Marks of a Chosen People," Hooton reflected on "the Jewish problem." Once again mingling biological and cultural evidence, Hooton concluded that the difficulties being experienced by Jewish people—in Nazi Germany and elsewhere—were basically self-inflicted: "The Jew possesses as part of his heritage, perhaps reinforced by the traditions of his people, a certain emotional intensity which expresses itself in modes of behavior alien to certain northwest European stocks—especially to Anglo-Saxons . . . [because] the peculiar merits of essentially Jewish culture can be preserved only through a maintenance of the traditional policy of inbreeding and social exclusiveness," Hooton proposed assimilation and interbreeding as the best solution to the "Jewish problem."

Not surprisingly, Franz Boas did not hold Hooton's racialism in high regard, admitting in 1926 that he ranked Hooton at the very bottom of American physical anthropologists when it came to his "contribution to the theory of anthropology." Hooton was well aware of Boas' earlier work on American-born immigrants and its devastating implications for racial typology. Although admitting that Boas had established that differences in skull shape *could* result from environmental, rather than hereditary factors, Hooton dismissed the argument by suggesting that Boas had worked with small and perhaps unstable populations. Sure, the average cephalic index of American-born individuals might differ from that of their parents, but Hooton doubted whether the difference would persist in subsequent generations if they were transplanted back to their homeland. Ignoring the fact that Harry Shapiro (Hooton's first Ph.D. student) had confirmed Boas' conclusions in his own early study of 1930s Japanese immigrant populations to Hawaii, Hooton continued to rely on cephalic index and other cranial measurements to reconstruct human heredity. Firmly convinced that enduring races existed and that they could be differentiated statistically, he published a study in 1939 correlating skull types with criminal behavior, and he retained his Pecos-style approach to racial typology until his death.

From 1913 until the early 1950s, Hooton trained virtually every physical anthropologist in America. He was an extraordinarily popular professor, drawing cartoons, writing poetry, and nurturing generations of students who called him "Hootie." His personal charm, his association with the nation's most famous university, and his dozens of publications made him a dominating figure. Some of his students agreed with his theories on racial determinism and heredity, others did not. But few publicly criticized his work, and mainstream physical anthropology continued within the framework of nineteenth-century traditional assumptions and methods. It was not until the 1950s that Sherwood Washburn's "new" physical anthropology finally vindicated Boas' criticism of racial typology, "racial essence," "racial genius," and "racial soul."

Debra Martin, a physical anthropologist at the University of Massachusetts, feels that Hooton's Pecos study "represents one of the many, many missed opportunities for skeletal biologists to examine, firsthand, the effects of colonization." The Pecos collection was unique because of its size and because the remains spanned the precolonial and colonial periods. By fixating on hereditary differences and perpetuating racial models developed two decades earlier, Hooton missed the real value of the Pecos remains—as evidence of the biological relationships between colonization, disease, and death. Although recording the obvious causes of death of the people who (however unwittingly) contributed their bones to his collection, he never looked into the larger patterns or considered how those patterns might have been influenced by the Euroamerican invasion. Both Hooton and Hrdlička were blind to the problems of racism, poverty, and disease plaguing Indian Country—outrageous rates of infant mortality, a life expectancy two decades less than the national average, rates of diabetes and tuberculosis several times higher than among the white Americans. Small wonder that "doing science" on the bones of dead Indians has been seen in Indian country as linked to white domination.

STEPHEN JAY GOULD TAKES ON MORTON

While Boas had concentrated on the cephalic index to discredit the idea of immutable racial differences, there was a second, lingering issue: the correlation of skull size with human intelligence. Morton's ladder of cranial sophistication stacked the human races in predictable order: whites on top, Indians in the middle, and blacks on the bottom. Moreover, he claimed that this pattern had been stable throughout human history, with whites enjoying a similar superiority over blacks in ancient Egyptian times.

Paleontologist Stephen Jay Gould attacked this problem in 1977, spending several weeks recomputing Morton's data. Since *Crania Americana* was mostly devoted to documenting the inferior intellect of American Indians, Gould started there. Morton had reported that 144 Indian skulls showed a mean cranial capacity of 82 cubic inches, several cubic inches below the Caucasian norm. Gould found that the American Indian average was in error. Morton's sample was heavily biased toward the Inkas of Peru, who showed a significantly smaller cranial capacity than the rest of the Native American sample. When Gould corrected the bias by averaging mean values for *all* tribes, the American Indian average rose to 83.79 cubic inches.

There were also problems with the average Caucasian cranial capacity. Whereas the Native American value had been mistakenly calculated too low, the Caucasian average was statistically inflated because Morton had excluded several small-brained Hindu skulls from his calculations. When Gould included the Hindu sample in the Caucasian total, the average cranial capacity dropped to 84.45 cubic inches. There was, Gould concluded, no statistically significant difference in cranial capacity between Caucasians and American Indians.

Although similar problems turned up in Morton's other calculations, Gould did not accuse Morton of premeditated fraud or deliberate manipulation. Because Morton published all his data and "made no attempt to cover his tracks," Gould declared that his procedures were honest, if misguided. Apparently Morton's belief in racial rankings was so strong that he unconsciously slanted his tabulations toward the "right answer."

RACE AND ANTHROPOLOGICAL ETHICS

In September 1997, the American Anthropological Association sent a memo to the U.S. Census Bureau stating that race could not be determined scientifically. A year later, the Executive Committee of the American Anthropological Association—the world's premier organization of professional anthropologists—issued a statement on race, which reads in part:

> In the US both scholars and the general public have been conditioned to viewing human races and separate divisions within the human species based on visible physical differences. With the vast expansion of scientific knowledge in this century, however, it has become clear that human populations are not unambiguous, clearly demarcated, biologically distinct groups. . . .
>
> Race . . . evolved as a world view [is] a body of prejudgments that distorts our ideas about human differences and group behavior. Racial beliefs constitute myths about the diversity in the human species and about the abilities and behavior of people homogenized into racial categories. . . . Racial myths bear no relationship

to the reality of human capabilities or behavior. Scientists today find that reliance
on such folk beliefs about human differences in research has led to countless errors.

Modern genetic theory has toppled the basic assumptions of racial taxonomy. Kenneth Kidd, a Professor of Genetics and Psychiatry at Yale Medical School, recently put it this way: "In lectures, I now say that human races do not exist if by race you mean a discrete category, a quantitatively different subgroup of humanity. When I look at DNA, I see no racial differences. There tend to be more DNA variations within each population group than between groups and such variation is present broadly around the world within every population. This contradicts the conventional wisdom of earlier this century when there was a tendency to think of populations as monomorphic with rare variants." That is, while biological variability is obviously real, "race" contributes relatively little to overall human variability—and those biological differences are not patterned into discrete population clusters (called "racial types").

But this does not mean, as some seem to think, that "race does not exist" or that "race has no meaning." Racism in America is a deeply embedded fact of history. "Folk beliefs about the fixed, immutable nature of biological 'race' are alive and well in American culture today," writes the anthropologist Yolanda Moses. "I am concerned that well-meaning educators may unwittingly buy into social Darwinist theories which will then be used to keep 'the other' (minorities and women) in their place."

SOME PROBLEMS WITH FORENSIC ANTHROPOLOGY

Kennewick Man has become a textbook example of why race science is bad science.
—Alan Goodman (1998), Anthropologist

Despite a century of criticism, some scientists continue to argue that race remains an appropriate model for describing and explaining human variability, and forensic anthropologists still widely employ the concept of race in their teaching and research. The forensic perspective compares unknown skeletons to modern (culturally constructed) racial groups to see what matches with what. Huge statistical databases of measurements divide up modern human populations into distinct racial types: Caucasoids have longer, more angular faces, with beakier noses; modern Mongoloids have rounder skulls and smaller noses, and so forth. Drawing upon these comparative measurements, forensic anthropologists can often work with law enforcement agencies to reconstruct the overall appearance of crime victims, and usually their reconstructions are pretty accurate. As the title of one article in *Social Science and Medicine* asked, "If Races Don't Exist, Why Are Forensic Anthropologists So Good at Identifying Them?"

Why indeed?

The paper's author, Norman J. Sauer, a forensic anthropologist at Michigan State University, argues that while race might be suspect scientifically, it still works. He and his colleagues claim an 85–90 percent success rate in identifying race from a human skull, which seems like a pretty good average. Forensic studies play an important role in understanding skeletal variations, particularly in criminal investigations. Because, statistically speaking, the dominant descendant groups living in the United States are European, African, and Asian—and there are indeed distinctive differences in cranial form between these modern groups. It is sometimes (but not always) possible to identify from which descent group a particular skull comes. The problems with Hooton's racial typologies, or with a modern cause célèbre like the Kennewick skull, arise when somebody unthinkingly extends these modern trends significantly back in time.

Alan Goodman argues that even the modern forensic studies may fall victim to spurious assumptions of immutable racial types. He reminds us of the severed leg that was recovered from the wreckage of the bombed-out Oklahoma City Federal Building in 1995. One of the world's foremost forensic anthropologists positively identified it as belonging to a "white male." More sophisticated testing later demonstrated that the leg actually came from a black female.

Forensic specialists make their matches by comparing unknown specimens against reference collections containing thousands of skulls and skeletons. But how was "race" determined in the skull libraries? Some of the comparative specimens were collected from archaeological cemeteries during the late nineteenth-century skull wars and "race" was assigned based on supposed archaeological or ethnological associations. Other skulls in the reference collections come from dissection laboratories in major teaching hospitals, where the "race" of record is based on the individual's own testimony before death, or from a death certificate or other legal documentation.

In other words, the baseline racial labels in the reference collections reflect little more than folk stereotypes. The underlying processes of human variability—natural selection, genetic drift, disease, acclimatization, stress, and so forth—produce only gradual trends. They do not cluster in discrete "racial types." As Boas stated half a century ago, racial classifications are merely social constructs loosely based on certain biological traits. "Race" depends mostly on the experience and prejudices of the observer.

PROBLEMS WITH THE C-WORD

We disagree with the notion that this individual is Caucasian. Scientists say that because the individual's head measurement does not match ours, he is not Native American. We believe that humans and animals change over time to adapt to their environment. And our elders have told us that Indian people did not always look the way we look today.

—Armand Minthorn (1996), Umatilla tribal spokesman

In the first wave of national publicity, anthropologists were quoted as describing Kennewick Man's "Caucasoid traits," meaning his long, narrow face with narrow cheekbones and a protruding upper jaw. In fact, Kennewick Man looked so "Caucasoid" to Jim Chatters that he initially mistook him for a nineteenth-century European settler. This meant that Chatters, quite properly, approached the Kennewick skull from a forensic, rather than evolutionary perspective. After the startlingly old radiocarbon date came in, Royce Rensberger wrote in the *Washington Post* that because of the "Caucasoid look . . . the Kennewick skull might alter conventional views of how, when, and by whom the Americas were peopled." In this widely read article, picked up around the world, the words "Caucasoid" and "Mongoloid" were repeated two dozen times.

In a *New York Times* story published two months after the Kennewick discovery, science writer Timothy Egan states flatly in his second paragraph that Kennewick Man had "Caucasian features, judging by skull measurements." He then quotes Chatters' caution that "this finding does not necessarily mean that white people were in North America before Indians. . . . Rather, [Chatters] said, it points to the possibility of mixed ancestry for today's American Indians," meaning that there may have been multiple migrations into ancient America. But then, ignoring Chatters' specific warning, Egan repeated the term "Caucasian" six more times and suggested that the Kennewick discovery "adds credence to the theories that some early North Americans came from European stock."

Rensberger and Egan are respected science writers, but both passed along to their readers the mistaken assumptions that identifiable, immutable human races exist today, that the same races existed 10,000 years ago, and that these determinations can be reliably identified by skull measurements. Maybe they just thought the race story made better copy. Or maybe they were misled by Chatters' use of the terms "Caucasoid," and "Caucasoid-like," as he lapsed into colloquial speech to explain why he decided to run the radiocarbon test in the first place: "I've got a white guy with a stone point in him."

Chatters was hardly the only scientist to call Kennewick Man a "Caucasoid." Among researchers interested in the peopling of the New World, there has been a surprising reluctance to acknowledge the fact that significant morphological changes can occur in relatively short periods of time. Speaking of Kennewick Man (among other finds), the physical anthropologist George Gill, one of the eight scientists suing over the Kennewick skeleton, publicly declared that "examining these earliest remains shows me that some were Caucasian." A Smithsonian Institution Web site even suggested possible connections between the ancient "Caucasians" of America and "the mysterious Ainu people, an isolated Caucasoid group who live in northern Japan." Small wonder that the American press—and the American public—became confused about the racial implications of Kennewick Man.

Equating race with biology is bad science and has caused enormous confusion and hard feelings. "I really do object to saying there is such a thing as a Caucasoid trait," Goodman reiterates. "You can find amazing changes in cranial size just within certain groups that lived in the same area." He suggests that in Rensberger's ill-informed use of racial terminology, "the hands of the anthropological clock had just been put back 100 years." One wonders how, if he were alive, Boas would react to this news. Would he be shocked that 9,400-year-old Kennewick Man looks different from contemporary Native Americans? Would he be pleased that the shopworn Caucasoid-Mongoloid-Negroid racial typology—a relic from the eighteenth century—is still around? Probably not.

From an evolutionary—rather than a "forensic"—perspective, is it hardly surprising that Kennewick Man does not look like a modern American Indian. Why should he? Why should anybody who lived 10,000 years ago look like somebody living today? The earliest migrants into America were presumably few, with relatively little genetic diversity; subsequent migrations and extended periods of reproductive isolation at this early point in North American history would presumably increase the differences between pioneer Americans and other populations of the world. Consider how the American landscape has altered since the days of Kennewick Man—staggering climatic changes, major shifts in the distributions of plant and animal communities (which, of course, led to major changes in human diet), the domestication of plants (including maize, beans, and squash), massive demographic change (with some pre-Columbian settlements approaching modern levels of urban crowding), the introduction of devastating European diseases, the adoption of a modern, western-style diet—each of which can change the way a skull looks.

In North American Indian populations (and, indeed, human populations worldwide), there has been a distinct tendency for skulls to become more globular ("rounder") and less robust over the last 10,000 years. This being so, no experienced physical anthropologist should be surprised that the Kennewick skull has a longer, more robust face than recent Native Americans. That these attributes are still sometimes interpreted in racial terms indicates that the typological approach is still alive, if only here and there, among modern physical anthropologists. Although forensic anthropologists can often produce spectacular results in separating modern "races," this success requires very specialized assumptions that are wholly inappropriate when projected into the deep past.

At the level of molecular archaeology—the analysis of ancient DNA—terms like "pure Caucasoid" or "pure American Indian" have little meaning. No combination of genetic traits, molecular or otherwise, is "pure." No such combination is universally present in one racial grouping yet entirely lacking in all others.

Goodman stresses several key points:

- There are no pristine and unchanging racial types.
- Indisputable racial types did not exist in the past.
- Terms like "Caucasoid" and "Mongoloid" have little scientific utility.
- It is hardly surprising that Kennewick Man fails to fit into such imperfect and inappropriate racial categories.
- Race simply fails as a scientific shorthand for organizing human biological variability.

How, then, can racially loaded terminology be applied to a skull that is 9,400 years old? When somebody says that Kennewick Man is "Caucasoid" or "Caucasoid-like," that statement calls up racial stereotypes left over from colonial days. It may be true that in scientific circles, terms like "Caucasoid" refer only to morphology, rather than ancestry. Relying on dictionary definitions overlooks the racial connotations that invariably arise when speaking to the American press corps. In the first quantitative analysis of Kennewick Man published in a scientific journal, Chatters complained that newspaper accounts had "confused the description of the remains as 'caucasoid-like' with an assertion that the skull was European." The result, he felt, led to unwarranted speculations "that this find suggested migration of people directly from Europe to North America in the latest Pleistocene or early Holocene." Before a professional audience at the Society for American Archaeology meetings, Chatters said, "Nobody is talking about white here." But that's precisely what most nonscientists think when somebody says "Caucasoid."

As scientists repeatedly used everyday racial terminology to describe the Kennewick bones, they inadvertently stirred up some of anthropology's most hateful and threatening ghosts—the legacy of scientific racism. Lawrence Straus, an archaeologist at the University of New Mexico, considers Chatters' use of "Caucasoid" and "Caucasoid-like" to be "dangerous." Donald Grayson, an archaeologist from the University of Washington, agrees, pointing out that "the use of the term *Caucasoid* really is a red flag, suggesting that whites were here earlier and Indians were here later, and there's absolutely no reason to think that." Adeline Fredin, Director of the Colville Tribe's History and Archaeology program, goes even further: "Whenever you get an individual that jumps right up—from the instant that he gets ahold of this human remains—and says 'Aha! It's Caucasian, it's not Native American,' you know you've automatically set an opposition in place."

Reflecting on his experiences with Kennewick Man, Chatters has candidly acknowledged, "Now that I know that people are so upset about the word 'Caucasoid,' I'd probably use it a lot less—if at all." He justifies his use of such racial shorthand by stating it was "necessary to use a term with such incendiary connotations" because no other words seemed to do the job. Several anthropologists have taken exception to this statement, suggesting that plenty of precise nonracial terms are available to describe human remains.

So how should scientists handle the race question? It is scientifically appropriate to suggest that physical traits on the Kennewick skull might point to biological connections outside America, and perhaps even hint at a complex history of human migrations into the Americas. But this is very, very different from calling a 9,400-year-old skeleton a "Caucasoid" because the word itself overshadows the scientific intent and inadvertently raises instead the emotional connotations of race-based language in modern America. Unfortunately, using the C-word in archaeology has became the anthropological equivalent of a witness using the "n-word" in the O. J. Simpson homicide trial. Some words are so powerful that their use preempts further discussion: use of (and then lying about) the "n-word" rendered Officer Mark Fuhrman's sworn testimony hateful and bogus. In the aftermath of Kennewick, any scientist (or science writer) using the term "Caucasian," "Caucasoid," or "Caucasoid-like" in a public forum to describe a 9,400 year-old skull is both practicing bad science and painfully naive about the power of racial language in modern America.

The careless use of racially charged language not only demeans legitimate anthropological science; it also plays directly into the hands of those who would use race in a hateful way. According to Goodman, the Asatru Folk Assembly—who have filed their own lawsuit over the Kennewick skeleton— "is not, as many seem to think, a harmless bunch of spiritualist crazies and weirdos. Rather, their leaders have extensive neo-Nazi connections." Louis Beam, who has also commented on the case, is a former "Ambassador at Large" for the Aryan Nations. In his broadly circulated article "Dead 'Indians' Don't Lie" Beam cites public statements by scientists on Kennewick-Man-as-Caucasian to support his view that that America was first settled by whites (and, by implication, rightfully "belongs" to their Aryan descendants). He "jokingly speculates" that "this was the first incidence of 'cowboys and Indians' with the Indians winning." So viewed, Kennewick Man becomes the Great White Hope and this is why the far right promotes a detailed scientific investigation as "a means by which this long-dead kinsman of ours can tell his saga and renew his glory."

There is no more important issue facing modern anthropology than clarifying the concept of race—what it means and what it doesn't. "In the absence of reasonable anthropological explanation," Yolanda Moses warns, "many people tend to fall back on what they know, or what they think they know . . . raising the potential for reasonable, modern, people to get back into a nineteenth-century biologically determinist mode of accepting the notions of fixed racial, gender, and class hierarchies all over again." Anthropologists have done a poor job of explaining human biological variability in language that everyday people can understand, and as the Kennewick episode makes so clear, even well-meaning academics get tongue-tied when it comes to race.

Franz Boas, the resolute grave robber who did more than any other scientist to refute scientific racism, embodied the paradoxes that continue to torment anthropologists today. Although modern anthropology has soundly repudiated its founding doctrine, a legacy of racialism hangs on.

MOST VISITORS COME to natural history museums to see the dinosaur bones, gems and meteorites, and dioramas of exotic wildlife and faraway cultures. Little more than a decade ago, few museum goers were aware of the formidable research collections stored behind the scenes, of the tens of thousands of Indian skulls and skeletons in the research collections.

Some of the Cheyenne skulls long stored in the Smithsonian Institution's collection facility had been carted away from the 1864 Sand Creek Massacre; down the aisle were the Pawnee skulls painstakingly prepared by B. E. Fryer after the Mulberry Creek Massacre of 1869. The Blackfeet remains Dorsey exhumed were until recently stored in Chicago's Field Museum. The bones of "Peary's Eskimos" were curated in New York's Museum of Natural History. These modern skeletal libraries have never been a secret, but many expressed surprise when told of them. "When I was first made aware of the thousands of Native American human remains housed in the Smithsonian Institution and other great museums and scientific institutions," writes Senator Daniel Inouye, "I was shocked and appalled. I questioned whether the human remains of Germans, of Japanese, of the English, the French, or the Spanish would be treated in the same manner. The answer was a resounding and certain 'no'."

The Senator was misinformed. Museums in America and around the world have long stockpiled skeletons of German, Japanese, English, French, and Spanish, among many others. The brain of John Wesley Powell, founder of the Bureau of American Ethnology, has been stored in the Smithsonian for a century, alongside similar anatomical specimens from around the world. Nineteenth-century scientists collected human remains wherever they could, sometimes by legitimate means, sometimes not. Claiming that Native Americans Indians were singled out for unique treatment is a myth, a stereotype that has at times become a rhetorical tool for those promoting the cause of Indian reburial.

The truth should be enough.

It is certainly true that thousands of Indian skeletons were curated in America's natural history museums, virtually all of them obtained without consent of their Native American descendants. Indian people were justifiably horrified when they learned the scale of the museum holdings and the sometimes shocking circumstances under which the skeletons were acquired. "To many Native Americans," wrote Douglas Preston in a 1989 *Harpers Magazine* article, "the collecting of their ancestor's bones and bodies by museums is a source of pain and humiliation—the last stage of a conquest that already had robbed them of their lands and destroyed their way of life."

Federal legislation now mandates the return of "culturally affiliated" remains to tribes. But the very existence of these enormous skeletal collections has driven a wedge between anthropologists and Indian people. Throughout Indian Country, native people still resent what they see as an academic arrogance that permitted anthropology museums to store the skeletons of dead Indians for the good of science.

Some also see a lingering racism in the conflation of American Indians with the rest of America's natural history. W. Richard West, Jr., Director of the National Museum of the American Indian (himself a Cheyenne descendant), tells of how he once asked a clerk in a bookstore for help in finding a book about American Indians. "Believe it or not," West writes, "she referred me to the *Nature* section! It's as if we Native Americans were considered to be something less than human—something apart from the family of man. By the same token, it was not unusual when I was a child to walk into a museum and find Indians displayed next to dinosaurs and mammoths—as if we too were extinct."

From a modern perspective, the callous disregard demonstrated by Jefferson, Hrdlička, and Boas was racist, elitist, and disrespectful of the dead. Modern attitudes in anthropology are very different. Few if any contemporary anthropologists are racists, and none, to my knowledge, engage in the kind of out-of-control grave robbing that was common in the nineteenth century. Most are trying to do the right thing. Still, anthropology's long romance with scientific racism has left an undeniable legacy. Thousands of Indian skulls are still curated in America's museums, and the reasons they were brought there reflect archaeology's roots in the crass racial determinism of the nineteenth century. It is small wonder that many Indian people still associate archaeology with grave robbing.

Part III

DEEP AMERICAN HISTORY

As Gods might, the Europeans believed they had created the New World by their "discovery" of it. If that was so, why couldn't they just as boldly "invent" the creation myths of its origins? They did.

—Stan Steiner (1987)

ORIGIN MYTHS FROM
MAINSTREAM AMERICA

12.

NOT LONG AFTER Columbus' triumphant return home, Europe began to buzz with a new question: Where did those "Indians" come from?

Columbus thought that maybe they lived on the threshold of the Garden of Eden. The Bible clearly stated that every living human was descended directly from Adam and Eve. Since only Noah and his immediate family survived the flood, the Indians either descended directly from Noah's family or were subhuman. Until the publication of *On the Origin of Species*, most Euroamerican thinkers agreed that human beings were a fairly recent creation and that the distribution of people across the globe could be attributed to specific migrations of Biblical peoples.

How, then, had the Indians fallen so far from their civilized state? Some believed that sin had reduced Indians to savagery; others blamed the American environment. Either way, as Indians were forced to wander in an untamed wasteland, suffering privation and beleaguered by risk, they had lost their knowledge, their religion, and all the rudiments of society they once enjoyed.

In 1642, Dr. John Lightfoot, master of St. Catharine's College and Vice-Chancellor of Cambridge University, published a treatise with the delightful title *A Few and New Observations on the Book of Genesis, the most of them certain, the rest probable, all harmless, and rarely heard of before.* Lightfoot also published a chronology of the Creation, concluding that "heaven and earth, centre and circumference, were created all together in the same instant and clouds full of water . . . this took place and man was created by the Trinity on October 23, 4004 BC at nine o'clock in the morning." Centuries later, archaeologist Glyn Daniel would dryly reflect, "We may perhaps see in these dates and time a prejudice of a Vice-Chancellor for the beginning of an academic year and the beginning of an academic morning, but at least, Lightfoot did provide an exact and absolute chronology which must have been very comforting."

So, if there was only a single Biblical creation and it took place in 4004 BC, then the Indians must have come into America after that date. By the nineteenth century, accounting for the Indian presence had become something of a cottage industry. Ignatius Donnelly suggested in *Atlantis: The Antediluvian World* that they came from the fabled sunken continent. Voyaging Egyptians and Vikings were cited as proto-Americans. *The Book of Mormon* declared that Indians had migrated from the Near East about 500 BC Other groups were nominated as well—Phoenicians, Basques, Greeks, Mongols, Romans, Persians, even the Japanese. Petroglyphs throughout the New World were variously read as Norse runes, Egyptian hieroglyphs, Hebrew, Arabic, and Phoenician characters. In *Mound Builders of Ancient America,* Robert Silverberg notes that "the dream of a lost prehistoric race in the American heartland was profoundly satisfying, and if the vanished ones had been giants, or white men, or Israelites, or Danes, or Toltecs, or great white Jewish Toltec Vikings, so much the better."

A youthful America, seeking its place in the world, was looking for a monumental history comparable to Schliemann's highly publicized finds at Troy and Mycenae. Properly embellished, maybe Pueblo Bonito in Chaco Canyon and Cliff Palace at Mesa Verde could rival the sensational finds of the Old World. As Professor F. V. Hayden's nineteenth-century manual on the West suggested, the larger ruins of the American Southwest confirmed that "in size and grandeur of conception they are equal to any of the present buildings of the United States, if we except the Capitol at Washington, and may without discredit be compared to the Parthenon and the Colosseum of the Old World."

A RACE OF (NON-INDIAN) MOUNDBUILDERS

The red man came —
The roaming hunter tribes, warlike and wild,
And the mound-builders vanished from the earth.
The solitude of centuries untold,
Has settled where they dwelt.

—*William Cullen Bryant (The Prairies, 1883)*

Always a man of contradictions, Thomas Jefferson saw America's future as a medium-size agrarian republic without ambitions for world power. Yet with a single stroke of his pen, Jefferson's Louisiana Purchase doubled the size of the United States—the New Republic was now the size of Europe. Americans weren't even sure how much land they'd annexed.

Although unsure of the constitutionality of his acquisition, Jefferson clearly understood that "the *idea* of America always existed beyond the boundaries of the moment." Something in the psychological makeup of America required a constant distending of borders and advancing into new territory. Purchasing the western lands was only part of the issue: Expanding America into the remote hinterland required more than military force and political negotiation. It required that the new territory be annexed into the American psyche.

To do this, Jefferson convinced Congress to authorize a secret expedition westward, and in 1802, Jefferson sent his handpicked representatives to the Missouri Valley and beyond. Meriwether Lewis and William Clark were asked to find an all-water route to Cathay, directly across the American continent. This was, of course, precisely the same task assigned young Columbus by Ferdinand and Isabela. Jefferson instructed Lewis and Clark to make detailed accounts of the natural history they encountered on the way, including the conditions of the Indians and any "monuments" they might find. He also warned them to look out for live mammoths—for which, he recounted in *Notes on the State of Virginia*, there is "traditional testimony of the Indians that this animal still exists in the northern and western parts of America . . . he may as well exist there now." Privately, Jefferson also asked Lewis to collect some Indian children, that they might be "brought up with us, & taught such arts as might be useful to them."

The Lewis and Clark expedition was perhaps the world's most successful and exhaustive geographical adventure, collecting a wealth of botanical, min-

Excavating an ancient Indian mound in the Mississipii River Valley, from a panorama (1850).

eralogical, ethnographic, and archaeological specimens. As they renamed the rivers, mountains, and valleys, they took symbolic possession of the new American West. As they collected and categorized various natural specimens from the new territory, they engaged in what the ethnologist Curtis Hinsley has called "a discourse of domination through ordering." Lewis and Clark imposed a Euroamerican order on the new territory: choosing and selecting, naming, and categorizing. In this way, Jefferson cleverly situated his Louisiana Purchase into the national imagination, affirming a conquest and proprietorship over the distinctive natural resources of the American West—including its aboriginal inhabitants. The study of natural history became a tool for establishing the agenda of American expansion westward.

On a winter's night in 1804, William Clark found himself at the site of an ancient fortification where the Mississippi and Missouri rivers joined, near present-day St. Louis. Here was ample evidence of large-scale ancient constructions—huge residential areas, open plazas, protective palisade walls, and more than one hundred earthen mounds. A single gargantuan earthwork dominated the area. Today it is known as Monks Mound, the largest mound ever constructed in the Americas and perhaps the largest in the world, covering a full city block and containing 22 million cubic feet of earth. In the course of their heroic journey, Lewis and Clark encountered more strange and ancient "mounds," "ancient graves," and "hillforts." Subsequent expeditions reported earthworks shaped like birds, bears, and great snakes. What were they to make of such constructions?

Each of these monuments actually existed, and many still do. Driving across Ohio, you can see dozens of Moundbuilder earthworks, many erected to commemorate the dead. In Collinsville, Illinois, you can climb atop Monks Mound—if you're comfortable at the height of a 10-story building.

As Euroamericans dug into these enigmatic earthworks, they found ancient graves with strange and sometimes magnificent artworks. Many were crafted from exotic materials—mica from the Appalachian Mountains, volcanic glass from Yellowstone, chalcedony from North Dakota, conch shells and shark teeth from the south Atlantic, copper from the Great Lakes. Fashioned into mystical and exotic shapes, the finds demonstrated an extraordinary level of craftsmanship. During the late nineteenth century, questions about these antiquities eventually crystallized into a single, fundamental quandary: *Who were these ancient American builders of mounds?*

Few ascribed such high-tech achievements to ancestors of the American Indians, who were seen as just too backward. Nineteenth-century Indians were thought incapable of fashioning metal tools and ornaments, weaving cloth, or growing the crops necessary to support such an advanced civilization. Because there were not enough Indians to account for the abundance of mounds and earthworks, America's ancient monuments had obviously been erected by an older, "higher" culture.

The mystery deepened when inscribed stone tablets turned up inside some of the mounds. A circular stone with strange-looking inscriptions was allegedly unearthed from West Virginia's Grave Creek Mound in the 1820s. Several bizarre slate tablets were said to have been found in the 1870s inside a mound chamber near Davenport, Iowa—one looking for all the world like an ancient calendar stone. Another had crude scenes of animals, mounds, and Indians. These highly publicized, Old World-looking inscriptions reinforced the idea that America had once been inhabited by sophisticated, literate pre-Indians. (Most of these finds were hoaxes, although one went undetected for more than a century.) So complete was the mystery that, in 1875, the esteemed historian Herbert Bancroft could write that "most and the best authorities deem it impossible that the moundbuilders were ever the remote ancestors of the Indian tribes."

So arose the myth of the American Moundbuilders. The tens of thousands of earthworks and mounds dotting the eastern American landscape suggested that a vanished civilization—highly intelligent and almost certainly white—had inhabited the country before Indians arrived. Perhaps ancestors of the very same Bloodthirsty Redskins who now menaced the American frontier had victimized these First Americans, accomplished non-Indians who mysteriously perished in antiquity.

The Moundbuilder myth was promoted by some of America's most powerful leaders. New York Governor De Witt Clinton argued in 1820 that Vikings had built the earthen mounds of western New York State. Texas hero Sam Houston opined, "I have often come across fortified works which bear evidence of the existence of a people who had reached a fairly high state of civilisation. Whence did that people come? Wither did it vanish? There is a mystery there. But one cannot doubt that it existed, and nothing indicates that the Indians of our day are the remnants thereof." In his 1830 message to Congress, President Jackson explained, "In the monuments and fortresses of an unknown people, spread over the extensive regions of the west, we behold the memorials of a once powerful race, which was exterminated, or has disappeared, to make room for the existing savage tribes. Nor is there anything in this, which, upon a comprehensive view of the general interests, is to be regretted." The Moundbuilder scenario provided Jackson a much-needed pretext for forced removal of Southeastern Indians to Oklahoma: after all, if the ancestors of the Creek and Cherokee had decimated an earlier, more civilized population, they deserved no better fate themselves.

The Moundbuilder myth became an epic creation story and won broad acceptance by scholars and the American public. If America was originally white, not red, then the new republic could rightfully view its spirited Indian adversaries as savages who had decimated the true First American culture. "What delighted the public most keenly," writes Robert Silverberg, "was the stirring depiction of a great empire dragged down to destruction by hordes of barbarians," a perspective that exposed a virulent anti-Indian sentiment and spawned a not-so-subtle rationale for European appropriation of Indian lands. "Even as the U.S. Army drove Indian people west," writes archaeologist Randall McGuire, "white scholars and preachers tried to rout their ancestors from the history of the nation."

Not every mainstream American assumed that the glorious race of Moundbuilders was necessarily white. Many believers merely hoped they were; but even if they weren't white, at least the Moundbuilders must have been more akin to the great civilizations of Mexico and Peru than to the scruffy Indians still living in the United States.

THE RED SONS OF ISRAEL

Another popular origin tale equated Native Americans with misplaced Jews. The Lost Tribe of Israel theory was heavily promoted by a number of high-profile American clergymen, including William Penn, Roger Williams, Cotton Mather, Jonathan Edwards, and Joseph Smith. Although a few had some personal experience with Indian people, most Lost Tribe advocates combined biblical doctrine with second-hand testimony supplied by helpful missionaries. As one of the few "ethnographic" texts available to the general public, the Bible was a ready source of parallels.

Some pointed to similarities in language, architecture, and religious rites between Hebrews and American Indians. Others looked for deeper parallels, such as feasts of the first fruit, sacrifices of the first-born in the flock, purification ceremonies, and division into tribes. One authority interpreted syphilis—endemic in America and spreading rapidly to Europe—as a particularly virulent form of biblical leprosy. Louis Hennepin, a Flemish Monk, noted that Indians lived in "a form of tents, as did the Jews;" both anointed themselves in oil, bewailed their dead "with great lamentations;" and both tribes were "subtle and crafty." Perhaps most important, Indians and Jews shared God's curse "laid upon them." In his *American Antiquities*, published in 1833, Josiah Priest wrote that "the opinion that the American Indians are descendants of the Lost tribes is now a popular one and generally believed." The Red Sons of Israel tale was especially appealing because it conveniently linked one missing group with the unknown origins of another—two puzzles solved for the price of one.

WANDERING CELTS

The legendary sixth-century Irish monk St. Brendan claimed to have sailed westward, landing in the "Promised Land of the Saints." In the nineteenth century, as today, some believed that he landed in North America. An account of the voyage, popularized a thousand years ago, contained credible descriptions of icebergs, volcanoes, and islands, revealing some knowledge of Iceland and perhaps Newfoundland. But Brendan also spoke of sea monsters who exhaled fire from their nostrils, and of monks hitching a ride on the back of a whale. Thinking it was an island, they did not realize their faux pas until their signal fire aroused the slumbering beast. Many wondered whether St.

Brendan's account was merely a medieval allegory or a sincere depiction of discovery. Or could it be both?

Other claims had more obvious political motivations. During the reign of Elizabeth I, the British crown suggested that the Welsh arrived in America about AD 1170. A much-embellished English ballad, originally published in 1584, celebrated the travels of Prince Madoc, who sailed to America, returned home, and eventually recruited thousands of Welsh colonists for a one-way voyage back again. Travelers' accounts and missionary records detailed numerous linguistic and biological parallels between the Welsh and the American tribes. Particularly graphic was the testimony published in *Gentleman's Magazine for the Year 1740*, which told how a Reverend Morgan Jones had been held captive among hostile Indians in the year 1660. Because the Indians spoke only Tuscarora and the good Reverend only Welsh, the reader shared his shock as he readily conversed with his captors. Obviously these Indians had learned Welsh from Prince Madoc, or perhaps were his direct descendants.

THE ARIZONA AZTECS

Geographical surveys conducted after the Mexican-American War—when the United States obtained huge tracts of land in the Southwest through treaty, purchase, and the occasional force of arms—recorded dozens of substantial ruins, fortresses and towns, enclosures, and "castles" along with the other natural riches of the area. While visiting Arizona's monumental Casa Grande, journalist J. Ross Browne marveled at how "this grand old relic of an age and people of which we have no other than traditionary accounts looms up over the desert in bold relief as the traveler approaches, filling the mind with a strange perplexity as to the past. What race dwelt here? By what people were these crumbling walls put together? How did they live? And where have they gone?"

While mapping the ruins of Canyon de Chelly and Chaco Canyon in 1849, Lieutenant J. H. Simpson asked his native guides who had constructed such impressive architecture. Some Navajos thought they had probably been "built by Montezuma and his people, when they were on their way from the north toward the south," fueling speculation about an early Aztec presence in the American Four Corners. Pueblo Indians maintained their own version of the Montezuma legend, likewise confirming that the Aztecs had built the ruins. But when some Zunis saw the ruins of Chaco Canyon for the first time, they reportedly said, "White men built these walls, Indians could not."

Eastern newspapers rhapsodized over the ruins in faraway Arizona and New Mexico territories; many educated Americans had read William Prescott's wildly popular *Conquest of America*, published in 1843, which extolled the exploits of Mexico's famed Aztec empire. Increasingly, the ruins in the American Southwest became associated with Montezuma and his visiting Aztec warriors. One large site in northern New Mexico became known as "Aztec Ruin," and a spectacular cliff dwelling south of Flagstaff was dubbed "Montezuma Castle" after the famed Aztec leader. Both names stuck—you can visit both sites today. A number of Indian agents and federal officials believed and actively promoted the Aztec-first theory. The *Legislative Blue Book of the Territory of New Mexico* for 1882 even claimed Montezuma as a native son, saying he was born at Pecos Pueblo, not far from Santa Fe.

The Aztec origin tale was particularly convenient for white Americans colonizing the Southwest, for whom the Pueblos posed a real threat to westward expansion. It was one thing to roust Plains nomads from their skin tipis, but quite another to force sedentary Pueblo farmers out of permanent four-storied adobe apartment buildings. But if the enchanting ruins and ancient Pueblo-style buildings had actually been built by Aztecs—tribes totally unrelated to nineteenth-century Pueblo people—then perhaps the Pueblos were newcomers without clear title to the land.

In the *United States v. Joseph* ruling of 1876, the United States Supreme Court translated myth into law by declaring that since Pueblo land was not an official Indian reservation, it could readily be bought and sold. Although a number of sympathetic federal officials opposed the ruling, the Supreme Court had effectively made available the Pueblo's land and water rights, including some of the Southwest's most arable acreage. Ever watchful for a chance to grab Indian land, Anglo speculators applauded the Arizona Aztec theory for helping to separate Pueblo people from their traditional lands.

ACROSS THE BERING STRAIT

Yet another origin story enjoyed a certain following in the eighteenth and nineteenth centuries and remains popular today. Thomas Jefferson was convinced by linguistic and geographic evidence that Indian people had moved eastward from Asia to America, "if the two continents . . . be separated at all."

But Jefferson did not originate the trans-Siberian theory. That distinction goes to Fray José de Acosta, a sixteenth-century Jesuit missionary stationed in Mexico and Peru. Writing in 1589—more than a century before the European discovery of the Bering Strait—Acosta speculated that small groups of hunters, driven from their Asiatic homeland by starvation or warfare, might have followed now-extinct beasts across Asia into the New World. Acosta argued that this slow, mostly overland migration took place perhaps two thousand years before Spaniards arrived in the Caribbean.

THESE MULTIPLE ACCOUNTS were not pitting science against Western religion, since most nineteenth-century explanations could be accommodated within the biblical wisdom of the day. Given the evidence then at hand, there was no rational, "scientific" way to choose between alternatives, and there was little in the Bering Strait theory that warranted special attention. Although periodically revisited, this Indian-first scenario remained a distinctly minority opinion for centuries. Tales of white First Americans and wandering Aztecs held far more appeal for an American public enthralled by the specter of a vast, sophisticated empire threatened by the barbarian hordes.

Hardly anyone cared what Indian people thought about their own origins.

THE SMITHSONIAN TAKES ON ALL COMERS

13.

NINETEENTH-CENTURY ANTHROPOLOGISTS eventually discovered that many of the negative characteristics attributed to American Indians—particularly their nomadic non-agricultural subsistence and absence of technical achievements, such as weaving and the use of metals—derived not from an inherent backwardness but from disruptions brought about by the European invasion. Once anthropologists began to understand the impact of the European invasion on Native America, they recognized that Indians were excellent candidates for having built the ancient American earthworks.

During the 1850s, Samuel Haven, librarian of the American Antiquarian Society, vigorously attacked the Moundbuilder theory, arguing that "the flint utensils of the Age of Stone lie upon the surface of the ground. . . . The peoples that made and used them have not yet entirely disappeared." In other words, American Indians of the remote past were not very different from Indians in the "ethnographic present." Although his monumental *Archaeology of the United States*, published in 1856, is today viewed as "a model of reasoned description and discussion in comparison with the speculative works that had dominated the literature until then," few contemporaries believed Haven's report.

The Moundbuilder controversy resonated so deeply with mainstreet America that in 1881 the U.S. Congress authorized $5,000 for the Smithsonian's Bureau of American Ethnology to resolve the issue once and for all. John Wesley Powell drafted Cyrus Thomas, an entomologist by training, to head up the Moundbuilder inquiry. Although Thomas began as a professed "believer in the existence of a race of Mound Builders, distinct from the American Indians," he would soon change his mind.

From his Washington headquarters, Thomas began a massive program to record and excavate mounds across the eastern United States, "like a general directing his troops from the rear lines." With Smithsonian field crews deployed from Dakota to Florida and from New England to New Orleans, artifacts were collected by the thousands. Not surprisingly, the Moundbuilder inquiry assumed a David-and-Goliath flavor, with friction building up between local amateur scholars and a heavy-handed Federal presence.

Thomas summarized the four frenzied field seasons in the twelfth Annual Report of the Smithsonian, published in 1894. He concluded, first, that many of the mounds had been constructed after initial Euroamerican contact, and second, that all of them could be attributed to the ancestors of the modern Native American. The report also concluded that the cultural level of those who built the mounds in no way surpassed that of Indian people living on the eastern seaboard during the sixteenth and seventeenth centuries.

AN EMERGING EUROPEAN
STONE AGE

Another issue facing American archaeologists in the mid-nineteenth century would strain relations between professional and avocational archaeologists even further.

In Europe, biblical explanations for the age and distribution of humanity had grown threadbare. The Garden of Eden theory of human origins received a jolt when some very crude stone tools were discovered in the ancient gravels of England and continental Europe. About 1836, Jacques Boucher de Perthes, a customs controller at Abbeville, France, began finding ancient axeheads in the Somme River gravels. Associated with those tools he also found the bones of mammals apparently long extinct. To Boucher de Perthes, the implication was obvious: "In spite of their imperfection, these rude stones prove the existence of [very ancient] man as surely as a whole Louvre would have done."

Few contemporaries believed him. By Lightfoot's strict biblical reckoning of the Creation, there simply hadn't been enough time for an extensive period of human antiquity. More important, if Boucher de Perthe's artifacts were truly contemporary with now-extinct animals, this implied the existence of some kind of pre-biblical world, which was decidedly unacceptable. These rude implements, therefore, must be something other than human handiwork. Perhaps these "tools" were meteorites. Maybe the stones were produced by lightning, elves, or fairies. One critic suggested that the chipped flints were "generated in the sky by a fulgurous exhalation conglobed in a cloud by the circumposed humour."

But Boucher de Perthes stuck to his guns. More chipped flints turned up in the French gravel pits at St. Acheul and across the Channel in southern England. The issue was finally resolved when the respected British paleontologist William Falconer visited Abbeville in 1859 to examine the disputed evidence for himself and pronounced it genuine; English geologist Charles Lyell, visiting a few months later, agreed with Falconer's assessment. After a paper was presented to the influential Royal Society of London backing the claims of Boucher de Perthes, several powerful natural scientists declared their support. The age of humanity—at least in Europe—reached well back into the Pleistocene, long before Earth had assumed its present climate.

So it was that 1859 became a banner year in the history of science. Not only was the remote antiquity of humankind accepted by many, but Darwin's *On the Origin of Species* even suggested the process by which modern people had arisen.. European archaeology became obsessed with the problems of remote geological time and the demonstration of long-term human evolution.

Boucher de Perthes found Paleolithic handaxes like this in the gravels of the Somme River, France.

WHY NOT AN AMERICAN PALEOLITHIC?

These European discoveries stoked the American imagination. During the 1870s, as evidence from Paleolithic Europe was piling up, some began wondering if a parallel history could exist in the Americas. If European prehistory could be turned on its head by a single well-documented find, why not that of the New World? Why not an American Paleolithic?

Once people started looking, they found plenty of Paleolithic-looking artifacts that closely resembled those of Europe. Although the geological contexts were often ambiguous, the American tools suggested a human presence in America during the Ice Age. The search for an American Paleolithic was in full swing by the late 1880s, with numerous scholarly books and articles on the topic. A physician named C. C. Abbott stirred the pot when, in the 1870s, he reported his discovery of rude implements in the Delaware Valley glacial gravels of his New Jersey farm. For the next two decades, Abbott argued that these crude tools of argillite weathering out of a riverbank looked "old"—very old, in fact. Abbott beamed over his discovery of "glacial man in America," and some even took to calling him "America's Boucher de Perthes"—not only because of his discovery of allegedly ancient artifacts, but also because of the struggles required to convince others. Abbott's artifacts, if that's what they were, became the flash point in the battle over the earliest American.

Opposing Abbott was William Henry Holmes of the Bureau of American Ethnology, who believed that the proper classification and ordering of the world's people required solid empirical data and universal standards of evidence. Holmes, who would come to epitomize the Smithsonian's dominating presence in American archaeology, attacked the Abbott Farm discoveries on several counts. He drew on the geological principle of uniformitarianism: The first step in knowing the past is to know the present. In his classic 1890 research at Piney Branch Creek in Washington D.C., Holmes collected thousands of so-called "paleoliths" that were strewn about—large, crude artifacts that looked exactly like the Old Stone Age tools from St. Acheul and elsewhere. Holmes' detailed examination of the stoneworking technology showed that the Piney Branch artifacts were not old at all—they just looked that way. To be sure, some of the crude tools looked like ancient European artifacts, but these "rude tools," Holmes argued, were actually "failures," unfinished rejects made by relatively recent Indian flintknappers, but discarded instead of being worked into their intended final form. Holmes demonstrated how stone tools were produced stage-by-stage and illustrated the products involved in each step.

Holmes' work at Piney Branch established his credentials for scientific caution and intelligence. It also held an important lesson for the so-called American Paleolithic: Form alone could not predict age. To draw trans-Atlantic analogies was not only inappropriate, Holmes admonished, it also displayed an embarrassing ignorance of how stone tools are actually made. He emphasized the importance of understanding the geological context in which old-looking artifacts were found. Crude-looking stone tools alone were not enough. To make a valid claim for the American Paleolithic, those rude artifacts must be found in demonstrably Pleistocene-age sediments. Holmes also stressed finding artifacts in "primary" geological contexts (meaning that the date of the strata reflected the age of the artifact) as opposed to "secondary" contexts, as when streams wash later rocks into earlier deposits. Furthermore, even when artifacts were securely located in "primary" contexts, investigators still had the problem of assessing the age of the deposits.

When human skeletal remains turned up in apparently ancient contexts, Holmes deferred to his student and colleague Aleš Hrdlička, a trained physician and specialist in human evolution and anatomy. Hrdlička believed in an Asian origin of American Indians; but since he thought that Neanderthals represented the next-older (Pleistocene) stage of humanity (rather than a separate species), any purportedly Pleistocene-age human bones in America should look like the genuinely ancient bones of Europe—the Neanderthals. To Hrdlička, this meant that any anatomically modern skeleton in America automatically belonged to relatively recent American Indians—regardless of its geological context.

As Holmes and Hrdlička grew increasingly relentless in their criticism of supposed early finds, a familiar scenario developed for evaluating early-man claims: A find is made, a claim for extreme antiquity is entered, scientific luminaries descend on the site and pronounce their verdict, then the profession follows suit. Holmes and especially Hrdlička both made careers as traveling curmudgeons—erstwhile protectors of scientific virtue.

The two men brought the formidable reputation and resources of the Smithsonian Institution to bear on the issue, sometimes using their influence to block publication of opposing viewpoints. Archaeologist Alfred Kidder later suggested that Holmes and Hrdlička "actually frightened away" alternative viewpoints. Frank H. H. Roberts, another Smithsonian archaeologist, admitted that the "question of early man in America became virtually taboo, and no anthropologist, or for that matter geologist or paleontologist, desirous of a successful career would tempt the fate of ostracism by intimating that he had discovered indications of a respectable antiquity for the Indian." Nels Nelson, an archaeologist at the American Museum of Natural History, cautioned students wishing to study the subject that perhaps it was best simply to "lie low for the present." Most archaeologists did just that, restricting their research to the less contentious, later periods in the American past.

WHERE ARE ALL THE NATIVE AMERICAN ARCHAEOLOGISTS?

14.

THEODORE ROOSEVELT, the first President inaugurated in the twentieth century, was described by one historian as "the archetypical 'good guy,' combining the best of the inherited English tradition of gentlemanly honor with a riproaring taste for adventure which is quintessentially American." With his Tiffany silver Bowie knife, fringed buckskin shirt, and alligator boots, Roosevelt managed to combine an aristocratic style with a no-nonsense image of frontier America. In the first volume of *The Winning of the West* (1889), he warned the sentimentalists that the Indians had no real title to America because they had never effectively occupied the land. It was unthinkable to Roosevelt that America's grasslands and forests be withheld from civilized homesteaders by the claims of a few savages. Roosevelt's Indians were a treacherous and brutal lot, and he told chilling tales of "the hideous, unnameable, unthinkable tortures practiced by the red men on their captured foes." It was the long-suffering frontiersman, Roosevelt reminded Americans, who had been wronged," . . . a stern race of freemen who toiled hard, endured greatly, and fronted adversity bravely, who prized strength and courage and good faith, whose wives were chaste and who were generous and loyal to their friends."

The myth-making ran deep, burnishing the images of American heroes and brushing aside stories of those with different perspectives. Historian Frederick Jackson Turner argued in the 1890s that, "rightly viewed," the issue of slavery becomes a mere "incident" in American history. *The Spanish Borderlands*, by Herbert Bolton, dismissed Indians as "children," and his protege, John Francis Bannon, relegated Native Americans to the catchall category of "Borderland irritants." Mainstream historians promoted "the great unifying myths that define the dreams, characteristics, and special history of America," and, in 1990, the conservative author Peggy Noonan cautioned that "if our retelling of the past is dominated by the compulsive skepticism of the modern mind, with its ill-thought-out disdain, then we will stop being America."

The paradox is that once the Indians no longer posed a threat, they were basically written out of mainstream American history. An element of Indian imagery was still required, however, to make the concept of America actually work. "History seemed for Roosevelt," says Alan Trachtenberg, "the westward experience, a foreclosing event, an inevitable advance from low to high, from simple to complex, and in more senses than one, from 'Indian' to 'American'. . . . In this 'progress,' this proof of 'America,' the profoundest role was reserved not for the abundance of land but for the fatal presence of the Indian. . . . 'Civilization' required a 'savagery' against which to distinguish itself."

Archaeology became, for Roosevelt's generation, a way to document the course of American culture from one evolutionary stage to the next—from "Indian" to "American"—and, in the process, validate the doctrines of progress and Manifest Destiny. Archaeologists and historians usually obliged them, admits the historian Frederick Hoxie, providing the American public "with an image of Indian people and Indian history that conformed to the power relationships of their day." In effect, the Roosevelt administration challenged American archaeologists to help write the national narrative. It was clear to all that Indians were vanishing and so were the archaeological traces of their history. Railroads had opened up the American West to tourism and created a demand for Indian curios. Public and private museums scrambled to document and collect Indian culture before it disappeared. Looters—and the occasional museum expedition—were plundering archaeological sites at a record clip. In the early 1890s, for instance, the Swedish naturalist Gustaf Niles Adolf Nordenskiold dug up several boxes and barrels of artifacts from newly discovered ruins near Mesa Verde. As he shipped his take from Durango, Colorado, to the Swedish Consulate in New York, en route to Stockholm, local newspapers raised a fuss over the foreigner who was digging up and exporting America's ancient past. Although briefly arrested on a warrant sworn out by the local Indian Agent, Nordenskiold and his artifacts were eventually permitted to pass on to Sweden. Paradoxically, Nordenskiold's account of his excavations, *The Cliff Dwellers of the Mesa Verde* (published in 1893) is universally considered to be the best scientific monograph of the nineteenth century on Southwestern archaeology, setting a standard unequalled for two decades.

The House of Representatives' Committee on Public Lands recognized the threat of uncontrolled excavation of archaeological sites and, in 1906, pointed out that "practically every civilized government in the world has enacted laws for the preservation of the remains of the historic past, and has provided that excavations and explorations shall be conducted in some systematic and practical way so as not to needlessly destroy buildings and other objects of interest." Suitably prodded, Congress enacted the Antiquities Act of 1906, reflecting Roosevelt's passion for conserving and studying natural history, protecting America's remote past, and ensuring continued access for a fast-growing scientific community.

The Antiquities Act fixed in law what had been an American reality for a century. From at least the time of Thomas Jefferson, white intellectuals had looked to archaeology to answer the nagging question of American Indian origins. "Archaeologists" throughout most of the nineteenth century were well-educated hobbyists, who drew upon their general educational background to make sense of what they found. But they were not sufficiently maverick to embrace the idea of Indian people with long and culturally significant histories of their own. For such amateurs, Lost Tribes, mythical Welsh sailors, and ancient (non-Indian) Moundbuilders made more intuitive sense as the *real* First Americans.

Toward the end of the nineteenth century, as the Smithsonian Institution campaigned to turn archaeology into a profession, it almost incidentally established the American Indian as responsible for creating America's archaeological record. Cyrus Thomas had marshaled the Smithsonian's prestige and considerable resources to establish that the Moundbuilders and Indians were the same people at different times. In their battle against an American Paleolithic, Holmes and Hrdlička effectively made the same case, but from the bottom up. If the First Americans were Indians who migrated from Asia—rather than European-style Neanderthals—this meant that the very earliest part of the American history was distinctly Indian as well.

After a century of give-and-take, authority came to those with professional training who were affiliated with one (or more) of America's rapidly growing natural history museums. Not surprisingly, considerable tension developed between professional and avocational archaeologists, particularly when it came to the hotly disputed issue of Indian origins.

The 1906 Antiquities Act recognized a new archaeological establishment by permitting only professionally sanctioned archaeologists to remove antiquities from federal lands. The legislation specifically charged the Smithsonian Institution to administer the new permitting process. The bill also empowered the President to designate key archaeological sites as national monuments. The Smithsonian became the official repository for duplicate copies of fieldnotes, photographs, and any collections made without regulatory compliance. By criminalizing unauthorized artifact collecting on federal lands, the 1906 law effectively quashed amateur access to the American past. Indians, who almost universally lacked the requisite training, were, by definition, amateurs. A series of antiquities-related acts followed over the next half-century or so: establishment of the National Park Service in 1916, the National Environmental Policy Act (NEPA) of 1969, the Archeological Resources Protection Act of 1979, and so forth. These congressional acts helped professionalize American archaeology and preserved many archaeological sites for future generations. But they also encouraged generations of professional archaeologists to view the archaeological record of America as their exclusive intellectual property because, by law, it essentially was.

This impression was reinforced during the mammoth flood-control programs initiated by the federal government in the 1940s. In clear violation of their treaty rights, and without prior consultation, several Indian tribes were forced to give up their best land and move onto marginal prairie lands elsewhere on their reservations. Although federal law had supposedly established the doctrine of tribal self-determination, Indian leaders were simply ignored in every phase of the negotiations. So confident was the Army Corps of Engineers in its ability to acquire Indian land through eminent domain that it sometimes began constructing its dams on tribal land even before opening formal negotiations with the tribal leaders. In *Dammed Indians*, the historian Michael Lawson shows how the 1944 Pick-Sloan Plan for the Missouri River Basin, developed by the U. S. Army Corps of Engineers and the Bureau of Reclamation, ended up flooding more than two hundred thousand acres of valuable Sioux bottomlands in what Lawson called "arguably the single most destructive act perpetrated against an Indian tribe by the United States during this century."

The Pick-Sloan Plan was, however, a boon for archaeology. Through the

George Gillette, Chairman of the Fort Berthold Indian Tribal Business Council, weeps as secretary of Interior J.A. Krug signs a contract confirming the forced sale in 1948 of 155,000 acres of the North Dakota reservation's best lands to the government for the Garrison Land and Reservoir Project. Of the sale, Gillette said, "The members of the tribal council sign this contract with heavy hearts. . . . Right now the future does not look so good for us."

Inter-Agency Archaeological Salvage Program, a project coordinated by the Smithsonian Institution and the National Park Service in conjunction with sixteen regional museums and universities, hundreds of archaeological sites were identified and investigated within the reservoir areas. By 1970, over ninety major sites had been extensively excavated, ranging in age from pre-ceramic occupations to relatively recent Indian villages. Most Indians saw the archaeologists simply as handmaidens to the Army Corps, helping to wrest Indian homeland from control of the tribes. But as Lawson notes, "Whether or not the tribes are willing to acknowledge the fact, several of these studies have contributed greatly to our knowledge of Plains Indian culture, and many were directly relevant to the history of the Sioux."

The generation of post-World War I scholars that followed Holmes and Hrdlička, including Alfred Kidder, Nels Nelson, and Clark Wissler, defined a "new archaeology" grounded in stratigraphic principles and a more rigorous interpretation of archaeological materials. Falling in line with the scientific-minded Boasian agenda for the rest of anthropology, archaeologists deliberately sought out allies in the generalizing social sciences, especially economics, political science, and sociology. By the 1970s, few archaeologists had any sustained contact with Indian people.

Scientific authority conferred a certain power over history. American archaeologists came to perceive themselves as sole proprietors of, and reigning authorities on, the remote Indian past. When archaeologists appeared as expert witnesses in court cases, their testimony carried more weight than that of tribal elders. Archaeologists wrote the books about First Americans, gave the public lectures, and taught the classes. Archaeologists generally controlled access to museum collections of Native American objects from that very distant past. One archaeologist has recently stated, "All origin myths are equally absurd, but some are more politically correct than others." Another expressed a similar viewpoint in a particularly vivid oxymoron: "I don't think that . . . oral traditions are worth the paper they're written on."

This is why American Indians did not figure into American archaeology for most of the twentieth century. Beginning with the Antiquities Act of 1906, only professionally trained experts could do archaeology on federal lands. Although archaeology in North America consisted almost entirely of Indian artifacts and sites—with only a recent veneer of Euroamerican material culture—there was no recognition, in 1906 (or for decades after), that Indian people might have religious, spiritual, or historical connections to the material record of their own past. That past belonged with "natural history" rather than American history. With the Antiquities Act, Congress had legally defined the American Indian past as part of the larger public trust, like Yellowstone and the American bison.

BREAKTHROUGH AT FOLSOM

15.

DESPITE OPPOSITION FROM Smithsonian archaeologists, many Americans remained intrigued by several well-publicized archaeological finds hinting that the First Americans might have arrived sometime during the Pleistocene—a geological epoch that began two million years ago, during which mammoths and mastodons, giant bison, and saber-tooth cats roamed across a landscape dominated by massive ice sheets. Some accepted these conclusions at face value, arguing that—sometime within the last 25,000 years—late Pleistocene people must have hunted the giant game animals that once populated America. With few exceptions, however, these "early man advocates" were amateur relic and fossil collectors—impassioned, committed, but increasingly marginalized. They were countered at every turn by the big guns of nineteenth-century American archaeology—establishment men well positioned in the major museums of the land—who contended that American Indians probably arrived in America no earlier than the Moundbuilders, Pueblo Indians, and the Classic Maya, all of whom left easily recognizable archaeological traces dating from the last couple of thousand years.

At the dawn of the twentieth century, it was obvious to all who cared that more sites must be investigated. Whenever solid evidence did turn up—undisturbed associations of artifacts with extinct animal bones in sediments of Pleistocene age—everyone recognized that these associations should be submitted to various scientific critics for verification. Only then would Ice Age Americans receive scientific accreditation.

This is exactly what happened at Wild Horse Gulch, about eight miles west of Folsom, New Mexico.

GEORGE MCJUNKIN'S BONE PIT

In late August 1908, while riding across the Crowfoot Ranch, George McJunkin saw storm clouds rolling across the afternoon sky. An experienced ranch hand and first-rate naturalist, he knew the danger signs: a sudden cloudburst could threaten the town of Folsom, wedged in a narrow canyon directly downstream.

Overnight, the splatter of raindrops became walls of water. McJunkin's rain gauge overflowed, as heavy cottonwood trees toppled from the eroding riverbanks. Dogs barked and howled in the darkness. The water picked up speed as it funneled beneath a railroad bridge, then hit the town of Folsom with deadly force. Somebody had alerted Sarah Rooke, the town's telephone operator, of the floodwaters headed her way. Hurrying into the tiny telephone office attached to her house, Rooke dialed her phone subscribers one after another, warning them about the flood. Many packed up quickly and were saved. A wall of liquid mud thirteen feet high roiled through the streets and destroyed half the town's buildings, sweeping away any townsfolk in its path. Rooke stayed at her post, ignoring the danger, until the phone line went dead.

The final death toll in Folsom reached seventeen, but dozens more would have perished without Rooke's dogged heroism. Rescuers searched the smashed ruins of her small house, but she was nowhere to be found. Six months later, a rancher found her remains sixteen miles downstream.

As foreman of the Crowfoot Ranch, McJunkin rode out a few days later to assess the flood damage to the upland pastures. Along a gully called Wild Horse Arroyo, he saw that the water had scoured a ditch ten feet deep. While piecing the fence back together, McJunkin glimpsed something bright white protruding from the steep arroyo wall. Using his barbed-wire clippers, he dug out a large fossilized bone. McJunkin knew right away that this bone was not cow. It looked more like bison. In all his days as a professional buffalo hunter, however, he had never seen a bone this large. Over the years, McJunkin returned to his Bone Pit, as he called it, retrieving more washed out bones, which he displayed on his mantel. A self-taught natural scientist, McJunkin had stockpiled a first-rate library, but nothing showed bones like these. He tried writing to specialists about his finds, but nobody wrote back.

A few years later, McJunkin drove to Raton, about 30 miles west of the Crowfoot Ranch, to have repairs made on an antique chuck wagon. While waiting for blacksmith Carl Schwachheim to finish the work, McJunkin noticed a curious fountain decorated with a huge set of interlocked elk antlers. McJunkin remarked that he had found some skulls from ancient animals robust enough to hold up those antlers. Like McJunkin, Schwachheim was a self-educated amateur naturalist who kept a detailed journal of observations about the birds, animals, and flowers of the New Mexico mountains.

Although McJunkin provided directions to the Bone Pit, Schwachheim never quite found the time to make the two-day trip by horse-drawn wagon or on horseback. But he did share the story with a friend, Fred Howarth, another eager amateur naturalist and fossil collector (who happened to own a car). On December 10, 1922, Schwachheim and Howarth organized a small party to explore the Crowfoot Ranch site. McJunkin had died the previous January, but his detailed directions led them directly to the Bone Pit. Schwachheim recorded in his journal that they "dug out nearly a sack full [of bones] which look like buffalo & Elk." Returning home, the two men spread the bones across Schwachheim's kitchen table, comparing them with descriptions in his paleontology books. They knew then that the bones belonged to a very big bison.

"SOMETHING IN THE NATURE OF AN ANTICIPATED SURPRISE"

Schwachheim and Howarth tried for years to interest the State of New Mexico in the find, but without success. Then, in January of 1926, they dovetailed a trip to deliver cattle to Denver with a visit to the Colorado [now Denver] Museum of Natural History. Jesse D. Figgins, the director of the museum, turned the bones over to paleontologist Harold Cook, who identified them as an extinct species of bison.

For some time, Figgins and Harold Cook had been looking for traces of Pleistocene man. They were particularly interested in the Lone Wolf Creek

site, outside Colorado City, Texas, where man-made stone tools were apparently associated with the bones of extinct bison. Both men believed that the
Lone Wolf Creek evidence proved that humans had been there 500,000 years
ago—a bold statement for 1925, when few scientists admitted a human antiquity in America of more than a few thousand years.

Neither Figgins nor Cook was actually present when the Texas finds
were made, and the excavator, not realizing the importance of leaving things
in place, let the spear points drop out of the matrix block containing the
bones. Lacking credible eyewitnesses or clear photographs, Figgins was reluctant to push the Texas evidence too strongly; he knew that Aleš Hrdlička,
czar of American skull science, would quickly dismiss any find lacking solid
supportive documentation. But as Figgins wrote to a colleague, "Sooner or
later, we're going to find human artifacts associated with fossil animals!"

The fossilized bones from Folsom compelled the Denver scientists to
take a closer look. The four men—Figgins, Cook, Schwachheim, and
Howarth—went to Wild Horse Arroyo in March 1926, and again in April.
Figgins and Cook decided that their museum should support excavations
there to acquire some fossil bison skeletons for exhibition. They hired
Schwachheim to remove the six feet of overburden; then, in June, Figgins'
son Frank joined the excavation team. The clay matrix was so hard in places
that they sometimes had to blast their way through.

That summer, as Schwachheim and the younger Figgins dug away at the
Folsom Bone Pit, Hrdlička published an article in the July issue of *Scientific
American* summarizing current knowledge about Pleistocene Man in America.
Despite the lifelong efforts of several prominent archaeologists there was
"not a scrap of bone or implement that can generally and with full confidence
be accepted as geologically ancient," Hrdlička concluded." . . . As to the antiquity of the Indian himself, that cannot be very great."

"AND THE DURNED THING IS RIGHT BESIDE A BISON RIB"

Within days after reading Hrdlička's article, Schwachheim recorded in
his journal: "Found part of a broken spear or large arrow head near the base of
the fifth spine . . . it must have been in the skeleton of the smaller [bison] &
just inside the cavity of the body near the back. It was found 8 1/2 feet beneath the surface with an oaktree growing directly over it 6 inches in diame-
ter showing it to have been there a great length of time." The senior Figgins

was in Denver at the time, but when he got word of the find, he described his feelings as "something in the nature of an anticipated surprise."

Figgins shared the good news with the American Museum of Natural History's distinguished paleontologist Barnum Brown: "Last week I had the shocking news that an arrowhead had been found associated with a bunch of dorsal vertebra of the New Mexico *Bison*. . . . Unfortunately, the shaft end is missing, but seemingly, only a small part of it. . . . I am having the boys scan every particle of the dirt they remove—first with the prospect of finding the missing part, and to discover any other artifacts." They would not have to wait long because the missing point fragment turned up shortly.

But Figgins faced a new worry. "Now I am in doubt whether to write it up or to keep it quiet. If I keep quiet I will be accused of hampering the advance of science and Hrdlička's chest will keep on swelling, and if I do write it up, I will be suspected, if not accused, of lying. And the durned thing is right beside a Bison rib." After considerable debate, Figgins and Cook decided to announce their finds in companion articles in *Natural History*, the flagship journal of the American Museum of Natural History. The article, Figgins later admitted, was motivated in large measure by his personal desire to "arouse Dr. H. and stir up all the venom there is in him. . . . Everyone seems to think Hrdlička will attack [and if he] tears a chunk of hide off my back . . . there is nothing to prevent my removing three upper and lower incisors, black one eye and gouge the other, after I have laid his hide across a barbed wire fence."

Despite the bravado, Figgins and Cook ran into a solid wall of doubt and disbelief. Maybe the strata had been jumbled in the geological past. Maybe the excavators inadvertently mixed ancient strata themselves. Maybe the flaked stones were much later than the bones, having fallen into the excavation from above. In truth, there was no particular reason to trust their judgment.

"DR. HRDLIČKA WAS NOT HAPPY"

Figgins traveled eastward the following spring to show his Folsom artifacts to critics at the Smithsonian Institution and elsewhere. He was disarmed by Hrdlička's "courteous" reaction. Although expressing his reservations about the age of the Folsom finds, Hrdlička encouraged Figgins to continue his excavations—stressing the importance of leaving future finds undisturbed in the original matrix, to be authenticated by specialists.

Hrdlička then took Figgins down the hall, to show the Folsom artifacts to his colleague Holmes (without telling him where they came from). After briefly inspecting the stone tools, Holmes declared them to be "undoubtedly foreign—European—both in material and workmanship." When Hrdlička explained that the artifacts had actually been excavated in New Mexico, an elated Figgins struggled to "retain a fairly straight face and dignified demeanor. So much for the great Dr. Holmes . . . Dr. Hrdlička was not happy." A chagrined Holmes then admitted to Figgins that "he would never believe men and those prehistoric mammals were contemporaneous . . . until arrowheads were found imbedded in the bones of the latter in such a manner as to prohibit question that they were shot into them while the animal was still living. Not having arrowheads so imbedded, I left Dr. Holmes happy in his determination to oppose any and all evidence likely to interfere with his personal theories."

Not everyone was so skeptical. Barnum Brown effusively praised the excavations, but echoed Hrdlička in stressing the importance of leaving future finds in place for examination by others. Brown was so enthusiastic that he convinced the American Museum to co-sponsor the 1927 excavations at Folsom.

That August, Schwachheim found another fluted point, stuck between two bison ribs. This time, the bones and spear point were still embedded in

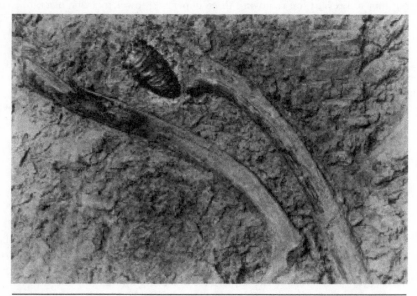

Folsom spear point embedded between the bones of extinct bison, near Folsom (New Mexico) in 1927.

the original matrix—clear evidence that they had been deposited together. Leaving the new finds exactly as he found them, Schwachheim dashed off a note to Figgins, then drove his wagon at breakneck speed to get his letter onto the evening train to Denver. Taking Hrdlička's advice to heart, Figgins dispatched a flurry of telegrams, urging specialists to come to Folsom and satisfy themselves as to the legitimacy of the association. At this point, Barnum Brown was working at Grand Junction, Colorado, and on September 4, 1927, he accompanied Figgins to the excavations at Wild Horse Arroyo. Although Brown was not present when the key find was made—he stayed around just long enough to have his picture taken at the site—he was immediately convinced. "The artifacts are substantially contemporaneous with the Bison."

Figgins had also sent a telegram to Pecos, New Mexico, where A. V. Kidder had convened a conference of prominent archaeologists. Frank H. H. Roberts, a young archaeologist with the Bureau of American Ethnology, first visited the site on September 4, then returned with Kidder, one of America's most respected archaeologists, on September 9. They too were convinced: The artifacts and the extinct animal bones must have been deposited at the same time.

The Folsom site provided clear-cut evidence that ancient hunters had killed and butchered perhaps thirty now-extinct buffalo (*Bison antiquus*). Subsequent archaeological investigations indicate that, on a fall day nearly 11,000 years ago, a group of hunters entrapped a bison herd in a dead-end tributary headcut of Wild Horse Arroyo. After dispatching the trapped animals with their stone-tipped spears, the hunters butchered the bison where they fell, creating an extensive bone bed. Although the Folsom hunters undoubtedly retrieved many of their spears, a number of spear tips remained embedded in the bison, particularly in the deepest carcasses.

To date, archaeologists have recovered at least two dozen of these distinctive spear points from the site. Following standard scientific precedent, to the discoverer went the right to name the finds. Figgins, well aware of scientific protocols, called McJunkin's Bone Pit the "Folsom site" and characterized the distinctive artifacts recovered there as "Folsom points."

"IN MY HAND I HOLD THE ANSWER ..."

In 1927, the big news was the clear-cut contemporaneity between Folsom spear points and extinct animal bones. A month after visiting Folsom,

Kidder delivered a lecture at the Southwest Museum in Los Angeles, telling his audience he believed that the "first human adventurer came to this continent . . . across the Bering Straits, and that his first journey to the New World took place at least fifteen or twenty thousand years ago"—quite a departure from Hrdlička's gloomy *Scientific American* assessments published only a few months earlier. Although the news from Folsom reached the Smithsonian quickly, Hrdlička was in transit to Europe to receive the Huxley Medal and lecture to the Royal Society on the Neanderthal Phase of Man.

Hrdlička delivered his opinions on the Folsom find the next year. Speaking at the New York Academy of Medicine, he reaffirmed his statement that no skeletal remains existed anywhere in North America to support great human antiquity; and despite the best efforts of prominent archaeologists, Hrdlička claimed nobody had yet discovered convincing evidence of ancient Americans. Nels Nelson, who followed Hrdlička, disagreed and suggested that perhaps the matter could be resolved within an hour by some earnest discussion. Barnum Brown then clinched the argument by showing off some of the newly discovered Folsom points, which he apparently kept stowed in his desk drawer. Brown crowed, "In my hand I hold the answer to the antiquity of man in America. *It is simply a matter of interpretation.*" Although Hrdlička's rejoinder at the New York meeting is not recorded, he continued to denounce the Folsom finds, stressing the uncertain dating of the deposits and arguing that Indian people throughout the Americas commonly used stone points. In fact, Hrdlička would argue until his death that the evidence at Folsom was not sufficient to establish a Pleistocene age for the deposits. These bison, after all, might "not have been extinct very long."

Except for the diehard Hrdlička, scientific controversy over Ice Age man in America evaporated virtually overnight. Once the Folsom associations were verified, the floodgates opened. In the next decade, at least half a dozen additional *bona fide* Paleoindian sites cropped up. After decades of abiding by Holmes and Hrdlička's short chronology, archaeologists now beheld a time span at least three times that long. At the recent end lived the modern American Indians. At the early end lay the Folsom finds. In between was a huge "chronological chasm"—where presumably the immediate and more ancient ancestors of American Indians remained to be found.

THE PALEOINDIAN SEQUENCE
AT BLACKWATER DRAW

Now that archaeologists knew what to look for—the bones of extinct animals—evidence of the First Americans poured in. Just 150 miles down the road from Folsom came another startling New Mexico discovery in 1932. A road construction crew digging in a gravel pit at Blackwater Draw (near Clovis) plowed up a large, extremely well made stone tool, buried next to a huge animal tooth. Decades later, archaeologist George Frison called it "the most significant Paleoindian site in North America."

Hearing of the Blackwater Draw discoveries, archaeologists from the Academy of Natural Sciences of Philadelphia and the University of Pennsylvania Museum began serious work there in 1933. E. B. Howard, and his young protege John Cotter, led the charge. They found that the wind-blown brownish sand overlying the site contained evidence only of relatively recent pottery-making people. But distinctive Folsom spearpoints and extinct animal bones turned up in the underlying bluish-gray sands, in places where the top sands had been blown away. Howard described these Folsom points as "the finest examples of the stone-flaking art." Their chief characteristic was a longitudinal groove (the "flute") running along each side (or sometimes just one face). The secondary flaking was extraordinary, showing remarkable control. Although only about two inches long, some Folsom spear points had up to 150 minute sharpening flakes removed from their surface.

Between excavation seasons at Blackwater Draw, Howard traveled to Europe and Russia to study museum collections from Siberia in a search for Folsom prototypes. Finding none, he concluded that if Folsom point technology was not imported from elsewhere—as seemed to be the case—it must have evolved in America. Because such an extraordinarily well made artifact tradition could not have sprung up overnight. Howard concluded that the distinctive Folsom points must have been "preceded by other cruder forms which have not yet come to be recognized."

The real breakthrough at Blackwater Draw came in 1937, when Howard and Cotter excavated *below* the Folsom strata, looking for those earlier, cruder artifacts. In a basal stratum of mottled sand, they found, associated with butchered mammoth bones, a new kind of spearpoint, which Cotter and Howard named Clovis, after the nearby New Mexico town. As suspected, Clovis points indeed differed in several important ways from the later Folsom artifacts. According to Cotter, the Clovis points from Blackwater Draw were "typically long and heavy for the Folsom pattern. It might not be amiss to suggest here that a difference in 'calibre,' i.e., weight and dimensions, is evident in weapon points of the Folsom Complex, presumably dependent on intended use. The heavier and larger points evidently being intended for the mammoth, the medium-sized points with more extensive channeling for bison and game of moderate size." This was the first time that elephant-hunting Clovis remains were found below (and hence older than) the bison-hunting Folsom artifacts. Today, archaeologists use the term *Paleoindian* to distinguish these Clovis and Folsom occupations from later Native American populations (sometimes called *Neoindians*). The Blackwater Draw excavations established the basics of the Paleoindian sequence that archaeologists still use today.

Over the next half century, archaeologists defined the Clovis complex as the earliest well-documented culture in Native America. Clovis sites in western North America consistently date between 11,500 and 10,900 years ago. In eastern North America, Clovis-like point assemblages seem to date somewhat earlier. These sites contain thousands of diagnostic stone tools—not just the signature Clovis points, but also specialized tools used to process various extinct animal parts. The most distinctive Clovis-age fossil is the Columbian mammoth, but bones of horses, camel, bison, turtles, and various small mammals also show up at Blackwater Draw.

Clovis spear points from the Wenatchee site (Washington).

The Folsom complex appeared roughly 10,900 years ago and survived for about six centuries. Mammoths were extinct by Folsom times, and the Blackwater Draw hunters mainly targeted a now-extinct form of bison, plus the occasional pronghorn antelope and mountain sheep. Not as widespread as Clovis, Folsom remains are confined to the Great Plains, American Southwest, and the central and southern reaches of the Rocky Mountains.

THE CLOVIS-FIRST HYPOTHESIS

Although Paleoindian skeletal remains are rare, all of the available bones belong to fully evolved *Homo sapiens*. Fossil bones from archaic hominids (such as Neanderthals) are entirely absent in the Americas. Archaeologists today believe that modern humans evolved elsewhere and that the earliest immigrants to America brought with them certain basic cultural skills: language, fire making, flint chipping, and serviceable means of procuring food, shelter, and clothing. They may have brought with them kin-group social organization and beliefs about magic and the supernatural.

These First Americans were called *Clovis* because that is where archaeologists first encountered them. They have been hailed as courageous hunters who made magnificent spear points with long, even elegant "flutes." As the highly mobile big-game hunters spread across their new American paradise, it took them only a few centuries (between 11,200 and 10,900 years ago) to colonize the continent from west to east. Some archaeologists believe that the Clovis people were instrumental in exterminating the wooly mammoths and other Pleistocene megabeasts.

The Clovis-first scenario suggests that the first Americans arrived sometime during the final part of the Pleistocene. Twenty thousand years ago, ice blanketed one-third of Earth—three times the area covered today. Huge ice sheets covered nearly all of Canada and extended across the present Great Lakes into the eastern United States. In places, these ice masses were two miles thick. Monumental Pleistocene glaciers locked up so much water that the world's oceans dropped markedly, exposing a massive unglaciated tract known as the Beringia (the Bering Land Bridge), which connected Siberia to modern Alaska. Beringia was a flat, well-vegetated grassland capable of supporting both the giant animals of the late Ice Age and the ancient hunters who crossed into the area from Asia. During the Pleistocene, reindeer, wolverines, and lemmings all lived in places that today would be too warm for them, and muskox, now found only in the Arctic, ranged into Mexico.

The skull of a 10,000-year old walrus, no doubt an inhabitant of frigid waters, has been uncovered on the Virginia coast.

The late Pleistocene glaciers began to recede as the climate warmed up. Although scientists still debate the causes of these dramatic shifts, it seems likely that Earth's tilt and its orbit about the sun must have changed, increasing the amount of sunlight reaching the planet. As summers warmed up, water from melting glaciers poured back into the oceans, and sea levels rose again, eventually submerging much of the exposed continental shelf. By 12,000 years ago, shrinking continental ice sheets exposed an ice-free corridor that stretched from the Yukon to Montana. The Clovis-first model holds that the first Americans walked through this ice-free passageway southward onto the Great Plains. Although archaeologists still debate when the first Americans arrived, most agree that Paleoindian hunters had already crossed from Siberia into central Alaska by at least 12,000 years ago. Increasingly, however, archaeologists are expanding traditional notions of a simple Siberia-to-Alaska migration.

The Clovis-first model dominated American archaeology for five decades, but this hardly implies a consensus within the scientific community—far from it. Each decade, a number of potential pre-Clovis sites have been advanced, and while most of these claims for ancient man have been rejected and forgotten, some have not. Some observers see the Paleoindian scene as having been policed by a "Clovis mafia"—intellectual descendants of the Holmes-Hrdlička tradition—who consistently and forcefully rejected all claims of earlier evidence. As archaeologist James Adovasio puts it, all the pre-Clovis candidates "have gotten their 15 minutes of fame, then disappeared into obscurity."

BUSTING THE CLOVIS BARRIER

16.

THE MAPUCHE INDIANS of southern Chile tell of the first people in their land. "Our ancestors looked at every path closely and deliberately. They tried them all as many times as they thought necessary. Many paths were long and led nowhere. Some paths were joyful journeys and made the people strong. Others weakened the people and made them curse their lives. We often ask our ancestral spirits if we Mapuche are now choosing the right path. They say time will give us the answer."

Here, in the Mapuche homeland, time seems to have directed archaeologist Tom Dillehay to the right path. Against all odds, Dillehay finally broke the Clovis barrier at a site he calls Monte Verde ("Green Meadow").

FIRST EXPLORATIONS

Tom Dillehay was drawn into the Clovis/pre-Clovis fray in 1976, when a team of local lumbermen was cutting roadways through the cool upland forest. As they stripped back the brush along Chinchihuapi Creek they uncovered some large bones and buried wood. The landowners, Gerardo Barria and his family, took some of the bones to the Southern University of Chile, in Valdevia, where paleontologists identified them as mastodon—Ice Age elephant. The university conducted a small field exploration, recovering additional mastodon bones, some curiously smoothed wooden artifacts, and one large flaked quartzite tool.

The paleontologists asked Dillehay, then teaching at the Southern University of Chile, to look over the bones for any signs of butchering or other human alteration. Looking closely, Dillehay saw, for the most part, recent cuts and scrapes—shovel marks, pick fractures and the like—but the bones also showed unmistakably ancient cut marks and fractures that suggested humans had indeed worked over these bones while they were still green.

By themselves, these cut marks were not enough to justify a full-scale field expedition. But when he realized that more than three-quarters of the bone fragments were ribs, Dillehay wondered if the non-rib bones had perhaps been carted off by ancient hunters. Maybe Monte Verde was a kill site, a place where ancient human hunters had killed and field-butchered the mastodons. During a three-week exploratory field season at Monte Verde in 1977, Dillehay found what he considered "irrefutable and unquestionable evidence of human activity"—worked wooden artifacts, broken stone, and flaked tools associated with worked and unworked mastodon bones. Despite this, he and his Chilean students remained uncomfortable with the nature of the evidence.

Like most archaeologists familiar with First American sites, Dillehay had a stone-tool-first mentality: First establish the age of the site by finding old-looking stone tools (like Folsom or Clovis points), then look at the rest of the artifacts and animal bones to figure out what went on there. The stone tools at Monte Verde were pretty disappointing by North American archaeological standards. No clear-cut Paleoindian spear points turned up in the initial excavations (and none would appear later). Although Monte Verde seemed to be a very ancient site, the stone tools were a problem and the case for its antiquity would have to be made through organic remains—worked wood, plant parts, and even chunks of preserved mastodon meat and skin.

Dillehay returned to Monte Verde the next year on a "spaghetti budget," financed in part by the Southern University of Chile and the Museum of History and Anthropology and also from his own savings. This time, he got sufficient archaeological evidence to warrant a year of support from the

National Geographic Society (and eventually, a succession of research grants from the National Science Foundation). The newfound funding allowed Dillehay to assemble a team of specialists—which would ultimately swell to eighty members—to explore the site. Eventually, an impressive suite of radiocarbon dates confirmed that Dillehay had something special at Monte Verde. The site dates were roughly 12,800 to 12,400 years old—a full 1,500 years more ancient than the oldest known Clovis occupation. To complicate matters still further, a stratigraphically earlier level yielded dates nearly 20,000 years older than that.

Conventional archaeology is almost entirely a matter of stone and bones, plus the occasional lump of charcoal usable for radiocarbon dating. The ancient occupations at Monte Verde were buried beneath a thick, protective peat bog. Because bogs are water-saturated, the organic remains are spared destructive changes in humidity and moisture. Because oxygen cannot penetrate the depths, bacteria do not attack the skin and wooden remains buried there. As a result, the conditions at Monte Verde resembled those that preserved Scandinavia's famous mummies—the Bog People. This is why, after draining the bog and stripping off the peat, Dillehay and crew recovered much more than just stones and bones.

Preserved on the 12,500-year-old surface were 38 chunks of animal meat and hide, 11 specimens of wild potato, 4 kinds of exotic seaweed, and 180 architectural elements, wooden lances, and mortars. The archaeologists mapped at least a dozen huts on this surface, including a sixty-foot-long tent-like structure that could house twenty to thirty people—maybe year-round. Framed with logs and planks, the superstructure was covered by wet mastodon and paleo-llama hide and anchored by wooden stakes. Skins also covered the floor inside, where families maintained some degree of privacy by defining their living spaces with hide-covered walls.

To the west stood a wishbone-shaped structure, made of wooden uprights set into a sand and gravel foundation stabilized with hardened animal fat. Mastodons had been butchered inside, and the inedible hide and bones fashioned into tools and building materials. Incredibly, inside the west building were some 23 kinds of medicinal plants, suggesting that healing may have also taken place here. The wet clay floor of Monte Verde preserved three human footprints—from a bulky teenager or, perhaps, a smallish adult who once walked the banks of Chinchihualpi Creek.

HIGH PROFILE SKEPTICS

When the National Geographic Society agreed to bankroll the Monte Verde dig, it also asked Junius Bird of the American Museum of Natural History to visit the site and personally verify Dillehay's assessment of the site's antiquity. Bird, the acknowledged dean of Paleoindian research in South America, had spent five decades trailing the First Americans. In the early 1930s, he and his new wife Peggy traveled to remote Tierra del Fuego on a curious mixture of scientific exploration and personal adventure. With only a worn out Model T Ford for transportation and no immediate source of gasoline, Bird harnessed a more abundant energy source—the wind. Rigging a makeshift sail across the back of the Model T, the Birds literally sailed their Ford across the pampas. Junius was actually disappointed when, near the end of the journey, local officials filled the tank with gas. He had relished the drama of entering town under full sail.

Perhaps the real-world prototype for Indiana Jones, Junius Bird arrived at Monte Verde early in the 1979 field season. After observing the excavations and inspecting previous finds in the field lab, Bird filed his report with the National Geographic Society. Although expressing confidence in Dillehay's ability to direct excavations under difficult field conditions, Bird had some serious reservations about the archaeology. He questioned whether the "artifacts" were indisputably cultural materials and thought it possible that later materials had worked their way downward from more recent deposits. Everything considered, Bird thought the antiquity of Monte Verde was questionable, and hearing this, the National Geographic Society cut off Dillehay's funding.

Years later, Dillehay responded that Bird's two-day visit unfortunately occurred very early in the field season, while the crew were setting up their grid system and screening dirt from the upper (non-human) layers. According to Dillehay, Bird's lab visit lasted only 45 minutes and "as far as artifacts were concerned, Bird spoke the truth. If he had stayed just two more weeks at the site, however, he would have seen us uncover the dramatic 12,500-year-old remains."

But the damage was done. Bird's reputation was sterling, and his opinion carried considerable weight with Paleoindian specialists, most of whom joined with him in questioning the Monte Verde evidence. Dillehay claims that at scientific conferences, "others would be introduced as doctor this and doctor that. I was always 'the guy who is excavating Monte Verde.' Some wouldn't even shake my hand."

Some of these critics suggested that the artifacts on the alleged 12,500-year-old surface must have been displaced from overlying, recent strata—maybe by burrowing animals or cracks in the sediments. Dillehay responded that there are no more recent strata at Monte Verde—the site was sealed by overlying layers of peat. Noting that the nearest "later materials" are buried one-third of a mile upstream, he argued that the possibility of contamination from later materials is zero. Some archaeologists, accustomed to seeing very different stone tool assemblages, were disappointed in the collection from Monte Verde, and Dillehay admitted that, by United States standards, the stone tools at Monte Verde were not particularly diagnostic of early humans. But in South America, the bola stones (spheroid throwing stones) and unifacial stone tools he found are now recognized as existing early and everywhere.

Other archaeologists expressed concern over the small sample of unambiguous artifacts, the possibility that the radiocarbon dates might be contaminated, and the prospect that floodwaters (rather than First Americans) might have brought the wood and bone artifacts into the site. Responding to each charge, Dillehay complained about the negativity of the "Clovis Police" and railed at what he called "Instant Analysis and Opinion-hurling . . . [by archaeologists] too anxious to write the obituary of the site."

For more than a dozen years, Dillehay was joined in defending Monte Verde by the geologist Mario Pino and archaeologists Jack Rossen and Michael Collins. They invited other qualified archaeologists to visit the site, but hardly anyone showed up. "In one publication," Dillehay protested, "Monte Verde is foundering and floundering. In the next publication, the site is under siege, on the defensive and rejected. All this takes place without a site visit and consultation of all the evidence." Even senior Chilean archaeologists failed to visit Monte Verde during the decade-long excavations. Dillehay readily admits that such site visits would have been difficult, in part because of the oppressive military government of General Augusto Pinochet during the 1970s and 1980s and also because of the remote location. Visiting Monte Verde was a time-consuming and costly undertaking, so nobody did.

"THE CLOVIS CURTAIN HAS FALLEN"

The controversy perked along until 1997, when a blue-ribbon panel of archaeologists, supported by the Dallas Museum of Natural History and the National Geographic Society, finally went to Monte Verde for a first-hand look. The team, which consisted of several archaeologists openly skeptical of Dillehay's claim, asked the same basic questions as those who had visited the Folsom site nearly seventy years before: (1) Are the "artifacts" truly man-made? (2) Are the sediments and their stratigraphic relationships correctly interpreted? (3) Are the associations between artifacts and extinct animals valid?

Beginning at Dillehay's University of Kentucky lab, they inspected some of the Monte Verde artifacts and listened to presentations from several specialists. They also saw the celebrated 12,500-year-old Monte Verde human footprint, which had been removed intact in a block of sediment. Then, at the Southern University of Chile, they examined additional collections from the site. Finally, they traveled to Monte Verde itself. Unfortunately, the expert team could not investigate the primary occupation area because it had been destroyed by road construction and stream erosion. But they did examine neighboring areas, which still preserved remnants of the site stratigraphy.

After a week came the moment of truth. In a local saloon named *La Caverna*, team leader David Meltzer finally popped the question: Does everyone present agree that Monte Verde is 12,500 years old?

Everyone did.

In their final report, the panel expressed "complete unanimity" that the 12,500-year-old surface is clearly archaeological. They found "no reason to question the integrity of the radiocarbon ages," which not only were internally consistent, but also agreed with the regional chronology from non-archaeological contexts established through years of work by a diverse group of scientists. Although the stone tool assemblage from Monte Verde was disappointing, the mastodon and other extinct mammal bones had clearly been modified by humans. There was no question that the cordage was man-made, and many of the seeds and other ancient plant materials seem to have been introduced by human activities. The evidence did indeed support an antiquity of 12,500 years, and the tools looked nothing like Clovis—Monte Verde was declared to be definitely older.

For years, C. Vance Haynes of the University of Arizona had been the leading Clovis-first advocate. Although he was a member of the panel visiting Monte Verde and accepted the affirmation of the site, Haynes still sounded a note of caution, pointing out that Monte Verde "has just six [stone tools]. If it is as old as it looks, and the dates do look solid, then there should be others like it. Until we find those, there are still questions."

David Meltzer responded that Haynes' criticism is a red herring. Meltzer emphasizes that the human presence at Monte Verde is also supported by the cordage, the architecture, the human footprints, the anomalous and exotic plants remains and so forth. Why, adds Meltzer, since archaeologists needed only a single Folsom site in 1927, should we now require two or more Monte Verdes today? Although additional sites will surely help establish the pattern, they are not needed simply to establish the antiquity.

Although Monte Verde is only 1,000 years older than the generally accepted dates for Clovis, that difference is profound. Located 10,000 miles south of the Bering land bridge, Monte Verde suggests a fundamentally different history of human colonization than the Clovis-first model had allowed. *New York Times* science writer John Noble Wilford compares the Monte Verde vindication with aviation's breaking of the sound barrier. The Clovis-first hypothesis—the textbook story of First Americans pouring down from Alaska 12,000 years ago—was discredited. People may have arrived here thousands, maybe tens of thousands of years before that.

REVISITING MONTE VERDE

Just as this book was going to press (in October 1999) the always controversial field of First American archaeology took another unexpected turn. Stuart J. Fiedel published a detailed critique of Dillehay's research at Monte Verde, raising some serious questions about whether Monte Verde is indeed a viable pre-Clovis site.

After their high-profile visit to Monte Verde in 1997, the elite panel published its verdict confirming Monte Verde's antiquity. They praised Dillehay's long-awaited second volume just published by the Smithsonian Institution Press. One panel member paid a backhanded compliment, calling the report "analytical overkill . . . a milestone in American archaeology." Another wrote, "This is not just another archaeological monograph: it represents a historic turning point in our understanding of the initial peopling of the New World." The Society for American Archaeology gave Dillehay's two-volume set its 1998 Book Award, praising "the extreme care given to the site's excavation, analysis, and publication . . . [it] sets a new standard for all archaeologists." Someone even said that Dillehay's publication was so convincing that the panel's verdict was "anticlimactic and, ultimately, unnecessary." As they conferred their blessing on Monte Verde, the panel added a caveat urging "readers . . . to examine for themselves Dillehay's detailed volumes and draw their own conclusions." Two years later, someone did just that.

Fiedel's sharply worded critique closely analyzes the new Monte Verde report and compares its descriptions to those previously published in preliminary reports. He concentrates on the controversial stone tool assemblage from Monte Verde, concluding that inconsistencies in cataloguing, mapping, and reporting make it impossible to tell where the most important artifacts were found. Recalling the famous 1927 image of the spear point lying between extinct bison ribs at Folsom (reproduced on page 150). Fiedel asks "Where are the photographs, or even field drawings of the Monte Verde bifaces at the moment of discovery in their various locations?" Since chipped stone tools were so rare at Monte Verde, Fiedel suggests, their discovery "must have occasioned considerable excitement."

Fiedel also has trouble pinning down just where the radiocarbon-dated samples came from. He questions whether mastodon hide huts ever existed at Monte Verde and doubts that Dillehay had found chunks of mastodon meat. Fiedel argues that all of these problems, taken together, "raise doubts about the provenience of virtually every 'compelling,' unambiguous artifact." He criticizes the 1997 site visit, quoting Dillehay's comment that "in 1988 most of our site had been wiped out by a bulldozer blade" and suggesting that the "guest scholars could only inspect a remnant soil stub that at most only demonstrated . . . the site's natural stratigraphy." He suggests that "only Junius Bird actually witnessed the excavation of Monte Verde [and] he did not see convincing evidence of a human occupation." Fiedel's bottom line is this: "Unless and until the numerous discrepancies in the final report are convincingly clarified, this site should not be construed as conclusive proof of a pre-Clovis human occupation in South America."

The editors of *Scientific American Discovering Archaeology* circulated Fiedel's manuscript to the Monte Verde investigators and several other archaeologists for comment, which they published alongside Fiedel's critique. Dillehay and several of his colleagues concede some "editorial and factual errors," and thank Fiedel for bringing these mistakes to light. They do not deny that "inconsistencies in data analysis and interpretation exist in the publications" but suggest that "this is common in any long-term and interdisciplinary project." Then they apologize "for any misunderstandings that may be experienced by readers of the book" and promise that an errata sheet will soon appear on the Internet.

Dillehay and his colleagues also clarify their field strategies and explain the cataloguing and mapping systems. They continue to downplay the importance of the stone tool assemblage, accuse Fiedel of "[fixating] on bifaces and points," and warn that South American sites "should not be judged exclu-

sively by North American criteria." They disagree with Junius Bird's evalua-
tion, reiterating their view that "Bird never knew the excavated site."

The other comments on the Fiedel critique and Dillehay's response are
predictably mixed. Some defend Monte Verde by attacking Fiedel's credentials and questioning his right to speak among the archaeological elite. One
accuses Fiedel of having only "an elemental understanding of standard procedures in the long term interdisciplinary research and publication of a complex." After complaining about the tendency for such discussions to lapse into
personal attacks, another commentator complains of Fiedel's alleged "inability to dig one's way out of a sack." Adovasio claims that Fiedel "demonstrates
a near total failure to grasp the major methodological issues, let alone the tac-
tical nuances of excavations at a site like Monte Verde." In effect, says Adovasio, Fiedel has plunged into the "Clovis/pre-Clovis gunfight armed with an
experiential pocket knife." David Anderson, on the other hand, believes that
the problems raised by Fiedel are "real, numerous and extremely serious."
Feeling that an Internet posting of errata is insufficient, Anderson calls on the
Smithsonian Institution Press to produce a fully corrected second edition of
the Monte Verde volumes.

Vance Haynes reiterates his own discomfort with the 1997 site visit to
Monte Verde. When one of the sponsors told him that a consensus would be
required from the participating scientists, Haynes "found this to be an unreasonable request and replied that it was unlikely." When a consensus did
emerge in Chile, Haynes double-checked the specific proveniences of stone
tools in the Monte Verde monograph when he got home and, to his surprise,
"found these data to be inadequate and therefore unconvincing." After reading Fiedel's critique, Haynes adds several of his own reservations about where
the stone tools and radiocarbon samples really came from.

Any archaeologist who has ever tackled a complex, multi-year excavation—particularly before electronic databases became commonplace—can
only empathize with Dillehay and his associates. Provenience error and con-
fusions do happen: they always will. In December, 1999, the Monte Verde
team distributed a massive, point-by-point response to Fiedel's critique (available on the Web at www.uky.edu/projects/monteverde), addressing the major
criticisms and providing several additional photographs from the excavation—including shots of key artifacts as they were being uncovered. No
objective critic could ask for a more forthcoming response.

Minutia aside, Fiedel's criticisms raise some serious issues about quality
control in conventional archaeological discourse. Archaeologists are among

the few scientists who necessarily destroy their own data, and because so few excavations can accommodate a significant number of expert witnesses to verify the proficiency of those excavating—to say nothing of laboratory processing—most digs must be judged on the published results. Scientific publication of all sorts has traditionally relied heavily on "peer review" to maintain the highest standards. But how many "peers" can realistically be expected to grapple with the hundreds, sometimes thousands of pages required to report on complex excavations like Monte Verde? Those selected for peer reviews are usually the archaeologists with the heftiest reputations (and, not coincidentally, with the least time to conduct a substantive review). The danger is that key manuscripts—whether grant proposals, technical articles, or book drafts—will be simply rubber-stamped down the line, with judgments conditioned as much by interpersonal relations and accumulated reputation as by dispassionate objectivity.

The solution? With the advent of near-instantaneous electronic communication, it has become a relatively simple matter to ask colleagues to look over manuscripts in progress, to seek out errors before they become reified in print. Had Fiedel sent a draft of his criticisms to Dillehay, many of the issues he raised could have been readily resolved. Instead, Fiedel elected to rush his manuscript into print, ambushing Dillehay and his colleagues with a mishmash of shotgun criticisms—what *Science* termed "a belligerence rarely seen in scientific spats." By refusing to engage in pre-publication, person-to-person dialogue with the Monte Verde principals, Fiedel not only clouded the issue with irrelevant details but raised serious questions about his motivations. Was Fiedel critique primarily concerned with the pre-Clovis possibilities of Monde Verde? Or was it just another carefully timed headline grabber? Handled the way it was, who knows?

The new Monte Verde controversy raises deeper issues regarding the inner workings of archaeology as a science. As in the days of Holmes and Hrdlicka a century ago, some criticize the role of elite panels and traveling experts. Dillehay complained about the "instant analysis and opinion-hurling" of pre-Clovis skeptics like Junius Bird, and some are uncomfortable with the pro-Monte Verde verdict rendered by the 1997 visiting panel—each side complaining that legitimate data and alternative opinions are being quashed by the weight of accumulated authority and paleo-politics. Others, including Robson Bonnichsen, take a larger view, suggesting that the various Monte Verde challenges are signs of healthy science—reflecting the "many checks and balances in place to insure that good scientific procedures are followed." Final judgments, of course, reside in the eye of the beholder.

WHAT MODERN ARCHAEOLOGISTS THINK ABOUT THE EARLIEST AMERICANS

THE MONTE VERDE and Kennewick finds have scrambled the conservative world of First American archaeology. Most archaeologists now agree that humans arrived in the New World sometime before, say, 12,000 years ago. Monte Verde may well be earlier than Clovis, but nobody knows how much earlier. Several hundred feet to the south of the 12,500-year-old deposit is a second, earlier component where Dillehay has found some questionable stone tools and burnt wood, three clay-lined pits, and two radiocarbon dates suggesting an age of maybe 33,000 years. At this writing, he is planning further excavations on this very early stratum.

A wave of new finds suggests that the southern tip of South America may have been first occupied about the same time as North America, or even earlier. How could this be? Were people sailing to Tierra del Fuego as Clovis hunters were slogging southward from the Bering Straits?

The combined linguistic, genetic, and archaeological evidence still points to a Bering Strait crossing, but since Clovis may no longer be the pioneering New World population, the origins and ultimate spread of those Very First Americans remain a puzzle to be explored. The Pulitzer-prize winning science writer John Noble Wilford suggests that American archaeology has been plunged "into a new period of tumult and uncertainty over its oldest mystery, one critical to understanding how modern humans spread out throughout the world." The arrival of people in America was a critical turning point in the human past, "the last time in history when people occupied an entirely new land," writes Wilford, "alone and with little more than their own ingenuity and an eye on far horizons."

THE ICE-FREE CORRIDOR CLOSES

The Clovis-first story remained the archaeological party line for six decades. It went like this: maybe 13,000 years ago, America's first two-legged predators walked across the Bering Land Bridge to begin their arduous trek southward. For decades, the Clovis-first hypothesis posited an ice-free corridor, the original Pan-American highway, through which the First Americans moved southward between the massive continental glaciers into heartland America.

But if the Clovis curtain falls, as seems likely, the archaeological community will find itself without a dominant paradigm. Not only is there increasing evidence of pre-Clovis human presence, but more refined data also suggests that the ice-free corridor model may not be so useful after all. Science writer Diedtra Henderson parodies the Clovis-first theory as a "cartoon version" of human migration, "with Big Game Hunters breaking through the ice sheets (KAPOW!) and descending in blitzkrieg fashion (BAM!) into this New World." Harvard geologist Carole Mandryk goes even further, suggesting that the Clovis-first hypothesis is an academic fantasy developed by "macho gringo guys [who] just want to believe the first Americans were these big, tough, fur-covered, mammoth-hunting people. . . ."

Mandryk thinks that the long-favored ice-free corridor was basically inaccessible between about 30,000 and 12,000 years ago, but a new route— along an aboriginal Pacific Coast Highway—not only remained accessible but also provided valuable resources. New evidence of maritime adaptation— a people living almost entirely on seafood—has turned up, dating from 11,000 years ago in Peru and perhaps as early as 10,000 years ago in southern California's Channel Islands. Could this have been the route followed by the Monte Verde ancestors?

Mandryk and others propose an initial entry along the Pacific shoreline, and she cites oral histories of Northwest Coast Indians that seem to describe the post-glacial environment and events, a tree-covered land with sea levels much lower than at present. Creation stories from the Haida people of British Columbia tell of a time, long ago, when their islands were much larger, surrounded by grassy plains. But then the oceans rose, and a supernatural "flood tide woman" forced the Haida to move their villages to higher ground.

The geological record seems to agree. About 11,000 years ago, the islands off British Columbia were probably twice their present size. For a thousand years at the end of the Pleistocene, the oceans rose an inch a year. That's nearly 85 feet! Today, geologists are using high-resolution sonar technology to explore the flooded shorelines, and someday remote submarines may search for the long flooded campsites.

A PALEOLITHIC FRENCH CONNECTION

The Clovis-first model postulated a migration from Siberia about 12,000-13,000 years ago, but there seem to be no ancestral Clovis sites in Asia. Where did this culture come from? As Bruce Bradley puts it, "We've got to do better than to simply say that people walked across the Bering Strait, and *voila. . . I* became Clovis overnight."

Today, there is much discussion of a Paleolithic French Connection—a view that ties American Clovis to a European ancestry through the Solutrian culture, which developed in France and stretched down the Iberian peninsula. The Solutrean culture (20,000-14,000 years ago) is a little older than Clovis, but not much. This suggested Solutrean-First American connection is not new. In 1919, Nels Nelson suggested in *Natural History* that traces of Solutrean-style technology could be found in North America, and in 1933—before the finds at Clovis turned up—he reiterated this theme, suggesting that "we have in America very faint traces of the Solutrean culture stage, of which the Folsom, N.M., discovery may be an example."

Today one of the world's premier flintknappers, Bradley will tell you that Clovis and Solutrean technologies are very, very similar. Although this idea has been around for decades, Dennis Stanford, a Smithsonian Institution archaeologist, says the idea that Clovis technology might have originated in Europe "would have been hooted right out of the lecture hall if we had said that a few years ago." No longer. Vance Haynes, the most cautious member of the Monte Verde panel, sees important parallels between Clovis and its contemporary in Europe. "There are just too many similarities" for the resemblance to be coincidental, he says.

Bradley stresses that his technological studies deal with very complex decision-making strategies, not just the "simple stuff" of making a stone tool. Frustrated that even his professional colleagues "haven't got it," Bradley suggests a linguistic analogy: "Just as languages have syntax and structure, allowing words to express an idea or concept, so do flaking technologies." The Clovis and Solutrean flintknapping cultures developed over a very long period and carried deep intuitive meaning for their makers. Each step in the process—the strategy of removing thinning flakes, the spacing of individual flakes, how the flintknapper supports his work, the tools used to make tools, and so forth, is culturally specific. "If Solutrean and Clovis technologies were languages," says Bradley, "they would be like Portuguese and Spanish." Bradley suggests that the oldest artifacts in the Arctic and Siberia—from where the supposed ancestors of Clovis originated—are "to Clovis as Chinese is to Spanish! I have yet to hear any explanation of how one gets from Chinese to Spanish!" Skeptics, of course, question Bradley's analogy between stone tool making and grammar. For one thing, speakers of a language enjoy considerably more flexibility in forming words and syntax than does the flintknapper making a Clovis point (given the mechanical constraints involved).

To Bradley and Stanford technology is only a piece in the larger puzzle. Where Vance Haynes might see nine similarities in Clovis and Solutrean technologies, Bradley sees dozens of simple, artifact-level parallels. "I don't know what scale he is looking at," Bradley admits. As a parting shot, he adds, "If the French Solutrean were found in northeastern Asia, there would be nobody asking . . . whether Clovis was related."

Stanford wonders whether the European Solutrean people could have been adapted to a maritime economy and thus familiar with watercraft. "It wouldn't take too much for an intelligent person to learn how to handle the ocean and perhaps even get to North America," he suggests. But he also cautions that "this is really an off the wall kind of idea right now but it's one that I don't think we should ignore." Clovis people, says Stanford, were probably familiar with water travel. "If you look at the distribution of Clovis sites in the East, they seem to be associated with the large rivers and you can follow them up and down these rivers and I think it's a matter of time before we find a site where there are boats preserved." Stanford thinks that crossing the late Pleistocene oceans in a skin-covered boat is a possibility. While Haynes still favors the Bering Strait entry, he does admit that the French Connection is "not outrageous. The upper Paleolithic people of the Old World must have known boat technology pretty well. It's another working hypothesis to add to the hopper."

If any consensus can be said to exist among archaeologists, it would be that the earliest Americans were characterized by multiple origins and numerous migrations: by this view, late Ice Age America may have been the original melting pot.

LINGUISTIC PERSPECTIVES

The linguist Joseph Greenberg of Stanford University has analyzed sets of cognates (words held in common) in nearly every known American Indian language—a gargantuan task—in an effort to correlate language families with ancient migrations. He has concluded that Native Americans arrived in the New World in three distinct groups—speakers of the Amerind, Na-Dene, and Eskimo-Aleut language families—with the Eskimo-Aleut and Na-Dene populations arriving relatively recently.

This reconstruction suggests that the earliest wave of immigrants—the large "Amerind" language family—must have arrived about 12,000 years ago; Greenberg identified these as the people of the Clovis complex. These ancestral American Indians spread throughout most of the Americas and, according to Greenberg, gave rise to virtually all the indigenous languages spoken throughout the Western Hemisphere.

This model has come under heavy fire. One linguist called Greenberg's classification "distressing. . . . 'Amerind' is discounted by nearly all specialists." Others worry about how the individual languages were compared, how similarities due to language contact were filtered out, and the possibility of multilingualism among these groups. Why do linguistic differences necessarily reflect migration histories? Lingering questions such as these have made many wary of accepting the Greenberg's reconstructions of historical linguistics without solid archaeological support.

More recent linguistic research by Johannna Nichols, Professor of Slavic Languages at the University of California, Berkeley, suggests a different picture. Nichols defines a total of 143 Native American language stocks, each mutually unintelligible to all the others. Working from a premise that about 6,000 years are required for two languages to diverge sufficiently from a common ancestral tongue to become distinct, Nichols concludes that roughly

60,000 years would be needed for the 143 Native American language stocks to develop from a single ancestral language. Even allowing for multiple migrations, her calculations still require a minimum age of 35,000 years to account for Native American linguistic diversity.

When somebody pointed out that archaeologists have not found sites that old, Nichols shrugged, "As a linguist, that's not my problem."

MOLECULAR ARCHAEOLOGY

Like its parent discipline, molecular biology, the new field of molecular archaeology addresses the ultimate physiochemical organization of life, focusing on the molecular basis of human inheritance. Although not yet two decades old, molecular archaeology has already yielded unexpectedly precise answers to questions long explored through more conventional means.

This powerful approach began in 1984, when Allan Wilson and his research team at the University of California, Berkeley, became the first to identify genetic materials from old tissue. When they cloned DNA from the 140-year-old skin of quagga—a recently extinct African beast resembling a zebra—the Berkeley team showed the world that DNA could survive after the death of an organism. The next year, Swedish researcher Svante Pääbo cloned DNA from a 4,400-year-old Egyptian mummy. Not long thereafter, Pääbo pushed the barrier back still further by extracting ancient DNA from human brain tissue miraculously preserved at the Windover site in Florida.

Some 7,000 to 8,000 years ago, ancient Native Americans at Windover buried their dead in a spring that flowed through an ancient limestone sinkhole. Water levels fluctuated seasonally, with a maximum depth of less than 4 feet. In the soft bottom, deposits were preserved among the several distinct strata of peat—compact, dark brown organic material built up from the partial decay and carbonization of vegetation. In the mid-1980s, Glen Doran of Florida State University dug into these peat levels and found extremely well preserved skeletons. Some were even still held in place by large stakes, probably placed there at the time of burial to keep the bodies from floating to the surface.

The low oxygen level and neutral pH in such boggy conditions were also perfect for preserving soft tissue. More than 60 well-preserved human brains turned up at Windover, including the one used by Pääbo as his source of ancient DNA. Geneticists were particularly excited about the large numbers of brains because they provided the first chance to examine gene frequencies across an entire ancient population. Microbiologists at the University of Florida were surprised to find how little the genetic makeup of the Windover population had changed during the thousand years that the burial ground was used, possibly a sign of ancient inbreeding.

The work at Windover signaled the birth of molecular archaeology as a viable way to explore the human past. Molecular archaeologists have concentrated on "mitochondrial DNA (mtDNA)," the genetic material contained within the small energy-producing bodies found in each cell. So far, genetic comparisons of widely separated contemporary American Indian groups strongly suggest that these people diverged from a common genetic ancestor between 15,000 and 40,000 years ago.

Geographically, this divergence must have occurred after people entered the New World. Some molecular archaeologists believe that the initial group moving out of northeastern Asia into Alaska created a severe genetic "bottleneck"—a population so small that there is only limited genetic diversity among the descendants. Thus, they argue, the genetic differences between Asian and Native American populations must generally postdate this separation. Consequently, the genetic distance between populations becomes a valid estimator of the time elapsed since their initial migration. One early estimate placed this separation between 21,000 and 42,000 years ago.

Another recent study analyzed mitochondrial DNA samples from living people in seven linguistically related tribes in Central America (the so-called Chibcha speakers). Assuming that this homogeneous group separated from other American Indian tribes 8,000 to 10,000 years ago—obviously a whopping assumption—their mtDNA must have mutated at a rate of 2.2 percent per million years (which works out to 0.0022 to 0.0029 percent per 1,000 years—a very small quantity to gauge accurately). These same investigators then looked at mitochondrial DNA from 18 other tribes scattered throughout the Americas. Using the mutation rate they derived from the Chibcha speakers, they estimated how long ago all these tribes had diverged from a common ancestor. The answer turned out to be 22,000 to 29,000 years ago, once again suggesting a pre-Clovis presence in the Americas. Critics emphasize the degree to which these dates require an unconfirmed assumption: that the observed genetic diversity began *after* these tribes crossed the Bering land bridge into the New World. If instead the tribes split up someplace in Asia, then the biological clock would have begun ticking earlier.

Here the linguistic evidence becomes important. Following Greenberg's (admittedly controversial) language families, some molecular archaeologists have even argued that more than 95 percent of all Native Americans—the speakers of the Amerind languages—are descended from a single pioneering founder population that crossed the Bering Strait together in the late Ice Age. The same genetic evidence suggests that the Eskimo-Aleut and Na-Dene people, who are today mostly confined to the northern rim of North America, may derive from later migrations out of Asia, perhaps 7,500 years ago.

BY ANY SCIENTIFIC measure, American archaeology has made huge strides in understanding Indian origins since Thomas Jefferson dug into his Virginia burial mound. Dozens of key sites have been discovered and methodically excavated. Intricate theories had neen framed to account for the data, then discarded when contradictory evidence turned up. Increasingly sophisticated dating technology is allowing archaeologists to assign dates to previously undatable bones and artifacts. Increasingly precise geo-archaeological reconstructions demonstrate the nature of ancient American environments. Molecular archaeology has opened entirely new ways to approach biological variability without calling up obsolete nineteenth-century racial classifications.

Right now, almost everything relating to the First Americans seems to be up for grabs – an unsettling reality for textbook writers, but an unmistakably positive sign that archaeological scientists are doing their job—maintaining critical attitudes and avoiding the pitfalls of orthodoxy.

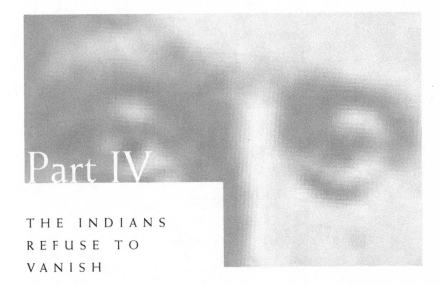

Part IV

THE INDIANS
REFUSE TO
VANISH

Not long before the Civil War a young cadet wrote an essay for his ethics class at West Point in which he lamented the coming death of what he called "a noble race," the Native Americans. The Indians were a vanishing race, he wrote, and he eulogized their death with sorrow and compassion.

That young cadet was George Armstrong Custer. He was wrong. It was he, not the Indians, who soon would vanish.

—Stan Steiner (1987)

"BE AN INDIAN AND KEEP COOL"

ON JULY 6, 1912, less than one year after Ishi stumbled out of the northern California chaparral, the straw-hatted United States Olympic contingent paraded into Stockholm Stadium, ready to battle the world's best athletes. American chances looked slim. The European sports community derided the American athletes as over-specialized mongrels, capable of excelling perhaps in one or two events, but not very good athletes overall. Some even stated publicly that, as castoffs from the continent, the Americans lacked the heart and eugenic fitness of world-class European athletes.

In an unprecedented move, the Scandinavian host countries successfully lobbied to introduce two new Olympic events, the pentathlon and decathlon, designed to showcase the all-around prowess of the Scandinavian athlete. Their homefield advantage secure, the northern European teams looked forward to embarrassing an outclassed American team.

"A REAL AMERICAN IF THERE EVER WAS ONE"

But the United States had a surprise of its own. Aboard the *SS Finlandia* as it steamed toward Stockholm, a solitary figure in khaki knickers and a cardigan sweater had spent his days running lap after lap under the watchful eye of Glenn "Pop" Warner, legendary football coach at the Carlisle Institute. Jim Thorpe, a Sauk and Fox Indian from the Oklahoma Territory, was coming to compete.

The Olympiad began with the pentathlon, a grueling five-event contest. Thorpe won four events the first day, scoring three times the points of his closest competitor and he easily captured the gold medal. Then, while other pentathletes recuperated, Thorpe entered the high jump and long jump, sharpening himself for the upcoming decathlon, to be held six days later. Thorpe won four decathlon events outright; his point total set an Olympic record that would stand for three dozen years. Moments after Thorpe won the final event, King Gustav V placed a laurel wreath on his head and presented him with his second gold medal, telling him "Sir, you are the greatest athlete in the world." The unassuming Thorpe replied simply, "Thanks, King."

One proud American writer crowed that the Indian's astounding triumph not only "answers the charge that Americans specialize in athletics. . . . It also answers the allegation that most of our runners are of foreign parentage for Thorpe is a real American if there ever was one." Thorpe returned home a hero, honored by ticker tape parades, banquets, theater parties, and laudatory speeches. He received a letter of congratulation from President William H. Taft, proclaiming, "Your victory will serve as an incentive to all to improve those qualities which characterize the best type of American citizenship."

Nobody recorded Thorpe's reaction to the President's praise, which today rings curiously hollow. A dozen years would pass before American Indians were granted United States citizenship.

INDIANS DISCOVER TWENTIETH-CENTURY AMERICA

Thorpe's Olympic victories came during a critical period of transition, when American Indians announced they were here to stay. Nobody knows how many were living in America in 1492. Although some scholars reckon there were about 18 million people in pre-Columbian North America, most prefer much lower figures—two million is widely accepted as reasonable. What is beyond dispute is the massive loss of life that resulted from European contact with the Americas. One count records only 237,000 Indians living in the United States in 1900. Since the dawn of the twentieth century, the Native American population has increased as dramatically as it had once fallen. In one century, the United States Indian population shot up by an amazing 555 percent. The myth of the Vanishing American turned out to be just that.

Native Americans of the early twentieth century set out to define new ways of interacting with the non-Indian world. "They saw avenues open before them for an *Indian* discovery of non-Indian America," writes Frederick Hoxie. "Discovery thus presented Indians with interests and public positions from which they could launch their own voyages of exploration. Those voyages, in turn, would help both tribal communities and the larger public define a path leading form the 'ancient way' to the twentieth century." Like all discoverers, Thorpe's generation named the objects and people they found from their own distinctive perspective, setting the terms of the new encounter and reversing a four-hundred-year history of Indians being defined as "discovered" objects. For the first time, a number of influential Indians took hold of their own imagery and turned it around for their own benefit.

"AT HOME ON EITHER SIDE OF THE BUCKSKIN CURTAIN"

Arthur C. Parker, one of America's leading Indian intellectuals of his time, wore many hats, some of them feathered. He was a folklorist, ethnologist, writer of children's books, historian, museum director, advocate for Indian rights, and American archaeologist of the first order.

Parker was born in western New York in 1881 on the Cattaraugus Reservation of the Seneca Nation. His great uncle was Ely S. Parker—Iroquois leader, engineer, military secretary to General Grant during the Civil War, and Lewis Henry Morgan's highly respected collaborator on *League of the Ho-de-no-sau-nee*. Arthur Parker's maternal grandmother was an Anglo New Englander whose Congregationalist family helped establish the local mission school. He grew up in a household that proudly mingled Indian and white values, where portraits of distinguished Seneca ancestors in Indian dress hung next to those of white New Englanders. Local Indian beadwork and arrowheads decorated the bookshelves, crammed with Devonian-age fossils from the rocky cliffs of Cattaraugus Creek—all collected from those secret places where Seneca elders told Parker the Little People live. He learned to hunt with bow and arrow and expressed an early interest in the natural history of the reservation. Parker spoke Seneca as a second language. Indian friends and relatives would spend long hours in the parlor, telling young Arthur the tribal stories and passing along the rich oral tradition of the Senecas.

When he was eleven, his parents moved to White Plains, an affluent suburb of New York City, and his life turned upside down. Young Parker missed his Cattaraugus homeland, but he pursued his childhood interest in natural history as best he could, spending considerable time at the American Museum of Natural History that was only an hour's train ride away. Put off by the antiquated exhibits, he wrangled his way behind the scenes, entering a world of "spicy dust and mothballs, but mostly of mystery and greatness." The curatorial staff befriended Parker and patiently identified his collections of artifacts, fossils, and birds' eggs.

"In the early nineties," Parker recalled, "I was permitted to examine the skeletal material at the American Museum of Natural History, to discuss the 'bones' with . . . Hrdlička and finally to have some systematic guidance from Professor F. W. Putnam." Although he studied for the ministry after graduating from public high school, Parker kept up his contacts with curators at the American Museum, particularly Putnam, one of America's most influential anthropologists and Alice Fletcher's mentor at Harvard.

The archaeologist Mark Harrington, one of "Putnam's boys," invited the fourteen-year-old Parker to join him on a dig at Long Island's Oyster Bay in 1903. Later that summer, they worked together digging on the Cattaraugus Reservation, an arrangement that worked well for both. Harrington's new assistant provided him access to the reservation, and Parker was proud of returning home in his new role of fledgling museum archaeologist.

This early dig experience convinced him to undertake a career in archaeology. This decision came at a fateful time, when museum-based anthropology faced competition from a more "academic," more "scientific" brand of anthropology being taught in the large universities. Aware of this shift, Parker deliberately chose the museum world, selecting the genial and outgoing Putnam as mentor over the "awesome," but icy Professor Boas at Columbia.

In 1904, Parker joined the New York state government as an ethnologist attached to the state library. The next year, he became the first State Archaeologist, affiliated with the New York State Museum in Albany. Digging at the Ripley site, an Erie Indian village and mortuary site in Chautauqua County, Parker excavated and analyzed dozens of human burials in 1906. His final report on the excavations has been called a landmark in the history of American archaeology—the first time an archaeologist had interpreted his excavation findings based on first-hand knowledge of local Indian life.

Parker became a leading museologist (a term he coined). Arguing that museums are "the university of the common man," Parker went on to become Director of the Rochester Institute of Science, New York State Indian Commissioner (1919-20), and in 1935 the first President of the Society for American Archaeology (SAA), the premier professional archaeological organization in North America.

Parker saw no conflict between his Seneca heritage and his professional responsibilities as an archaeologist. He used his influence as state archaeologist to help various Indian causes and excavated to help clear up disputed land titles. Drawing upon his expertise in physical anthropology, he often assisted homicide police. In one case, he determined that bones recovered by the police were not those of a murder victim but of an Iroquois leader who had been buried two centuries before. "We have been able to defend the Iroquois from harmful influence and notify them of impending legislation," Parker wrote. "That a museum of archaeology should do this is most fitting and demonstrates that we are capable of acting as an intermediary not only between the Indians of today and their past history, but between the Indian and the white man of today."

INDIANS AS TWENTIETH-CENTURY CULTURE BROKERS

Jim Thorpe and Arthur Parker, each in his own way, tried to span the social and racial gulfs between early twentieth-century Indians and non-Indians—Thorpe through his athletics and Parker through his museum-based anthropology. But there was a larger problem: If anthropologists like Boas and Kroeber were right, that learned culture mattered more than racial heritage, then what happens to a minority, Indian or otherwise, when that cultural behavior is modified? Are assimilated Indians still Indian?

Parker cared about his Indianness and thought it important to transmit this knowledge to white America. He transformed himself into a tribal storyteller, somebody whose knowledge of the past provided a unique twist on the present. He stepped beyond tribal distinctiveness, drawing upon a body of pan-Indian knowledge to counteract negative stereotypes and imagery. Parker emphasized the positives in conventional Indian symbolism to defend native people from early twentieth-century attacks by educators, missionaries, bureaucrats, land-grabbers—and anthropologists arguing for the destruction of "tribalism."

In a classic comment, Parker offered this advice for those seeking to escape the blistering July heat of urban America:

> Be an Indian and keep cool. Are you tired of work and sick of the city? What's the answer? Simply be an Indian—cut out the work and take the first trail for the timber. Nobody knows how to enjoy the big outdoors like an uncontaminated redskin and no one better likes a prolonged vacation. Take your cue from the kids on the street. The boys know no greater delight than to play Indian and even the girls dress up like Red Wings and Mineehahas. It's natural to be an Indian in this country, so the scientists say, and the sooner imported Americans understand this the sooner the race will be improved.

Accepted that America had long viewed her Indians as symbols, "Parker did not hesitate to don a literary headdress," writes Philip Deloria, "in order to challenge and redirect American constructions of Indianness."

In 1911, Parker joined Francis La Flesche and several other self-made Indian intellectuals to establish the Society of American Indians (SAI), the first formally chartered Indian organization in America. A succession of Indian-based national organizations, including the American Indian Association (founded in 1922) and the National Congress of American Indians (established in 1944), tried to enlighten the American public about Indian culture, preserve native cultural values, and promote legal protection for tribal treaty-rights.

Patterned after Euroamerican reform groups such as the Lake Mohonk Conference, the Society of American Indians advanced a national rather than tribal agenda, promoting self-help, personal enterprise, education and the breakup of the reservation system as critical to Indian success in America. They criticized Indians who went "back to the blanket," slipping back into a traditional culture the SAI saw as "clannish" and regressive. Parker spoke for the SAI leadership when he wrote that "the true aim of educational effort should not be to make the Indian a white man, but simply a man normal to his environment. . . . No nation can afford to permit any person or body of people within it to exist in a condition at variance with the ideals of that nation. . . . The Indian should accustom himself to the culture that engulfs him . . . developing the great ideals of his race for the good of the greater race, which means all mankind."

The SAI was heavily influenced by the anthropological ideas of the day.

Parker, La Flesche, and several other founding members were trained professional anthropologists, and a number of ethnographers joined the SAI as non-
voting (that is, non-Indian) members. Although Boas had begun his
two-pronged campaigns against racial determinism and unilineal evolution,
his message was not picked up by the SAI, whose leaders were steeped in
Morgan's theories of social evolution. Sounding every inch like the social
Darwinist he was, Sherman Coolidge, founding president of the SAI, argued
that "we have reached a time when the white people are pretty well educated
to the fact that the Indian can be civilized, can be Christianized, can be a
good man."

Parker was also raised with the doctrine of racial determinism, which was
incorporated into the platform of the SAI. To Parker, racial consciousness
formed the rationale for a national, pan-Indian identity. "Today there is a
growing consciousness of race existence," he wrote. "Today as perhaps never
before all men of the aboriginal peoples feel themselves members of the red
race or of aboriginal ancestry. No man should seek to destroy the special genius that race ancestry gives him. The God of nations did not give races distinctive racial endowments and characteristics for naught. And now, with a
coming race-consciousness the American Indian seeks to go even further and
say, 'I am not a red man only, I am an American in the truest sense, and a
brother man to all human kind."

This was a time when many saw America as struggling to maintain its
identity in the face of large numbers of European immigrants. The melting
pot concept was seen as critical in breaking down the new cultural diversity
and converting the new immigrants into productive, hard-working American
citizens. Parker not so discreetly played off his own authentic Indianness
against what he saw as the rootlessness of "imported Americans," races he
characterized as ignorant and artificial. Parker's racialist views reflected the
growing concern that immigrants were devaluing and diluting the American
spirit. If these unlettered immigrant newcomers were ever to help America,
Parker argued, a week of camping and "living like an Indian" under the tute-
lage of real Indian counselors might be just what they needed.

THE POWER OF INDIAN COSTUME

Since the days of the Boston Tea Party, non-Indians have found something in Indian dress that has helped them define and shape the national
identity. Both Morgan and Cushing promoted their science while dressed up

as Indians. By the 1920s, 30 million Americans were active members in 800 or so fraternal orders that incorporated Indian lore and costumes in their secret ceremonies. For these non-Indians, "real Indians" were those immortalized in Noble Redman imagery; mainstream Americans tended to see well-educated, middle class Indians like Arthur Parker as having lost their authenticity and, in the process, most of their appeal as Indians.

Indian people saw conflicting meanings in their traditional mode of dress. For Jim Thorpe—a direct descendant of legendary war chief Black Hawk—Indian costume and tradition were ways of capitalizing on his Indianness and his athletic prowess. As "the greatest gridiron warrior of all time," and one of the first professional superstars, Thorpe played out his Indianness on the football field. When a group of team owners established the National Football League in 1920, they unanimously elected Thorpe as its first president.

In 1922, Jim Thorpe helped establish the Oorang Indians, the world's first all-Indian pro football team. Although many thought "Oorang" was a tribal name, it was really just a made-up term that sounded Indian. But the players were all authentic Indians, and the press loved Indian names such as Wrinkle Meat, Bear Behind, Joe Little Twig, and Laughing Gas.

Each football game was an all-Indian showcase. After Coach Thorpe's pregame pep talk, the Oorangs roared onto the field, war bonnets and buckskins concealing their football uniforms. At halftime, the Oorang players pulled on their Indian garb to stage their halftime spectacle. Some players demonstrated fancy tomahawk and knife throwing, while others did rope tricks and Indian dances. Thorpe's Indians tracked live raccoons and coyotes, occasionally even treeing a black bear; and if time permitted, Long Time Sleep wrestled the bear.

Throughout their brief and colorful history, the Oorang Indians drew sellout crowds and provided the fledgling National Football League with a badly needed public relations boost. The curious amalgam of imagery—the Noble Redmen, the proud warriors, the Wild West Show in cleats—provided what one writer called "a kind of whoopee-cushion comic relief." Incredibly, the imagery took in some of the country's leading sport writers who despite the team's only average won-lost record speculated that perhaps the Oorang Indians were the greatest football team ever assembled.

Omaha scholar Francis La Flesche took a different road, believing that the early twentieth-century Indian was best presented in "civilized" dress because "the paint, feathers, robes and other articles that make up the dress of the Indian, are marks of savagery to the European, and he who wears them however appropriate or significant they might be to himself, finds it difficult to lay claim to a share in common human nature."

One chairman of the Hopi tribe took still another view. Emphasizing the degree to which treaty-guaranteed rights to lands and services were grounded in the stereotypes of the period in which the treaties were signed, he argued that these images—misleading as they were—must be preserved to convince Congress to ensure those rights not protected directly by the Constitution. Should Indians become indistinguishable from whites, Congress might begin to assume that assimilation was complete, and step away from defending the treaty-guaranteed rights. "Is [our sovereignty recognized] simply because we look like Indians, we speak our language, we live like Indians?" he asked. "Once that's all gone, we are part of the mainstream of society." To dress, live, and speak like a native was critical to the continued sovereignty and survival of the Hopi people.

19.

AN INDIAN NEW DEAL: FROM ABSOLUTE DEPRIVATION TO MERE POVERTY

> *It may be hard for us to understand why these Indians cling so tena-*
> *ciously to their lands and traditional tribal way of life. The record*
> *does not leave the impression that the lands are the most fertile, the*
> *landscape the most beautiful or their homes the most splendid examples*
> *of architecture. But this is their home—their ancestral home. There*
> *they, their children and their forebears were born. They, too, have their*
> *memories and their loves. Some things are worth more than the costs of*
> *a new enterprise.*
>
> —*United State Supreme Court Decision,*
> *Federal Power Commission v. Tuscarora Indian Nation (1960)*

JOHN COLLIER GREW up a miserable child in Georgia. His mother died young and his father killed himself. He spent his early life searching for meaning, he wrote years later, but found mostly disenchantment.

Professionally trained as a social worker, Collier spent a difficult dozen years in New York City's settlement houses, futilely trying to establish community organizations that would localize political, economic, and cultural decision-making. Then, fed up with this gritty and thankless existence, he made his way westward to help Pacific Coast immigrants and migrant workers, only to run afoul of the California government during the "Red scare" of 1920s, when anyone trying to help the poor was considered a possible anarchist or Bolshevik.

Collier ended up in New Mexico, where he ran head-on into the Noble Redman. At Taos Pueblo, the bohemian reformer found his American ideal— "a magical habitation full of magical people." The Pueblo people of Taos lived lives vastly different from his own, and Collier believed he'd found an Indian culture ethically and aesthetically superior to that of mainstream America. Collier saw in this Indian heritage an ancient-yet-contemporary counterbalance to the dismal urban world dominated by machines and bureaucrats. He had finally found his lifework: America's native cultures were clearly worth saving, and he was the one to save them. "They had what the world had lost," Collier wrote, and "what the world has lost, the world must have again, lest it die."

PUEBLO INDIANS TAKE ON WALL STREET

The Pueblo people had long been a legal anomaly set apart from the other Indian tribes of America. In *United States v. Joseph*, the Supreme Court had ruled, in 1876, that the Pueblo Indians were neither bound nor protected by federal restrictions relating to tribal lands. But by the 1920s, the Pueblos were in trouble. Thousands of trespassers had stolen their lands, and because of the 1876 ruling, they had no recourse to government protection. In fact, the federal government was itself carving out sections of tribal holdings for its own use, even seizing Blue Lake, the ancient sacred site of the Taos people. Time after time, tribal leaders asked the federal government to restore their traditional land.

When New Mexico became a state in 1912, the enabling legislation specifically spelled out that the Indians in that state owned their own land. This meant that the Pueblo Indians now enjoyed the same legal status as tribes throughout the rest of America, and, in *United States v. Sandoval* (1913), the Supreme Court formally recognized this extension of federal control over New Mexico's Indians (thereby nullifying the earlier *Joseph* decision). Although this ruling should have returned Blue Lake to Indian hands, the Interior Department took exception and enlisted the help of New Mexico Senator Holm Bursum, who sponsored legislation that would grant non-Indian claims on more than sixty thousand acres of Pueblo land—thereby undermining both tribal autonomy and the Pueblo land-base.

In 1922, the All Pueblo Council drafted a position paper that spoke for many Indian groups: they had lived "in a civilized condition before the white man came to America," and they appealed to the sense of decency and fair-play of mainstream Americans to help them preserve "everything we hold dear—our lands, our customs, our traditions." For the first time since their successful 1680 revolt against Spanish rule, individual Pueblo tribes banded together to defeat the Bursum Bill. In 1923, a delegation of Pueblo leaders visited New York City to seek support in their battle. Wrapped in their traditional blankets, befeathered Pueblos sang and drummed their way onto the floor of the New York Stock Exchange. The businessmen—many seeing "real" Indians for the first time—joined their cause in droves, flooding Congress with supportive telegrams.

By that time, Collier was employed by the General Federation of Women's Clubs, working as a field representative for the Indian Welfare Committee. Collier rallied the two million members of federation to join the fight against the Bursum bill. He also organized the American Indian Defense Association in 1923 as another response to the Pueblo crisis. The battle over the Bursum Bill was Collier's entree into national-level politics and he loved it. Lobbying ferociously on behalf of Pueblo Indians, Collier also helped craft a Pueblo Lands Board to save other Indian lands.

The Bursum Bill was roundly defeated by a visceral, gut-level response to real Indian people. Playing up their own Indianness, the Pueblos aroused a deeper kind of support, sometimes based on images and symbols, if not always reality. The myth of the Vanishing Savage was in full retreat, replaced by individual Indians and tribes actively staking out a future for themselves.

COLLIER HUMANIZES THE BUREAU OF INDIAN AFFAIRS

Like the miner's canary, the Indian marks the shift from fresh air to poisoned air to our political atmosphere; and our treatment of Indians, even more than our treatment of other minorities, marks the rise and fall of our democratic faith.

—*Felix Cohen (1942), Attorney*

In 1923, an elite panel known as the "Committee of 100" convened to advise on federal Indian policy. Although their report supported assimilation as a general goal, it also called for greater sensitivity to Indian customs and urged Congress to protect tribal land. The federal government followed up three years later by commissioning the respected and nonpolitical Brookings Institute to undertake a thorough study of Indian policy. Its 1928 report, commonly called the Meriam Report, was highly critical of previous government policy, condemning the Dawes Act of 1887 as a thinly disguised plot to separate Indian people from their land. It also urged that tribal governments be formally incorporated, that Indian boarding schools be closed, and that federal policy be redirected to promote cultural pluralism in lieu of assimilation.

Collier hailed the Meriam Report as evidence that Indian tribes were in desperate straits. Having established his *bona fides* as an advocate for Indian America, he argued that the Bureau of Indian Affairs should be safeguarding Indian interests rather than dismantling the tribal land-base. In 1929, the Senate ordered an investigation of its own, and for three years, Collier led delegations of senators to most of the major Indian reservations. They were appalled at what they saw.

Margaret Mead agreed. With her husband Reo Fortune, she conducted a three-month study of Omaha Indians during the summer of 1930. "It was a devastating experience for both of us," she later recounted in her autobiography, *Blackberry Winter.* "We had both worked in living cultures [of the Pacific Islands] . . . but this was a culture so shrunk from its earlier style, from the time when the Omaha had been buffalo-hunting Plains Indians, that there was very little out of the past that was recognizable, and still less in the present that was aesthetically satisfying." Mead saw the reservation as "infuriating and depressing" and came away from her Omaha fieldwork with" . . . the dismal sense that the people were going backward . . . Drunkenness was rife. Broken homes, neglected children, and general social disorganization were evident everywhere . . . I had the unrewarding task of discussing a long history of mistakes in American policy toward the Indians [and] prophesying a still more disastrous fate for them in the future." Although the allotments encouraged by Fletcher were supposed to set the stage for family-based agricultural economy, farming never really took hold among the Omaha, and Mead documented the aftermath of a failed policy.

The Omaha, of course, had been the pioneering effort to establish land allotment as federal policy. During the Great Depression, the failure of the Dawes Act of 1887 was starkly evident nationwide. When the legislation was passed fewer than 5,000 American Indians were landless; four decades later, when Mead visited the Omaha, that number had risen to 100,000. The statistics for land loss under allotment were even more alarming, as emphasized by Congressman Edward Howard in 1934: "In 1887 our Indian wards numbered 243,000. They owned 137,000,000 acres of land, more than one-third good farming land and a considerable portion of valuable timberlands. Today they number about 200,000. Their land holding has shrunk to a mere 47,000,000 acres . . . almost one-half [of which is] desert or semiarid lands of limited use or value." In 1887 the Indian trust fund totaled $29 million; yet despite the addition of $500 million dollars during intervening years, the Indian trust had shrunk to $13.5 million by 1934. The annual death rate for Indians in 1887 was about eighteen per thousand; by 1934, it had climbed to twenty-six per thousand—more than twice the death rate of the general population.

When Franklin Delano Roosevelt won the 1932 election, 15 million Americans were unemployed and the country cried out for reform and change. Shortly after his election, Roosevelt received a letter signed by six hundred educators, urging his immediate attention to the dreadful circumstances in Indian Country, where the level of poverty verged on starvation, the illiteracy rate had reached 30 percent, and more than 90 million acres of tribal land had recently been lost: "We do not believe we are exaggerating when we suggest that your administration represents almost a last chance for the Indians."

A month after President Roosevelt took office, John Collier's controversial appointment as Commissioner of Indian Affairs was confirmed by Congress. Harold L. Ickes, FDR's new Secretary of the Interior, supported Collier against his critics: "I do believe . . . that no one exceeds him in knowledge of Indian matters or his sympathy with the point of view of the Indians themselves. I want someone in that office who is the advocate of the Indians. The whites can take care of themselves, but the Indians need some one to protect them from exploitation." After years of harassing the BIA, Collier now headed it—and his takeover signaled a major shift in federal philosophy toward Indians.

During his crusade against the Bursum Bill, Collier had solicited advice from both Franz Boas and Alfred Kroeber, asking their help in framing an Indian policy to restore tribal authority and cease the allotment policies from the Dawes Act era. An applied anthropology unit was formed in the Bureau of Indian Affairs, the BIA preferentially hired Indians, and Indian input was actively solicited at all levels. Collier's new administration reflected a new respect for Indian traditions, urging that Boasian-style cultural relativism be introduced into federal management plans at all levels.

Collier also brought Felix S. Cohen on board. Cohen, a lawyer who had been active in the American Indian Defense Fund, eventually became the country's foremost scholar on Indian law, which he synthesized in his monumental *Handbook of Federal Indian Law*. While at the BIA, Cohen helped Collier frame a major piece of legislation that reversed the assimilation policies of the past and reaffirmed the importance of the tribal concept. The resulting Indian Reorganization Act (IRA) of 1934 incorporated most of the recommendations of the Meriam Report, melded with many of Collier's own ideas.

Five decades later, Vine Deloria, Jr. would call the Indian Reorganization Act the "only bright spot in all Indian-Congressional relations." The IRA changed federal policy in several important ways, granting Indians the power to operate as tribal entities and restoring rights that had been systematically undercut since treaty-making was abandoned in 1871. By dismantling the Dawes Act, the IRA helped Indians retain their land base. It also set out a blueprint for establishing new tribal governments—with their own constitutions and extended powers—and helped foster a healthy economic base by encouraging Indian-owned businesses. No longer did the federal government assume that the Indians would simply vanish. Collier encouraged tribes to organize for their common welfare, to formally incorporate, and to adopt constitutions, by-laws, and law codes on the United States model. In so doing, the IRA imposed a federal structure on tribes, for the most part ignoring traditional self-governing institutions. In Deloria's view, the IRA helped the tribes move "from absolute deprivation to mere poverty."

Although marching in the long parade of Euroamericans who imposed their vision of Indians upon Indians— passionately wanting to help— Collier insisted on defining the terms, viewing Indian Country as his own "ethnic laboratory of universal meaning." He attacked social Darwinism, rejected Morgan's evolutionary sequences that culminated in Western civilization, and helped create a vision of a pluralistic American future, with Indian and mainstream cultures surviving side-by-side.

In framing the IRA, Collier drew upon his early experiences in the Pueblo Southwest, seeking to incorporate a Pueblo-style model of close-knit communalism in national Indian policy. In this, the culmination of the Roosevelt administration's "Indian New Deal," Congress did not formally abandon assimilation as a goal, but it transferred considerable authority to tribal governments. Whereas the Dawes act had attempted to replace native forms of government with eventual individual membership in the American body politic, Collier set up tribes as separate constitutional assemblies modeled on the U.S. government.

But when Collier convened a series of Indian congresses around the country to rally support for the bill, he encountered deep political splits between (and sometimes within) Indian tribes. To Collier's chagrin, many Indians wished to continue under the previous allotment policies. The Hoopas of California, for instance, rejected the Indian Reorganization Act because they wished to continue handing out small allotment tracts to tribal members.

Collier also learned that his draft plan for Indian reorganization sometimes conflicted with more traditional forms of government and with established treaty relations. The Seneca Nation was quite satisfied with its Treaty of Canandaigua, signed by George Washington in 1794. They had been guaranteed that they could elect their own government, and many Senecas saw the Indian Reorganization Act as threatening these guarantees. As Seneca leader Alice Jemison put it, the IRA "provides only one form of government for the Indian and that is a communal or cooperative form of living. John Collier said he was going to give the Indian self-government. If he was going to give us self-government he would let us set up a form of government we wanted to live under. He would give us the right to continue to live under our old tribal customs if we wanted to."

In 1933, Collier traveled to the Rosebud Reservation in North Dakota to explain his Indian New Deal to Sioux representatives. "The present administration is not merely willing for you to govern yourselves," Collier told them, "We are determined that you shall and must do it if we have the power to insist." He soon found that the Lakota living on the Pine Ridge and Rosebud reservations had their own ideas about what self-determination might look like. Some enthusiastically embraced the New Deal forms of self-government, arguing that the IRA-style constitution established workable tribal councils to govern the reservations. The so-called "old dealers" questioned the authority of the New Deal councils, arguing that traditional tribal leadership would be taken over by educated, but largely landless mixed-bloods. Collier's "decoloniation" created a legacy conflict that is being played out to this day.

Collier's reign at the BIA has been called a complex mix of "good intentions and ironic results, of a simple vision crashing into a complex reality." Traditional Indians from almost all tribes strongly criticized the new tribal organizations, but according to Vine Deloria, Jr. and Clifford Lytle, "many of the old customs and traditions . . . had vanished during the interim period since the tribes had gone to the reservations. The experience of self-government according to Indian traditions had eroded and, while the new constitutions were akin to the traditions of some tribes, they were completely foreign to others."

While sometimes imperfect, the new tribal constitutions provided for self-government by Indian residents on the reservations, prohibited further breakup of Indian land, and provided for land consolidation programs by tribal councils. "The Indian New Deal wasn't perfect," writes John Echo-Hawk, Director of the Native American Rights Fund, "but its results were fundamentally beneficial for Indian people. The Indian Reorganization Act reversed the direction of American Indian policy." The pattern of history changed from the erosion of Indian sovereignty to its restoration and revival.

Collier's experience characterizes, to some degree, the paradox faced by non-Indians—politicians, lawyers, historians, and even archaeologists—who try to "help the Indians:" There are few successful roadmaps to follow. "Helping Indians" smacks of the paternalistic intrusions that Collier so wanted to avoid yet couldn't. Should the non-Indian just back off and leave well enough alone in Indian Country?

Do the various tribal governments established under the Indian Reorganization Act genuinely represent their respective tribes, or are they puppet governments run for a select few? Whatever the answer, Collier established the tribal structure that would politically define Indian Country from that time forward—a fact that, six decades later, would have a major impact on reburial legislation.

TRIBAL SOVEREIGNTY REINFORCED AND REDEFINED

The IRA gave native tribes a distinct voice in Indian politics and redefined the nature of sovereign relationships between Indian tribes and the United States government. "That is, such rights were not *granted* by the United States as part of their guardian-ward relationships," emphasizes Philip Deloria, "but had been *retained* by the tribes through their treaties."

The IRA reiterated and reinforced the principle, established by court decisions a century before, that many Indian tribes have powers equal to those of the states, yet remain subordinate to the federal government. In his landmark judicial ruling of 1831, Chief Justice Marshall recognized Indian tribes as "distinct, independent, political communities." In so ruling, Chief Justice

Marshall likened the relationship between the federal government and Indians to that between guardian and ward: a tribe has some aspects of national sovereignty and retains certain rights—those of a childlike ward—that are protected by the "parental" United States government. Despite the fact that the Supreme Court has continually reaffirmed the concept that Indian tribes should be treated as nations foreign to the United States both culturally and politically, it remains difficult for most Americans to understand this principle. This is why many people mistakenly continue to view Indians as simply another racial minority.

As Deloria and Lytle write in *The Nations Within*, "American Indians are unique in the world . . . they represent the only aboriginal peoples still practicing a form of self-government in the midst of a wholly new and modern civilization that has been transported to their lands." The United States government had assumed a broad authority in dealing with a tribe and its interests, including an obligation to protect that tribe from an invasion by third parties (including individual states). Congress retained exclusive power to regulate commerce with foreign nations—and with Indian tribes. None of the fifty states has inherent power to deal with Indians at all. This is why Tim Giago, publisher of *Indian Country Today*, equates state legislation affecting Indians with "letting France make laws that also become law in Italy."

Throughout his term as Indian Commissioner, Collier continued to alienate many in Congress, reflecting a nationwide debate over policies between those favoring total Indian assimilation and those encouraging cultural pluralism. With the onset of war, Congress underfunded and weakened the Indian reorganization program and, in 1945, Collier resigned.

Today's tribal governments are almost entirely a twentieth-century invention—largely the brainchild of John Collier—but the very concept of tribal sovereignty implies a direct continuity over long periods of time. As Philip Deloria puts it, tribal sovereignty" is, after all, a recognition in law of the fact that Indian societies were here first."

THE TERMINATION BACKLASH: FROM AMERICAN INDIANS TO INDIAN AMERICAN

America took a distinctly conservative turn in post-World War II America. Traditional Indian-style "communalism" smelled to some like *communism*, and a McCarthy-conscious Congress took aim at the Bureau of Indian Affairs appropriations. In its fervor to fight communism on the homefront, Congress began to suspect that perhaps one red was just like another. This conservative philosophy arrived at the BIA in the person of Dillon S. Myer, who became Commissioner in 1950. Myer had achieved national prominence as Director of the War Relocation Authority (1942–1946), where he was responsible for operating, then dismantling the Japanese-American relocation centers. Myer saw distinct parallels between the two jobs: both Japanese internment camps and Indian reservations were established as short-term facilities to incarcerate the inmates. Once the reason for incarceration was gone, the facilities should be phased out as rapidly as possible. Supported by Presidents Truman, Eisenhower, and a powerful bloc of conservative congressmen known as the "terminationists," Myer set out his plan to terminate the Indian reservation system by selecting tribes adequately assimilated and sending them on their way.

In 1952, Indian Commissioner Myer sent a memo to all BIA employees saying that he was reversing Collier's efforts to preserve tribal land, culture, and Indian autonomy: "I want to emphasize that withdrawal program formulation and effectuation is to be a cooperative effort of Indian and community groups affected, side by side, with Bureau personnel. We must lend every encouragement to Indian initiative and leadership." Myer also added, ominously, "I realize that this will not be possible always to obtain Indian cooperation . . . We must proceed even though Indian cooperation may be lacking in certain cases." It was about this point that Harold Ickes called Myers "a Hitler and Mussolini rolled into one."

The Eisenhower administration apparently forgot the past failures associated with Indian assimilation and wanted to turn the Indians loose to fend for themselves. The basic thinking was pretty easy to follow (if only because it was so familiar): if we integrate Indians *as individual Americans*, then the federal government can once and for all get off the reservation. Like the Dawes advocates decades earlier, those supporting termination said they were "liberating" Indians from meddlesome government interference and, in the process, saving some dollars from the burgeoning Indian budget. This policy was implemented by Congress in 1953 in legislation called House Concurrent Resolution 108 and Public Law 280. Throughout Indian Country, it was known simply as "termination"—the day when America's Indian tribes got the pink slip.

Under the conservative leadership of Senator Arthur V. Watkins of Utah, Congress met in joint sessions to begin the termination process. "Watkins' idea was to get rid of as many tribes as possible before the 1956 elections," says Deloria. "He feared that if the Great Golfer were not reelected the movement would be stopped by a President who might pay attention to what was happening in the world around him."

House Concurrent Resolution 108 eventually mandated termination of federal responsibility over all the Indians of California, Florida, Iowa, New York, and Texas, plus the Klamath, Menominee, Flathead, Osage, Potawatomi of Kansas and Nebraska, and the Turtle Mountain Band of Chippewa. Senator Watkins started termination proceedings at home, focusing on several small Paiute bands in southern Utah. Because the Paiutes were too poor to attend the hearings in Washington, they only belatedly learned that they had been "freed from Federal supervision and control." Federal termination meant that tribal property would be divided among enrolled members and their long-term relations with the federal government were severed. They were no longer exempt from federal taxes and they became subject to state laws.

Perhaps the most publicized termination case involved the Menominee Tribe of northeastern Wisconsin. Their successful forestry operation and lumber mills not only employed a large proportion of the tribe, but it enabled the Menominee tribal government to pay for most of their own services; on the eve of termination, the total federal cost of the Menominee tribe to the federal government was $144,000 (roughly $51/Indian). Because they presented an image of moderate prosperity—and most tribal members were literate in English—the Menominees became prime candidates for termination.

President Eisenhower signed the Menominee termination act on June 17, 1954, authorizing a payment of $1,500 to each tribal member. They set December 31, 1958, as the effective termination date, after which Menominee tribal members were no longer eligible for federal services provided to Indians; they were, instead, subject to the laws of the state of Wisconsin.

Virtually overnight, the termination policy turned the Menominee from a tolerably successful Indian reservation into Wisconsin's poorest county. The tribal economy collapsed with the federal pullout, as the Menominee found themselves unable to compete without the tax exemptions and federal services previously provided. The tribe could not afford its health program, and the Menominee hospital quickly shut down (after which infant mortality shot up and tuberculosis became a major health menace). Educational problems soon developed and within six years of tribal termination 14 percent of Menominee County was on welfare. The State of Wisconsin estimated that the county needed a transfusion of $10 to $20 million just to bring it up to the standards of the other Wisconsin counties. The federal War on Poverty was eventually forced to step in, pouring in millions to keep Menominee County afloat.

The two thousand Klamaths living on the timber-rich Siletz and Grand Ronde reservations in Oregon were next, phased out in August 1954. Said Congress: "It is our belief that the Klamath Tribe and the individual members thereof have in general attained sufficient skill and ability to manage their own affairs without special Federal assistance." Because Congress wanted to terminate the Klamath tribe as quickly as possible, the hastily drafted legislation inadvertently mandated the immediate clear-cutting of $80 million worth of timber. When somebody explained to the Senate and House Committee members that clear-cutting would drop enough timber onto the Oregon economy to destroy the local economy, the legislation was quickly amended. Such was the frenzy attending the tribal termination movement in the early 1950s.

For their part, the Klamath tribe was sharply factionalized over termination. Wade Crawford (once the superintendent under Collier) led one faction, which actually lobbied for the termination of the tribe; those choosing this path received a per capita payout of $43,000 each in 1961. Those who remained in the tribe (by retaining shares in a corporate trust until 1975) received a payout of about $150,000 each. In return for terminating their tribe, the Klamaths lost their federal recognition and their federal health and education programs. The Native American community also commonly considered them outcasts.

Tribal termination resulted in a wholesale relocation of Indian people from reservations into urban enclaves—a shift supported by job training and employment counseling that was designed to get them "off the blanket" and onto mainstreet America. Indian enclaves grew up in all major American cities, and the Bureau of Indian Affairs promoted an urban version of Indian assimilation designed to eliminate the remnants of the tribal structures.

In the 1960s, the Area Redevelopment Administration, authorized by Congress to fulfill President John Kennedy's promise to revitalize Appalachia (West Virginia), made Indian reservations eligible for grants. Indians asked why the U. S. government wanted to invest money in constructing community halls and tribal offices, when tribal "termination" remained the official federal policy. Richard Nixon formally closed the door on termination in 1970.

THE RED POWER OF
VINE DELORIA, JR.

20.

Had the tribes been given the choice of fighting the cavalry or the anthropologists, there is little doubt as to whom they would have chosen ... A warrior killed in battle could always go to the Happy Hunting Grounds. Where does an Indian laid low by an anthro go? To the library?

—*Vine Deloria, Jr.* (1988)

THE 1971 DIG in Welch, Minnesota, was going pretty much like all others, mostly dust and discouragement, but the students still felt lucky to be there. They slaved for weeks, learning to move dirt scientifically. They dug in square pits, wrote detailed fieldnotes, and took routine photographs. They screened everything, picking out even the tiniest bones and artifacts. They catalogued and classified, looking for clues to what life had been like in the ancient Indian village that once stood here.

Then the Indians showed up. Representing a new protest group called "AIM"—the American Indian Movement—they confiscated excavation equipment, burned the fieldnotes, and backfilled the excavation trenches. Clyde Bellecourt, their leader, announced that the Indians of Minnesota were deeply offended because archaeologists were disturbing graves of their ancestors. No more digging would be permitted.

Then, like the dress-up Mohawks at the Boston Tea Party, the Indians from AIM offered to pay for any damage caused by their protest.

The archaeologists, shocked and irritated, complained about "five weeks of work down the drain." Tears welled up in one student's eyes as she explained how careful they had been. Another excavator, preparing for a career in archaeology, said that the activists had made her lose respect for all Indian people and that these citified Indians were simply ignorant about their own past. A third said that the Indians just did not understand—archaeologists are "trying to preserve Indian culture, not destroy it." The AIM radicals did not care what the archaeologists said. They couldn't see how archaeologists were showing respect to Indian people by digging up their dead ancestors.

Russell Means, the self-described "most controversial Indian leader of our time," remembers his first glimpse of AIM Indians. "I couldn't help notice the way they were dressed and their haircuts—parted on one side and combed into waves falling across the other side, the way Indian boarding-school students had once been forced to wear their hair. They wore beaded belts, sashes, chokers, moccasins, headbands, and lots of Indian jewelry. I thought, what are they trying to prove? Those guys looked ridiculous, all dressed up like Indians. I asked somebody, 'Who are those guys?' 'They're from the American Indian Movement in Minneapolis,' he answered."

Unlike the Boston Tea Party, the Minnesota protest was staged by real Indians—dressed up like real Indians. Their mostly peaceful acts of civil disobedience illustrated a deep dissatisfaction with the Federal government and their own lack of representation. In the 1971 Minnesota confrontation, the Indians of AIM were reestablishing claims on their own heritage, showing the world that Indians were very much alive.

DID CUSTER DIE FOR YOUR SINS?

Any of the Minnesota students with a current issue of *Playboy* stashed under the mattress could have spotted the next incoming round. Those who were mystified that protest against white domination targeted an innocent archaeological dig would soon have the mystery cleared up. Vine Deloria, Jr., a Standing Rock Sioux law student had just published an extract from his soon-to-be-released blockbuster, provocatively entitled *Custer Died for Your Sins: An Indian Manifesto*. Deloria's book exploded on the scene in 1969—trashing academics, missionaries, Congress, the Bureau of Indian Affairs, and most other non-Indians who frequented Indian Country.

Particularly stinging was Deloria's Chapter 4—"Anthropologists and Other Friends"—a humorous, take-no-prisoners indictment of anthropological research in Indian country. In Deloria's hands, the term "anthro" became a clever slur, soon to be picked up by angry young Indians across the land (some of whom had never actually encountered an anthro first-hand). To Deloria, the Anthro-American was a meddlesome academic who "infests the land of the free, and in the summer time, the homes of the braves."

"Indians," Deloria teased, "are . . . certain that Columbus brought anthropologists on his ships when he came to the New World. How else could he have made so many wrong decisions about where he was?" He also suggested that, like religious missionaries, anthros were "tolerably certain that they represent ultimate truth" when they set themselves up as the authoritative sources on tribal cultures. He questioned how they had become the custodians of the Indian past.

Deep down, said Deloria, anthros are motivated mostly to climb the academic totem pole. "Reduction of people to ciphers for purposes of observation apparently appears to be inconsequential to the anthropologist compared with the immediate benefits he can derive, the production of further prestige, and the chance to appear as the high priest of American society, orienting and manipulating to his heart's desire." Archaeologists carted off Indian bones and artifacts to faraway museums and wrote complex ethnographies and site reports that were intrusive, irrelevant, and insulting to Indian people. All "amateur" inquiry—research that did not fit this absurd world and therefore was not sanctioned by the academy—was frowned upon and derided.

Furthermore, Deloria argued, anthropology's commitment to "pure research" had forced Indian tribes into unfair competition with academics for funding from private foundations and federal agencies. Anthropological research was especially wasteful, he said, because the "scholarly productions are so useless and irrelevant to real life." Deloria's anthros dwelt only on the past, seeking "authenticity" and ignoring the interests of modern Indian people. Archaeologists in particular were perpetuating myths and images that had structured white perceptions of Indian people for centuries. For them, the only good Indians were the dead ones. He challenged anthropologists to "get down from their thrones of authority and PURE research and begin helping Indian tribes instead of preying on them."

Deloria was infuriated at the anthropologists' silence during those critical days in 1954, when Congress was terminating federal services to Indians. Why, he asked, should Indians maintain an ethnographic zoo for the professional pleasure of academics that had so miserably failed to support tribal interests? After decades of "pure research" on the reservations, why couldn't the anthros have said *something* in support of Indian rights?

Deloria clearly expressed his view that the so-called "alliance" between anthropologists and Indians had long been imbalanced and contradictory. He brought up anthropology's long-term colonial associations and scoffed at the anthropologists' claim of scientific objectivity. Deloria branded archaeologists as exploiters of Indian people, accused them of perpetuating long-standing Indian stereotypes, and asked them to stop digging up his ancestors.

RED POWER ON ALCATRAZ

Custer Died For Your Sins and the American Indian Movement were hardly the first time Indians had spoken out on their own behalf. While the bloody military campaigns involving freedom-fighters like Sitting Bull and Geronimo remain the best-known Indian response to the white invasion, native people of the nineteenth century resisted mainstream domination in multiple ways: Sequoyah developed his own syllabary to publish a newspaper and books in Cherokee; Paviotso Paiute Sarah Winnemucca spoke on the East Coast lecture circuit to promote the well-being of her people; Wanapum medicine man Smohalla and Paiute prophet Wovoka promoted their visionary message of salvation in the famous Ghost Dances of 1870 and 1890; and Arthur Parker had helped establish the Society of American Indians in 1911. Each one in his or her own way promoted pan-tribal resistance to exploitation by outsiders.

The termination debacle of the 1950s had brought a new unity of Indian purpose, sparking a number of Indian protests and conferences that emphasized the need to protect the tribal land base and promote cultural pluralism in the United States. By the 1960s, Indian activists had a track record of successful social protest. The Indian fish-ins of the Pacific Northwest and the successful fight by Taos Pueblo for the return of sacred Blue Lake typified a focus on measured, obtainable goals with clear-cut solutions. When Vine Deloria Jr. was selected as executive director of the National Congress of American Indians (NCAI) in 1964, he called for qualified Indians with the necessary skills to assure the success of federal social and economic programs in bringing prosperity to Indian Country.

The skyrocketing urban Indian population, fostered in large measure as a byproduct of termination, brought large numbers of native people in contact with the militant wing of the 1960s civil rights movement. The American Indian Movement was formed initially in response to police brutality in urban Minneapolis. AIM members patrolled the streets in a media-based counterattack, documenting with cameras episodes of police brutality against Indians. These emergent Red Power advocates joined forces with broader civil rights concerns. The largely reservation-based constituency of the NCAI, on the other hand, had problems with the urban activists and their confrontation politics, and a split of sorts developed between the two perspectives. Deloria warned in *Custer* against merging Indian concerns with the broader civil rights movements, but the off-reservation factions continued to build ties with black militant groups.

The 1968 Poor People's March on Washington drove a wedge between moderate and militant Indians. In November 1969, a group calling themselves "Indians of All Nations" began a 19-month occupation of Alcatraz Island, in the middle of San Francisco Bay. Millions of Bay Area residents saw "The Rock" daily, and headlines across the nation made Alcatraz ground zero for the growing Red Power movement.

Four months after the Alcatraz takeover, Deloria told a reporter that while he was not against militancy, he was against stupidity. He considered the occupation to be entirely irrelevant because the Alcatraz activists lacked any meaningful backup in Washington to effect real change. "You can sit on the rock for the next 100 years," Deloria warned, "but if you have nobody carrying that paper through the government agencies, then how do you expect to get title to it, see?" As the Alcatraz occupation dragged on, Deloria received a memorable call from the Nixon White House, ordering him to "get those Indians out of that prison or we'll throw them in jail!" As Indians observed at the time, without decent housing, water, or employment opportunities, Alcatraz looked more like an Indian reservation than the federal prisons then in service.

For Deloria, the Alcatraz takeover became "an Indian version of the Poor People's March," a symbolic protest with ill-defined goals and without specific solutions. The newspapers said that the Indians occupied Alcatraz because they were entitled to the island as a federal surplus property provision of the 1868 treaty of Fort Laramie. Calling this interpretation "a myth," Deloria said that the Alcatraz sit-in, "in legal terms . . . meant nothing." The NCAI had refused to endorse the Poor People's March because, in Deloria's words, its leaders were "unable to articulate specific solutions and see them through to completion."

According to historian Troy Johnson, AIM leadership entered the national scene only after visiting the Indian occupation of Alcatraz. They saw the power of the press, and how Indian imagery could be used to manipulate it. They also realized the reluctance of federal bureaucrats to punish Indians engaged in civil disobedience. As "Indians of All Tribes, Inc." focused on the Alcatraz occupation, "AIM seized the historical moment and became the premier national Indian activist group," Johnson wrote, "sponsoring a series of protests that would continue throughout the decade and encourage others to speak up for themselves and for their rights."

AIM had reversed the agenda of Parker's Society of American Indians. Although both movements promoted Indian goals and identity at a national level, the emphasis on tribal sovereignty, retention of treaty rights, and self-determination for reservations had replaced the previous calls for assimilation and abolition of reservations. An emphasis on traditional tribal values replaced Parker's reliance on racial determinism. "Going 'back to the blanket' carried positive rather than negative connotations," writes the anthropologist Jeffrey Hanson, "and the outer, visible Indian replaced the inner Indian of the SAI."

The occupation of Alcatraz from 1969 to 1971 was followed by the 1973 takeover of Wounded Knee on the Oglala Lakota (Sioux) Reservation, where Dennis Banks, Russell Means, and 250 AIM supporters faced off against federal marshals. The flashy imagery of Alcatraz and Wounded Knee played well in the world of urban Indians. According to Means, "about every admirable quality that remains in today's Indian people is the result of the American Indian Movement's flint striking the white man's steel. In the 1970s and 1980s, we lit a fire across Indian country. . . . Thanks to AIM, for the first time in this century, Indian people stand at the threshold of freedom and responsibility." Richard West and Kevin Gover take exception to Means, suggesting that while AIM "probably never had the influence in the Indian community that the American media believed it had, it did reflect accurately the frustration and anger felt by all Indians, at least to some degree."

DO THE WASHINGTON REDSKINS HONOR INDIAN PEOPLE?

Beginning in the 1960s, the Red Power movement confronted the power of names head-on. Deloria joined several other Indians leaders in calling attention to the demeaning stereotypes and misleading Indian imagery assigned by the non-Indian mainstream, focusing in particular on the American sports and advertising industries. In 1968, the National Congress of American Indians launched a campaign to address stereotypes found in print and

other media, urging America's high schools, colleges, universities, and professional sports franchises to "do the right thing" by taking a hard look at the
racist implications of appropriating Indian names and images. The next year,
Dartmouth College changed its mascot from the "Indians" to the "Big Green";
in 1971, Marquette University abandoned its "Willie Wampum" mascot; in
1972, Stanford University teams stopped being the "Indians," Dickinson
State switched from the "Savages" to the "Blue Hawks," the University of
North Dakota stopped being the "Fighting Sioux," and the University of Oklahoma retired its "Little Red" mascot. In 1996, Miami University of Ohio
quit being "Redskins" and, in March 1999, the Crayola Company announced
that it was dropping the color "indian red" from its 64-crayon box. Emphasizing that the name was based on a reddish-brown pigment commonly found in
India, a Crayola spokesman maintained that the "indian red" crayon had
nothing to do with American Indians, but "if it confuses children, it's something that should be reevaluated."

Not all Americans were willing to give up their Indian imagery without a
fight. There is today no single word more offensive to Indian people than the
term "redskins," a racial epithet that conjures up the American legacy of
bounty hunters bringing in wagon loads of Indian skulls and corpses, literally—the bloody dead bodies were known as "redskins"—to collect their payment. For years, Deloria and others have emphasized that such racial slurs
would never be permitted for other ethnic groups in America. When they
asked the National Football League to change the Washington team's name
to something less offensive, they were told that the term is only meant to
"honor" native people—the equivalent to using the n-word to name a sports
team, then claiming it was done to "honor African-Americans."

In *Red Earth, White Lies*, Deloria recounts the curious tale of Marge Shott,
former owner of the Cincinnati Reds baseball team. When Shott made some
derogatory remarks about African Americans and Jews in a *private* conversation, she was suspended for a year from baseball. When Jimmy the Greek, a
popular sports telecaster, suggested on a national broadcast that African
Americans had longer muscles extending up their backs because slave owners
bred them that way, he was summarily fired. Thousands of Indians were out-
raged when actress Jane Fonda was shown on national television supporting
her husband Ted Turner's Atlanta Braves with an enthusiastic rendition of the
"Tomahawk Chop."

"We have been lectured by every redneck peckerwood who can man a
typewriter about how harmless these names and symbols are," complains Deloria. Where are all the protests of racism when Indian people are the sub-

jects? Although this cavalier attitude stems from stereotypes through which America has long defined Indians, Deloria notes that the problem has been exaggerated by scientists who "may not have intended to portray Indians as animals rather than humans, but their insistence that Indians are outside the mainstream of human experience produces precisely these reactions in the public mind. . . . The constant drumbeat of scientific personalities manipulating the public's image of Indians by describing archaeological horizons, instead of societies, speaking of hunter-gatherers instead of communities, and attacking Indian knowledge of the past as fictional mythology, has created a situation in which the average citizen is greatly surprised to learn that Indians are offended by racial slurs and insults."

In 1992, Deloria joined Suzan Shown Harjo and six other Indian leaders to press the mascot issue by suing the Washington Redskins football team. "This is one of the last vestiges of overt racism right out in public in America, and it happens on a weekly basis during sports season," said Harjo. "This is the worst name you can call Native Americans in the English language." In *Harjo et al. v. Pro Football, Inc.* the co-petitioners asked the federal government to cancel trademark protection for the team's name, on the grounds that federal law was not designed to protect those making money from using offensive language. Framing the context as "protection against racism" vs. "profit from racism," Harjo, Deloria, and the others pressed their case for seven years until a federal panel ruled in their favor in April 1999. The ruling meant that marketing and merchandising of the Washington Redskins logo would no longer receive trademark protection (it is now pending appeal).

Several newspapers, including the *Minneapolis Star Tribune, Seattle Times*, and *Portland Oregonian*, recognizing the racial overtones involved, refuse to print the term "Redskin" in reporting the results of sporting events. U.S. Senator Paul Simon asks, "Can you imagine tolerating a halftime dance at a football game of a Catholic priest or Jewish rabbi with vestments on, holding a chalice or Torah? It is a small thing but small things are important."

These battles over mascots and Indian imagery underscore the power of naming in mainstream America; and Indians across the country are trying to reclaim that power. In the early 1980s, Papago leaders informed the Bureau of Indian Affairs that they wished to have their tribal name changed to Tohono O'Odham in subsequent official correspondence because the former "Papago" did not like being called "bean-eaters." The tribe's name was officially changed to Tohono O'Odham soon thereafter. A decade later, several members of the Navajo Nation made a similar request, asking to be known by the traditional name, Diné, which means simply "people;" but so far, the tribe's name remains "Navajo." Some Sioux Indians prefer to be known as Dakota or Lakota because "Sioux" is a French adaptation of an Ojibwe or Chippewa word meaning "enemy."

A similar problem has cropped up with the term "Anasazi," used for more than 60 years by archaeologists to denote the Indian people living at Chaco Canyon and elsewhere in the Four Corners between about AD 200 and 1600. The Anasazi people are considered by most archaeologists to be ancestors of the modern Pueblo groups in New Mexico and the Hopi people of north-western Arizona. In the last few years, a number of Pueblo people have ex-pressed concern over the term "Anasazi." Why, they ask, should their ancestors be known by a Navajo term meaning "ancient enemy"? Although a number of substitute terms have been suggested, many archaeologists today use the term "ancestral Pueblo" instead of "Anasazi."

Indian people also sometimes object when the term "prehistoric" is used to characterize their ancient past. In a European framework, "history" means written records, and for most of the Americas, such documentation did not begin until the arrival of Columbus. But most tribes maintain rich oral tradi-tions, which describe in detail their remote past, and today, some scholars substitute the terms "precolumbian" or "precontact" for the era formerly called "prehistoric." This is why, except for direct quotes from historical sources, you'll not find the word "prehistoric" anywhere in this book.

REFUSING   TO   WALK   THE   BERING
STRAIT   AND   NARROW

> *There's a real feeling that we've been here forever. The Bering Strait theory makes logical sense, but it doesn't override the traditional belief at all. That comes first.*

> —*Larry Benallie* (1996),
> Archaeologist and member of the Navajo Nation

In the very first sentence of *Red Earth, White Lies*, Deloria says, "Like almost everyone else in America, I grew up believing the myth of the objective sci-entist." He then goes on to compare the codification and repetition of scien-tific "truths" to the myths that have emerged from the Judeo-Christian tradition. The more he read, Deloria says, the more he became convinced that scientific arguments are largely based on authority rather than fact, and on manipulation rather than objective reading of the data. He defines science as that "collection of beliefs—some with considerable evidence, some lacking proof at all—which reflects data gathered by a small group of people over the past five hundred years with the simple belief that phenomena have been objectively observed and properly described because they have sworn themselves to sincerity."

In recent years, Deloria has attacked several popular scientific theories, striking particularly hard at the proposition that the populating of America occurred across the Bering Straits, which he considers a farcical "smear tactic" against Native Americans. "The Bering Strait theory is tenaciously held by white scholars against the varied migration traditions of the natives and is an example of the triumph of doctrine over facts," Deloria argues. "If the universities were controlled by the Indians, we would have an entirely different explanation of the peopling of the New World and it would be just as respectable for the scholarly establishment to support it."

Deloria uses the Bering Strait theory to illuminate the smoldering resentment felt by many Indians against science. He says that the recent Kennewick and Monte Verde discoveries only highlight how little science really knows about Indian origins. Archaeologists, he argues, have yet to find either the African Eve's cradle or to locate the frozen superhighway that delivered the first Americans across the Bering Strait from Asia. "Excavating ancient fireplaces and campsites may be exciting," Deloria suggests, "but there are no well-worn paths which clearly show migratory patterns from Asia to North America, and if there were such paths, there would be no indication anywhere which way the footprints were heading."

According to many Indian creation accounts, native people have lived in the Americas since emerging onto Earth's surface from a spiritual underworld. Deloria suggests that many have a cultural memory of traumatic continental and planetary catastrophes, keeping this information alive in tales deliberately constructed to preserve and to entertain. Calling science "the dominant religion," Deloria goes well beyond promoting the truth-value of oral tradition. He launches a full-scale attack on western science: "Like any other group of priests and politicians . . . scientists lie and fudge their conclusions as much as the most distrusted professions in our society—lawyers and car dealers." Here are some alternatives proposed by Deloria as antidotes to the standard teachings of natural history and conventional science:

"**Humans and some creatures we have classified as dinosaurs were contemporaries.**"

Oral traditions from the Pacific Northwest discuss oversized animals in their lakes and rivers. Deloria concludes that because current research suggests that some dinosaurs were warm blooded with instincts not unlike modern mammals, "there is no reason to hesitate suggesting that some of these creatures, described as animals or large fish by observers, were surviving individuals of some presently classified dinosaur species."

"There were mammoths or mastodons still living in the eastern United States at the time the Pilgrims landed."

Deloria believes that mammoth bones found on the surface must date to the historic period because "they could not have lain on the ground for thousands of years without suffering complete decay or dissolution." He takes Thomas Jefferson at his word on the matter and cites a British Columbian Indian story to the effect that they built lakehouses on stilts to protect themselves from mammoths.

"Radiocarbon Dating is a Sham"

Deloria believes that radiocarbon dating is "grossly inaccurate" and that scientists routinely instruct radiocarbon lab personnel in preferred results. He claims that radioactive materials washing downstream from the Hanford Atomic Energy plant have hopelessly contaminated the Kennewick bones, "making a test of anything there absurd."

Scientists in Deloria's view are "incredibly timid people" crippled by an excessive reverence for authority and orthodoxy. "Many subjects, no matter how interesting, are simply prohibited because they call into question long-standing beliefs." Prestigious people are permitted to dominate entire fields of inquiry, which are "populated by little people trying to protect their status [and] some areas of 'science' have not progressed in decades." He singles out—correctly, in my view—the historian Samuel Eliot Morison and the physical anthropologist Aleš Hrdlička as heavy-handed zealots who dominated conventional academic inquiry in their day, defending the intellectual *status quo* at all cost and quashing research proposals designed to explore alternative possibilities.

Ideas like these are increasingly being endorsed by large numbers of fundamentalist Christians and liberal activists. This broad constituency joins Deloria in rejecting current theories of human evolution as unfounded dogma, at least in part because the archaeological finds contradict traditional belief systems—Biblical or otherwise. These are strange bedfellows: Native American communities, right-wing Christian groups, and left-wingers. It is just this curious coalition that was instrumental in the passage of reburial legislation by the U. S. Congress.

LEGISLATING THE
SKULL WARS

21.

In the larger scope of history this is a small thing. In the smaller scope
of conscience, it may be the biggest thing we have ever done.
—*Congressman Morris Udall (1990), sponsor of the*
NAGPRA legislation

THE 1971 CONFRONTATION in Minnesota triggered a nationwide dialogue over whether archaeologists should dig up dead Indians. At the time,
many tribes seemed lukewarm about the issue unless it affected them directly.
A number of tribes, including Zuni, Navajo, Makah, and Pequot, operated
their own archaeological research programs, and they were accustomed to
making sure that archaeologists serve the tribal interest.

In the late eighteenth century, Thomas Jefferson wrote that "the dead
have no rights" and two centuries later, some anthropologists are reiterating
the same message: "I explicitly assume that no living culture, religion, interest groups, or biological population has any moral or legal right to the exclusive use or regulation of ancient human skeletons since all humans are
members of a single species," writes Douglas Ubelaker, a bioarchaeologist
with the Smithsonian Institution. "Ancient skeletons are the remnants of

unduplicable evolutionary events which all living and future peoples have the right to know about and understand. In other words, ancient human skeletons belong to everyone."

As the reburial issue heated up throughout the 1970s and 1980s, the Indian attitude toward archaeologists hardened. Archaeologist Larry Zimmerman tells a story about excavations on the Crow Creek Sioux reservation, in South Dakota. When some local tribal members asked him what he was doing, Zimmerman replied that looters had vandalized the site, and that he was digging to protect the past. The Indians said that they did not understand the difference between looters and archaeologists. "What is the difference if you dig burials with a trowel or a bulldozer?" asked Chick Hale, a Prairie Potawatomi spokesman. "Is it any better to go into a bank and steal the money all at once, or is it better to steal it a penny at a time?" Over time Zimmerman came to see the importance and sincerity of other perspectives, and became one of the very first archaeologists to advocate a more sensitive approach to Native American remains.

Indian leaders began to complain that whereas non-Indian graves are protected from desecration, grave robbing, and mutilation by criminal statutes in all fifty states, these same protections were not extended to the Indian dead. Instead, Indian graves were defined as "'nonrenewable archaeological resources' to be treated like dinosaurs or snails, 'federal property' to be used as chattel in the academic marketplace, 'pathological specimens' to be studied by those interested in racial biology, or 'trophies or booty' to enrich private collectors," write Walter R. Echo-Hawk and Roger C. Echo-Hawk, (Pawnee attorney and historian, respectively). As Echo-Hawk saw it, "If you desecrate a white grave, you wind up sitting in prison. But desecrate an Indian grave, you get a Ph.D. The time has come for people to decide: Are we Indians part of this country's living culture or are we just here to supply museums with dead bodies?" Indians declared that Native American concern for the dead must override scientific objectives.

Archaeologists were particularly sensitive to such criticisms. Some defended their profession by citing well-documented cases of red-on-red violence and of Indians desecrating the bones of other tribes. Historian Francis Parkman, for example, recorded a Crow war party's treatment of five Sioux corpses that had been ritually buried in trees. After dislodging the grave bundles and kicking them apart, the Crows held rifles against the skulls and blew them to pieces. Is this behavior acceptable, archaeologists asked, just because the ghouls happened to be Indians?

What about Arthur Parker, a Seneca Indian? In his role as New York State archaeologist, Parker personally excavated hundreds of Iroquois Indian burials. Why, archaeologists asked, should modern Indians be so appalled at archaeologists disturbing the old graves when their ancestors had done so all along? Several museum-based anthropologists pointed out the number of Indians who had willingly sold sacred and ceremonial artifacts to museums. As their traditional world fell apart in the late nineteenth century, many Indian people made the difficult choice to entrust their heritage to museums for long-term safekeeping.

Many archaeologists dismissed 1960s Indians as unauthentic, believing that American anthropology was being unjustly vilified by a cadre of "Professional Indians," career-building activists whose biology was their sole credential. Professional Indians seemed to be opportunists who advocated Indian perspectives on controversial topics more for their own personal advancement than from any deep-felt commitment to the issues. But the profession of archaeology almost uniformly misread the depth of belief among many elders and spiritual leaders who were deeply concerned about their dead. Many archaeologists believed that Indians had no real knowledge of their own history. and were just lashing out in resentment at the highly trained non-Indians who knew more than they did. Many agreed with archaeologist Clement Meighan who warned, "if archaeology is not done the ancient people remain without a history and without a record of their existence." Archaeologists argued vigorously during the 1980s against any potential legislation that would protect the "religious beliefs" of Indian people when no other religious group in America was granted such protection. According to archaeologist G. A. Clark "It is simply a fact that most of the pre-contact aboriginal cultures of the New World would have vanished without a trace were it not for archaeology (and the occasional presence of a western observer to record observations about them)." As for the Professional Indians who made their living touting a contrived connection with past religions and traditional spirituality, most archaeologists saw them as phony. Few Indian people, they argued, any longer held these beliefs. In fact, most Indian knowledge of these traditions, they said, is derived from archaeological collections and anthropological scholarship—the very body of scholarly knowledge that the Professional Indians were now attempting to destroy.

This is why many archaeologists felt that the "Deloria problem" was basically educational. If they could just enlighten the Indians about what they were doing, then the Indians would recognize how important science really was—and stop complaining about archaeologists conducting legitimate science. When confronted by Deloria and the AIM activists, most archaeolo-

gists believed—and many still do—that if the Indians would just listen to archaeologists, they could learn a great deal about their own past.

Throughout the 1970s and 1980s, archaeology's response to *Custer Died
for Your Sins* was mostly a knee-jerk defense of the status quo. Even in the face
of increasingly strident criticism, as someone said, anthropologists continued
with "business as usual, only *more* so." As one archaeologist put it, the Red
Power protests and the calls for repatriating artifacts and reburying bones
have a bright side—after all, "it's good that Native Americans are finally starting to care about their pasts."

"I AM A FUTURE ADULT MEMBER OF THE OMAHA TRIBE..."

Most bills presented before the United States Congress die a slow and
painful death, victims of political compromise and bureaucratic red tape. In
the late 1980s, however, it had become increasingly clear that the reburial
and repatriation issues were not going to disappear, thanks in large part to the
impact of the American civil rights movement, the increasingly effective lobbying efforts from Indian Country, and the alliance of Native Americans with
mainstream religious organizations. Red Power groups correctly sensed that
this was a battle they could win, and faced with the almost certain passage of
federal legislation, several museums began internal audits of their collections
to locate materials that seemed to be "culturally inappropriate" and to seek
out ways to return those remains "proactively," before the law required them
to do so.

In 1988, a delegation of Omaha leaders approached the anthropologists
at Harvard. They knew that Alice Fletcher had been convinced that the
Omaha tribe would soon vanish into the Great American melting pot, and
the influential La Flesche family as well as many other Omahas had agreed
with her. All of them were wrong because the Omaha did not vanish. Exactly
a century after Yellow Smoke turned over the Sacred Pole of the Omahas to
Fletcher and La Flesche, his descendants stood in a small courtyard outside
the Peabody Museum, and the Omaha people respectfully asked that their
consecrated religious artifacts be returned to them.

As with many nineteenth-century museum acquisitions, there are some
lingering questions about how the Sacred Pole actually came to the Peabody
Museum. In *The Omaha Tribe*, Fletcher and La Flesche explain that "influences
were brought to bear" by Iron Eye La Flesche to prevent the sacred items' bur-

ial. Even today, considerable oral tradition survives among the Omaha about what these "influences" might have been. Some believe the transfer was not entirely voluntary, that perhaps La Flesche took the pole without Yellow Smoke's consent.

While the Peabody staff debated the merits of the Omaha repatriation request, Ian W. Brown, curator in charge of the artifacts, received a number of letters from Omaha school children, pleading with him to return their Sacred Pole. Brown was particularly moved by the letter from Cary Alice Wolf that began "I am a future adult member of the Omaha tribe. . . ." Cary's letter went on to say that her grandmother "wrote two books on the Omaha language and I am learning the old ways of my fathers and my people. Our young generation of Omahas do cherish the sacred ways. We will take care of and keep the Sacred Pole for our future children. Just as our elders have kept and are teaching us the ways now, we will teach the future Omahas."

After some months of deliberation, the Peabody Museum decided that, although not legally required to do so, they would return the Omaha Sacred Pole. In an emotional presentation at the annual Omaha Powwow in Macy, Nebraska, the Peabody Museum formally returned the Sacred Pole and 280 other sacred artifacts to Doran Morris, Tribal Chairman of the Omaha and Yellow Smoke's great-great-grandson.

The Sacred Pole comes from another era. Yellow Smoke and the other keepers perished more than a century ago. The last renewal ceremony for the Sacred Pole took place in 1873, and the last buffalo hunt a year later. The modern Omaha scored a victory in getting their most sacred artifact returned, but there is some doubt about how to treat the Venerable Man. To them, he remains alive with meaning, and modern Omaha leaders still debate the necessary protocols and rituals required of them. The Omaha people still remember the death of Iron Eye La Flesche shortly after his son Francis, the anthropologist, recorded the legend of the Sacred Pole. Although some still fear the Venerable Man, most apparently believe that if he is treated like a respected elder, his power will help the tribe to continue their spiritual renewal.

The Omaha were long considered one of America's vanishing Indian tribes. After spending her "infuriating and depressing" summer with the Omaha in 1930, Margaret Mead called them a "broken culture." But the Omaha still live in Nebraska, and they retain the traditions of prayer and ceremony, the belief in the power of dance and song, and the stories of their tribal past. They have survived as a people and as a sovereign nation. Today, the Venerable Man resides at the Center for Great Plains Studies in Lincoln, awaiting a move to an Omaha cultural center to be built on the reservation.

THE PASSAGE OF NAGPRA

In 1990, Congress passed and President George Bush signed into law landmark legislation called the *Native American Graves Protection and Repatriation Act* (NAGPRA). A significant triumph for Indian people, NAGPRA permits living Indians to exercise their traditional responsibilities toward the dead. The late Northern Cheyenne Elder William Tallbull put it this way: "How would you feel if your grandmother's grave were opened and the contents were shipped back east to be boxed and warehoused with 31,000 others and itinerant pothunters were allowed to ransack her house in search of 'artifacts' with the blessing of the U.S. government? It is sick behavior. It is un-Christian. It is [now] punishable by law." As Judge Sherry Hutt pointed out in congressional testimony, rather than extending special rights to Native Americans (which would violate the 14th Amendment), NAGPRA awards an equal protection of property rights already extended to other Americans. She calls NAGPRA "one of the most significant pieces of human rights legislation since the Bill of Rights."

NAGPRA covers several basic areas of concern. First, it recognizes the importance of tribal consent when dealing with Indian graves on tribal lands and requires "consultation" with tribes over remains found on federal lands. NAGPRA mandates that, by November 16, 1993, all museums and universities receiving federal funds (personal collections are not included) send a summary of Native American sacred and ceremonial objects and unassociated funerary items to Indian tribes potentially affiliated with those artifacts. Two years later, on November 16, 1995, these same institutions were required to file an inventory of Native American human remains and associated grave goods with culturally affiliated tribes. Indian tribes shown to be culturally affiliated with these artifacts and remains could then request their return. The National Park Service provided museums a listing of 771 tribes, bands, and nations to which the appropriate inventories should be sent. Only federally recognized native groups appear on the list; tribes recognized only by state-level governments and those whose federal standing is pending are not covered by the legislation.

The bill also mandates an intensive and continuing interaction between archaeologists and tribal representatives. At first, these interactions were tinged with mistrust and apprehension. For decades, many Native American people felt uncomfortable visiting public museums where their cultural heritage was on display. Some Indian people saw NAGPRA as placing them on equal footing with museum and university officials. Other Native American

representatives believed that NAGPRA unfairly favored the museum community, hindering native people in gaining control over materials that rightfully
belonged to them (and which in their view should never have left Indian land
in the first place).

The bill made its heaviest impact on archaeologists working on federal or
tribal lands, but even those working on private land became involved, because most archaeologists were wary of dissolving collections long held in
the public trust; such behavior is contrary to every museum charter. Many
collections contain pieces specifically commissioned for exhibit and study.
Museums argued that, far from robbing Native people of their heritage,
ethnographers and archaeologists have attempted to preserve this heritage
for the common good. Still, museums across the country are complying with
the new law of the land.

THE BONES GO HOME

Suzan Shown Harjo, then executive director of the National Congress of
Americans Indians, had protested in the late 1980s to the *Los Angeles Times* that
the Smithsonian was holding the skulls of her Cheyenne relatives hostage. "It
wasn't enough that these unarmed Cheyenne people were mowed down by
the Cavalry at the infamous Sand Creek massacre; many were decapitated
and their heads shipped to Washington as freight." Harjo tried to imagine the
reactions of her ancestors when they returned home, "finding their loved
ones disinterred and headless."

More than 125 years after they were first shipped east, the Smithsonian
Institution returned the remains of the Sand Creek massacre victims to their
Cheyenne descendants. Tribal members packed cedar chips around the bones
and reburied the blanket-wrapped remains in a cemetery in Concho, Oklahoma. For the Cheyenne, the return was a formal admission by the federal
government that the skulls and skeletons should never have been seized from
the battlefield in the first place. It fell to the living to make it right with the
dead.

In another noteworthy case of cooperation, Smithsonian scientists and a
delegation of Blackfeet representatives together resolved the problems raised
by fifteen skulls sent from the Blackfeet reservation to the Army Medical College in 1892. The Blackfeet were concerned because their ancestors had been
at war with neighboring Indian groups in the late nineteenth century. What if
enemy skulls had been misidentified as Blackfeet?

To avoid an unacceptable mixing of spirits, they asked for assurances that only legitimate Blackfeet remains were being returned for reburial. Accordingly, bioarchaeologists at the Smithsonian conducted a battery of tests on the remains, returning only those thought conclusively to be Blackfeet. These remains were subsequently reinterred in Montana, where a monument was erected on the Blackfeet reservation.

Some tribes chose not to deal directly with human remains at all. The Eastern Shoshone people on the Wind River Reservation in Wyoming did not wish their ancestral remains repatriated because they questioned the accuracy of museum records. The Zuni people asked that the skeletons removed from tribal lands remain under museum curation.

Phillip Walker, a physical anthropologist, has worked with the Chumash Indians of southern California for a quarter century. The Chumash have long designated an individual as *liwimpshit*, a tribal member intimately familiar with the human skeleton. "These medical practitioners not only could set bones, but they could also arrange all the bones of a human skeleton properly, and determine whether those ancestral bones had once belonged with a man or a woman." These traditional practices opened up some common ground between Walker and the Chumash, serving as a basis to insure that bioarchaeological research could be conducted within an environment showing proper respect for the dead. Together, they established a specially designed subterranean ossuary at the University of California, Santa Barbara, where tribal remains are stored and protected—and available for bioarchaeological research under the supervision of their Chumash descendants.

Many Chumash say that they can gain a deeper understanding of tribal history from these collections. The thought of losing that, when so much has already been lost is not appealing. "The basis of the arrangement we have with the tribe," writes Walker, "is the mutual trust and respect we have built over the years through working together to prevent the destruction of archaeological sites and grave robbing."

THE PUEBLOS RETURN TO PECOS

On May 22, 1999 in the largest repatriation and reburial of the twentieth century, the Pecos and Jemez Pueblo people welcomed home the remains of nearly 2,000 of their ancestors. One thousand Pueblo people and well-wishers walked alongside the 53-foot-long eighteen-wheeler carrying the remains for the final mile of a 2,200 mile-trip that had started out in Massachusetts, where the bones had been stored and studied for more than seven decades. Three days earlier, an honor guard of two hundred had left on foot from Jemez Pueblo, seventy miles west of Pecos. Working their way eastward—through the chilly Jemez Mountains, across the Rio Grande, and into the Sangre de Cristo Range—they were backtracing the path of their ancestors who in 1838 had abandoned Pecos to join relatives at Jemez. As they walked, five and six abreast on the two-lane road, War Chief Pete Toya said simply, "We are real grateful, happy and proud that our ancestors are on their way home."

Their destination was a long rocky ridge where for eight centuries the powerful Pecos Pueblo had stood. There was no dispute over cultural affiliation: the Jemez and Pecos people had long been linked by biology, language, and spiritual beliefs. Disease and warfare during the Spanish colonial period reduced the population at Pecos until, in 1838, the handful of survivors relocated to Jemez. In 1936, the United States Congress formally recognized that the two tribes had merged. Although the Pecos descendants retained a certain autonomy, the Pueblo of Jemez was named as their legal, cultural, and administrative representative. Thanks to actress Greer Garson, whose Forked Lightening Ranch abutted Pecos Pueblo, the site became a National Monument in 1965.

When NAGPRA was signed into law, the people of Jemez Pueblo began discussing how to bring the remains of their ancestors back to Pecos. About the same time, as prescribed by the new law, James Bradley, Director of the Robert S. Peabody Museum in Andover, contacted Jemez representatives, saying simply "We have a lot of your stuff." The Jemez replied in equally simple language: "We know, let's talk."

Walking alongside the truck carrying the bones was Ruben Sando, the Governor of Pecos Pueblo. He carried with him the ceremonial cane of authority presented to the Pueblos by Spanish King Philip III in 1620—the same year the Pilgrims splashed ashore at Plymouth Rock. Raymond Gachupin, now the Governor of Jemez Pueblo compared the gathering to a celebration, like a "whole family getting together at Christmas, a reunion. You feel fulfilled." Not far away, 87-year-old Juan Ray Tafoya quietly wept, his grandson Bryan whispering softly to him in their native Towa language, the traditional tongue of the Jemez people. "He wants to walk the last mile," explained Bryan, "It's spiritual to him." And so he did.

The Pecos repatriation was difficult for archaeologists. The collections had been stored at Harvard University in Cambridge and the Phillips Academy in Andover since the 1920s. The esteemed archaeologist A. V. Kidder had dug them up in then-revolutionary excavations, and some say Kidder's work at Pecos provided a "Rosetta stone" for understanding the basics of Southwestern archaeology. These were the same skeletons that Earnest Hooton had studied, and many physical anthropologists had worked on the bones since. The Pecos collection had long been the largest available skeletal population from a single Indian community. Although the Pecos skeletons are well studied, the prospect of what might have been done with newer technology, newer theories, and newer science will always bother museum scientists, whose job descriptions call for preserving museum specimens, not disposing of them. No matter how culturally, social, or politically appropriate, the Pecos repatriation entails a loss to science. But a number of scientists believe that the sacrifice is warranted given the human component involved in archaeology. After all, archaeology and paleontology have rather different ethical mandates.

The two thousand skeletons were buried in an unmarked area in the National Park at Pecos.

THE NEW YORK ESKIMOS RETURN TO GREENLAND

Rather different emotions greeted the bones of the six Greenland Eskimos, Minik among them, who in 1897 had sailed into New York harbor aboard Robert Peary's ship *Hope*, and lived at the American Museum of Natural History while working with Franz Boas and Alfred Kroeber. Canadian author Kenn Harper heard their story while traveling in Greenland in 1977. A decade later, his book, *Give Me My Father's Body*, called the story to the attention of the American press once again. Although NAGPRA does not apply to international repatriations, the American Museum of Natural History decided, in 1992, to explore the possibilities of returning the Eskimo skeletons to Greenland for (re)burial.

Acting on behalf of the museum, Edmund Carpenter, an anthropologist specializing in Eskimo studies, and Jorgen Meldgaard, an archaeologist with the Danish National Museum, met with town officials at Qaanaaq, the Greenland village presently occupied by descendants of the six New York Eskimos. Their plan for reburying the remains was met with unexpected silence. Although the Qaanaaq Eskimos expressed an interest in continued anthropological research, none seemed particularly interested in discussing a return of the bones. Finally, after a delay of nine months, Pastor Hans Johan Lennert of

Qaanaaq's Lutheran Church agreed to conduct the reinterment, but apparently only after a Danish bishop pressured him.

The Royal Danish Air Force flew the four tiny coffins containing the skeletons to Thule, and Carpenter accompanied them to Qaanaaq in August 1993. After a service in the modern glass-fronted church, a pickup truck took the remains of Qisuk, Nuktaq, Atangana, and Aviaq to the Lutheran cemetery where they were buried beneath a cross and a bronze plaque that begins, "They Have Returned." After the service, everyone shook hands.

Ted Carpenter and his wife, Adelaide, asked the community about their reaction to the service, one resident said simply, "Embarrassment." Carpenter believes that "The whole service was really for us," that the Eskimo were only participating in the reburial ceremony as a courtesy to their American and Danish guests. The people of Qaanaaq knew that Qisuk and the others had left Greenland because they wanted to; they liked Admiral Peary, and he had treated them well in the past. Once in New York, Peary disappeared, and the four had died. When the strangers arrived for a church service so many years later, the Eskimos at Qaanaaq went along because they did not want to upset anyone.

"How do you feel" the Carpenters asked Qaqqutsiaq, Minik's last surviving relative, "about the return of the bones?"

"If that's what [the museum people] wanted," replied Qaqqutsiaq, "it's alright. If [the bones] had stayed where they were [in New York], that would have been alright, too."

"May I record you saying that?"

"No, I'll soon be dead," replied the 94-year-old, "and I don't want my voice left behind. And no photographs. I want nothing left."

Qisuk, Nuktaq, Atangana, and Aviaq were not Christians, but many of their modern descendants in Qaanaaq are, and so, they believed, were the strangers who brought the bones from New York. They knew that the Christian religion places great emphasis on respecting and burying the bodies of the dead.

But the Polar Eskimos' religion—the tradition in which Qisuk and the others were raised—attributed only evil properties to the dead. This is why, in 1897, they told Alfred Kroeber that the bodies and personal effects of the deceased must quickly be discarded and not discussed again. Although the modern people of Qaanaaq were too polite to say so, many felt that Qisuk would not have wanted his bones brought back home. Polar Eskimos of his day tried to avoid the remains of their dead.

WHO'S GOT ISHI'S BRAIN?

Yet another reburial story was played out in the strange saga of Ishi's brain.

Since his death in 1916, the poignant story of the last "wild man" in America had faded from the public eye. Then came an Ishi revival of sorts, sparked by the 1961 publication of *Ishi in Two Worlds* by Theodora Kroeber (Alfred's second wife and companion for four decades). The book, which tells Ishi's story without melodrama or romanticism, was an instant hit. *Ishi in Two Worlds* still enjoys brisk sales, making it the University of California Press' all-time top seller.

In his mid-eighties when Theodora wrote the book, Alfred Kroeber agreed to share his memories of Ishi but refused to participate directly in the writing. "This was, to be sure, the teacher keeping his finger out of the student's pie," Theodora Kroeber wrote later, but it "was more than that: the old sense of pain and hurt returned with these recollections as readily as the indubitably happy and comic and fulfilling memories. I knew then that Kroeber would never have written Ishi's biography. He had lived too much of it, and too much of it was the stuff of human agony from whose immediacy he could not sufficiently distance himself."

During the 1990s, two documentaries and a made-for-television movie brought the Ishi story to an entirely new American audience. In *The Last of His Tribe*, Native American actor Graham Greene starred as Ishi, and Jon Voight played a melancholy young Kroeber. Ishi's burial urn, placed in a cemetery near San Francisco, became something of a tourist attraction.

In May 1997, as part of the NAGPRA review of human remains, Arthur Angle of the Butte County Native American Cultural Committee announced plans to rebury Ishi's remains in his tribal homeland near Mt. Lassen. Citing Ishi's belief that the body must be whole for the spirit to reach the land of the dead, however, the committee refused to proceed without the brain, which had been removed at the 1916 autopsy. Angle wrote to California Governor Pete Wilson, stating his intentions and soliciting help in locating the long-missing brain, which they believed was preserved somewhere in the University of California system.

The staff of the Phoebe Hearst Museum of Anthropology, appropriately located in Kroeber Hall on the Berkeley Campus, launched a detailed investigation into the whereabouts of Ishi's brain. The staff reported that all the existing records suggested that Kroeber and his colleagues had firmly opposed treating Ishi as a specimen. They could find no record that Ishi's brain was anywhere at Berkeley and suggested it had been cremated with the rest of the body. However, it might have been transferred the University of California Medical School in San Francisco.

At this point, administrators at the University of California asked Nancy Rockafellar, research historian in the History of Health Science Department, to investigate. Rockafellar got in touch with Orin Starn, a Duke University anthropologist who was researching a book about Ishi. Starn found a long-ignored file at Berkeley indicating that when Kroeber arrived back in California, Ishi's brain was waiting for him. Seven months after Ishi's death, Kroeber wrote to Aleš Hrdlička at the Smithsonian Institution: "I find that at Ishi's death last spring his brain was removed and preserved. There is no one here who can put it to scientific use. If you wish it, I shall be glad to deposit it in the National Museum Collection." Hrdlička quickly replied that he would "be very glad" to add Ishi's brain to his collection, which already contained more than two hundred human brains (including that of John Wesley Powell). Ishi's brain was shipped to the Smithsonian Institution on January 5, 1917.

In January 1999, the curatorial staff of the National Museum of Natural History confirmed that Ishi's brain was indeed stored at the Smithsonian's offsite curation facility in Silver Springs, Maryland. Smithsonian officials had not known that anybody was looking for it. Four months later, the Smithsonian's Museum of Natural History offered to return Ishi's brain to the Redding Rancheria and Pitts River Tribes of northern California under the conditions of federal repatriation legislation.

Ishi's death had deeply affected Kroeber. There can be no doubt about that. But sometime between forbidding the autopsy and his October letter offering Hrdlička the brain, Kroeber changed his mind. Did he come to see some scientific merit in preserving the brain, or was he simply looking to cement his personal and professional relationship to Hrdlička, the most important physical anthropologist of the day? Whatever the answer, Kroeber's curious behavior reflects the classic Jeffersonian paradox: his unfeigned devotion to Ishi his friend, weighed against his scientific perception of Ishi as a priceless scientific specimen.

Part V

BRIDGING THE CHASM

To archaeologists, the idea of consulting with potential specimens must seem annoying. For Native Americans, it's yet another version of this country's oldest and deadliest game: Cowboys and Indians.

—Gary White Deer (1997)
Choctaw Nation of Oklahoma

TRIBAL AFFILIATION AND SOVEREIGNTY

22.

Repatriation is the most potent political metaphor for cultural revival that is going on at this time. Political sovereignty and cultural sovereignty are linked inextricably, because the ultimate goal of political sovereignty is the protecting of a way of life. As separate polities, tribes can tax and regulate, and exercise jurisdiction. But it is equally important, perhaps even more important, to protect Indian ways of life and ways of thinking.

—*W. Richard West, Jr. (1996, Southern Cheyenne),*
Founding Director of the National Museum
of the American Indian

IF ISHI WAS truly the last of his tribe—as both he and Kroeber firmly believed in 1911—how could his remains be "culturally affiliated" with any person living in 1999?

DETERMINING CULTURAL AFFILIATION

In dividing up skeletal and cultural materials, NAGPRA states that cultural affiliation was to be decided by "a preponderance of the evidence based upon geographical, kinship, biological, archaeological, linguistic, folkloric, oral tradition, historic, or other information or expert opinion." No priority is assigned to these very diverse criteria.

In those instances where a court is called upon to adjudicate the issue of cultural affiliation, the judge will listen to all sides and make a determination based upon the weight of evidence. Although archaeologists and historians have traditionally enjoyed priority over native people in giving "expert testimony," NAGPRA shifts the balance. No longer is the scientific position privileged by the courts; this is not equivalent to "beyond a reasonable doubt" or "scientific certainty." Preponderance, involving as it does only 51 percent confidence, has opened up the dialogue on establishing cultural affiliation, paving the way for oral tradition and native perspectives to weigh in more heavily than before.

Each action under NAGPRA requires a choice: *culturally affiliated* or *culturally unidentified*. Does "the preponderance of the evidence" place a collection in one category, or the other? Where no affiliation can be assessed, it falls to the Department of Interior to issue regulations that will decide ultimate disposition. But with bones the age of Kennewick Man, it may be impossible (at least with current technology) to find any ancestral affiliation.

The issue is ultimately legal because, in the memorable words of Felix Cohen, federal law "dominates Indian life in a way not duplicated in other segments of American society." According to Vine Deloria, Jr., overall patterns in Indian law can be perceived only in hindsight because federal Indian policy has always been "expediency grounded only in the political considerations of the moment and without any lasting understanding of the nature of the peoples, laws, governments, or responsibilities." As a result, currently acceptable definitions of Indians and Indian tribes are fundamentally political in nature—their purpose being to determine which groups have a quasi-sovereign relationship with the United States government and which individuals are eligible for various governmental programs.

The problem facing archaeologists is to assign identities to the remains of the past using the political definitions of the present.

WHAT'S AN INDIAN?

This seemingly innocent question goes to the heart of the matter. For centuries, Euroamerica has taken the meaning of "Indian" as self-evident. When George Catlin went westward into Missouri River country to paint Indians in the 1830s, he did not need a legal definition to identify his subjects. Decades later, when Edward Curtis did the same with a camera, he knew exactly what a real Indian looked like, and he photographed hundreds of them. Defining Indians was easy as long as they differed markedly from mainstream Americans—as long as they looked physically different, dressed in different clothes, spoke a different language, and acted differently from white Americans. Today, however, it is necessary to step behind the obvious images and seek the Indian people's own definitions of Indianness, as well as those of the governmental agencies charged with administrating Indian policy.

The United States Census Bureau currently defines Indians using a criterion of "self-identification," and Scott Momaday agrees, to a point. "An Indian is somebody who thinks of themselves as an Indian," says Momaday, "But that's not so easy to do and one has to earn the entitlement somehow. You have to have a certain experience of the world in order to formulate this idea. I consider myself an Indian; I've had the experience of an Indian. I know how my father saw the world, and his father before him."

But Indian self-identification has a distinct downside because many Indians complain about imposters, those belonging only to what Rayna Green terms "the tribe called Wannabee." Because they "feel" like an Indian, the logic goes, therefore they are. Cherokee has long been the most favored Wannabee identity, but Apache ancestry seems to be gaining ground in California.

One demographer estimates that one in every thirty-five Americans today claims some degree of Indian ancestry which, taken to its literal extreme, suggests that Indian self-identification has the potential of swelling the North American Indian population from roughly two million to a whopping seven million people. Authentic Indians—however this difficult term is constructed—generally greet Indian Wannabees with a mix of resentment and derision.

Legal definitions are even more complex. As Steven Pevar points out in *The Rights of Indians and Tribes*, different laws use different definitions of Indian, and some don't define the term at all. Federal courts have sometimes relied on a two-part test: first, the Indian community must recognize this person as Indian (following Momaday's statement quoted above), and second, the person must have some definable degree of "Indian blood" (meaning some identifiable Indian ancestry). But even these standards carry tremendous confusion and inconsistency. Some federal laws define an Indian as anyone of "Indian descent"; others require one-fourth or even one-half Indian blood. Ambiguity like this means that someone may be sufficiently Indian to receive educational benefits, but not Indian enough to qualify for the tribe's medical plan.

WHAT'S AN INDIAN TRIBE?

By not specifically defining "Indian," NAGPRA implies that the term designates anyone who has been accepted as a member of a "federally recognized" Indian tribe. In this way, NAGPRA emphatically respects the sovereignty of tribal authority. There is also a provision for recognizing *individual* "Indians," who may or may not belong to recognized tribes. These individuals are still entitled to make NAGPRA claims as lineal descendants (if they can trace their ancestry through an unbroken chain of kinship relations). But setting aside the issue of lineal descendants as individuals, the law defines as "Indian" anybody who belongs to an "Indian tribe," a definitional shift that places a tremendous burden on that deceptively simple word *tribe* (which itself has multiple definitions and shades of meaning).

The word "tribe" has long been a problem for anthropologists. In one widely cited study, Morton Fried of Columbia University defined "tribes" as loosely organized sets of villages or migratory camps with some central leadership, but with little or no coercive power. According to Fried, members of a tribe speak the same basic language, share an ideological unity, and use a distinctive name for themselves. Tribes generally have a cultural network that includes common ritual and religious beliefs, a subsistence network linking economic production, distribution, and consumption, and a kinship network stipulating that people marry within the tribe.

Fried believed that tribes are secondary phenomena resulting from contact with more powerful societies: "So-called tribal groups . . . are not social organizations whose integrity receded into a remote past; rather," he argued. "the tribalism displayed is a reaction to more recent events and conditions. . . . What it amounts to is [that a tribe is] created by governmental action, its members showing considerable diversity in culture, language, and in physical type." But this forces one to ask if "tribes" only result from Euroamerican contact, what went before?

Further, as the anthropologist William Sturtevant points out, it is almost impossible to determine the existence of a tribe from documentary evidence; we simply know too little about the various cultural, economic, and kinship networks to make an informed decision. If it's difficult for an ethnohistorian to infer tribal structure from documents, how likely is it that archaeologists can define "tribe" on the basis of excavated remains? How do you dig up "the same basic language," an "ideological unity," or a "distinctive name?"

These problems aside, it is hard to overemphasize the importance of "tribe" to generations of attorneys, judges, juries, lawmakers, and bureaucrats. As Felix Cohen stressed in his classic *Handbook of Federal Indian Law*, the notions of tribe and tribal status have been critical in establishing relations between the United States government and Indian communities. The legal concept of tribe derives from a 1901 Supreme Court decision, *Montoya v. United States*, which defines an Indian tribe as "a body of [1] Indians of the same or a similar race, united in [2] a community under [3] one leadership or government, and [4] inhabiting a particular though sometimes ill-defined territory." In this and subsequent decisions, the court clearly distinguished *tribe* from *band* and *nation*, concluding that "the word 'nation' as applied to the uncivilized Indians is so much of a misnomer as to be little more than a compliment."

Unsatisfactory as the term might be, "tribe" is the fundamental unit of Indian law. Because of pro-Indian sympathies in Congress, federal agencies were not allowed simply to overpower Indian tribes; they were mandated to sign treaties with tribes, as they would with any other sovereign power. The term "tribe" is common in the pre-1871 treaties that effectively chartered modern Indian societies and established the basis for treaty-guaranteed rights. The Indian Reorganization Act of 1934 established various political entities known as "tribes" in large parts of the United States.

There is also the common-sense definition of tribe, the meaning of the term as used by many Indian people. "As I use it and as I understand other Indian people using it," writes Vine Deloria Jr., the word *tribe* "means a group of people living pretty much in the same place who know who their relatives are. I think that's the basic way we look at things."

In practice, each of these definitions is difficult to apply to repatriation cases, in part because today's tribal governments are largely the products of John Collier's lobbying during the 1930s. To complicate matters, each Indian tribe is entitled to establish its own membership requirements. The Salish-Kootenai Tribe, for instance, is comprised mostly of mixed-bloods and barely escaped termination in the 1950s. In 1960, they tightened their blood quantum requirement to one-quarter. For them, defining a blood quantum was more important to tribal sovereignty than a sense of community. This strategy was devised by many tribes to keep pro-termination factions from packing tribal councils with 1/8th-bloods who would vote to terminate (and hence receive a payoff from tribal assets).

But there is no blood quantum requirement for Cherokee tribal membership because, says Russell Thornton, their "large, dispersed mixed-blood population enabled them to achieve 'political power' as a tribe and to protect a 'core' of more full-blood, more traditional Cherokees." The Onondaga, Seneca, and Oneida (of New York, but not Wisconsin), tribal membership is accorded only to individuals born of an enrolled mother; this is why Arthur Parker was not born a Seneca. For the Tohono O'Odham of Arizona, all who reside on the reservation are automatically members. The Yakima tribe permits children to be born elsewhere, but parents must establish residence by returning to the reservation at least once every five years; tribe regulations also require that a member have at least one-quarter Yakima blood and belong to one of the fourteen original bands.

In 1910, somewhat more than half of the 265,683 registered Indians in the United States were full-bloods. Today, many tribes have no full-bloods at all. When the Sault Ste. Marie Band of Chippewas discarded its blood requirement in 1975, enrollment jumped from 1,300 to 21,000. Most tribes require that a person have at least one-fourth tribal blood to become a member; some demand as much as one-half, others only one-sixteenth. While these criteria establish tribal membership, they do not necessary determine Indianness for other purposes. When the Tonawanda Band of Senecas banished five political dissidents from the tribe, their names were stricken from the tribal rolls. Not only were these five heretics no longer Seneca tribal members by law, they were no longer Indians.

To further confuse matters, many tribes today accept Indian blood from other tribes as valid, but list the children as having all tribal blood. Here's an example: Vine Deloria, Jr., is 3/8th Standing Rock Sioux. When his brother (also 3/8th) married an Oglala Sioux woman (who was 3/4 blood), their children became 9/16th Oglala—tribal rules mandated that their Standing Rock blood disappeared altogether.

This extensive range in tribal self-definition has become a major issue in NAGPRA cases because the concept of tribal sovereignty assumes that tribes have remained in the same place over long periods of time. Sometimes historians can trace tribal roots back for centuries; sometimes they cannot. Sometimes archaeologists can find material residues tracking tribal histories well back in time; sometimes they cannot. Sometimes archaeological and historical research confirms Deloria's assumption of tribes "living pretty much in the same place," sometimes it does not. Sometimes, in the language of NAGPRA, the "geographical, kinship, biological, archaeological, linguistic, folkloric, oral tradition, historic, or other information or expert opinion" leads to a single verdict on cultural affiliation based on "preponderance of the evidence," sometimes it does not.

K E N N E W I C K   M A N   R E V I S I T E D

> *I haven't seen this level of viciousness before, and you should remember that I was working in the Clinton White House.*
>
> > —*Speaking of NAGPRA,* Jay Stowsky (1996),
> > *Director of Research and Policy, University*
> > *of California, Berkeley*

The hope was that NAGPRA would redress centuries of injustice by establishing legal processes through which Native American tribes and lineal descendants could reclaim human remains, sacred objects, funerary remains, and items of cultural patrimony. Having been drafted after years of wrangling and negotiation, the final bill attempted to balance the conflicting interests of Indian tribes, museums, and archaeologists. In the Congressional debate over NAGPRA, Senator John McCain stressed the importance of achieving this balance:

> *I believe this bill represents a true compromise. . . . In the end, each party had to give a little in order to strike a true balance and to resolve these very difficult and emotional issues. . . . I believe this legislation effectively balances the interest of Native Americans in the rightful and respectful return of their ancestors with the interest of our Nation's museums in maintaining our rich cultural heritage, the heritage of all American peoples.*

A decade later, many people question how effective this compromise really was.

Thomas Killion, who heads the repatriation office at the Smithsonian's National Museum of Natural History, notes that "NAGPRA wasn't the quick fix that some people may have envisioned when the legislation was passed. I don't think the people who passed the law or the tribes realized how difficult and complex the process would be. . . ." Today, nearly everyone seems unhappy with some aspect of the law.

With the Kennewick find, archaeologists' worst fears about NAGPRA were realized—that the 1990 legislation would be stretched into deep time, thereby preventing science from studying remains that were not affiliated with any modern tribe. During the years of pre-NAGPRA lobbying, archaeologists and museum officials had gone to great lengths to argue against universal reburial, trying to ensure that NAGPRA would not close down legitimate research on ancient remains. Yet this is exactly what may happen at Kennewick. In the view of Richard Jantz, "If we lose Kennewick Man, then every ancient skeleton in the United States could be lost to this law."

The eight scientists filing suit (including Jantz) have argued that the federal government has failed to show that the skeleton meets the statutory definition of Native American. "Kennewick hits [NAGPRA] right where it's weakest," says David Meltzer. "The law requires remains to be repatriated to the lineal descendants . . . but proving lineal descent at that distance is no easy task." It is, in fact, rare that archaeology can do this at a time depth of 500 years, much less 10,000. But NAGPRA also provides for establishing relationship through "cultural affiliation," which requires a reasonable assurance of "shared group identity" between a past group represented by human remains and/or objects with a modern Indian tribe. But given what is known from modern population biology, the very notion of tracking fixed, enduring, bounded ethnic groups is outmoded and quaint, if not a little racist.

NAGPRA is predicated on the argument that archaeologists can often identify ancient antecedents of contemporary Indian tribes. For nearly two centuries scientists have favored a theory that America was first populated by people walking across the Bering Straits from Asia, spreading out and settling down in simple linear fashion. Most scientists now agree that the picture is much more complicated. Current research emphasizes the great time spans and massive geographic areas involved, plus new information from archaeology, linguistic, and biological studies.

The definition of "Native American" is also at dispute in the Kennewick case. The Department of Interior asserted in court that any remains in the United States older than 500 years old are Native American; but in September 1999, Judge Jelderks asked if the 500-year-old rule applies even when the remains in question are morphologically different from modern tribes. When government attorneys confirmed this position, the court commented that current definitions seem to imply that a 10,000-year-old European would be Native American, no matter where his parents came from. The court also cautioned that NAGPRA did not appear to refer to such ancient remains. This is how things stood as this book went to press.

Archaeologists must determine whether or not newly discovered human remains are Native American; if they are, then NAGPRA comes into play and cultural affiliation may become an issue. Property rights law is not necessarily dependent on cultural affiliation. Such are the problems of projecting tribes, as political units, back in time across archaeological landscapes. Sometimes tribes have demonstrable antiquity; sometimes they do not. The irony is that archaeologists often have a central role in determining the cultural affiliation of remains—a circumstance that "infuriates any Indian who really understands this irony," adds Deloria.

Tribes are frustrated that the language of NAGPRA draws so heavily on the perspectives of archaeology and history to determine cultural affiliation. NAGPRA says that federal agencies and museums must make a good faith effort to reach a decision as to whether a given set of remains is culturally affiliated with a present day, federally recognized Indian tribe. Although NAGPRA does attempt to provide some balance by including oral history and folklore in the mix, many Indians feel that decisions still reflect a "White Man's mythology." In their view, tribal traditions derive from a spiritual base that cannot be challenged from a scientific perspective.

Why, they ask, is the burden of proof placed on Indians to defend their beliefs and practices when similar burdens are not placed on other religions? "How can devout Jews prove, to the secular mind, that religious circumcision has any religious significance at all?" asks Deloria. "Do Christians actually believe that the bread and wine they consume at Mass are the body and blood of Jesus? A simple scientific lab test could dispel this superstition." The Constitution was supposed to treat all religions equally, he argues, but under NAGPRA, Indians find themselves forced to defend their faith publicly against an array of scientific evidence marshaled by museum directors, archaeologists, National Park Service personnel, and state historians. Many Indians deeply resent the long-standing Boasian premise of scientific anthropology—that because scientists have objectively studied Indian religion, they must, therefore, know things that tribe members don't. "How can any scholar, no matter how well educated," asks Deloria, "possibly know more about the religious beliefs, feelings and practices than a practitioner of a religion?"

The key issues in the lawsuit over Kennewick Man, then, boil down to these:

- *Is Kennewick Man subject to NAGPRA?*

- *What are the legal meanings of "Native American" and "indigenous"?*

- ✪ *Is there evidence of a biological or cultural linkage between Kennewick Man and modern Indian tribes?*

- ✪ *Does NAGPRA apply to an ancient population that may not be directly related to modern Native Americans?*

- ✪ *Are scientific study and repatriation of remains mutually exclusive or can both objectives be accommodated?*

At this writing, the matter has yet to be resolved. U.S. Magistrate John Jelderks in Portland, Oregon is hearing the case. Sherry Hutt, a Superior Court judge in Phoenix, Arizona, believes that no private individual—including a scientist—has the right to claim government property for study. According to Hutt, only descendants or those judged to be culturally affiliated under the provisions of NAGPRA have the legal standing to claim the remains. Although the Corps of Engineers was entitled to take appropriate action at first, Hutt feels that if the remains are established as Native American, any further actions would require permission of the individual or tribe with the authority to grant such approval.

Ultimately, the Kennewick dispute is not a matter of religion v. science, or even Indians v. scientists. At its heart, the matter of the Kennewick skeleton involves political power and property rights: "Permission to pursue scientific research," Hutt testified before the Senate Select Committee on Indian Affairs in 1999, "must come from the party with the right to grant it."

DOES KENNEWICK MAN THREATEN TRIBAL SOVEREIGNTY?

In a *60 Minutes* segment, television journalist Leslie Stahl suggested that Kennewick Man "could turn out to be the missing link between what we thought to be the truth and what is actually the truth—a truth, if it is the truth—that the Indians are not happy with and would just as soon leave well enough alone." In the same program, James Chatters proposed that tribal opposition to further testing was "based largely on fear, fear that if someone was here before they were, their status as sovereign nations, and all that goes with it—treaty rights, and lucrative casinos . . . could be at risk." Although noting that Indians dismissed such charges as "nonsense," this widely watched program left the distinct impression that if Kennewick Man turned out to be non-Indian, tribal sovereignty would be directly threatened.

Setting aside Kennewick Man's alleged racial affiliation, this implication is simply false. One of the most important principles in American Indian law is the concept of "reserved sovereignty." A 1905 Supreme Court ruling (*United States v. Winans*) concluded that when signing a treaty with the United States, all Indian tribes reserved a right that was superior to and prior to the rights of other the citizens in the territory. The Court explicitly noted that "a treaty was not a grant of rights *to* Indians, but a grant of rights *from* them—a reservation of those not granted." This means that only those rights and privileges specifically spelled out in a given treaty were being ceded: All other rights were retained.

No Indian treaty has ever contained a provision that would nullify the agreement should it be discovered that the tribe's ancestors were not the first people here. The centuries of recognizing native sovereignty will not be undone or replaced simply by documenting the presence of early non-Indians. This is a critical and often misunderstood point about Kennewick Man: When Europeans arrived, they recognized existing native people as the sovereign inhabitants of the continent. Period. No new finds will change that relationship.

But does this mean that tribal sovereignty is irrelevant to the Kennewick controversy? Not at all.

The Kennewick matter raises formidable questions about tribal rights with regard to human remains and archaeological sites, treaty rights and Indian land claims, and especially the contemporary religious use of tribal and federal land. These issues are complex, and simply to assert that tribes are politically motivated in the Kennewick Man dispute would be to misstate the complexity of the reburial and repatriation issues.

UMATILLA SOVEREIGNTY AND TREATY RIGHTS

For two centuries, North American Indians ceded huge tracts of their homelands in exchange for treaty-guaranteed sovereignty. In 1855, the Umatilla joined other Columbia River tribes to sign a treaty with Isaac I. Stevens, Governor of Washington Territory, relinquishing specific tracts of land in exchange for protection and certain goods and services. But the tribes reserved for themselves other rights and privileges that included hunting, fishing, and gathering rights on the very lands they were ceding.

There is no evidence that, during treaty negotiations or at any time thereafter, the Umatilla ever ceded the rights and properties of their dead and their possessions. In fact, subsequent Executive Orders and legislative acts have verified that the Umatilla and other tribes of the Columbia Plateau retain the legal right to continue religious practices on Federal lands within their traditional homeland. These tribes never relinquished their religious responsibilities to care for the dead, their property, and their general well-being through prayer, ceremony, offerings, and other means. Only tribal members are qualified to fulfill these sacred and ceremonial obligations.

This is an important point because Kennewick Man was found on such ceded Federal land—within the traditional Umatilla homelands along the Columbia River, but on a tract administered by the Army Corps of Engineers. This is why ethnographer Deward Walker argues that any attempt to reduce the Kennewick dispute to a "scientific" debate over DNA testing and tribal affiliation will be invalid. In his view, the issue is one of human rights and First Amendment prerogatives—not scientific property rights.

A BACKLASH AGAINST SOVEREIGNTY

In the twentieth century, Indians became America's favorite underdog, the First Americans who lost almost everything to the European invasion. Today, some Indian leaders boast that it has been two decades since Congress passed a major law over tribal objections.

But reservation gaming—the tribal cash crop of the 1990s—has severely tested the limits of tribal sovereignty, state jurisdiction, and tribal worldviews. The principle of sovereignty has helped some tribes make billions in profit from gambling casinos. This generation of richer Indians is more experienced in the exercise of tribal power.

A great deal of resentment has surfaced against these "rich Indians." Political opponents are no longer shy about attacking these new sources of Indian revenue and power. Across the American West, ranchers find it hard to accept that a neighboring Indian tribe enjoys preferential treatment in the matter of precious resources, especially land and water. Some civil rights advocates are uncomfortable that—under the doctrine of tribal sovereignty—certain tribes fail to measure up to international standards of due process, equal protection and human rights as recognized in the United States Constitution and international law. Animal protection groups find themselves increasingly at odds with tribes, using sovereignty and treaty-guaranteed rights as a basis for hunting endangered and threatened species. Arguments over treaty-guaranteed fishing rights in Minnesota have prompted some animal rights groups to threaten a lobbying effort aimed at rescinding those treaties.

Amidst these other factors, the late twentieth-century prosperity of some Indian tribes seems to have fostered a visceral backlash against tribal sovereignty, including a series of highly publicized attacks on the centuries-old right of Indian self-government. Several pieces of legislation recently introduced in Congress have been designed to limit Indian holdings. The Supreme Court has been shrinking the concept of Indian Country, providing states with increased power to limit the profitable Indian gaming industry.

Some just resent the power Indians have over them. Others say that the concept of Indian sovereignty—parallel nations within individual states—conflicts with the core concept of one country.

The anti-sovereignty movement seems to be gaining momentum in Kennewick territory. The state of Washington has seen increasingly violent confrontations over nineteenth-century treaty rights that the whites don't remember—but the Indians do. For three decades, first as Washington State attorney general and now as senator, Slade Gorton has called Indian sovereignty "an anachronism" and argued that citizens of the United States should not have their rights limited by separate governments within the United States. "I find nothing in any Indian treaty" says Gorton, "that says they must be continuously supported by the Federal taxpayers."

During the summer of 1997, *The New York Times* reported that a Senate Indian Affairs Committee field hearing held in Seattle provoked "ancient hatreds and old-fashioned shouting." The hearing was held to vet a bill newly introduced by Senator Gorton that would effectively abolish sovereign immunity for the nation's several hundred Indian tribes. "Making a case out of what happened to your grandfather," Gorton warns, "is not the best way to decide public policy." Although property owners claimed that the bill would "level the playing field" for non-Indians, Indian leaders say it would doom many poorly funded tribal governments.

Then there are the larger implications. If property rights can be taken from Indian tribes, from whom else might they be taken? Does the Fifth Amendment apply only to non-Indians?

This is why reserved rights, repatriation and reburial are at the heart of these larger issues involving sovereignty. Indian leadership is under pressure to find ways to protect the economic and political gains of the past century.

Many tribal leaders believe that compromise will be misconstrued as a sign of weakness. The implications of the Kennewick lawsuit reach far beyond the specifics of the case itself, and many tribal leaders believe that compromise of any sort will be misconstrued as a sign of weakness.

SPEAKING OF ORAL TRADITION

23.

THE KENNEWICK CONTROVERSY highlights yet another serious conflict in interpreting the NAGPRA criteria of "a preponderance of the evidence." Many archaeologists today feel that based on a preliminary assessment of the biological, archaeological, and linguistic evidence, Kennewick Man cannot be associated with any living group—including the Umatilla. They believe that the best evidence relates the bones to humanity at large rather than any specific tribe.

But Armand Minthorn of the Umatilla tribe says that if Kennewick Man "is truly over 9,000 years old, that only substantiates our belief that he is Native American. From our oral histories, we know that our people have been part of this land since the beginning of time. . . . Some scientists say that if this individual is not studied further we, as Indians, will be destroying evidence of our own history. We already know our history. It is passed on to us through our elders and through our religious practices." To Minthorn, a "preponderance of evidence" would include the widespread oral traditions that place Indian populations in the Columbia River area prior to Kennewick Man. This argument would require that Indian oral traditions be considered as valid as the speculations of linguist Johanna Nichols and the facial reconstruction of Kennewick Man that looks to some like British actor Patrick Stewart. Supporters of the Umatilla case criticize such "scientific speculation" as inadmissible evidence, and argue that the bones belong to the Umatilla.

Here, then, is the nub of the conflict: What are the relative merits of evidence about the past? If tribal tradition outweighs scientific criteria, then it is difficult to argue with the position of Walter Echo-Hawk: "We don't expect everyone to share our beliefs, but it doesn't take the wisdom of Solomon to understand that our dead deserve to rest in peace. . . . All we're asking for is a little common decency. . . . We're not asking for anything but to bury our dead."

If scientific evidence and tribal traditions are held comparable, then Alan Schneider (lawyer for the *Bonnichsen et al.* lawsuit) makes a telling point when he worries that the "subtly implied message is that somehow Native Americans own the history of this country. What's going on here is not a question of whether Native Americans can believe or follow their traditions, but it's a question of whether all of the rest of the country can be required to follow their traditions."

We are thus back to weighing the merits of scientific evidence against the "insider's" view of Native American culture. Thomas Jefferson had little difficulty accepting "traditionary testimony of the Indians," including accounts of mammoths still alive in the American West (and, as we saw, Deloria takes Jefferson at *his* word). A number of late nineteenth-century archaeologists believed that Native American oral traditions provided a viable link between ancient ruins and the Indian people who still lived in America.

By the early twentieth century, when ethnologists and archaeologists began to question seriously whether mythology and folklore contained any real "historical" value, Lowie effectively slammed the door on such "insider's" perspectives in his 1915 denunciation: "I cannot attach to oral traditions any historical value whatsoever under any conditions whatsoever." Today, after decades of following Lowie, a number of archaeologists are taking a second look at native oral traditions, asking once again whether these accounts might provide otherwise unavailable perspectives on events of importance to them. Even if they do not care to revisit the issue, the requirements of NAGPRA insist that they must.

IS ARCHAEOLOGY A REAL SCIENCE?

Assessing the relative merits of oral tradition is only one aspect of a deeper conflict over the relationship of archaeology to the "harder" sciences. Like the Boasian design for anthropology, archaeology developed its own brand of "physics envy," reflected in a certain starry-eyed longing for a systematic, if sometimes formulaic approach to the past. As such, American archaeology has constructed for itself a kind of objective, "scientific" perspective that would explain and predict archaeological findings within a theoretical framework—in this case, within a theory of human cultural development.

Although this "new archaeology" began shortly after World War I, the trend became dominant only in the 1960s when another generation of "new archaeologists" intensified their quest for cross-cultural regularities and correlations that would transcend the specifics of individual cultures. In this way, "explicitly scientific archaeology" became one of the generalizing social sciences such as economics, political science, and sociology. Its stated goal, to create universally valid generalizations about the human condition, was meant to lead to the improvement and management of contemporary societies by providing hard, objective evidence about the past. The politics of the present were dismissed as irrelevant; as scientists, archaeologists were to avoid passing moral judgments on people, past or present.

When asked about this, American Indians have often expressed their puzzlement over modern archaeology's strident insistence on this generalizing approach to human behavior. This almost clinical hypothesis-testing agenda seemed, to many Indian people, to preclude the use of archaeology for investigating the specific historical events of real interest to them. With their unrelenting focus on ecology and subsistence, archaeologists since the 1960s have effectively ignored (and belittled) the cultural and religious traditions of interest to Indian people. Science-based archaeology sent an unspoken message to Indian Country: We intend to use the archaeology of Native America for ends that have no particular relevance to Native Americans. Today, a number of archaeologists believe that the heavy-handed pursuit of law-like generalizations unintentionally alienated the very Native American communities that Euroamerican archaeologists wanted most to study.

In his stinging 1969 indictment of anthropology in *Custer Died for Your Sins*, Vine Deloria, Jr. clearly identified serious structural problems within the hard-science approach to anthropology. As Thomas Biolsi and Larry Zimmerman have put it, "Long before anyone in anthropology had heard of

Michel Foucault or Pierre Bordieu, Deloria had put his finger directly on what would later be called discursive formations, symbolic capital, and the micropolitics of the academy." Echoing Deloria's criticisms, the postmodern critique goes something like this: Facts are hopelessly contaminated by theory, and scientific theories are always politically and morally based doctrines. The method of science is narrow, requiring that everyone talk and argue in certain approved ways. Science tries to control the mind and limits one's ability to question authority. Science is sexist and driven by authoritarian male egos. It maintains an imperialist arrogance, brushing aside beliefs and understandings from other times and other cultures. At its heart, science is also capitalist, serving the interests of big business and the military-industrial complex. Although science has proven effective for producing goods and profits, a scientific perspective cannot uncover any truths not already anticipated by its own highly restrictive way of thinking. The ultimate objective of science (in this view) is a totalitarian control of human lives.

The postmodern spirit of pluralism (though not the entire agenda) has penetrated American archaeological practice, creating a highly diverse set of research agendas expressed in a less authoritarian manner. More and more, American archaeology calls for and welcomes multiple perspectives on the past. No longer do most archaeologists believe in absolute value neutrality, or transcendent objectivity. These concepts derive from an outdated philosophy of science. Today, most archaeologists believe—along with most philosophers of science—that science is part of culture, not outside it. Values, properly employed, can be productive rather than contaminating.

The real problem posed by relativism and multiple pasts is that judgments seem arbitrary and that there are no viable means for deciding between alternative views. At its extreme, this anarchic vision holds that no intellectual criteria are necessary to evaluate theories or to judge between them. This is because, the extremists argue, no theory can ever be "objectively" judged to be better than any other. Although few archaeologists today embrace this extreme relativism, there is clearly an element leaning in that direction in postmodern archaeology.

This, then, is the central issue in the Kennewick controversy. The 1990 NAGPRA legislation requires that cultural affiliation of human remains be judged based on numerous criteria—geography, kinship, biology, archaeology, linguistics, folklore, and so forth—without saying which of these incredibly diverse sources is to be preferred. The language of NAGPRA gives us no hint of how we are to choose among different worldviews in actual decision making. The "preponderance of evidence" criterion provides no way to resolve the conflicts between scientific and traditional belief systems whose notion of "evidence" may be entirely incompatible. As a result, the NAGPRA legislation, as written, leaves the door open for racialist arguments and assertions by authority from both sides.

The Kennewick Man conflict also reflects a worldwide concern with conflicting heritage claims and the larger issues of intellectual property rights. The controversy really revolves around ownership of the past—not just the objects of the past, but the broader perceptions of it as well.

ARCHAEOLOGY REDISCOVERS ITS HUMANISTIC ROOTS

For more than a century, archaeology prided itself in its scientific perspective, which was thought to provide an elegant and powerful way of allowing people to understand the workings of the visible world and the universe beyond. The goal of science is to develop theories that can be criticized and evaluated, to be eventually modified or even replaced by other theories that better explain the data. The scientific method relies heavily on the twin concepts of objectivity and testability. All archaeologists profess to believe in certain scientific fundamentals: in honest and careful scholarship, in generalizations backed by firm data, and in full consideration of negative evidence. But they are more than data-gathering automata; they may use creative imagination to solve problems of interest about the human past. Many archaeologists today acknowledge the degree to which they are historically situated and so reflect the stereotypes and images of their era. Many also stress the importance of bringing more humanistic perspectives to their understanding of the past.

In general, humanists tend to emphasize the dignity and worth of the individual. Humanists believe that the value of their contributions lies in their being intuitive, synthetic, and idiosyncratic. This is rather different from the scientific goal of making observations that are replicable by anyone with sufficiently rigorous training. By employing more subjective methods, humanists stress reality as perceived and experienced. A researcher's personal mental characteristics or attitude heavily conditions the result of a humanistic study.

The world has changed considerably since American archaeology began. Colonial powers have largely vanished, the so-called "primitive" is gone, the geopolitical landscape has become violent and hostile to archaeologists, funding is more difficult to obtain as university and institutional priorities have shifted. Archaeology has steered away from seeing itself as the "natural science of society." Some archaeologists now reject all causal viewpoints in their quest for understanding different worldviews, symbol systems, values, religions, philosophies, and systems of meaning. A newer brand of interpretive archaeology has abandoned notions of overarching theory or systematic research on "the other." In its place is proposed a closer consideration of cultural context and the meaning of social life to those who enact it. Instead of looking for regularities, postmodern archaeology seeks to explain the exceptions.

This means that archaeological evidence can be fully appreciated only in its specific historical contexts. Some archaeologists have even turned away from traditional "scientific" fieldwork to embrace instead the tenets of postmodernism—that all truth is relative and all perceptions are mediated by one's cultural and sexual identity. Postprocessual critics point out, quite correctly, that much of explicitly scientific archaeology rigidly adhered to rote rules of evidence and interpretation.

To understand the past, many archaeologists today believe, one must develop more empathetic, particularistic approaches—considering not only human reasoning and decisions but also such highly subjective elements as affective states, spiritual orientations, and experiential meanings. These empathetic approaches assume that the inner experience of human beings is worthy of study both for its own sake and as a clue for interpreting the human past. In other words, many archaeologists today seek a return to the "insider's" perspectives of Cushing, Fletcher, and La Flesche.

It is simply incorrect to assume that the history written by historians and/or anthropologists is value-neutral, an objective telling of events that took place back in time. Like it or not, the historical disciplines are the products of Western tradition, and even anthropologists, protest as they·might, are the prisoners of their own cultural backgrounds. Increasingly, science is coming to accept that anthropologists and native people sometimes reckon time on rather different time scales, and different cultures recognize different aspects of the same event as important to them.

So, returning to the question of whether "real" history might, indeed, be embedded in Native American oral traditions, one must ask "whose reality." Sometimes, oral traditions seem to contain a history that has some common "reality" to both native and western historians, a kind of history that can also be observed in the archaeological record. If so, then how do we articulate these diverse sources of information to paint a richer view of the past?

Examples are beginning to pile up. A few years ago, for instance, archaeologists working for the Mohegan Nation of Connecticut were called upon to document an alleged historical cabin site slated for destruction by a construction project. When asked, tribal elders not only pinpointed exactly where the cabin foundations were buried—in the complete absence of surface evidence—they also remembered the name of its occupant during the 1690s. Subsequent archaeological and documentary research completely verified the elder's recollections, three hundred years after the fact.

And consider the case of the Sand Creek massacre. Scientists and historians have long debated exactly where the infamous 1864 slaughter took place. Nineteenth-century maps are inaccurate, and despite repeated efforts, archaeologists have been unable to pinpoint the location of Black Kettle's ill-fated encampment.

Then, in 1998, Laird Cometsevah (a Southern Cheyenne leader) suggested that maybe the exact massacre location had never actually been lost. Maybe the location was recorded in tribal oral tradition. Enlisting the aid of U.S. Senator Ben Nighthorse Campbell (himself a Southern Cheyenne), Cometsevah convened a task force including the Sand Creek Descendants Association, National Park Service, state officials, and other tribal representatives. Together, they set out to track down the precise spot where his ancestors had been brutally slain, so that it could be declared a historical site of the National Park Service.

Studying aerial photographs, the Cheyenne elders finally agreed on a spot near Dawson's Bend, Colorado. The follow-up archaeological survey quickly turned up compelling evidence less than a mile to the north. "The clincher," said Doug Scott, field director of the archaeological survey, "was the discovery of 12-pounder cannonballs — the type used by the Colorado calvary in the engagement." Since Chivington's men were the only troops known to have turned their heaviest weaponry on a defenseless Indian village in this era, the case was finally closed. Scott's field crew found evidence of only defensive fighting by native people in and around the camp — further verifying that the "engagement" was indeed a surprise attack and massacre of the most brutal sort. The Sand Creek archaeological survey of 1998 also established, yet again, the power of native oral tradition in preserving "real history" across the generations.

Throughout the 1990s, native people and archaeologists have been increasingly willing to work with one another. Whereas many Indians once tended to ignore or reject requests from anthropologists to share their traditional knowledge, some tribal elders are now more willing to discuss these things, provided that the scientists take tribal goals into account in their research. For their part, a number of modern anthropologists are willing to grant that human memory can preserve key events over generations, perhaps for thousands of years.

As one anthropologist sees it, the long-standing conflict is resolved: "It is no longer a question of *whether* oral tradition includes historical knowledge, but how much is present, how long a time span it covers, and how valid it is."

HIDATSA ORIGINS: CONVERGING TRIBAL AND ARCHAEOLOGICAL VIEWS

Not all archaeologists shared Lowie's glum view of oral tradition. Where viable Indian populations remained on the land, American archaeologists often maintained at least an informal curiosity about local tribal traditions— in North Dakota, for instance, where several extraordinarily well-preserved earthlodge villages were clustered along the banks of the Knife and Missouri rivers, just north of Bismarck. Three of these villages, today part of the Knife River Indian Villages National Historic Site, were once home to between 3,000 and 5,000 Hidatsa people. The unbroken archaeological record preserved there documents Hidatsa life in these settled farming communities from the time people first arrived about AD 1300.

The French explorer Pierre Gaultier de Varennes stopped at Knife River in the late 1730s, on his trading and exploring expedition along the Upper Missouri River. Then came eighteenth-century Euroamerican fur traders. The Knife River villagers, experienced traders, welcomed the newcomers into their earthlodges. Throughout the nineteenth century, they hosted a steady stream of colorful visitors including members of the Lewis and Clark expedition in 1804 and 1806, George Catlin in 1832, and Karl Bodmer in 1833–1834. These early visitors produced journals, maps, paintings, and drawings, recording Euroamerican impressions of traditional Hidatsa lifestyles. They also recorded a Hidatsa creation story, which had been handed down from generation to generation.

The story begins with a supernatural being who lived in a village in the clouds. Although everyone in this tribe also enjoyed an extraordinary range of metaphysical powers, hunters complained that there was not enough game to feed their families. One day, our hero heard the snorting of many bison. Peering through a hole in the clouds, he could see boundless herds of buffalo on Earth below. That made him want to settle there; so he transformed himself into an arrow, soaring downward from the sky. His arrow-shaped body stuck fast and was attacked by an evil adversary named Fire-Around-the Ankle, who set him on fire. The hero was badly burnt and from then on he was known as Charred Body.

After he freed himself, Charred Body settled on a rise overlooking the Missouri River, where he constructed thirteen earth lodges. He returned to the clouds and recruited thirteen young couples to settle the new land. Bringing with them seed corn and the necessities for life below, the pioneers—themselves transformed into downward-shooting arrows—accompanied Charred Body to the new village. Hidatsa tradition holds that epic struggles took place between the supernaturals and villagers who already lived in this new land (perhaps early Mandan people). Charred Body's village prospered. The pioneering families intermarried and the population soared, eventually becoming the thirteen clans of the Hidatsa people.

This Hidatsa legend states that this first village of thirteen lodges was established on a river terrace overlooking Turtle Creek, about two miles below the present town of Washburn. Because of the legend, this creek is also known as Burnt or Charred Body Creek.

Archaeological research began in the Knife River area when Lewis Henry Morgan visited the area in 1862 to collect information on Hidatsa kinship, linguistics, and ceremonial activities. Morgan also studied the architecture and settlement layout of one earthlodge village shortly after the Arikaras had abandoned the site. More systematic research followed in the early 1900s when Orin G. Libby (of the newly formed State Historical Society of North Dakota) began mapping the archaeological sites at Knife River. Recognizing close ties between the archaeology and the native people living at the nearby Fort Berthold Reservation, Libby commissioned Sitting Rabbit, a Mandan, to prepare paintings of all the known villages, drawing together the information available from tribal elders. Libby then teamed a professional surveyor with Sitting Crow (Mandan), Holding Eagle (Hidatsa), and James Holding Eagle (also Hidatsa), who pointed out important connecting trails and cemetery areas. They also provided traditional information about the sites, some of which had been abandoned only six decades earlier.

During a survey in the 1940s, archaeologists recorded a site near the spot where Mandan-Hidatsa oral history suggested Charred Body had supposedly established the initial Hidatsa settlement, and the archaeologists named it "the Flaming Arrow site." Years earlier, ethnographer Alfred Bowers noted that thirteen lodge outlines were visible at the Flaming Arrow site and that Hidatsa traditions said these represented the original dwellings of the thirteen distinct lineages that comprised the ancient clan system of the Hidatsa (prior to the smallpox epidemics). But highway and railway construction damaged the Flaming Arrow site before much archaeology could be done there.

Intriguing new evidence suggests a previously unsuspected convergence between archaeological and traditional Hidatsa Indian knowledge. In 1983, when University of North Dakota archaeologists tested what remained at Flaming Arrow, they found some very unusual evidence buried there. First, they found that the houses were oval, quite unlike the rectangular or circular houses typical at nearby village sites. They were also puzzled to find that corn storage pits, a feature common on similar sites, were entirely absent at Flaming Arrow. The cord-roughened pottery was also unusual, more similar to ancient ceramics than to local wares. When archaeologists processed several radiocarbon dates on charred timbers from the buried house, the date came back about AD 1100—making Flaming Arrow the oldest Plains Village site in the region. Oral tradition had quite obviously preserved the memory of the Hidatsa's first Missouri River settlement.

MOUNT MAZAMA: CAN ORAL TRADITION SURVIVE FOR 7,500 YEARS?

In *Red Earth, White Lies*, Deloria offers a radical new alternative to standard science-based explanations of Native American origins. He argues that American Indians may have occupied the Western Hemisphere for an extremely long period of time, and that immense knowledge regarding past migrations, ancient geological and climatic events is preserved in the traditions of Native American tribes.

A number of Northwest Coast Indian tribes have legends that say that in times past, strange people came through their lands, strangers who did not look like them and practiced entirely different customs and ways of life. Although some believe that these long-standing Indian traditions complement interpretations of Kennewick Man as a non-Indian outsider, others retain a Lowie-like refusal to see anything of scientific value in oral tradition.

Deloria warns, "Until the academic scholars recognize the place of indigenous peoples and their traditions as well as the work of independent scholars, these conflicts will continue to occur." He points out that, for centuries, the Trojan War was believed to be a myth. Only when Heinrich Schliemann discovered and excavated the archaeological site of Hissarlik did the western world accept that Homer's poetic account was grounded in historical fact. Deloria argues that indigenous Americans witnessed significant geological events, and their accounts have been handed down across the generations, through oral myth and storytelling. He brings up the dramatic case of Crater Lake, in southeastern Oregon.

For some years, geologists struggled to explain how this spectacular lake came to be nestled in the summit of Mount Scott, at an elevation of nearly 10,000 feet. Today, scientists believe that at the end of the Ice Age, Mount Scott did not exist, and neither did Crater Lake. In its place stood Mount Mazama, a steep, peaked mountain extending perhaps a mile higher than the current lake. Mount Mazama may have looked something like Mount Shasta, 100 miles south, in California.

About 7,600 years ago, the 12,000-foot summit of Mount Mazama exploded violently, spewing tons of ash particles skyward and sending a superheated ash and lava slurry rushing down its slopes. Seventeen cubic miles of the mountain's interior poured over the countryside, the fiery lava avalanches flattened everything in their path, creating huge subterranean channels. Five or six miles below the surface, a hollow cavity remained in the heart of the mountain where the volcanic lava had once collected. Within days, the summit was so weakened that it collapsed almost straight downward, creating a caldera six miles wide and 4,000 feet deep. Rain and snow eventually created the Crater Lake that we see today. It is the deepest lake in North America.

Deloria thinks that the key elements of this 7,000-year-old story have survived in the Native American traditions of the area. A nineteen-year-old soldier, William Colvig, wrote down one such story, when he was stationed at Fort Klamath in 1865. In a conversation with eighty-year-old Chief Lalek, Colvig asked, "Why do your people never go up to the lake? Why are you afraid to look down upon its waters?" The old man told Colvig a story he had learned from his father, who had learned it from his father. Colvig later recorded the same tale from several other Klamath elders.

Chief Lalek begins the Klamath story like this: "A long time ago, so long that you cannot count it, the white man ran wild in the woods and my people lived in rock-built houses. In that time, long ago, before the stars fell, the spirits of the earth and the sky, the spirits of the sea and the mountains often came and talked with my people. . . ." Lalek then described the spirits living inside Mount Mazama and its sister mountain, Mount Shasta. The two massive peaks had openings that led to a lower world through which the spirits could pass. The Chief of the Below-World loved a Klamath chief's daughter, Loha, and demanded that she marry him. When this amorous overture was rebuked, the result did not sit well with the spirit, who threatened total de-struction of the people as revenge. "Raging and thundering," the story went, "he rushed up through the opening and stood on top of his mountain," terror-izing the people below.

At this point, the spirit of Mount Shasta intervened as a cloud appeared over the peak of Shasta, and the two mountains engaged in a horrible com-bat: "Red-hot rocks as large as the hills hurtled through the skies. Burning ashes fell like rain. The chief of the Below-World (Mazama) spewed fire from its mouth. Like an ocean of flame it devoured the forests on the mountains and in the valleys. On and on the Curse of Fire swept until it reached the homes of the people. Fleeing in terror before it, the people found refuge in the waters of Klamath Lake."

The Klamaths then decided that someone should be sacrificed to calm the chaos. Two medicine men climbed Mount Mazama and jumped into the caldera: "Once more the mountains shook. This time the Chief of the Below-World was driven into his home and the top of the mountain fell upon him. When the morning sun arose, the high mountain was gone. . . . For many years, rain fell in torrents and filled the great hole that was made when the mountain fell. . . ."

Chief Lalek ended his story this way: "Now you understand why my peo-ple never visit the lake. Down through the ages we have heard this story. From father to son has come the warning, "look not upon the place . . . for it means death or everlasting sorrow."

Deloria emphasizes the parallels between the pre-1865 Klamath ac-count—recorded decades before the first scientist explored Crater Lake—and the modern geological explanation, which dates only to the 1920s. In both, Mount Mazama was destroyed in a catastrophic explosion, character-ized by superheated avalanches, a massive cloud of volcanic dust, the dra-matic collapse of the peak into the belly of the mountain, and the formation of a new deepwater lake atop the truncated mountain.

Did native people actually see Mount Mazama erupt 7,400 years ago? Deloria thinks so, drawing upon the extensive archaeological evidence show-ing the presence of a major Native American population in southeastern Ore-gon at that time. Or is it possible that Indians figured out Crater Lake the same way Euroamerican geologists would later, and that it was not a case of collective memory passed down for 7,500 years? Many Indians are pretty good observers of natural history in their own right: Couldn't they have seen an eruption in more recent times in one of the Cascade ranges and put the story together for themselves?

Archaeological research solidly demonstrates that native people *could have* witnessed the drama. People have lived within what is now the State of Oregon for at least 11,000 years, perhaps as long as 13,000 years. Recently, archaeologists working near Paulina Lake, about 75 miles northeast of Crater Lake, have uncovered the remains of a 9,400-year-old house—the oldest dwelling yet found in North America. The house itself was buried under volcanic ash from the Mount Mazama eruption. Archaeological evidence like this clearly shows that it is at least plausible that human eyewitnesses saw the eruption.

But could an oral tradition survive for nearly 7,500 years? If the Klamath story about Crater Lake is *not* an eyewitness account, Deloria asks, how did the Klamath elders come up with a sophisticated, pre-1865 version of the event— long before geological science had developed its explanations of volcanic explosions and centuries before a geologist had ever set eyes on Crater Lake?

Further, the Mount Mazama eruption is unusual in the geological record. Most volcanic eruptions simply blow off the top of a mountain. Sometimes— as in the recent case of Mount Saint Helens—they blow out the side as well. How could the Klamaths have known that Crater Lake is a rare case in which the top of a volcano collapsed directly downward into the active caldera?

But there is a problem here. With his stridently anti-science position, Deloria demands an extraordinarily high level of evidence on the part of archaeological science. Obviously, as the previous discussion of the ongoing dispute over Monte Verde clearly indicates, archaeologists do not always achieve that standard. But in his passionate advocacy for archaeologists to include native traditions as valid history—which makes good sense to me— Deloria seems to accept much lower standards of evidence than those he requires from science.

Is Deloria willing to turn his searing criticisms of science on his own historical reconstructions from native tradition? Or has tribal tradition earned a special measure of respect simply from the fact that the tales have survived over the ages?

A SPECTRUM OF ORAL TRADITIONS

The specifics of Native American origin tales vary widely, but deep down, the stories share several similarities. Innumerable Native American oral traditions, for instance, refer to the existence of dangerous "monsters" and giant animals in ancient times. Other origin stories are set during a prehuman period, when animals and birds ruled the world. Roger C. Echo-Hawk notes that paleontologists, not coincidentally, describe late Ice Age America as a realm dominated by giant animals—mammoths, mastodons, and giant sloths, which towered over their human predators.

Echo-Hawk believes he has identified a "spectrum of oral traditions" with potential for shedding light on the late Pleistocene world of his ancestors: memories of Arctic Circle patterns of solar behavior, transition to lower latitude diurnal/nocturnal cycles (as First Americans moved southward), remembrances of European and New World glacial ice sheets, sea level changes during the last Ice Age, human relations with the now-extinct megafauna of the New World, references to glacial lakes, and the onset of Holocene (post-Pleistocene) seasons. Could these traditional tales reflect an ancient reality, when great creatures, no longer on this earth, made the New World a dangerous place for the ancestral Native American? Echo-Hawk believes so.

He also notes that in many Indian traditions, a great flood covered Earth at an ancient time that many stories associate with the end of the age of monsters. Could these tales reflect the end of the most recent Ice Age, some 12,000 years ago, which doubtless involved some cataclysmic flooding? As the glaciers melted, the sudden release of a massive ice sheet into the ocean would have brought episodes of worldwide flooding. Echo-Hawk urges the study of archaeological evidence concurrent with an exploration of Native American oral traditions.

He also warns that serious researchers must be cautious about uncritically accepting oral traditions as literal characterizations of past events. He considers Deloria's *Red Earth, White Lies* "fringe literature" because it dismisses out-of-hand the findings of geologists, physicists, and archaeologists and substitutes a faith-based reliance on oral information, bolstered by selective use of science. Echo-Hawk argues instead for a "partnership ecology," a return to more fruitful interaction between Indians and archaeologists. Deloria accuses Echo-Hawk of "sucking up" to the archaeological elite by telling them what they want to hear.

Various tribes react differently to the use of oral tradition for scholarly research. The Hopi tribe has encouraged archaeologists to employ such knowledge, particularly when tribal advisors are involved as collaborators. The Navajo Nation is also enthusiastic about melding their oral traditions with scientific evidence from tribal sites. The Zuni Nation forbids the use of oral tradition in scholarly research, except in a very limited fashion by researchers employed by the tribe and for purposes that Zuni cultural advisers consider acceptable. The Hualapai Tribe, seeing oral traditions as critical to their cultural heritage, expresses some discomfort when outsiders obtain too much knowledge. The Hualapai request that only appropriate tribal members conduct research into oral history, to be certain that sensitive information can be controlled and that the tribe can be assured such information is used only for appropriate purposes.

Although research into oral tradition and the archaeological record have some parallels, there is one important difference: Whereas archaeologists can often find corroborative information in traditional tales, rarely do Indian people feel the need to corroborate their own oral history. Some Native Americans also point out that, in the past, archaeologists have mined traditional sites to collect artifacts. There is increasing concern that archaeologists might now wish to appropriate tribal traditions in the same way.

SEEKING COMMON GROUND

The specifics of NAGPRA highlight the differing histories that have evolved for ancient Native America. One was written down in books, taught in schools, and exhibited in museums—this is mainstream history reflecting the perspective of the outsider, the conqueror of continents. An entirely different history exists in Indian Country, a history handed down by Indian people from elder to child as tribal tradition, language, spirituality, ritual, and ceremonies—even in jewelry and personal ornamentation.

Slowly recognizing the validity of both historical pathways, archaeology in America has changed significantly in recent years—from the scientific study of ancient things toward the systematic study of people and their history. It is no longer merely the study of material culture. Archaeologists no longer conduct their inquiry in a vacuum; today, many archaeologists are actively consulting and involving Indian people.

Archaeology and oral tradition differ, of course, in how observations are made and interpreted. Western science relies on discrete observational units and measurable variables that can be analytically combined and/or held constant. Native observations arise from people who view themselves within a holistic environment and societal framework. These are separate ways of knowing the past, but they tend to converge in a broad sense because certain important issues tend to dominate both realms—migrations, warfare, land use, ethnicity, and so forth. Because different standards apparently apply to how relevant information is collected, evaluated, and used, however, the two ways of knowing will never completely coincide.

AN ARCHAEOLOGY WITHOUT ALIENATION

24.

Our history, identity, and tribal sovereignty are indistinguishable from the land. From time immemorial, it has always been so.
[We have begun] the process of reclaiming our ancestral lands and identity as distinct, self-governing peoples. Today, we are continuing to restore our ancestral land base.

—*Exhibit label in the Tamástslikt Cultural Institute (1998)*

THE CONFEDERATED TRIBES of the Umatilla recently opened their $18 million dollar Tamástslikt Cultural Institute; the name means "interpreter" in the Walla Walla language. Tamástslikt is located at the foot of the Blue Mountains, about seven miles east of Pendleton, Oregon, part of the Wildhorse Resort that also includes a casino, a 100-room hotel, a 100-space RV park, and an 18-hole golf course. The Tamástslikt Cultural Institute is the only Indian-owned museum along the Oregon Trail, and the Umatilla are anxious to tell their story to the thousands of tourists who travel this way each summer.

In their signature exhibition, the Umatilla concisely describe how they feel about their own tribal history:

THE POWER OF HOME: WE WERE, WE ARE, WE WILL BE

> In the beginning, all the world was alive. The living beings were constantly at war. Eventually, the most powerful ruled the land. Then along came tspilyáy (Coyote). Tspilyáy wandered the land bringing order. A new time and a new kind of people were soon approaching. In this way, everything was made ready. Now, we the Natítayl (The People), have arrived. The Creator has planted us here on this earth. As our children listen to the deeds of tspilyáy and of times past, our story also begins.

This simple narrative of Red Creationism continues an oral tradition the Umatilla believe reaches back 10,000 years. They know how time began and how their tribe was created. To suggest otherwise is to disrespect their religion.

But Donald Sampson, former Chairman of the Board for the Confederated Tribes of the Umatilla Indian Reservation, points out that this traditional creation story does not require a wholesale rejection of science. "In fact, we have anthropologists and other scientists on staff and we use science every day to help protect our people and the land." But Sampson adds, "We reject the notion that science is the answer to everything and that science should take precedence over the religious rights and beliefs of American citizens." Rebecca Tsosie, a Native American and executive director of the Indian legal program at Arizona State University agrees: "Western science gives us a way of knowing the world, a noble goal, but it's not the only way to establishing something as the truth."

Like Sampson, many other American Indians accept the possibility of scientific inquiry into Indian origins, and several express confidence in the Bering Strait theory. Some look back to World War II, when non-Indian American soldiers sometimes mistook the famous Navajo Code Talkers for Japanese soldiers. They saw similar features in Navajos and Japanese—dark hair, darkish skin, and high cheekbones. To complicate matters, Japanese soldiers sometimes took uniforms from dead GIs and tried to sneak across American lines. The mix-up made life even more dangerous for the Code Talkers. Did any of them wonder whether their bodies might reflect some ancient Asian connection?

"These are early photographs of me which might have been made thirty thousand years ago on the Bering Strait land bridge; just wide of the prehistoric camera's eye there stands a faithful dog of the chow strain, dragging a travois."
—N. Scott Momaday

N. Scott Momaday, the first Native American author to win a Pulitzer Prize, certainly wonders about this: "As a child, especially, my features belied the character of my ancient ethnic origin. . . . And as recently as my undergraduate days someone . . . asked me from what part of Asia I had come. 'Northern Mongolia,' I replied. In Hobbs, New Mexico, in 1943, I was suspected of that then dreadful association. Nearly every day on the playground someone would greet me with, 'Hi'ya, Jap,' and the fight was on. Now and then two or more patriots would gang up on me"

Beyond his personal belief in a deep "racial memory" of Asian roots, Momaday is familiar with—and convinced by—the scientific evidence indicating that Indians migrated to America from Asia perhaps 20,000 years ago. In a 1996 Op-Ed piece in *The New York Times*, Momaday criticized the Indian creationists, as he does creationists of all kinds, and pointed out, "Science has unlocked countless doors, has allowed human beings to see themselves with a clarity not available to our forebears."

Momaday agrees with Tsosie and Sampson that a belief in science is not enough. "Archaeologists and anthropologists, especially, have given science a bad name in the Indian world." Despite his personal belief in an Asian ancestry for Indian people, Momaday knows that scientific desecration of Indian spiritual life has created long-lasting resistance toward additional scientific study. "Native Americans will resist. They feel they must. At stake is their identity, their dignity and their spirit."

This public affirmation of scientific research provoked a peppery response from Deloria, who accused Momaday of spending "the last thirty years carefully hidden at white literary circles enjoying the celebrity that being an Indian brings." Suggesting that Momaday's *New York Times* piece "borders on the incoherent," Deloria wrote, "I had always assumed that there was considerable evidence for the human crossing of the Bering Strait so a couple of years ago I began to look for articles on the theory. I couldn't find any . . . There is no great body of evidence supporting the Bering Strait! Period. I demand that if Scott Momaday knows where all this evidence is, has read it, and therefore made a rational decision regarding it, everyone else—Indian and white—should have the same rights. So would Scott please provide us with a list of the articles and books most supportive on the Bering Strait theory? These would assuredly provide interesting reading."

Refusing to rise to the bait, Momaday only reiterated his "deepest respect" for Deloria and suggested that "He and I can and should disagree from time to time; after all we are both independent thinkers. But I will not fight with my brother." Momaday took the occasion to restate his conviction that "the Bering Bridge 'theory' is not a theory at all ". . . there were human migrations across the Bering land bridge in prehistoric times." For his part, Deloria complained that ". . . to the audience Scott appears rational and I do not, simply because I have questioned this sacred cow—so readers have sympathy with his article which basically says that fundamentalist Indians are ruining science when the 'science' they are ruining is just utter chauvinistic nonsense."

This exchange highlights the central thesis of this book: We have argued that the Skull Wars cannot be seen as a simple conflict between modern science and traditional religion. The lingering issues between Indians and archaeologists are political, a struggle for control of American Indian history. Although Deloria and Momaday disagree about the relative merits of scientific knowledge and the role of Red Creationism, they agree on the most basic issue of all. The American academic community—led by grave-digging archaeologists—has robbed the Native American people of their history and their dignity. In different ways, Momaday and Deloria both urge Indians to take back control over their own heritage because in so doing, they will also gain control over their own identities.

This book has presented several episodes that suggest a long-term antipathy toward archaeologists in Indian Country. There is plenty of cultural baggage here, and it is important that we visit each other's history. The history of Indian-anthropology interactions is extraordinarily complex, and not entirely negative. Without taking anything away from Deloria's *Custer Died for Your Sins*, painting this history as red vs.white creates yet another series of stereotypes (which we can well do without).

Contrary to Deloria's blanket assertions in *Custer*, anthropologists were not completely silent about the termination policies of the Truman and Eisenhower administrations. Although the American Anthropological Association never took a formal stand against post-War federal policy, several anthropologists—the names of Alexander Lesser, Sol Tax, D'Arcy McNickle, and Philleo Nash come most readily to mind—fiercely lobbied in support of Indian tribes and the doctrine of self-determination.

An interesting 1973 exchange highlights these conflicting directions within anthropology. Four weeks after the outbreak of the Wounded Knee II unpleasantness in 1973, archaeologist Sally Binford wrote an open letter to the membership of the American Anthropological Association, suggesting that "the silence on the part of anthropologists about events there is deafening." Without referring directly to *Custer Died for Your Sins* (published four years before), Binford argued that anthropologists had long profited "directly or indirectly" from American Indians: "We study the artifacts looted from their kivas; we teach students their kinship systems and we dig up their burials. Native Americans have, without compensation, provided the data for countless MA and PhD theses. Perhaps it is time we paid our dues." Binford went on to suggest that concerned anthropologists donate to the Wounded Knee Defense Fund to help the more than one hundred Indians then incarcerated for their part in the Wounded Knee protests.

We do not know how many anthropologists contributed to the Defense Fund, but her letter drew an angry response from Leslie White, one of the most distinguished anthropologists of his day. White, who had conducted extensive fieldwork at Acoma Pueblo and elsewhere in the American Southwest between 1926 and 1957, expressed his deep resentment at being accused of ripping off Native Americans. Noting that he was removed from the University payroll while conducting fieldwork, White said "I do not believe that my researches ever injured Indians, deprived them of anything of value or harmed them in any way." None of his research monographs were copyrighted, and "I never received a cent in royalties. I was out of pocket on every field trip I ever made."

White took exception to Binford's accusations that Indians were forced to work for nothing: "No informant ever helped me without compensation," he said, "sometimes in kind and sometimes by an hourly wage." White denied knowing any anthropologist who looted artifacts from kivas, and told how he personally had rescued ancient ceramic vessels and ceremonial paraphernalia from unscrupulous traders and looters. "These precious elements of Pueblo culture are now preserved in museum collections where they may be studied by scholars and admired by the public—and where the Indians know they are safe." According to White, "members of the mea culpa chorus miss one point and a vital one: many Indians want to have a record made of their rapidly disappearing culture, a description and interpretation of their cultural identity— as communicated by the Indians themselves to the ethnographer. . . . Devoted Indians helped me to make these studies and others treasure them as reminiscences of their lives and of their mothers and fathers. I do not see how I could have rendered these Indians a greater service."

We have already noted how anthropologists like Fletcher, Cushing, Boas, Kroeber, among many others, used their political clout to help out American Indians (as least as they perceived such help was warranted). Even Lewis Henry Morgan—whose now-discarded theory of social evolution informed the disastrous Dawes Act of 1887—was personally dedicated to the betterment of Indian people.

Only two weeks after Custer and his Seventh Cavalry troops were annihilated by Sitting Bull and the combined Indian forces at the Little Bighorn, Morgan wrote an impassioned and quite unpopular letter to *The Nation*, published on July 20, 1876, blasting the virulent anti-Indian sentiments being expressed around the country. Morgan laid blame for the tragedy on failed federal policies that led to the crisis in the first place: "The press are now opening upon the Indians generally, and with a hue and cry in particular for the extermination of those tribes who have dared to raise their hands against the gallant soldiers of the Republic who were in the field in obedience to its commands." Morgan criticized the media's use of the term "massacre" to describe the fight, and accused General Custer of foolishly trying to "rout this encampment, men, women, and children, and kill all those who resisted without hesitation and without remorse. Unfortunately for General Custer and his men, they encountered the bravest and most determined Indians now living in America. . . . We admire the gallantry of General Custer and his men; we mourn their loss; but who shall blame the Sioux for defending themselves, their wives and children, when attacked in their own encampment and threatened with destruction. This calamity is simply a chance of war, nothing more and nothing less. For its moral character we must look to the motives which prompted our government in its commencement." Strong words from somebody too commonly perceived as writing off the Vanishing American as doomed by evolution. Morgan ended his wildly unpopular defense of Indians with a plea against revenge, saying, "the good name of our country cannot bear many wars of this description."

This is why we must not view the history of Indians and anthropologists in simplistic racial terms. Although the Kennewick controversy suggests that perhaps Indians and archaeologists must always remain enemies, Kennewick is only one model of Indian-archaeologist interactions. Once the fundamental dilemma has been defined—that archaeologists no longer exercise sole control over the ancient American past—perhaps the two sides will be freed to form new partnerships and build new bridges.

We now turn to a couple of widely separated archaeology programs— one on Alaska's Kodiak Island and the other on the Mashantucket Pequot Reservation of eastern Connecticut—that illustrate how Native Americans are developing their own archaeological projects in tandem with oral history programs to retrieve a past directly relevant to tribal members.

DIGGING AFOGNAK

Archaeologists have not always been welcome on Kodiak Island. Village elders still remember the archaeological dig in the 1930s, when Aleš Hrdlička dug up their ancient burial grounds. Some of the elders still call him "old hard liquor."

Kodiak Islanders buried their dead here for about three thousand years before they moved to other sites on the island around AD 1500. In the largest single-site dig ever conducted in Alaska, Hrdlička and his team excavated hundreds of graves and removed thousands of associated artifacts. At the time, this single collection comprised more than five percent of all the human skeletons curated in the Smithsonian Institution.

Hrdlička saw the Kodiak Island bones and artifacts as an important resource, the only way for anthropologists to reconstruct the thousands of years of cultural and biological history of Alaska's native peoples. The Alutiiq people living on Kodiak Island did not share Hrdlička's commitment to science, and they were shocked when he dug up hundreds of their ancestors and shipped them away to a museum they had never seen. The Alutiiq remember Hrdlička as a man who respected neither the living nor the dead.

Their resentment simmered for decades until the Kodiak Islanders requested in the 1980s that the bones and funerary objects be returned home for reburial. Tendered well before the passage of NAGPRA, this simple request for repatriation is now termed "a watershed event in the history of social science" because it forced curators and archaeologists to confront the ethical and moral problems raised by their excavations in Native American burial grounds.

Emotions ran high as the Smithsonian Institution refused the request, emphasizing the scientific importance of the collection and questioning the relationship between the modern people of Kodiak Island and the ancient skeletons dug up by Hrdlička. Offended by what they saw as an insensitive response, the Tribal Council continued to press for return of their ancestral bones. Finally, after years of spirited controversy, the Smithsonian finally agreed to hand over several hundred human skeletons and funerary objects to the Kodiak Island peoples. In the fall of 1991, priests from the Russian Orthodox Church officiated at the reburial ceremony. Village elders sang hymns in Alutiiq, Russian, and English. Leaders from the tribal council and Smithsonian Institution spoke as the remains were returned to the Kodiak soil.

Even as the repatriation struggle was going on, Amy Steffian, then a graduate student at the University of Michigan, asked the tribe for permission to dig further at Hrdlička's old site. She suggested that additional excavations could provide important clues about modern Alutiiq identity. When approached in this respectful and above-board manner, the community leaders not only granted her permission to excavate but even offered her a research grant from the Kodiak Area Native Association's bingo fund.

Here's yet another paradox in the anglo-Indian relationship: while heatedly battling for the return of archaeological and skeletal materials from the Smithsonian, these same Kodiak Island villagers were generously encouraging—and even helping to finance—archaeological research at the very same site.

Today, Steffian serves as curator of the Alutiiq Museum, an outgrowth of the Kodiak Area Native Association's Center and Heritage program, an organization founded in 1987 to develop an island-wide strategy of archaeological research and to promote educational programs on Alutiiq culture, language, and arts. Eight native corporations fund and govern the Alutiiq Museum; they also oversee their own archaeological research projects, employing professional archaeologists to work with crews of native people. The Alutiiq Museum curates the resulting collections and displays key artifacts in a native-governed repository. The artifacts repatriated from Hrdlička's excavation are today stored and available for study in the Alutiiq Museum.

The museum also provides professional and technical support to the *Dig Afognak* archaeological program, organized and staffed through the Afognak Native Corporation. The museum and the archaeological programs have produced new career opportunities for native people who have long participated in local excavations and more recently worked as archaeological laboratory technicians. A number of the Alutiiq students involved in the archaeology program are now pursuing college degrees in history and anthropology.

Dig Afognak offers the opportunity to live and work with native people in the remote wilderness of the Kodiak archipelago, a 20-minute floatplane ride from the city of Kodiak. Dig participants live in heated platform tents, dine in a large field kitchen, and bathe in a native-style sauna. Through *Dig Afognak*, Alutiiq people overcame their long-standing resentment of archaeologists like Hrdlička. Instead, they established new relationships with a different generation of archaeologists who have worked with them to establish their own program of archaeology and tourism.

"Our hearts were deeply touched by the work of our ancestors, and we determined that we needed to take responsibility for the excavation of the many sites located on our Native lands," says a spokesman for the Afognak Native Corporation. "To make the research circle complete, we decided to take the step of inviting the interested public . . . to join us as a *Dig Afognak* participant."

THE MASHANTUCKET PEQUOT: REBUILDING WHAT WAS TAKEN AWAY

One of the world's largest casinos is owned and operated by the tiny Mashantucket Pequot tribe of eastern Connecticut. To some, the Foxwoods Resort Casino, located halfway between New York City and Boston, epitomizes the worst in Indian gaming. One critic has grumbled about these "bingo Indians [who are] a disturbing illustration of the strange coinages that may result from the combining of gambling wealth and the ideology of tribal sovereignty in groups that in an ethnographic sense are, at most, only marginally Indian." But others see the "retribalization" of the Pequots as a uniquely American success story, an example of persistence and tenacity.

For thousands of years, the Pequot people had lived along the rivers and valleys of southeastern Connecticut. They became active fur traders during the seventeenth century, trading with Dutch and English settlers and becoming powerful players in the wampum-based economy of the time. In 1637, however, the Pequot nation was crushed by troops from the Massachusetts and Connecticut colonies in one of the bloodiest battles of America's Indian wars. Hundreds of men, women, and children were slaughtered in less than an hour. The survivors of the so-called Pequot War eventually found their way to a reservation near the town of Groton (the northern half of which became Ledyard, where the reservation exists today), where many accepted Christianity and intermarried with local black and white residents. In *Moby Dick*, Herman Melville wrote, "Pequod [Pequot], you will no doubt remember, was the name of a celebrated tribe of Massachusetts Indians, now as extinct as the ancient Medes."

But the Pequots were not extinct. Their 3000-acre reservation had been sold off piecemeal by the colony (and later, the state) to maintain the tribe, and by the mid-nineteenth century only 213 acres were left. The 1910 census recorded 66 survivors. In the 1970s, only two sisters, Elizabeth George Plouffé and Martha Langevin Ellal remained on tribal lands. When the two sisters died, 50 Pequot members vowed to pull the tribe back together, drafting a tribal constitution in 1974 and electing Richard L. "Skip" Hayward as Tribal Chairman. For the next several years, he personally tracked down distant relatives throughout eastern North America, urging the Pequot people to come back home.

The tribal council rounded up trailers for the returnees, and scratched to find a way for tribal members to make a living. They tried pig farming, selling firewood, and marketing maple sugar. They opened a pizza parlor, established a hydroponic lettuce farm, and operated a sand and gravel business.

Meanwhile, the Tribal Council built a claim for federal recognition, basing its claim on genealogy and continued occupancy of the land. The federal government recognized their tribal status in 1983 and settled the long-standing land claim by appropriating $900,000 for the purchase of 800 acres of lost tribal land. This is how the present-day Pequots reconstituted themselves as an official Indian tribe, simultaneously becoming a corporate business enterprise and a "sovereign" tribal state.

After three years of intense debate, the tribe opened a high-stakes bingo hall in 1986. For the first time, they had sufficient cash flow to build up the reservation infrastructure, including a centralized water system and better electrical service. A year later, the United States Supreme Court ruled that as sovereign nations, Indian tribes could legally operate casinos on their lands. With private backing, the Mashantucket Pequot built the Foxwoods Resort Casino, today the largest gaming operation in the Western Hemisphere.

The success of Foxwoods led to further business ventures, including the Pequot River Shipworks, which designs and builds state-of-the-art passenger ferries, and the Mashantucket Pequot Academy for management and business training. The Tribal Council also provides full scholarships to tribal members, completely supporting education from preschool through Ph.D. "We want to build a community and pass what we've built down to future generations," said Theresa Bell, a Pequot tribal representative. "We want to rebuild what was taken from us three hundred years ago."

By the late 1990s, Pequot tribal businesses had created more than 12,000 new jobs in southeastern Connecticut and awarded more than $145 million in contracts to non-tribal businesses. In 1995 alone, it turned over more than $150 million in revenue from gaming to the State of Connecticut. They also made substantial philanthropic contributions in support of the Native American Rights Fund, the Special Olympics, the D.A.R.E. antidrug program, and the Old Mystic Baptist Church. In 1994, the Mashantucket Pequot Tribal Nation donated $10 million to help establish the new National Museum of the American Indian. This was the largest single donation ever received by the Smithsonian Institution.

"Never doubt the old adage that money talks," says *Newsday*. "In the case of the Mashantucket Pequot Indian tribe, it's talking about the past." With the sudden wealth from the Foxwoods gambling palace, the tribe also had the wherewithal to reclaim and reconstruct its history and that of neighboring tribes. In 1982, the Pequot Tribe entered into a long-term relationship with Kevin McBride, an archaeologist at the University of Connecticut. The resultant Mashantucket Pequot Ethnohistory Project combines oral history, archival research, and archaeological excavations. The Ethnohistory Project undertook a walking survey of the entire 1,400-acre reservation, recording all aboveground archaeological evidence and locating more than 250 archaeological sites that span 11,000 years.

Workers installing a pipeline near a Foxwoods Casino parking lot discovered the most important find on Pequot land, the Sandy Hill site, in 1989. The 9,000-year-old site contains evidence of a dozen or more large pithouse structures, ancient stone tools, and well-preserved vegetable remains providing clear-cut evidence of a people living on cattails and hazelnut (and they probably collected turtles and hunted caribou). There is evidence that these people lived in a sedentary village—at least during the winter—much earlier than previously thought.

Beginning in 1984, tribal leaders began planning a museum to tell the story of Pequot history, culture, and identity. McBride was hired as director of research and he worked with tribal member Theresa Bell and anthropologist Jack Campisi to design the new museum's exhibits. McBride drew heavily upon results from the Mashantucket Pequot Ethnohistory Project. More than two hundred artisans, consultants and contractors from fifty Indian nations contributed to the new museum. They shared their oral histories and served as actors in the specially produced films.

In August 1998—on the 361st anniversary of the Pequot Massacre—the Mashantucket Pequot Museum and Research Center opened to the public, a 200-million-dollar facility housing a series of permanent exhibits recounting Mashantucket Pequot history, culture, and changing ways of life from the late Ice Age through the twentieth century. High-tech approaches are everywhere: A scent machine brings to mind a smoky campfire, a touch-screen computer explains the strategy of a caribou hunt, a computer linked to 110 speakers constantly remixes sounds of dogs, geese, and crickets. It is as large as Washington's Holocaust Museum and 20 percent larger than the Smithsonian's new National Museum of the American Indian.

The museum emphasizes multiple perspectives throughout, as in the hall illustrating creation stories from the Navajo, Kiowa, Mojave, Lakota, Iroquois, Ojibway, and Kwakwakáwakh (Kwakiutl). Alongside these cases are photographs of Monte Verde and Meadowcroft Rockshelter, with explanations of the Bering Strait theory of American Indian origins. "Every culture has its own beliefs about the origins of the cosmos and of human beings." the label copy explains. "Among tribal nations, such stories also offer explanation for social customs and for the way the tribe lives. They are more comprehensive than scientific explanations for how people came to North America— they are intended as metaphors for existence."

The Research Center houses a library devoted to American and Canadian native histories and cultures. Downstairs are state-of-the art research laboratories where twenty archaeologists and specialists are developing ethnographic and archaeological collections that shed light on the history of the Mashantucket Pequot people. They are also compiling a database of artisans involved in making such traditional objects. According to McBride, the aim is to create a one-of-a-kind research center on Native American culture history.

The Mashantucket Pequot Museum opened to rave reviews. *The New York Times* wrote, "No one can say the glory of native culture is a past phenomenon. The nation's museum professionals are watching with awe." *Connecticut*

Magazine called it "magnificent. Brings the Native American story vividly to life." *The Washington Post* calls the Pequot museum "a fascinating look into the history of American Indians, non-Indians and New England, and well worth the visit."

One of the stated aims of the Mashantucket Pequot Museum is to break down false imagery, and the exhibits look far beyond the white-created stereotypes of Indian people. True to this aim, the Pequots have also put aside the stereotypical confrontations between Indians and professional archaeologists during the late twentieth-century. Rather than replaying the stale archaeologist-as-enemy scenario, the Mashantucket Pequot tribe recognized the potential of conducting archaeological excavations on their reservation land to bring their past alive.

ARCHAEOLOGISTS AND INDIANS increasingly agree on certain key issues: The American past is important—we should attempt to understand it and preserve whatever remains of it. Many tribes maintain large and effective archaeology programs employing both white and Indian archaeologists. Several tribes sponsor their own museums that display archaeological materials. The Society for American Archaeology (SAA) sponsors a Native American Scholarship Fund—named after Arthur C. Parker, the SAA's first President—encouraging Indian people to train as professional archaeologists; it is funded, in part, from royalties earned on books written by archaeologists about the Native American past. Indian people are increasingly involved in archaeological meetings and publications—not merely as "informants," but participants and collaborators.

Archaeology has provided evidence in support of litigation for land claims, evidence that sometimes turns the tide in a tribe's favor. Some tribes have used their own archaeology to promote tribal sovereignty, a central social and political issue throughout Indian Country. For some tribes, archaeology has important financial benefits; more than ten percent of the Indian tribes in America today have their own archaeology programs. The largest of these, sponsored by the Navajo Nation, has an annual budget of $7,000,000 and employs 150 people in its historic preservation and archaeology departments – making it larger than any comparable state or federal program. Some native groups are conducting archaeology to encourage tourism, to inform educational programs, and to preserve sacred sites on their own land.

Archaeologist Duane Anderson has recently pointed out that one of the biggest flaws in the NAGPRA legislation is that it ignored all the positive models of communication and cooperation among American Indian groups, government agencies, archaeologists, and museums. By opting instead for a paternalistic, "radical, top-down solution," NAGPRA not only resulted in massive expenses to the tribes and museums involved but made the high-profile clash over Kennewick virtually inevitable.

The Kennewick controversy highlights the difficulties in asking the court system to resolve such disputes. To be sure, the eight scientists filing the Kennewick Man lawsuit felt a sense of urgency, even desperation. But as the argument over Kennewick Man came to be seen only in terms of "winners" and "losers," it overshadowed the search for a relationship based on mutual respect and consensus.

EPILOGUE

TWENTY-FIRST-CENTURY American archaeologists must do a better job. Here's one way to do it.

When Terry Fifield became the Forest Service archaeologist for Alaska's Prince of Wales Island, he felt as though he'd been preparing for this assignment his entire life. He had studied both geology and anthropology in college, had worked on various digs in the American Southwest, and wrote his M.A. thesis at Eastern New Mexico University. The formal part of his archaeological training was now complete.

Another side of Fifield's education began when he took a seasonal job in 1985 with the Alaska Native Claims Settlement Act (ANCSA) Projects Office in Anchorage. Working with a seasoned team of archaeologists and ethnographers, Fifield's assignment was to find key historical sites and cemeteries from a list selected by regional native corporations. Once such a site had been located, Fifield and his team began recording its archaeological characteristics and interviewing knowledgeable native elders in nearby villages.

Whenever possible, Fifield and colleagues accompanied the elders on a personal site visit. "It was a unique experience," he says, "to have people who had lived at the site actually tell you what that square hole was and why the structure had been moved to the other end of the village." A 75-year-old woman from Lime Village went with him to her grandfather's fish camp, where she took him around the ruins and showed him the fish weir. Two brothers took Fifield to a Yukon River campsite near Kaltag where as children they had spent a few months each year. As they joked and wandered around the "archaeological site," they spoke of long-forgotten people and events; Fifield mostly just listened and kept his tape recorder running. Once, a tribal elder showed him dozens of shallow oval depressions at an abandoned campsite. She said they were unmarked graves from 1911, when an epidemic carried away half of her village. Fifield still remembers the pain on her face as she told him the story.

In 1988, he visited an historic village site in Chichigoff Harbor on Attu Island, accompanied by an Aleut elder who, as an 18-year-old in 1942, had been captured and taken to Japan during the Japanese invasion of the Aleutian Islands. The man had not been back to the village since then. Fifield watched him wander aimlessly about the site, which had been alternately occupied and bombed by Japanese and Americans, looking for his father's grave and the place where the church had once stood. Failing to find much of anything familiar, the elder just sat on the edge of a bomb crater while Fifield and the lands assessors busied themselves making detailed notes about what the old man could remember and plotting the boundaries of the traditional village to figure out how much the acreage was worth. The next day, the Aleut elder said that he did not care to return to his village any more.

His experiences with Alaska natives took Fifield far beyond his graduate school training. At places like Kaltag and Chichigoff Harbor, he learned something of archaeology's human dimension and began to understand, for the first time, the role that archaeological and historical research could play in the lives of native people. Over the years, Fifield became increasingly involved in consulting with southeast Alaska tribes, at first working mostly with local groups, but increasingly joining with regional planners to help manage their ancestral sites on lands owned by Sealaska, a native-run corporation, and the U.S. Forest Service.

In 1994, Fifield and his family moved to Prince of Wales Island, eventually finding a home in Klawock, a small community in remote southeast

Alaska. The village has been there for centuries, and seventy percent of its inhabitants are today of Tlingit heritage. Fifield knows that whenever an artifact turns up around Klawock or a skeleton is discovered in one of the nearby caves, it likely belonged to one of his neighbor's ancestors. For years, he has regularly attended the local tribal council meetings and made it his personal policy to share immediately all information about archaeological investigations and discoveries on the island. This is small town living, with maybe 5,000 people spread across the island's eleven villages. Nearly half of the population live in the mostly native communities of Klawock and Hydraburg, where chance encounters at the grocery store often turn into informal consultation sessions.

" I T ' S A H O M E L Y L I T T L E C A V E "

In 1993, as a Forest Service archaeologist, Fifield began working with a team of researchers and spelunkers, members of the Tongass Cave Project who were documenting and mapping the hundreds of caverns and fissures that riddle the limestone bedrock of the many islands in the Southern Alexander Archipelago. Crawling into one cave on Prince of Wales Island, Kevin Allred, a project leader, found some old-looking bear bones protruding from the cave floor. The next summer, Allred invited Timothy Heaton, a paleontologist from the University of South Dakota (Vermillion) who had been conducting research on the ancient mammal populations on Prince of Wales Island, and he eagerly agreed to join the project. When Heaton submitted samples for radiocarbon dating, one of the bear bones turned out to be 41,000 years old, and some seal bones dated to 17,565 years ago—the very peak of the ice age. Raving that "this cave has delivered one record-setting find after another," Heaton convinced the National Geographic Society to sponsor a major paleontological investigation in 1996. The team camped on the beach and hiked each day over snags and deadfalls to reach the cave site. Worming their way through the dank passages, they systematically collected bone samples from the cave's multiple chambers.

Early in the dig, Heaton found a stone spear point well inside the cave, but he figured a wounded animal must have brought it inside before it died. Then on the Fourth of July (one day before the dig would shut down), Heaton's helmet lamp flashed across a small concentration of human-looking bones—down the same passage where he had found the spear point. Looking more closely, he found several artifacts lying near a mandible, three vertebrae, and a carnivore-chewed pelvis fragment. Fred Grady, an exhibit preparator on vacation from the Smithsonian, agreed that the bones were human. They looked really old.

"Oh my God!" Grady later exclaimed, "We weren't expecting it because we had bear bones that were 30,000 or 40,000 years old. We *were* just expecting a lot of animal bones." Well aware of their obligations under NAGPRA, the excavators stopped digging. That night, they radioed a cryptic message: "Important artifact found: Terry must come on the morning flight."

Fifield arrived the next day. After confirming the presence of human remains, he immediately looked up the presidents of the Klawock Cooperative Association and the Craig Community Association, the two local tribal authorities. With the help of Cheryl Eldemar of the Central Council of the Tlingit and Haida Tribes of Alaska, representatives of the Tribal Councils of Klawock, Craig, Kake, and Hydaburg were all invited to discuss the situation and decide what to do. "Right away, we went to them," Fifield noted later. "We said, 'We want your ideas. We'll put Native interns in the field. We'll put your questions into the research design. What do you want to know?'"

At first, the tribal leaders expressed their discomfort in handling human remains. Some thought that the excavations should stop, and the bones should go back to where they had been found. They were also concerned that an increased public interest in the caves might pose a threat to the sacred sites of the Tlingit and Haida people. Everyone involved—the archaeologists, the resource managers, and the tribal members—also worried about site security. Humans had apparently not walked on the water-saturated silts of the cave floor for millennia, and careless disturbance could destroy an accumulated long-term record of environmental change. Buried, waterlogged bones and other organics could easily be crushed by thoughtless visitors.

As the conversation progressed, the elders became more curious about how old the remains might be. Were these the bones of an ancestor to modern Tlingit or Haida people? Or did they come from a different group no longer living on Price of Wales Island? Gradually, the elders came to question the propriety of stopping excavations before anybody knew who this person really was. They agreed that the potential increase in knowledge about their oldest ancestors overwhelmed all other concerns. "In the end," says Fifield, "the weight of curiosity . . . about this person's culture and environment carried the day."

On July 11—a week after the human bones had been discovered—the Klawock Cooperative Association (the tribal government of Klawock) unanimously approved a resolution supporting the analysis of the artifacts and human remains already recovered. They also authorized additional excavations, requesting that they be kept abreast of new finds. The next day, the Craig Community Association approved a similar resolution, adding that they requested review prior to all media releases.

By this time, James Dixon, a former curator at the University of Alaska Museum and now at the Denver Museum of Natural History, had agreed to spearhead the archaeological project. He submitted minute samples of human bone for radiocarbon dating and was shocked by the results.

The human mandible returned a radiocarbon date of 9,730 years, and fragments of the pelvis dated to 9,880 years ago. When these two statistically indistinguishable dates are adjusted for the presence of certain carbon isotopes, they suggest a corrected age of 9,200 years, making the Tongass Forest bones the oldest reliably dated human remains ever found in Alaska—or all of Canada, for that matter.

For the next several summers teams of archaeologists and volunteers recovered a rich record of ancient life in this area. They found that the bones and teeth belonged to a man in excellent health, who died at the age of about 23. Maybe he was killed while hunting bears inside the cave, but that is pure speculation. Additional isotope analysis of the bones shows that most of his food came from the sea. The cave also yielded bones from eight mammal species now extinct on Prince of Wales Island, plus several tools of stone and a bone tool that has been radiocarbon dated to 10,300 years old.

Dixon believes that these early radiocarbon results "might just be the tip of an iceberg . . . it is my belief that some of the oldest archaeological remains preserved in North America will be found in the caves of southeast Alaska." He emphasizes the sophistication of marine mammal hunting between 10,000 and 9,000 years ago: Along this stretch of coast, "the table's set twice a day—at low tide and again at low tide." He also suggests that the New World was possibly first settled by people paddling along the north Pacific rim from Asia into western North America.

"It's a homely little cave," says Dixon, "It's not very pretty. But it is just a treasure chest of science."

" . . . A MODEL OF HOW WE CAN WORK TOGETHER"

Terry Fifield calls the Tongass Forest project "a model of how we can work together on important concerns. . . . We will continue to cooperate, sharing information and learning about the earliest beginnings of culture in southeast Alaska." These words—"cooperation", "sharing", "learning", and "together"—are not readily associated with the archaeology of the earliest Americans. It's tempting to think that perhaps Fifield, Dixon, and the others involved in the Tongass Forest excavations had learned from the tempestuous case of Kennewick Man. But the Tongass Forest remains were discovered on July 4, 1996—a few weeks *before* the Kennewick skeleton turned up.

The Tongass Forest and Kennewick cases define two pathways along which archaeologists, agency officials, and Indians interact. On Prince of Wales Island, where an infrastructure of cooperation was in place years before the critical find was made, tribal officials endorsed in-depth archaeological explorations only seven days after the first human bones turned up. By vivid contrast, the bones of Kennewick Man were confiscated within six weeks of their discovery and then locked up during years of high-profile legal wrangling.

One of these cases may well define the future (if any) of twenty-first-century archaeology. The question is: Which one?

EVERYONE INVOLVED IN the Tongass Forest excavations paid close attention to details. You may have noticed, for instance, that I have not given the name of either the site or the human remains. This is no accident. From the outset, tribal officials and archaeologists realized that the process of naming carries heavy baggage and should probably be avoided.

For recordkeeping purposes, the Tongass Forest cave was registered in the Alaska Heritage Resource Survey files as 49-PET-408, a modification of a trinomial system originally developed by the Smithsonian Institution and applied throughout the United States: "49" refers to Alaska (the 49th state admitted to the union), "PET" means that the site has been plotted on the Petersburg quadrangle sheet produced by the U.S. Geological Survey, and "408" indicates that the Tongass Forest cave is the 408th site recorded in this quadrangle.

For years, 49-PET-408 was informally known among project participants as "On Your Knees Cave," and paleontologists working there still sometimes use this name. Archaeologists, however, avoid the term in their public presentations. This simple difference in site naming practices reflects the deeper issues involved. The natural history model, in which scientists hold implicit intellectual property rights over their specimens—including the right to name their discoveries—is entirely appropriate in paleontology, where the specimens are mostly fossilized animal bones. But for American archaeologists, whose subject matter spans both the scientific and the human, the issues are more complex. Archaeologists cannot behave like paleontologists because their "specimens" are likely to be someone's ancestor.

At one point, one of the Tlingit interns (after talking to her aunt) thought that maybe the skeletal remains could be assigned the Tlingit name for "Maker of the Tools." But tribal elders pointed out that this name had previously belonged to a person long since deceased. Since nobody could be sure about the tribal affiliation of the 9,700-year-old man, the ancient name should perhaps be avoided as well. Although this approach will never produce a snappy name like "Lucy," nobody seems to regret the loss.

The media were not excluded from the Tongass Forest project, but they were not explicitly courted either. Everyone involved was rather guarded in their dealings with the press, refusing to allow reporters to set the agenda. Press coverage of this important find has been low-key. Occasional articles have appeared in the print media, and the archaeology was filmed for the NOVA television series and the History Channel. But there was never a public relations campaign to promote the Tongass Forest project. Although plenty of reporters have pressed for answers about whether the 9,700-year-old jaw bone is "Caucasian," Dixon and his colleagues are too savvy to fall into that racial trap. There have been no inflammatory headlines or contentious interviews, and to date, none of the principals has been profiled in *People* magazine.

From their long experience in the area, Dixon and Fifield knew that to work effectively with the tribes, archaeologists must bring more than their scientific reputations to the table. The project benefited from Fifield's long-term willingness to work with local native groups. Once, he had provided a boat to transport an ancient totem pole that a tribe wanted to replicate. Early in the project, Dixon arranged for the Denver Museum of Natural History to bring tribal delegations to Colorado, so that they could inspect the lab and storage facilities and meet those who would be doing the science face-to-face. The tribal councils were also invited to name Native American students to serve as paid interns on the project.

In a real way, the archaeologists ensured that the tribes joined the excavation as active players. The success of the Tongass Forest project also reflects well on the native Alaskan people involved, whose long-term relationships with Sealaska Inc. and other native corporations have finely tuned their sense for conflict resolution. According to Rosita Worl, an anthropologist of Tlingit descent, her people have a long-standing tradition of resolving conflicts through an orderly process. Only half-jokingly, she suggests that "the Tlingit may have dreamed up the original *Robert's Rules of Order*."

THERE IS TODAY deep concern over the future of archaeology, and throughout this book, I have used the Kennewick controversy to highlight some of the pressing issues facing both Indians and archaeologists. My point is neither to vilify those involved with Kennewick nor to lionize those working on the Tongass Forest project. NAGPRA remains a very murky piece of legislation, and clarifying it will be a bumpy political process. The Kennewick case, at its core, reflects legitimate and deep-seated differences in interpreting federal legislation. I have deep personal respect for the anthropologists and Native Americans involved in the Kennewick case; so far as I can tell, each of the aggrieved parties felt a personal and urgent need to press their case in the courtroom and in the court of public opinion. I understand that litigation will often follow in disputes over property rights, but I also question whether judges should be forced to carry the burden of defining the future of America's ancient past. By their very nature, lawsuits emphasize conflict rather than resolution. I hope that Indians and archaeologists can refrain from fixating on the legalisms of absolute rights, ownership, and control because if they continue to do so, all of us may well overlook the underlying issues that led to the passage of NAGPRA in the first place.

Many American anthropologists have long perceived themselves as champions of Indian rights, but what anthropologists think of themselves and each other is irrelevant. More important is how American Indian people see anthropologists and archaeologists. "The question is not what we have done as individuals, but rather what we have not done as an academic discipline," writes anthropologist Garrick Bailey. "We have failed to recruit and meaningfully integrate American Indians and other non-Western peoples into the profession of anthropology, and we have failed to convince American Indian peoples of the relevance of our discipline."

Correctly or not, many Native Americans still see anthropology and the greater academic world as rooted in Euroamerican imperialism. Why, after two centuries of interaction, do so many Indians still hold anthropologists in such low regard? Why can't anthropologists seem to shed the image of neo-colonial manipulators?

This is the central question behind *Skull Wars*: After all these years, why do so many Indians question the value of science, anthropology, and archaeology to their daily lives? Is the real problem with the scientists or the

Indians? Or both? Or are we just wasting our time in seeking the common ground?

AS A POSTSCRIPT, let me share a note that Terry Fifield sent while I was writing this last section. Terry had been more than helpful in providing the details surrounding the Tongass Forest find, and one day, not long after he had sent me a lengthy e-mail describing his experiences, he stopped by the newly constructed Gaan Ax Adi longhouse on the Klawock River, not far from his house. He ran into John Rowan, a member of the Heenya kwaan Tlingit people and the keeper of the local totem park, who was putting the finishing touches on an interior house panel he had carved over the summer.

"The stormy sky was breaking up a little," Terry wrote, "and there was great lighting on the Raven-Mink pole that stands in front of the under-construction carvers' shed. I stopped, at first, to take some photos. John teaches my kids carving and beginning Tlingit during the school year. We sat and talked about a lot of different things during a half hour conversation, sitting on a roughed out totem pole blank in the longhouse."

"I told him about the book you are writing and some of the things I mentioned in my note to you yesterday. He didn't say a lot, but he seemed pleased and relaxed. It was the kind of meeting that makes this relationship work. He will tell others and no one will be surprised or threatened when they hear of it later. The formal presentations to the councils and bureaucrats of all cultures are necessary for decision making. But the trust and the ideas are developed at a much more personal level. Just thought I would write that down. Maybe it conveys a feeling for the place."

Terry Fifield is not a typical American archaeologist at the millennium. Not many of us will watch our kids learn to carve a Raven-Mink totem pole or hear them practicing the Tlingit language. Fifield's experiences on Prince of Wales Island recall an archaeology of a century ago, a time when archaeologists had more personal contact with native people.

The Skull Wars, alas, seem far from over. Too many people are still talking past one another. But if archaeologists—of all people—can draw some lessons from the past, perhaps we can rediscover a more human side to our science and come to value once again the importance of face-to-face relationships with those whose ancestors we wish to study.

ACKNOWLEDGEMENTS

IT IS MY pleasure to acknowledge the assistance of those who helped with *Skull Wars*.

I am particularly grateful to that Sioux trickster Vine Deloria, Jr., for his detailed review of the manuscript and for contributing the Foreword. Although Vine and I disagree on many, many things, our disagreements remain cordial—partly because of the mutual trust developed over a decade of debate and dialogue, and also because we are both deeply disturbed by the chasm that continues to separate western science from Indian America. Each of us, in different ways, is trying to bridge that chasm.

I also thank James Chatters for his openness and willingness to spend hours working with me on this manuscript. The Kennewick experience has been extraordinarily difficult for Chatters, and, with Jim's help, I have tried to get beyond the media's distorted representations of the Kennewick affair. I have known Chatters for three decades; he's a first rate archaeologist. Although we sometimes view things differently, I sincerely hope that Jim feels he has been fairly treated here.

It has been my great privilege to work with William Frucht of Basic Books; more than once, Bill's editorial skill and encouragement carried the day. Kenneth David Burrows provided expert guidance throughout.

I am particularly grateful to Don Fowler, Frederick Hoxie, David Meltzer, and Lorann Pendleton—friends and colleagues who struggled through early drafts of the entire manuscript; their insightful comments have vastly improved the structure and content of the final manuscript. I also thank Paul Bochner, Bruce Bradley, Ian Brown, Robert Carneiro, Ted Carpenter, Donald Forsythe Craib, Tom Dillehay, James Dixon, Forrest Fenn, Terry Fifield, Alan Goodman, Martha Graham, Sherry Hutt, Ira Jacknis, Jerry Johnson, Rosemary Joyce, William Keegan, Roger Kennedy, Thomas Killion, Keith Kintigh, Clark Spencer Larsen, Kevin McBride, Robert McLaughlin, Frank McManamon, Alan L. Schneider, Gerald R. Singer, Anne Sidamon-Eristoff, Dennis Stanford, Amy Steffian, Deward Walker, Phillip Walker, Joe Watkins, and David Wilcox—each of whom commented on significant parts of earlier drafts, contributing new ideas and providing background materials. These people have a broad range of perspectives, and some of their suggestions were not accommodated. All errors of fact and interpretation must remain my own.

My staff in New York was terrific, as always. Margot Dembo improved draft after draft. Niurka Tyler, Lisa Stock, and Eric Powell helped with endless details.

I've had the good fortune to be a curator at the American Museum of Natural History for nearly three decades. Administrative philosophies have shifted somewhat over these years, but the Museum has always encouraged its scientists to pursue scholarship of the highest quality, no matter where those trails might lead. In the case of *Skulls Wars*, a couple of these trails ended rather close to home. I will always feel fortunate to have worked at an institution that values intellectual freedom and appreciates the importance of looking critically at history, including our own.

Finally, I thank my wife Lori and son Dave. Both were more than patient as I struggled through what became a rather difficult project.

ENDNOTES

PROLOGUE (PAGES XVII–XXXIX)

Anyone trying to make sense of the flap over Kennewick Man—the touchstone of this book—will be frustrated by the lack of solid scientific description. I've had little choice but to rely on popular media coverage, and since the role of the American press is one of the themes (problems, if you will) addressed here, the situation is hardly ideal. I have tried, with mixed success, to verify the accuracy of statements appearing in the media. Specifically, I have relied most heavily on information supplied on the Umatilla Web Page (especially Minthorn, 1996), on Chatters' publications on Kennewick (1997, 1998, 1999), and published updates from others directly involved in the lawsuit (e.g., Schneider 1998, 1999). I have also conducted my own interviews with several of the participants. But by and large, I've been forced to rely on news accounts, including the 60 *Minutes* transcript, various web pages on the subject (including those of the *Tri-City Herald* [www.tri-cityherald.com/bones] and *The Oregonian* [www.oregonlive.com/special/issues/ kennewick.html]), plus several high-profile articles such as those by Preston (1997b), Miller (1997), Lasswell (1999), Hastings (1997), Egan (1996), Rensberger (1997), Henderson (1997, 1998a, 1998b).

When this manuscript was completed, Judge Jelderks had not yet issued his final decision on the Kennewick matter. A number of reports and position papers have been issued by all sides, and I have made no attempt to reiterate all possible arguments and interpretations. Rather, I have tried only to emphasize the core of the conflict; a complete, objective analysis of the conflict is premature at this writing, and beyond the present scope. The reader seeking more detail should consult technical publications available from the Corps of Engineers and the Department of the Interior (esp. www.cr.nps.gov/aad/Kennewick).

"history written in bone . . ." Court decision, June 27, 1997.

"I like the way . . ." Hannah in *Tri-City Herald* (11/17/98).

"Bones are my thing . . ." Chatters in *People* magazine (11/30/98).

"I've got a white guy . . ." Chatters in Egan (1996).

"Was someone here . . ." *The New Yorker* (6/16/97).

"Europeans Invade America . . ." *Discover* magazine (February 1999).

"America Before the Indians." *U. S. News and World Report* (Petit 1998).

"When Columbus came . . ." *The Santa Fe New Mexican* (Easthouse 1997).

"barely unpacked before Columbus . . ." Deloria in Weaver (1997: 22).

"It's been like a . . ." Chatters (personal communication to the author, 9/30/99).

"On the physical characteristics . . ." Chatters in Preston (1997b: 73). On 9/30/99, Chatters informed me that he was misquoted: "The thing about Stockholm, New Delhi and Cairo is an incomplete quote . . . I went on to say he would be out of place in Tokyo or Beijing. It was a reference to major world cities (excluding New York or LA because they are so diverse). The point is he would be out of place among orthognathic, low nosed folk. My collaborator and I see the result as pretty generic Northern Hemisphere Homo sapiens, which is what you would expect to see in the early Holocene [that is, 10,000 years ago]."

"analogous to a book that they can read . . ." Court decision, Junen 27, 1997.

"Our oral history goes back 10,000 years. . . ." Minthorn (Egan 1996).

"proceed from the assumption. . . ." Schneider in Knickerbocker (1996). .

"The information from ancient . . ." editorial, *The Oregonian* (8/1/97).

"The tribe's fight . . ." Stahl in *60-Minutes* transcript.

"Kennewick Man is our kin . . . " Louis Beam in *The Runestone,* Summer, 1997.

"When his eyes meet mine . . ." Chatters in Preston (1997c).

"averaging tissue thicknesses . . ." Chatters (personal communication to the author, 9/30/99).

People are free . . ." Owsley in *60 Minutes* transcript.

"The ever changing scientific theories . . ." Big Boy (1999).

"Whose memories become history?" Korsmo (1999:131).

"the real Youth of the World" Rousseau in Dippie (1982:18).

"as the snow melts . . ." Dippie (1982:13).

The phrase "biologization" of history comes from Harris (1968:107).

"remains a major source . . ." Wolf (1994:1).

"Anglo-American East rise . . ." Dowd (1992:xvii-xviii).

"If aboriginal practices . . ." Korsmo (1999:128).

"Did you resist us? . . ." Korsmo (1999:120).

"Burdened by a linear, progressive . . ." Trask in Dirlik (1999:76).

"retribalization" Deloria in Vickers (1998:159).

"Until the majority of Americans . . . " Vickers (1998:10-11).

"perhaps no more insulting . . ." Johnson (1999:11).

On archaeology serving "the" public or just "a" public, from McLaughlin (1998a).

"hearing the Founders charged . . ." Bloom in Schlesinger (1998:62).

All Schlesinger quotes in this section from *The Disuniting of America* (1992:11, 17, 18, and bookjacket).

"we made a mistake in trying . . ." Reagan in Vizenor (1990:xxiii).

"A minority by conquest . . ." Limerick (1987:211).

"to wrest control over one's culture . . ." Goldberg (1997: 22).

On "Kennewick-Pasco-Richland Man" Johansen (1999).

PART I. NAMES AND IMAGES (PAGE 1)
"It is little wonder that Indian peoples . . ." Dorris in Thomas et al. (1993: 401).

CHAPTER 1. COLUMBUS, ARAWAKS, AND CARIBS:
THE POWER TO NAME (PAGES 3–10)
     The Columbian Quincentenary spawned an outpouring of perspectives on the earliest encounters between Columbus and the native Caribbean people. In this chapter, I have drawn from several key sources including John Noble Wilford's *The Mysterious History of Columbus: An Exploration of the Man, the Myth, the Legacy* (1991), David Henige's *In Search of Columbus* (1991), William Keegan's *The People Who Discovered Columbus: The Prehistory of the Bahamas* (1992), Samuel Wilson's *The Indigenous People of the Caribbean* (1997), and Paquette and Engerman's *The Lesser Antilles in the Age of European Expansion* (1996). See also Keegan (1989, 1996) and Tyler (1988). For some native views on Euroamericans, see Armstrong, (1971), Nabokov (1991), and Rosenstiel (1983).
     The issue of American Indian imagery is particularly well-handled by Robert F. Berkhofer in his superb *The White Man's Indian* (1978). I have also draw upon his *Handbook of North American Indians* article (1988). Other critical sources include Robert Bieder's *Science Encounters the Indian 1820-1880* (1986), Moffit and Sebastián's *Brave New People: The European Invention of the American Indian* (1996), and Dickason (1997). For native perspectives on American history, see *Native America: Portrait of the Peoples* (1994), edited by Duane Champaign. For a discussion of the relationship of historiography and American Indian history, see the papers in *Rethinking American Indian History* edited by Donald L. Fixico (1997).
     To interleaf with the discussions of Columbus, Michener, and Morison, I have reluctantly retained the now-classic distinction between "Arawaks" and "Caribs." But there are problems with both terms, and neither is retained in more modern discussions. Because the "Island Arawaks" of the Caribbean were culturally quite different from the "Arawaks" of mainland South America, anthropologists now prefer using the term "Taino" (meaning noble or good in the Arawak language). I must also note that there is some question whether "the taking" ceremony actually took place as described in Columbus' diary (see Henige 1991:108–110). Whether or not the scene was embellished, the outcome was identical for the indigenous people of America.

"[The natives] have often asked . . ." Williams in Berkhofer (1988:15).
"to bear witness . . ." Fuson (1987:76).
"God created these . . ." Las Casas in Berkhofer (1988:523).
The Morison quotes in this section are from Morison (1974:4, 106).
All Michener quotes are from *Caribbean* (1989:ix, 10, 19, jacket cover copy).
"the most maligned . . ." Josephy (1992:3).
"There never crossed . . ." Wilford (1991:179).
"barbaric peoples—enemies . . ." Davis and Goodwin (1990:38).
"great villains of West . . ." Keegan (1990:8).

CHAPTER 2. A VANISHING AMERICAN ICON (PAGES 11–25)
     Brian Dippie's *The Vanishing American* (1982) and Philip Deloria's wonderful *Playing Indian* (1998) were particularly important as background for this chapter. I also drew upon Hauptman's *Tribes and Tribulations* (1995, especially chapters 7 and 8). My discussion of George Washington's odd relationship with American Indians relies on Freeman's *Washing-*

ton (1968), Steiner's *The Vanishing White Man* (1987) Flexner's *Washington: The Indispensable Man* (1974), and Starkey's *European and Native American Warfare 1675–1815* (1998). My consideration of the American melting pot relies, in part, on Patricia Limerick's still-important *the Legacy of Conquest* (1987), plus Hertzberg (1979) and Dippie (1982). Other important sources for this chapter include *Killing the White Man's Indian* by Fergus M. Bordewich (1996), Richard Drinnon's *Facing West* (1997), and Schlesinger (1992, 1998). For more in Indian imagery, see *Wild West Shows and the Images of American Indians: 1883-1933* (1996) by L. G. Moses.

The phrase "Patriot Chiefs" comes from Josephy (1961).
"played out ideas . . ." Beard in P. Deloria (1998: 224).
"Had anyone asked . . ." Venables in Lyons and Mohawk (1992:75).
"When our ancestors . . ." Beard in P. Deloria (1998:224).
"Indians are the . . ." Washington in Freeman (1968:100).
"Being devoid of heavy . . ." Flexner (1974:97).
" . . . darted, with distraction of . . ." Cooper (1985).
Unless otherwise noted, the remaining Washington quotes in this section from Freeman (1968).
"assimilated to our . . ." Washington in Schlesinger (1998:30).
"The point of America . . ." Schlesinger (1992:13).
"determinedly turned three . . ." Jordan in Drinnon (1997:81).
"Made by the same . . ." Jefferson in Drinnon (1997:83).
"We shall with . . ." Jefferson in Bordewich (1996:38).
The remaining Jefferson quotes in this section are from Drinnon (1997:83, 96, 102).
"unite yourselves with us . . . " Jefferson quoted in Horsman (1988:36).
"The Indian could not hope . . ." Sheehan (1973:102).
"Jefferson's philanthropy was . . ." White in Thomas et al. (1993:261).
"civilizing the Indians . . ." Monroe in Drinnon (1997:115).
"poor children of . . ." Clay in Dippie (1982:8).
"merely asked the . . ." Drinnon (1997:116).
"Can it be cruel . . ." Jackson in Limerick (1987:193).
"this Trail of Tears . . ." Prucha (1984 :141).
"presidentially ordered death . . ." Stannard (1992:123).
The remaining quotes in this chapter were cited in Vickers (1998:16-17).

PART II. NINETEENTH-CENTURY SCIENTISTS (PAGE 27)
"It is important . . ." Blakey (1987:8).

CHAPTER 3. THE FIRST AMERICAN ARCHAEOLOGIST
(PAGES 29–35)
The critical source on Thomas Jefferson-as-anthropologist is, of course, his *Notes on the State of Virginia* (1954 [orig. 1787]); I have also drawn from Bernard Sheehan's *Seeds of Extinction: Jeffersonian Philanthropy and the American Indian* (1974), Joseph Ellis' *American Sphinx: The Character of Thomas Jefferson* (1996), Duman Malone's *Jefferson and the Rights of Man* (1951), Roger Kennedy's *Hidden Cities* (1994), Seller's *Mr. Peale's Museum* (1980), plus Bieder (1986), Chinard (1947), Lehmann-Hartleben (1943).

"the nation's first museum . . .": Kennedy (1994:219).

Except as otherwise noted, all direct quotation sections from Buffon and Jefferson in this section are from Jefferson (1954 [1787]).

"the probability of a . . ." Jefferson in Drinnon (1997:82).

"canine appetite" Jefferson in Peden (1954: xii).

CHAPTER 4. A SHORT HISTORY OF SCIENTIFIC RACISM IN AMERICA (PAGES 36–43)

In summarizing the difficult history of anthropology's racist background, I have relied especially on *The Rise of Anthropological Theory* by Marvin Harris (1968), *Race in Human Evolution* by Milford Wolpoff and Rachel Caspari (1998, especially chapters 2 and 3), Stephen Jay Gould's *Mismeasurement of Man* (1981), and Bieder (1986, chapter 3) and Berkhofer (1978). The best single source on Samuel Morton remains William Stanton's *The Leopard's Spots* (1960).

"Racial determinism was . . ." Harris (1968:80–1).

"the blacks, whether originally . . ." Jefferson in Harris (1968:80).

"the founder of anthropology" Gould (1981:32).

"Caucasian must, on every . . ." Blumenbach in Gould (1981:38).

"no scientific man in America . . ." Stanton (1960:144).

"Strange to say . . ." Morton in Bieder (1986:58-9).

"imagine a series . . ." Agassiz in Gould (1981:50).

Unless otherwise noted, the remaining quotes in this chapter come from Dippie (1982: 75, 76, 84–86).

"We of the South . . ." in Echo-Hawk and Echo-Hawk (1994:25).

"is clearly crazy," Nott in Meltzer (1998:71).

CHAPTER 5. DARWIN AND THE DISAPPEARING AMERICAN INDIAN (PAGES 44–51)

The key sources here are the original writings of Lewis Henry Morgan, particularly *League of the Ho-de-no-sau-nee, or Iroquois* (1851), *Systems of Consanguinity and Affinity of the Human Family* (1870), and *Ancient Society* (1877). The analysis of Morgan's theory of social evolution draws particularly upon Harris (1968, especially chapters 5, 6 and 7), Bieder (1986, Chapter 6), Hoxie (1984, Chapter 1), and P. Deloria (1998, Chapter 3).

"It can now be asserted . . ." Morgan (1877:5,7).

"Whatever interest I have since . . ." Morgan in Berkhofer (1978:52).

"We do not stir . . ." Morgan in P. Deloria (1998:176).

"Real Indian people . . ." P. Deloria (1998:91).

"Their memories were authentic . . ." P. Deloria (1998:91).

"as they were first seen . . ." Bancroft in Fowler (2000).

"commenced their career . . ." Morgan in Berkhofer (1978:53).

"will intermarry respectively . . ." Morgan in Bieder (1996:220).

"skulls and brains . . ." Morgan in Bieder (1996:176).

CHAPTER 6. THE GREAT AMERICAN SKULL WARS
(PAGES 52–63)

My account of the Sand Creek massacre is drawn from testimony and affidavits taken from various eyewitnesses to the slaughter, as cited by Hoig (1961, Appendix), Connell (1984:176-179), and Halaas (1995).

Several sources were important in tracing the early history of America's natural history museums, including Curtis Hinsley's *The Smithsonian and the American Indian* (1981), Douglas Preston's *Dinosaurs in the Attic* (1986), Steven Conn's *Museums and American Intellectual Life, 1876-1926* (1999), Richard Kurin's *Reflections of a Culture Broker* (1997, especially chapters 1, 2, 6, and 7), and *Museums, Objects, and Collections* by Susan M. Pearce (1992).

The collecting of Pawnee skulls is discussed by James Riding In (1992), Bieder (1992), and Gulliford (1996). The early career of Franz Boas is documented by George Stocking in *The Shaping of American Anthropology: 1883-1911: A Franz Boas Reader* (1974) and *Bones, Bodies, Behavior: Essays on Biological Anthropology* (1988) and Boas (1969). The competition for artifacts and skeletons on the Northwest Coast is discussed by Douglas Cole in *Captured Heritage: The Scramble for Northwest Coast Artifacts* (1995).

"extermination of the . . ." www.pbs.org/weta/thewest/wpages/wpgs400/w4chiv.htm m.
"the Cheyennes will . . ." Chivington in (Hoig 1961:83 and
    www.pbs.org/weta/thewest/wpages/wpgs400/w4chiv.htm).
"Scalps are what . . ." Chivington in Connell (1984:176).
"whoever gets this . . ." Agassiz in Preston (1986:21).
"cottage industry on . . ." Bieder (1986:67).
"Let me have . . ." Agassiz in Gulliford (1996:124).
"It is rather a . . ." Bieder (1986:66).
"diligently to collect . . ." Hammond in Gulliford (1996:132).
"squaw having remarkable . . ." Bieder (1992:28).
"two were injured a good deal . . ." Fryer in Riding In (1992:107).
"the American Indians . . ." Otis in Riding In (1992:109).
"It is most unpleasant . . ." Boas in Rohner (1966: 88).
The remaining Boas and Dorsey quotes in this section, unless otherwise noted, from Cole
    (1985: 108, 133, 168, 171, 175–176, 307).
"someone had stolen . . ." Boas in Rohner (1966:88).
"I am mad at myself . . ." Boas (1969:221).

CHAPTER 7. THE ANTHROPOLOGY OF ASSIMILATION
(PAGES 64–70)

Some conflicting perspectives on the role of Alice Fletcher can be found in *Blessing for a Long Time: The Sacred Pole of the Omaha Tribe* by Robin Ridington and Dennis Hastings (1997; see also Ridington, 1992); Joan Mark's *Four Anthropologists: An American Science in its Early Years* (1980), and Nancy Oestreich Lurie's "The Lady from Boston and the Omaha Indians" (1966a); see also Hoxie (1984, Chapter 1). For more on the Lake Mohonk and other reform movements, see Hoxie (1988), and Prucha (1984: Chapter 24).

"To free the slaves..." Limerick (1987: 196).
"A Convenient marriage . . ." Hoxie (1984:29).
"a chilling condensation . . ." Hoxie (1984: 24).
"Indians' Magna Carta" Hoxie (1984: 70).

"a mighty pulverizing . . ." Roosevelt in Nabokov (in Thomas et al. 1993:369).
"probably created more . . ." Nabokov (in Thomas et al. 1993: 366).
"dreadfully opinionated" Mark (1980: 62).
"the so-called Friends . . ." Limerick (1987: 196).
"Each one had uttered . . ." Mark (1980:61).

CHAPTER 8. THE ANTHROPOLOGIST AS HERO (PAGES 71–76)

This sketch of Frank Cushing relies heavily on *Zuni: Selected Writings of Frank Hamilton Cushing* (1979) and *Cushing at Zuni: The Correspondence and Journals of Frank Hamilton Cushing 1878-1884* (1990), both edited by Jesse Green and *The Southwest in the American Imagination* (1996), edited by Curtis M. Hinsley and David R. Wilcox, plus McGee et al. (1900), Mark (1976), Pandey (1972), and for a more contemporary look, see *A Zuni Artist Looks at Frank Hamilton Cushing* by Phil Hughte (1994).

"The past is a foreign . . ." Hartley in Basso (1996:3).
"the biggest fool . . ." Stevenson in Brandes (1965:6).
"Two months . . ." Cushing (1970:33).
"Rapidly the Indians . . ." Powell in Fowler (2000).
Unless otherwise noted, the remaining quotes in this chapter come from Green (1990:
    vii, 2, 3, 8, 9, 22-23, 26–27, 356, 358).
"preliminary hinterland where . . ." P. Deloria (1998:116).
"The pattern of Cushing's . . ." Simmons (1979:219).
"to a seat on . . ." Levi-Strauss in Hinsley (1981:192-3).

CHAPTER 9. COLLECTING YOUR FOSSILS ALIVE (PAGES 77–90)

According to Edmund Carpenter (1997:27, 29), the "tabloid account of Minik discovering his father's skeleton on display in the American Museum of Natural History . . . never happened. . . . he press. Behind this fiction were real people, real events, but by adding here, deleting there, journalists fashioned a mythic drama that would not die. Nor was it amenable to correction." The bones showed no signs of postmortem articulation, as would have been required for exhibition. Also, there is no surviving photograph of this display—not even a sketch—and the newspapers surely would have run one, had the bones ever been displayed. I agree with Carpenter here.

I should also mention that Carpenter (personal communication) thinks that Minik himself may have known that his father was not in the grave, because the bones were rendered at Lawyerville, where Minik was living. The discussion of Eskimo culture and history draws on Carpenter (1997).

The discussion of Ishi draws from T. Kroeber (1964, 1970), Heizer and Kroeber (1979), Wolf (1981). An excellent video presentation is also available on *Ishi: The Last Yahi* (1994), The American Experience, Shanachie Entertainment Group.

"I beg to suggest to you . . ." Boas in Harper (1986:33).
"So one day we all sailed away" Qisuk in *Time* (8/9/93).
"Peary asked if some of us . . ." Qisuk in *Time* (8/9/93).
Unless otherwise noted, the remaining Boas quotes in this chapter are from Harper
    (1986).
"Investigate and establish . . ." Boas in Cole (1995:147).
"We spent about two months . . ." A. Kroeber in T. Kroeber (1970:47).

"a Labrador half-breed Eskimo woman" A. Kroeber in T. Kroeber (1970:47).
"strong physically and psychically, dominant . . ." T. Kroeber (1970:50-51).
"visits the (supposed) grave . . ." Kroeber (1899:316).
"When you found . . . " Harper (1986:43-44).
"are exceptionally full . . ." Kroeber (1899:313).
"insisted that the boy . . ." Kroeber (1899:316).
"An upstairs room . . ." Harper (1986:91).
"I felt as . . ." Minik in *New York World* (1907).
"Boas and Hrdlička . . ." Carpenter (1997:29).
"the most uncivilized . . . " in *Ishi: The Last Yahi* (Shanachie Entertainment Group, 1994).
"Ishi received all . . ." Dippie (1982:208).
"Ishi himself is . . ." Kroeber in Hoxie (1984: 142).
The Kroeber and Waterman quotes in this section, unless otherwise credited, from T.
    Kroeber (1964:234-5).

CHAPTER 10. IS "REAL HISTORY" EMBEDDED IN ORAL
TRADITION? (PAGES 91–101)
    I recommend *The Mythology of Native North America* by David Leeming and Jake Page
(1998) and *A Dictionary of Creation Myths* by David Leeming and Margaret Leeming (1994).
For more on the Omaha and Francis La Flesche, see Boughter (1998), Ridington and Dennis Hastings (1997), and Liberty (1976, 1978). For a discussion of whether Joseph La
Flesche was an Omaha, see Clifton (1989:137) and Barnes (in Clifton 1990). On the scientific agenda developed by Franz Boas see Stocking (1974, part ix).

"What I know . . ." Hoxie (1992:983).
Unless otherwise noted, the La Flesche quotes in this section are from Fletcher and La
    Flesche (1911:251).
"one of the most . . . " Mark (1980:75).
"according to the canons . . ." Lowie in Mark (1980:121).
"in spite of their naively . . ." Lowie (1913:913).
"I did not . . ." Fletcher in Mark (1980:122).
"deep insight into . . ." Boas in Hinsley (1981:174).
"too much of the private . . ." La Flesche in Boughter (1998:234).
"The misconception of . . ." La Flesche in Hoxie (1992:983).
"the science of man" Boas (1940 [1899]:621).
"these subjects are . . ." Boas (1940 [1899]:621).
"These qualities have . . ." Kroeber in Harris (1968:253).
"Boas found anthropology . . ." Benedict in Harris (1968:253).
"there was a . . ." Fowler (2000).
"This work . . . can . . ." Fewkes (1900:579).
"the circle-squarers and inventors . . ." Lowie (1917:161).
"Native 'history' is . . ." Lowie (1915:599).
"oral tradition is . . . " Dixon (1915:600-601).
"as a matter of fact . . . " Swanton (1915:600).
"The habitual attitude of the Zuñi . . ." Kroeber (1917).
"I learned a great . . ." Kidder in Givens (1992:59-60).
"Zuñi traditional accounts of events . . ." Hodge in Lowie 1917:165).
"our equivalent branches . . ." Lowie (1917:163).

CHAPTER 11. THE PERILOUS IDEA OF RACE (PAGES 102–120)

The phrase used for the chapter title is from Wolf (1994). Contemporary views of race and anthropology are expressed in *Human Biodiversity: Genes, Race and History* by Jonathan Marks (1995), Eugenia Shanklin's *Anthropology and Race* (1994), and Elazar Barkan's *The Retreat of Scientific Racism* (1992). Jared Diamond's Pulitzer Prize-winning *Guns, Germs, and Steel* (1997) eloquently demonstrates the fallacy of projecting racial imagery into the human past. Two other important references include Michael Blakey's now-classic "Skull Doctors" (1987) and "Bioarchaeological Ethics" by Phillip Walker (1999). See also Moses (1997, 1999), Armelagos and Goodman (1998), Goodman (1996, 1997b, 1998), Haney Lopez (1996), and Harrison's "The persistent power of 'race' in the cultural and political economics of "racism." This chapter also draws from Gould (1981), Hooton (1930), Wolpoff and Caspari (1997), Stocking (1974, Part IV; 1988), Echo-Hawk and Echo-Hawk (1994), Harris (1999, chapter 5), Beam (1997), and Lesser (1981).

"It is ironic that . . ." Moses (1997:1).
"very striking and . . ." Boas in Stocking (1968:176).
"zero degree of . . ." Boas in Stocking (1968:177).
"Head form which has always been considered . . ." Boas (1911).
"the differences between . . ." Boas in Stocking (1968:191).
"America must be . . ." Coolidge by Harris (1999:68).
"struggling along—so . . ." Boas in Stocking (1968:166).
The Hooton quotes in this section derive from Hooton (1930:186, 348, 355, 356, 362).
"represents one of . . ." Martin (1998:175).
"The Jew possesses . . ." Wolpoff and Caspari (1997:148).
"contribution to the . . ." Barkan (1988:186).
"a historical decoupling . . ." Martin (1998:171).
"made no attempt . . ." Gould (1981:69).
"In the US both . . ." AAA Statement on Race, *Anthropology Newsletter* (1998:3).
"In lectures, I now say . . ." Kidd in Bronner (1998).
"Folk beliefs about the . . ." Moses (1999:265).
"Kennewick Man has . . ." Goodman in Egan (1998c).
"I really do object . . ." Goodman in Egan (1998c).
"We disagree with the notion . . ." Minthorn (1996)
"Caucasoid look . . . the Kennewick . . . " Rensberger (1997).
"Caucasian features, judging . . ." Egan (1996)
"examining these earliest . . ." Gill in a University of Wyoming press release (www.eu-rekaalert.org/E-lert/current/public_release/deposit/wyoming.htm 10/30/96).
"the mysterious Ainu . . ." Timreck and Goetzmann (www.nmnh.si.edu/arctic/html/introduction.html).
"the hands of the . . . " Goodman (personal communication).
"confused the description . . ." Chatters (1999).
"Nobody is talking . . ." Chatters in Egan (1998d).
Straus criticizing Chatters' use of Caucasoid in Henderson (1998b).
"the use of the term . . ." Grayson in Slayman (1996).
"to call the specimen . . ." Marks (1998).
"whenever you get . . ." Fredin in Henderson (1998b).
"Now that I . . ." Chatters in Henderson (1998b) and personal communication with the author.
"necessary to use . . ." Chatters (1998:19).

"Dead 'Indians' Don't Lie" by Louis Beam [http://www.louisbeam.com/kennewick.htm]
"Great White Hope" and "a means by which . . ." from Johansen (1999).
"When I was first . . ." Onouye in Echo-Hawk and Echo-Hawk 1994:i).
"To many Native Americans . . . " Preston (1989:67).
"Believe it or . . ." West in a promotional appeal produced by the National Campaign
    committee Office for the National Museum of American Indian (Nov. 1, 1992).
"knowledge of the life . . ." Boas (1940:v).
"much of twentieth-century . . ." (Stocking 1974:17)

PART III. DEEP AMERICAN HISTORY (PAGE 121)
"As gods might . . ." Steiner (1987:141).

CHAPTER 12. ORIGIN MYTHS FROM MAINSTREAM
AMERICA (PAGES 123–132)

On the mythical Moundbuilders, please see the following: Kennedy (1994:235);
Bieder (1986, Chapter 4); Trigger (1989, Chapter 3); Willey and Sabloff (1993:22); Silverberg (1968), Meltzer (1998). On Lost Tribe advocates, see the following: Steiner (1987:141) or Carpenter (1950:6). On the Aztecs in Arizona and New Mexico, see Lekson (1988), Fowler (2000, Chapter 2), McGuire (1997:68), and Hinsley (1992). On Fray Joseph de Acosta's suggested Asian origins for Indians, see (Jarcho 1959).

For a consideration of modern museum perspectives, see *Exhibiting Dilemmas: Issues of Representation at the Smithsonian* (1997), edited by Amy Henderson and Adrienne L. Kaeppler. For more on Angloamerican origin myths, see Ann Uhry Abrams' *The Pilgrims and Pocahontas* (1999). On Montezuma as a Native New Mexican: Lekson (1988:219).

"heaven and earth . . ." Lightfoot in Daniel (1962:19)
"We may perhaps see . . ." Daniel (1962:19).
"The dream of a lost prehistoric race . . ." Silverberg (1968: 57).
"in size and grandeur . . ." Brandes (1960:19).
"The red man came . . ." Bryant in Meltzer (1998:72).
"the idea of America . . ." Hinsley (1992:15).
"traditionary testimony of . . ." Jefferson (1954 [1787]:54).
"a discourse of domination . . ." Hinsley (1992:15).
"brought up with us . . ." Ambrose (1998:34).
"most and the best . . ." Bancroft in Winsor (1995:132).
"I have . . ." Houston in Hinsley (1996:180).
"In the monuments . . ." Jackson in Bieder (1986:112 n.).
"what delighted the . . ." Silverberg (1968:82).
"Even as the U. S. Army . . ." McGuire (1997:68).
"a form of tents . . ." Steiner (1987:142).
"The opinion that the American Indians . . ." Priest in Silverberg (1968: 83-84).
"this grand old . . ." Brandes (1960:14).
"The dream of . . ." Silverberg (1968:57).
"built by Montezuma . . ." Brandes (1960:12).
"White men built . . ." Judd in Lekson (1988:216).

CHAPTER 13. THE SMITHSONIAN TAKES ON ALL COMERS
(PAGES 133–138)

"the flint utensils . . ." Haven in Silverberg (1968).
"a model of reasoned . . ." Willey & Sabloff (1993:44).
"believer in the existence . . ." Silverberg (1968:173).
"like a general . . ." Silverberg (1968: 203).
"In spite of their . . ." Boucher de Perthes in Oakley (1964:94).
"generated in the sky . . ." (Daniel 1962:39).
"America's Boucher de Perthes" Meltzer (1993:45).
"The question of . . . ." Roberts in Willey and Sabloff (1993:55-6).
"lie low for the present" Meltzer (1993:50).
"Whether the price . . ." Willey and Sabloff (1993:56).

CHAPTER 14. WHERE ARE ALL THE NATIVE AMERICAN
ARCHAEOLOGISTS? (PAGES 139–144)

"the archetypical 'good guy,' . . ." Johnson (1997:615).
"the hideous, unnameable . . ." Roosevelt (1887).
"children" Bolton (1921:200).
"Borderland irritants . . ." Bannon (1974, heading of Chapter 8).
"the great unifying myths . . ." Noonan in Schlesinger (1998:62).
"History seemed for Roosevelt . . ." Trachtenberg (1982:26).
"with an image of . . ." Hoxie (1992:974).
"practically every civilized . . ." Trachtenberg (1982:26–27).
"arguably the single . . ." Lawson (1994:bookflap).
"whether or not the . . ." Lawson (1994:192).
"All origin myths . . ." G. A. Clark (letter in ACPAC *Newsletter* 2/97).
"I don't think . . ." Dean in Roberts (1996:86).

CHAPTER 15. BREAKTHROUGH AT FOLSOM (PAGES 145–156)

For more on the Folsom and Clovis finds, see David Meltzer's important "The antiquity of man and the development of American archaeology" (1983) and his *Search for the First Americans* (1993). Other references include Preston (1997a), Cotter (1938), and Folsom (1974, 1992). *The Fenn Cache* by George Frison and Bruce Bradley is a highly a readable overview of Clovis archaeology, accompanied by spectacular photographs of Clovis technology.

Recent excavations by David Meltzer and his team from Southern Methodist University provide new insights about the Folsom site. Meltzer has located a still-buried extension of the bone bed and, at this writing, is attempting to determine whether a Folsom-age camp or other activities were associated with the bison kill.

"dug out nearly . . ." Schwachheim in Folsom (1974:35).
"Something in the nature . . ." Figgins (1927:232).
"Sooner or later . . ." Figgins in Folsom (1974:36).
"not a scrap . . ." Hrdlička (1926).
"And the durned . . ." Folsom (1974:37).
"Found part of a . . ." Schwachheim in Folsom (1974:37).
" Last week I had . . ." Brown in Folsom (1974: 37).

"Now I am in . . ." Figgins in Folsom (1974:37).
"arouse Dr. H. . . ." Figgins in Meltzer (1991:32).
"Dr. Hrdlička was not happy" Folsom (1974:38).
"undoubtedly foreign—European . . ." Holmes in Folsom (1974:38).
"he would never . . ." Holmes in Folsom (1974:38).
"the artifacts are . . ." Brown in Folsom (1974:39).
"In my hand . . ." Brown in Meltzer (1983:36).
"first human adventurer . . ." Kidder (1927:5).
"not have been . . ." Hrdlička (1942:54).
"chronological chasm" Fagan (1987:52).
"the most significant . . ." Frison (1993:188).
"as the finest examples . . ." Howard (1936:319).
"preceded by other . . ." Howard (1936:319).
"a continent-wide . . ." Adovasio and Pedler (1997:573).
"the Clovis mafia" Petit (1998:59).
"have gotten their 15 minutes . . ." Adovasio in Petit (1998:58).

CHAPTER 16. BUSTING THE CLOVIS BARRIER (PAGES 157–166)

The archaeology of Monte Verde has been described in a two-volume technical report (Dillehay 1989, 1997a). Additionally, see Dixon (1999) and Meltzer et al.(1997).

"Our ancestors looked . . ." Dillehay (1997b:28).
"irrefutable and unquestionable . . ." Dillehay (1998:5).
"As far as artifacts . . ." Dillehay (1997a:32).
"others would be . . ." Dillehay in Begley and Murr (1999:56).
"Instant Analysis and . . ." Dillehay (1997a:3,4).
"In one publication . . ." Dillehay (1997a:4).
"The Clovis Curtain has fallen" Adovasio and Pedler (1997:578).
"complete unanimity . . . no . . ." Meltzer et al.(1997:660–661).
"has just six artifacts . . ." Haynes in Petit (1998:63).
On comparing to Monte Verde verification to breaking sound barrier, Wilford (1997).
Fiedel's critique and the responses to it were published as a Special Report by *Scientific American Discovering Archaeology* (November/December 1999); unless noted otherwise, all quotes in this section are taken from that publication.
"analytical overkill . . . a milestone . . ." Meltzer et al. (1997:754).
"this is not . . ." Grayson on book jacket of Dillehay (1997a).
"anticlimactic and, ultimately . . ." Adovasio and Pedler (1997:578).
"the extreme care given to . . ." *Society for American Archaeology Bulletin* (16[3]:17).
"readers . . . to examine . . ." Meltzer et al. (1997:660).

CHAPTER 17. WHAT MODERN ARCHAEOLOGISTS THINK ABOUT THE EARLIEST AMERICANS (PAGES 167–174)

For fairly up-to-date summaries of the archaeological evidence for the First Americans, I recommend Dillehay and Meltzer's *The First Americans: Search and Research* (1991) and West's *American Beginnings: The Prehistory and Palaeoecology of Beringia* (1996), edited by Frederick Hadleigh West. For a more readable, if somewhat dated, overview of the peopling of America, see Meltzer's *Search for the First Americans* or Brian Fagan's *The Great Journey* (1987).

Svante Pääbo (1993) provides an excellent and nontechnical overview of the potential for analyzing ancient DNA recovered in long-dead plants and animals. The Windover finds are discussed by Doran et al.(1986). Other good sources on molecular archaeology include Stone and Stoneking (1993) and Szathmary (1993). I particularly recommend Clark Spencer Larsen's *Bioarchaeology: Interpreting Behavior from the Human Skeleton* (1997).

"Into a new period . . ." Wilford (1999).
"with Big Game Hunters . . ." Henderson (1997).
"macho gringo guys . . ." Mandryk in Petit (1998:62).
"We've got to do . . ." Bradley in Easthouse (1997).
"There are just . . ." Haynes in Easthouse (1997).
"we have in American . . ." Nelson (1933:130); see also Nelson (1919).
All quotes from Bradley in this section are personal communications to the author.
The Stanford quotes in this section are from Stanford (1997).
"not outrageous. The upper . . ." Haynes in Easthouse (1997).
"As a linguist, that's . . ." Nichols in Petit (1998:62).

PART IV. THE INDIANS REFUSE TO VANISH (PAGE 175)
"Not long before the Civil War . . ." Steiner (1987:vii).

CHAPTER 18. "BE AN INDIAN AND KEEP COOL" (PAGES 177–185)
An important source in this chapter is Frederick E. Hoxie's "Exploring a cultural borderland" (1992). For a general overview of Indian-federal relationships, see Prucha's *The Great Father* (1984). On American Indian demography, see Thornton's *American Indian Holocaust and Survival: A Population History Since 1492* (1987). For a discussion of American Indians in sports, see Oxendine (1995). Britten (1997) discusses reservation conditions during the World War I period.

For more on the career of Arthur C. Parker, see W. Stephen Thomas' biography (1955), Hertzberg (1979:50), and Hanson (1997). On Parker's interpretation of the Ripley site as protohistoric Erie (an interpretation not currently accepted by archaeologists), see Fenton (1968: 17). For more on American Indian demography, see David Henige's *Numbers from Nowhere* (1998).

Unless otherwise noted, all quotes in this section from Bernotas (1992:13, 19).
"They saw avenues . . ." Hoxie (1992:976).
"At home on either . . ." Fenton (1968:2).
"spicy dust and mothballs . . ." Hertzberg (1979:52).
Unless otherwise noted, the remaining quotes in this chaper from Hanson (1997).
"Be an Indian . . ." Parker in P. Deloria (1998:124).
"Parker did not hesitate . . ." P. Deloria (1998:124).
"the power of costume" Hoxie (1992:992).
"the paint, feathers, robes . . ." La Flesche in Hoxie (1992:991.).
"Is [our sovereignty recognized] simply because . . ." Sheffield (1997:50).

CHAPTER 19. THE INDIAN NEW DEAL: FROM ABSOLUTE DEPRIVATION TO MERE POVERTY (PAGES 186–197)
Important references for this chapter include *The Nations Within: The Past and Future of American Indian Sovereignty* by Deloria and Lytle (1984) and *Termination Revisited: American Indi-*

ans *on the Trail to Self-determination, 1933-1953* (1999) by Kenneth Philp. On the reaction of the Pine Ridge and Rosebud Reservations to the Indian New Deal, see *Organizing the Lakota* by Thomas Biolsi (1992); see also Deloria and Lytle (1983, Chapter 1).

"It may be hard for us . . ." Deloria and Lytle (1983:21)
"a magical habitation . . ." Collier in Bordewich (1996:71).
"They had what . . ." Bordewich (1996: 71); Limerick (1987:201).
The Mead quotes come from *Blackberry Winter* (Mead 1972:190–192) and *The Changing Culture of an Indian Tribe* (Mead 1932:46) in which she disguised the Omaha tribe as "the Antlers."
"Like the miner's canary..." Cohen in Bordewich (1006: 20).
The statistics documenting the impact of the Dawes Act from Dippie (1982:314–315).
"I do believe . . ." Ickes in Prucha (1984:941).
The transcripts from Collier's congresses on the IRA have been edited by Vine Deloria, Jr. and will soon be published .
"many of the old customs . . ." Deloria and Lytle (1983:15).
"We do not believe . . ." Dippie (1982:304).
"in a civilized condition . . ." Hanson (1997).
"only bright spot . . ." Deloria (1988:48).
"from absolute deprivation . . ." Deloria in Marks (1998:279).
"ethnic laboratory of . . ." Collier in Limerick (1987:208).
"provides only one form . . ." Jemison in Thomas et al.(1993:413).
"The present administration . . ." Collier in Biolsi (1992:ixx).
"good intentions and ironic . . ." Limerick (1987:202).
"The Indian New Deal . . ." Echo-Hawk in Limerick (1987:209).
"American Indians are unique . . ." Deloria and Lytle (1984:2).
"That is, such rights . . ." P. Deloria in Thomas et al.(1993:415–6).
"letting France make laws . . ." Giago in *The Santa Fe New Mexican* (7/19/98).
"is, after all . . ." P. Deloria in Thomas et al.(1993:416).
"I want to emphasize . . ." Myer in Deloria and Lytle (1983:17).
"a Hitler and Mussolini . . ." Ickes in Prucha (1984:1031).
"Watkins' idea was to . . ." Deloria (1988:62).
"a large number of Indians . . ." Deloria and Lytle (1983:18).
"It is our belief . . ." U.S. Congress in Prucha (1984:1053).

CHAPTER 20. THE RED POWER OF VINE DELORIA, JR.
(PAGES 198–208)

The major works by Vine Deloria, Jr. include *Custer Died For Your Sins: An Indian Manifesto* (1988 [1969]), *God is Red: A Native View of Religion* (1992b), *Red Earth, White Lies: Native Americans and the Myth of Scientific Fact* (1995), *For this Land: Writings on Religion in America* (1999). In an unprecedented step, the American Anthropological Association celebrated the 25th anniversary of *Custer Died for Your Sins* at its 88th annual meeting, held in April 1989. The published papers presented at this session appear in *Indians and Anthropologists: Vine Deloria Jr. and the Critique of Anthropology* (1997), edited by Thomas Biolsi and Larry J. Zimmerman.

For discussion of the Red Power movement, see Smith and Warrior's *Like a Hurricane: Red Power from Alcatraz to Wounded Knee* (1996); Johnson's *The Occupation of Alcatraz Island* (1996) and also his *Contemporary Native American Political Issues* (1999); *American Indian Activism: Alcatraz to the Longest Walk* edited by Troy R. Johnson, Joane Nagel, and Duane

Champagne (1997), Cornell's *The Return of the Native* (1988) and *Alcatraz! Alcatraz! The Indian Occupation of 1969-1971* by Adam Fortunate Eagle (1992); and Hertzberg (1988).

On defining Indian identities, see *Tonto's Revenge* by Rennard Stickland (1997, especially Chapters 1 and 2), Champaign (1999, part I) and Vickers (1998).

"five weeks down . . ." Deloria (1992a:14).

"trying to preserve . . ." Deloria (1992a:14).

"most controversial Indian . . ." Means (1995: bookjacket).

"I couldn't help . . ." Means (1995:148).

Unless otherwise noted, all Deloria quotes in this section derive from Deloria (1988:79, 95, 99–100).

"You can sit . . ." Deloria in Johnson (1996:165–6).

"get those Indians . . ." Deloria (1992a:xi).

"an Indian version . . ." Deloria (1997a:46).

"a myth" Deloria (1997a:47).

"unable to articulate . . ." (Deloria 1997a:46).

"AIM seized the . . ." Johnson (1997:220).

"Going 'back to the blanket' . . ." Hanson (1997).

"about every admirable . . ." Means in Johnson et al.(1997:306).

"probably never had . . ." West and Gover (1988:290).

"if it confuses children . . ." in *New York Daily News* (3/10/99).

"This is one of the last vestiges . . ." Harjo quoted by the Associated Press (4/3/99).

"Can you imagine . . ." Simon in (www.siu.edu/~ppi/NPR980623.html).

Unless otherwise noted, all Deloria quotes in the rest of this chapter come from Deloria (1995: 20-21, 41-43, 50, 143, 241, 248).

'There's a real feeling . . .' Benallie in Johnson (1996)

"The Bering Strait theory . . ." and "excavating ancient fireplaces . . ." Deloria (1992c: 433).

"making a test of . . ." Deloria (1998).

CHAPTER 21. LEGISLATING THE SKULL WARS (PAGES 209–221)

For discussions on NAGPRA, see Thomas E. King's *Cultural Resource Laws & Practice: An Introductory Guide* (1998), *Battlefields and Burial Grounds*, by Roger C. Echo-Hawk and Walter R. Echo-Hawk (1994). *Reckoning with the Dead* edited by Bray and Killion, presents multiple perspectives on the Larsen Bay (Alaska) case, the first major repatriation and reburial claim in the United States.

For the purposes of this chapter, I only discuss the NAGPRA legislation. Parallel (but not identical) legislation as it applies to the various museums of the Smithsonian Institution. For present purposes, I have not here distinguished between the two. My discussion of tribes likewise does not address the issues of Native Alaskans and Hawaiians under NAGPRA. Congress sidestepped the tribal issue with Native Alaskans by lumping them under "Indian tribes." But when it came to "Native Hawaiian"—where no such legal concept previously existed—the NAGPRA legislation created considerable confusion.

Important references on reburial and repatriation include Stickland (1997, Chapter 85), Raymond (1999), D. Walker (1990), Ubelaker and Grant (1989), Mihesuah (1996a), Meighan (1994), McLaughlin (1998a and 1998b), *American Indian Culture and Research Journal* (1992 Special edition). For more on the Sand Creek Massacre repatriation, see Gulliford (1996:137) and Giarelli (1993).

"In the larger scope . . ." *American Institute for Conservation of Historic and Artistic Works News*, March 1998: 1A.

"I explicitly assume . . ." Turner (1986:1).

"What is the . . ." Hale in Zimmerman (1989b: 212).

"These medical practitioners . . ." Walker (1999).

"The basis of the arrangement . . ." Walker (personal communication to the author).

"nonrenewable archaeological resources . . ." Echo-Hawk and Echo-Hawk in Weaver (1997:15-16).

"If you desecrate . . ." Echo-Hawk in Vizenor (1990).

"If archaeology is . . ." Meighan (1985:20).

"It is simply . . ." Clark (1997).

"business as usual . . ." Terry Eagleton in Biolsi and Zimmerman (1997:6).

"I am a future . . ." Cary Alice Wolf in Ridington (1992:88).

"broken culture" Mead (1932:ix-xiii).

"How would you . . ." Tallbull in Swisher (1989).

"one of the most . . ." Hutt testimony before the Senate Committee on Indian Affairs (4/29/99).

"It wasn't enough . . ." Harjo in Vizenor (1990:62-3).

"We are real grateful . . ." Goldberg (1999).

"We have a lot . . ." Goldberg (1999).

"whole family getting . . . " Robbins (1999).

"He wants to walk . . ." Robbins (1999).

"How do you feel" and subsequent dialogue this section from Carpenter (1997:28).

"This was, to be sure . . ." T. Kroeber (1970:93).

PART V. BRIDGING THE CHASM (PAGE 223)
"To archaeologists, the idea . . ." White Deer (1997:38)

CHAPTER 22. TRIBAL AFFILIATION AND SOVEREIGNTY (PAGES 225–238)

Several important sources discuss the twin issues of tribal affiliation and sovereignty, including Pevar's *The Rights of Indians and Tribes: A Basic ACLU Guide to Indian and Tribal Rights* (1992), *The Arbitrary Indian: The Indian Arts & Crafts Act of 1990* by Sheffield (1997) and Deloria and Lytle's *The Nations Within: The Past and Future of American Indian Sovereignty* (1983). For a more skeptical view, see Clifton's *The Invented Indian: Cultural Fictions and Government Policies* (1990). Egan (1998b and 1998d) discusses the current backlash against tribal sovereignty. For more on authenticity, see Egan (1998e). For a discussion on blood quanta, see Pevar (1992:12) and Bordewich (1996:68).

"Repatriation is the . . ." West in Bordewich (1996:171–2),

"Law dominates Indian . . ." Cohen in Sheffield (1997:34).

"expediency grounded only . . ." Deloria in Sheffield (1997: 36).

"An Indian is somebody . . ." Momaday in Bordewich (1996:67).

On the Wannabees: Green (1988) and Sheffield (1997:87-94).

"So-called [contemporary] tribal . . ." Fried (1968).

"a body of [1] Indians . . ." Sturtevant (1983:10).

"As I use it and . . ." Deloria in Bordewich (1996:68).

"large, dispersed mixed-blood . . ." Thornton (1990142–143).

"I haven't seen . . ." Stowsky in Curtius (1998).
"I believe this . . ." McCain in the Congressional Record (10/26/90, p. S 17173).
"NAGPRA wasn't the . . ." Killion in Protzman (1998:134).
"Kennewick hits [NAGPRA] . . ." Meltzer in Henderson (1997).
"infuriates any Indian . . ." Deloria (personal communication).
"How can devout Jews . . . " Deloria (1999:200–-201).
"How can any scholar . . ." Deloria (1999:200).
"a treaty was not . . ." in Deloria and Lytle (1984:49).
"I find nothing . . ." Gorton in *The New York Times* (8/27/97).
"Making a case out of . . ." Gorton in Egan (1998a).

CHAPTER 23. SPEAKING OF ORAL TRADITION (PAGES 239–253)

The relationship of archaeology and Native American oral tradition is discussed in *Native Americans and Archaeologists: Stepping Stones to Common Ground*, edited by Swidler and others (1997). For a discussion on current relations between Indians and archaeologists, I recommend *At a Crossroads: Archaeology and First Peoples in Canada* (1997), edited by George P. Nichols and Thomas D. Andrews.

For more general discussions of recent theoretical shifts in archaeology, I recommend Alice Kehoe's impressive *The Land of Prehistory: A Critical History of American Archaeology* (1998), Patterson's *Toward a Social History of Archaeology in the United States* (1995), Tribber's *A History of Archaeological Thought* (1989), and my own *Archaeology* (1998). In addition, see Zimmerman (1989a) and Ferguson et al.(1996)

This chapter discusses only the origin legend of the Awatixa Hidatsa; other Hidatsa groups have different stories. For more on archaeology and Hidatsa oral tradition, see *People of the Willows: The Prehistory and Early History of the Hidatsa Indians* by Ahler, Thiessen, and Trimble (1991). For more on oral tradition and the Mt. Mazama eruption, see Deloria (1995), Briggs (1962), and Vitaliano (1973).

"If this individual . . ." Minthorn in 1996 press release from the Umatilla Nation.
"We don't expect . . ." Echo-Hawk quoted in Preston (1989: 75).
"subtly implied message . . ." Schneider in Hastings (1997).
"Long before anyone . . ." Biolsi and Zimmerman 1997:4).
"The clincher was . . ." Scott in Smiley (1999:22).
"It is no . . ." Cruikshank (1981).
All the quotes in the Klamath story about Crater Lake are from Clark (1952:53–55).
"until the academic . . ." Deloria (1995).
"spectrum of oral traditions . . ." Roger Echo-Hawk (1997:88).

CHAPTER 24. AN ARCHAEOLOGY WITHOUT ALIENATION (PAGES 254–267)

The views of Scott Momaday are explored in *Ancestral Voice: Conversations with N. Scott Momaday* by Charles L. Woodard (1989). For more on the Navajo code talkers, see Daily (1995: 41–42). For the details on the fall and rise of the Mashantucket Pequot tribes, see Hauptman and Wherry (1990). Silberman (1998) discusses the Mashantucket Pequot Museum.

For more on the relations between native people and archaeologists at Kodiak Bay, see Bray and Killion (1994).

"Our history, identity, and tribal sovereignty . . ." label copy in the Tamástslikt Cultural
    Institute, near Pendleton, Oregon.
"to be indigenous . . ." label copy in the Tamástslikt Cultural Institute.
"The Power of Home . . ." label copy in the Tamástslikt Cultural Institute
"In fact, we have . . ." Sampson (1997:26).
"Western science . . ." Tsosie in *The New York Times*, November 9, 1999.
"As a child . . ." Momaday (1976:85-60).
"Science has unlocked . . ." Momaday (1996).
"Archaeologists and anthropologists . . ." Momaday (1996).
"the last thirty years . . ." Deloria (1996).
"I had always assumed . . ." Deloria (1997b).
"He and I can . . ." Momaday in Burshia and Holm (1997).
" . . . to the audience . . ." Deloria in Tieri (1997:20).
"the silence on the part . . ." Binford (1973:2).
All the Leslie White quotes in this section are from White (1973).
All the Morgan quotes in this section derive from Morgan (1876:75, 76).
On anthropologists speaking out against termination, see Lurie (1998).
"Our hearts were . . ." *Dig Afognak* press release.
"Never doubt the . . ." Cooke (1998).
"a disturbing illustration . . ." and all other quotes in the next seven paragraphs from Bor-
    dewich (1996:110–111).
"Every culture has . . ." label copy in the Mashantucket Pequot Museum).
"No one can say . . ." and other newspaper quotes in this paragraph in *New York Times* ad-
    vertisement by the Mashantucket Pequot Tribal Museum.
"radical, top-down solution" Anderson (1998).

EPILOGUE (PAGES 268–276)
    Readers can learn more about the Tongass Forest excavations in *Bones, Boats, and Bison:
Archaeology and the First Colonization of North America* by James Dixon (1999). More technical
discussions can be found in Dixon et al.(1997), Fifield (1996), O'Hara (1998) and Fifield
et al. (1998).

Unless otherwise attributed, all quotes from Fifield are personal communications with the
    author.
"This cave has . . ." Heaton in Fifield et al.(1998:5).
"Oh my God!" Grady in O'Harra (1998).
"Important artifact found . . ." Heaton in O'Harra (1998).
"Right away, we went . . ." Fifield in O'Harra (1998).
"In the end, the weight . . ." Fifield in O'Harra (1998).
"might just be . . ." Dixon in Fifield et al.(1998:5).
"in southeast Alaska . . ." Dixon in O'Harra (1998).
"It's a homely . . ." Dixon in O'Harra (1998).
"a model of how . . ." Fifield in Fifield et al.(1998:5).
"the question is . . ." Bailey (1998: 24).

LITERATURE CITED

Abrams, Ann Uhry
1999.*The Pilgrims and Pocahontas: Rival Myths of American Origin.* Boulder, Co: Westview Press.
Adovasio, J. M., and D. R. Pedler
1997. Monte Verde and the antiquity of humankind in the Americas. *Antiquity* 71:573–80.
Ahler, Stanley A., Thomas D. Thiessen, and Michael K. Trimble
1991. *People of the Willows: The Prehistory and Early History of the Hidatsa Indians.* University of North Dakota: Grand Forks.
Alexander, Hartley B.
1933. Francis La Flesche. *American Anthropologist.* 35:328–331.
Ambrose, Stephen E.
1998. *Lewis & Clark: Voyage of Discovery.* Washington D.C.: National Geographic Society.
American Anthropological Association
1998. AAA statement on race. *Anthropology Newsletter,* September.
Anderson, Duane
1998. The NAGPRA experiment. *Anthropology Newsletter* 39(4): p. 28.
Anyon, Roger, T. J. Ferguson, Loretta Jackson, and Lillie Lane
1996. Native American oral traditions. *Society for American Archaeology Bulletin.* 14(2):14–16.
Armelagos, George J., and Alan H. Goodman
1998. Race, racism, and anthropology. *In* Alan H. Goodman and Thomas L. Leatherman, eds., *Building a New Biocultural Synthesis: Political-Economic Perspectives on Human Biology,* pp. 359–377. Ann Arbor: University of Michigan Press.

Armstrong, Virginia Irving (compiler)
    1971. *I have Spoken: American History Through the Voices of the Indians*. Athens, Ohio: Swallow Press.
Bahr, Donald, and Susan Fenger
    1989. Indians and missions: homage and debate with Rupert Costo and Jeanette Henry. *J Southwest*. 31:298–329.
Bailey, Garrick
    1998. NAGPRA, politics and control. *Anthropology Newletter*. April 1998.
Bannon, John Francis
    1974. *The Spanish Borderlands Frontier, 1513-1821*. Albuquerque: University of New Mexico Press.
Barkan, Alazar
    1988. Mobilizing scientists against Nazi racism, 1933-1939. *In* George W. Stocking, Jr., ed., *Bones, Bodies, and Behavior: Essays on Biological Anthropology*, pp. 180–205. Madison: University of Wisconsin Press.
    1992. *The Retreat of Scientific Racism: Changing Concepts of Race in Britain and the United States Between the World Wars*. New York: Cambridge University Press.
Basso, Keith F.
    1996. *Wisdom Sits in Places*. Albuquerque: University of New Mexico Press.
Beam, Louis
    1997. Evidence suggests whites settled Americas first. *Spotlight*, October 13.
Begley, Sharon, and Andrew Murr
    1999. The First Americans. *Newsweek*. April 26.
Beinart, Peter
    1999. Tribes: Anthropologists feud over Indian identity. *Lingua Franca*. May/June 9(4):34–41.
Berkhofer, Robert F., Jr.
    1978. *The White Man's Indian: Images of the American Indian from Columbus to the Present*. New York: Alfred A. Knopf.
    1988. White conceptions of Indians. *In* Wilcomb E. Washburn, ed., *Handbook of North American Indians*, Vol. 4: *History of Indian-White Relations*, pp. 522–547. Washington DC: Smithsonian Institution Press.
Bernotas, Bob.
    1992. *Jim Thorpe: Sak and Fox Athlete*. New York: Chelsea House Publishers.
Bieder, Robert E.
    1986. *Science Encounters the Indian, 1820-1880*. Norman: University of Oklahoma Press.
    1992. The collecting of bones for anthropological narratives. *Special Edition: Repatriation of American Indian Remains. American Indian Culture and Research Journal*. 16(2):21–36.
    1996. The representations of Indian bodies in nineteenth-century American anthropology. *American Indian Quarterly*. 20(2):165–179.
Big Boy, Marla
    1999. Colville Tribe on Kennewick. *AAA Newsletter*, May.
Binford, Sally R.
    1973. Aid for AIM: Wounded Knee Fund. *Newsletter of the American Anthropological Association*. 14(5):2.
Biolsi, Thomas
    1992. *Organizing the Lakota: The Political Economy of the New Deal on the Pine Ridge and Rosebud Reservations*. Tucson: University of Arizona Press.

Biolsi, Thomas, and Larry J. Zimmerman (eds.)
1997. *Indians and Anthropologists: Vine Deloria Jr. and the Critique of Anthropology*. Tucson: University of Arizona Press.

Blakey, Michael L.
1987. Skull Doctors: Intrinsic social and political bias in the history of American physical anthropology, with special reference to the work of Alex Hrdlička. *Critique of Anthropology*. 7(2):7-35.

Boas, Franz
1911. *The Mind of Primitive Man*. New York: Macmillan Company.
1940. *Race, Language and Culture*. New York: Macmillan Company.
1969.*The Ethnography of Franz Boas: Letters and Diaries of Franz Boas Written on the Northwest Coast from 1886-1931*, Ronald P. Rohner, comp. & ed., Hedy Parker, trans. Chicago: Chicago University Press.

Bolton, Herbert E.
1921. *The Spanish Borderlands: A Chronicle of Old Florida and the Southwest*. New Haven, CT: Yale University Press.

Bordewich, Fergus M.
1996. *Killing the White Man's Indian*. New York: Doubleday.

Boughter, Judith A.
1998. *Betraying the Omaha Nation 1790-1916*. Norman: University of Oklahoma Press.

Brandes, Ray
1960. Archaeological awareness of the Southwest, as illustrated in literature to 1890. *Arizona and the West*. 1:6–25.
1965. Frank Hamilton Cushing: Pioneer Americanist. Ph.D. Dissertation, Department of History, University of Arizona, Tucson.

Bray, Tamara, and Thomas Killion (eds.)
1994. *Reckoning with the Dead: The Larsen Bay Repatriation and the Smithsonian Institution*. Washington D.C.: Smithsonian Institution Press.

Briggs, Lyman J.
1962. When Mt. Mazama lost its top. *National Geographic*. 122 (July–December):128–133.

Britten, Thomas A.
1997. *American Indians in World War I*. Albuquerque: University of New Mexico Press.

Bronner, Ethan
1998. Inventing the notion of race. *The New York Times*. January 10.

Brooke, John Hedley
1991. *Science and Religion: Some Historical Perspectives*. Cambridge: Cambridge University Press.

Brumble, H. David
1998. Vine Deloria Jr., creationism, and ethnic pseudoscience. *Reports of the National Center for Science Education*. 18(6):10–13.

Burshia, Jodi, and Michael A. Holm
1997. RED INK talks with N. Scott Momaday. *Red Ink*. 5(2):16-17.

Carpenter, Edmund S.
1950. The role of archaeology in the 19th century controversy between developmentalism and degeneration. *Pennsylvania Archaeologist*. 20:5–18.
1997. Dead truth, live myth. *European Review of Native American Studies*. 11(2):27–29

Champaign, Duane (ed.)
1994. *Native America: Portrait of the Peoples*. Detroit, MI: Visible Ink Press.

Chatters, James C.

1997. Encounter with an ancestor. *Anthropology Newsletter* (January): 9, 11.

1998. Human biological history, *not* race. *Anthropology Newsletter* (February): 19, 21.

1999. The Kennewick Man: A first multivariate analysis. *Current Research in the Pleistocene* [in press]

Chinard, Gilbert

1947. Eighteenth century theories on America as a human habitat. *American Philosophical Society, Proceedings* 91.

Clark, Ella E.

1952. *Indian Legends of the Pacific Northwest.* Berkeley: University of California Press.

Clark, G. A.

1997. Letter in *ACPAC Newsletter,* February.

Clifford, James

1988. *The Predicament of Culture: Twentieth-Century Ethnography, Literature, and Art.* Cambridge: Harvard University Press.

Clifton, James A. (ed.)

1989. *Being and Becoming Indian: Biographical Studies of North American Frontiers.* Chicago: Dorsey Press.

1990. *The Invented Indian: Cultural Fictions and Government Policies.* New Brunswick: Transaction Publishers.

Cohen, Felix S.

1982. *Felix S. Cohen's Handbook of Federal Indian Law,* revised edition., Rennard Stickland et al., eds. Charlottesville, VA: Michie Bobbs Merrill.

Cole, Douglas

1995. *Captured Heritage: The Scramble for Northwest Coast Artifacts,* revised edition. Norman: University of Oklahoma Press.

Conn, Steven

1999. *Museums and American Intellectual Life, 1876-1926.* Chicago: University of Chicago Press.

Connell, Evan S.

1984. *Son of the Morning Star.* New York: Promontory Press.

Cooke, Robert

1998. Foxwoods' cache flow. *Newsday,* July 28.

Cooper, James Fenimore

1985. *The Leatherstocking Tales,* Vol. I. New York: Literary Classics of the United States.

Cornell, Stephen

1988. *The Return of the Native: American Indian Political Resurgence.* New York: Oxford University Press.

Cotter, John L.

1938. The occurrence of flints and extinct animals in pluvial deposits near Clovis, New Mexico. *In* Report on the Excavations at the Gravel Pit in 1936, Part 4. *Proceedings of the Philadelphia Academy of Natural Sciences.* 90:113–117.

Cruikshank, Julie

1981. Legend and landscape: Convergence of oral and scientific traditions in the Yukon territory. *Arctic Anthropology* 18(2):67-93.

Curtius, Mary

1998. Indian remains are bones of contention at Berkeley. *Los Angeles Times.* April 27.

Cushing, Frank H.

1890. Preliminary notes on the origin, working hypothesis and primary researches of the Hemenway. Expedition. *Seventh International Congress of Americanists.* 151–194. Berlin.

1970. [1882–1883] *My Adventures at Zuñi.* Palo Alto, CA: American West Publishing Company.

Daily, Robert

1995. *The Code Talkers: American Indians in World War II.* New York: Franklin Watts.

Daniel, Glyn

1962. *The Idea of Prehistory.* Baltimore: Penguin Books.

Davis, Dave D., and R. Christopher Goodwin

1990. Island Carib origins: evidence and nonevidence. *American Antiquity.* 55(1):37–48.

Deloria, Ella

1998 [1944]. *Speaking of Indians.* Lincoln: University of Nebraska Press.

Deloria, Philip J.

1998. *Playing Indian.* New Haven: Yale University Press.

Deloria, Vine, Jr.

1988 [1969]. *Custer Died For Your Sins: An Indian Manifesto.* Norman: University of Oklahoma Press.

1992a. Forward. *In* Adam Fortunate Eagle, *Alcatraz! Alcatraz! The Indian Occupation of 1969–1971,* pp. xii–xi. Berkeley: Heyday Books.

1992b. *God is Red: A Native View of Religion.* 2nd ed. Golden, CO: North American Press.

1992c. Afterword. *In* Alvin M. Josephy, Jr., ed. *America in 1492,* pp. 429–443. New York: Alfred A. Knopf.

1995. *Red Earth, White Lies: Native Americans and the Myth of Scientific Fact.* New York: Scribner.

1996. OK, Scott, where's the beef? *News from Indian Country.* Late December.

1997a. Alcatraz, activism, and accommodation. *In* Troy R. Johnson, Joane Nagel, and Duane Champagne, eds., *American Indian Activism: Alcatraz to the Longest Walk,* 45–51. Urbana: University of Illinois Press.

1997b. "Scientific Folklore" A conversation with Vine Deloria, Jr. *News from Indian Country.* Mid January.

1998. Do scientists have rights to all finds? *The Denver Post.* November 29.

1999. *For This Land: Writings on Religion in America.* New York: Routledge.

Deloria, Vine, Jr., and Clifford Lytle

1983. *American Indians, American Justice.* Austin: University of Texas Press.

1984. *The Nations Within: The Past and Future of American Indian Sovereignty.* New York: Pantheon Books.

Diamond, Jared

1997. *Guns, Germs, and Steel: The Fates of Human Societies.* New York: W. W. Norton & Company.

Dickason, Olive P.

1997. *The Myth of the Savage: And the Beginnings of French Colonialism in the Americas.* Edmonton: University of Alberta Press.

Dillehay, Thomas D.,

1989. *Monte Verde: A Late Pleistocene Settlement in Chile.* Vol. I: *Paleoenvironment and Site Context.* Washington: Smithsonian Institution Press.

1997a. *Monte Verde: A Late Pleistocene Settlement in Chile.* Vol. II: *The Archaeological Context and Interpretation.* Washington: Smithsonian Institution Press.

1997b. The Battle of Monte Verde. *The Sciences.* 37(1):28–33.

Dillehay, Tom D., and David J. Meltzer (eds.)
    1991. *The First Americans: Search and Research*. Boca Raton, FL: CRC Press.
Dippie, Brian W.
    1982. *The Vanishing American: White Attitudes and U. S. Indian Policy*. Middletown, CT: Wesleyan University Press.
Dirlik, Arif
    1999. The past as legacy and project: Postcolonial criticism in the perspective of indigenous historicism. *In* Troy R. Johnson, ed., *Contemporary Native American Political Issues*, pp. 73–98. Walnut Creek, CA: AltaMira Press.
Dixon, E. James
    1999. *Bones, Boats, and Bison: Archeology and the First Colonization of North America*. Albuquerque: University of New Mexico.
Dixon, E. James, Timothy H. Heaton, Terence E. Fifield, Thomas D. Hamilton, David E. Putnam, and Frederick Grady
    1997. Late Quaternary regional geoarchaeology of southeast Alaska Karst: A progress report. *Geoarchaeology*. 12(6):689–712.
Dixon, R. B.
    1915. Dr. Dixon's reply. *American Anthropologist* 17: 599.
Doran, Glen H., David N. Dickel, William E. Ballinger, Jr., O. Frank Agee, Philip J. Laipis, and William W. Hauswirth
    1986. Anatomical, cellular, and molecular analysis of 8,000-yr-old human brain tissue from the Windover archaeological site. *Nature* 323:803–806.
Dowd, Gregory Evans
    1992. *A Spirited Resistance: The North American Indian Struggle for Unity, 1745-1815*. Baltimore: Johns Hopkins University Press.
Drinnon, Richard
    1997 [1980]. *Facing West: The Metaphysics of Indian-Hating and Empire Building*. Norman: University of Oklahoma Press.
Easthouse, Keith
    1997. Were Europeans here before Indians? *The Santa Fe New Mexican*. August 10.
Eastman, Charles A.
    1916. *From the Deep Woods to Civilization*. Boston: Little, Brown, and Company.
Echo-Hawk, Walter R.
    1997. Forging a new ancient history for Native America. *In* N. Swidler, K. Dongoske, R. Anyon, and A. Downer, *Native Americans and Archaeologists*, pp. 88-102. Walnut Creek, CA: AltaMira Press.
Echo-Hawk, Roger C., and Walter R. Echo-Hawk
    1994. *Battlefields and Burial Grounds*. Minneapolis: Lerner Publications Company.
Egan, Timothy
    1996. Tribe stops study of bones that challenge history. *New York Times*. September 30.
    1998a. New prosperity brings new conflict to Indian Country. *The New York Times*. March 8.
    1998b. Backlash growing as Indians make a stand for sovereignty. *The New York Times*. March 9.
    1998c. Old skull get white looks, stirring dispute. *The New York Times*. April 2.
    1998d. Indian sovereignty. *The New York Times*. April 12.
    1998e. Indian reservations bank on authenticity to draw tourists. *The New York Times*. September 21.

Ehrenreich, Barbara, and Janet McIntosh
1997. The New Creationism: biology under attack. *The Nation.* June 9.
Ellis, Joseph J.
1996. *American Sphinx: The Character of Thomas Jefferson.* New York: Alfred A. Knopf.
Fagan, Brian M.
1987. *The Great Journey: The Peopling of Ancient America.* London: Thames and Hudson, Ltd.
Farris, Glenn J.
1989. Recognizing Indian folk history as real history: A Fort Ross example. *American Indian Quarterly.* XIII(4):471–480.
Fenton, William N.
1968.Introduction to *Parker on the Iroquois* by Arthur C. Parker. Syracuse, NY: Syracuse University Press.
Ferguson, T. J., Roger Anyon, and Edmund J. Ladd
1996. The representations of Indian bodies in nineteenth-century American anthropology. *American Indian Quarterly.* 20(2):251–273.
Fewkes, Jesse Walter
1896. The prehistoric culture of the Tusayan. *American Anthropologist.* 9:151–173
1900. Tusayan migration traditions. *Nineteenth Annual Report of the Bureau of American Ethnology for the Years 1897-1898,* Part 2, pp. 573–634.
Fifield, Terence E.
1996. Human remains found in Alaska reported to be 9,730 years old. *Society for American Archaeology Bulletin* 14(5): 5.
Fifield, Terence E., E. James Dixon, and Timothy H. Heaton
1998. Tribal involvement in investigations at 49-PET-408 Prince of Wales Island, Southeast Alaska. *AAA Newsletter.* May.
Figgins, J. D.
1927. The antiquity of man in America. *Natural History.* 27:229–239.
Fletcher, Alice C., and Francis La Flesche
1911. The Omaha Tribe. *Twenty-seventh Annual Report of the Bureau of American Ethnology.* Washington D.C.: Government Printing Office.
Flexner, James Thomas
1974. *Washington: The Indispensable Man.* Boston: Little, Brown, and Company.
Folsom, Franklin
1974. The story behind the Folsom site. *The American West: The Magazine of Western History* XI(6):34–39.
1992. *Black Cowboy: The Life and Legend of George McJunkin.* Niwot (Colorado): Roberts Rinehart Publishers.
Fortunate Eagle, Adam.
1992. *Alcatraz! Alcatraz! The Indian Occupation of 1969-1971.* Berkeley: Heyday Books.
Fowler, Don
2000. *A Laboratory for Anthropology: Science and Romanticism in the American Southwest, 1846-1930.* Albuquerque: University of New Mexico Press.
Freeman, Douglas Southall
1968.*Washington.* New York: Simon and Schuster.
Fried, Morton H.
1968. "On the concepts of 'tribe' and 'tribal society.' *In* June Helm, ed., *Essays on the Problem of Tribe,* June Helm, pp. 3-20. Proceedings of the 1967 Annual Spring Meetings of the American Ethnological Society. Seattle: University of Washington Press.

Frison, George C.
  1993.Modern people in the New World. *In* Göran Burenhult, gen. ed., *The First Humans: The Illustrated History of Humankind*, Vol. 1, pp. 184–205. San Francisco: Harper San Francisco.
Frison, George, and Bruce Bradley
  1999. *The Fenn Cache: Clovis Weapons and Tools.* Santa Fe, NM: One Horse Land & Cattle Co.
Fuson, Robert H. (translator)
  1987. *The Log of Christopher Columbus.* Camden, Me: International Marine Publishing Co.
Giarelli, Andrew L.
  1993. The return of Cheyenne skulls bring a bloody Western story to a close. *High Country News.* November 15.
Givens, Douglas R.
  1992. *Alfred Vincent Kidder and the Development of Americanist Archaeology.* Albuquerque: University of New Mexico Press.
Goldberg, Carey
  1999. Pueblo awaits its past in bones from Harvard. *The New York Times*, May 20.
Goldberg, David Theo
  1997. *Racial Subjects: Writing on Race in America.* New York: Routledge.
Goodman, Alan
  1996. The resurrection of race: The concept of race in physical anthropology in the 1990s. *In* L. T. Reynolds and L. Lieberman, eds., *Race and Other Misadventures: Essays in Honor of Ashley Montague in his Ninetieth Year*, pp. 174–186. Dix Hills, NY: General Hall Publishers.
  1997a. Bred in the Bone? *The Sciences*, March/April, pp. 20–25.
  1997b. Racializing Kennewick Man. *Anthropology Newsletter*, October, pp. 3,5.
  1998. Archaeology and human biological variation. *Conference on New England Archaeology Newsletter.* 17:1–8.
Gould, Stephen Jay
  1981. *The Mismeasure of Man.* New York: W. W. Norton and Company.
  1999. *Rock of Ages: Science and Religion in the Fullness of Life.* New York: The Ballantine Publishing Group.
Green, Jesse (ed.)
  1979. *Zuni: Selected Writings of Frank Hamilton Cushing.* Lincoln: University of Nebraska Press.
  1990. *Cushing at Zuni: The Correspondence and Journals of Frank Hamilton Cushing 1878-1884.* Albuquerque: University of New Mexico Press.
Green, Rayna
  1988. The tribe called Wannabee. *Folklore.* 99(1):30–55.
Grinde, Donald A., and Bruce E. Johansen
  1995. *Ecocide of Native America: Environmental Destruction of Indian Lands and Peoples.* Santa Fe: Clear Light Publishers.
Gulliford, Andrew
  1996. Bones of contention: the repatriation of native American human remains. *In* Clara Sue Kidwell and Ann Marie Plane, eds., *Representing Native American History. The Public Historian.* 18(4):119–143.
Haederle, Michael
  1997. Burying the past. *American Archaeology*, Fall, pp. 14–18.

Halaas, David Fridjoff
    1995. 'All the Camp was Weeping': George Bent and the Sand Creek Massacre. *Colorado Heritage*, Summer, pp. 2–17.
Haney Lopez, Ian F.
    1996. *White by Law: The Legal Construction of Race*. New York: New York University Press.
Hanson, Russell R.
    1997. Ethnicity and the looking glass: The dialectics of national Indian policy. *American Indian Quarterly*. 21(1):195–208.
Harper, Kenn
    1986. *Give Me My Father's Body: The Life of Minik, the New York Eskimo*. Frobisher Bay, NWT: Blackhead Books.
Harris, Marvin
    1968. *The Rise of Anthropological Theory*. New York: Thomas Y. Crowell Company.
    1999. *Theories of Culture in Postmodern Times*. Walnut Creek, CA: AltaMira Press.
Harrison, Faye V.
    1995. The persistent power of "race" in the cultural and political economics of "racism." *Annual Review of Anthropology*. 24:47–74.
Haskell, Thomas L.
    1977. *The Emergence of Professional Social Science: The American Social Science Association and the Nineteenth-Century Crisis of Authority*. Urbana: University of Illinois.
Hastings, Doc
    1997. Allow researchers to examine bones when there are no living descendants. *Insight*. 13(47): 24, 36.
Hauptman, Laurence M.
    1995. *Tribes and Tribulations: Misconceptions about American Indians and Their Histories*. Albuquerque: University of New Mexico Press.
Hauptman, Laurence M. and James D. Wherry (eds.)
    1990. *The Pequots in Southern New England: The Fall and Rise of an American Indian Nation*. Norman: University of Oklahoma Press.
Heizer, Robert F., and Theodora Kroeber (eds.)
    1979. *Ishi the Last Yahi: A Documentary History*. Berkeley: University of California Press.
Hellman, Geoffrey
    1968. *Bankers, Bones and Beetles: The First Century of the American Museum of Natural History*. Garden City, NY: The Natural History Press.
Henderson, Amy and Adrienne L. Kaeppler (eds.)
    1997. *Exhibiting Dilemmas: Issues of Representation at the Smithsonian*. Washington D.C.: Smithsonian Institution Press.
Henderson, Diedtra
    1997. Kennewick Man: new branch of the human family tree? *Seattle Times*, December 23.
    1998a. Ancient bones seem to say Kennewick Man was homicide victim. *Seattle Times*, March 27.
    1998b. Scientist digs up controversy with Kennewick Man. *Seattle Times*, June 10.
Henige, David
    1991. *In Search of Columbus*. Tucson: University of Arizona Press.
    1998. *Numbers from Nowhere: The American Indian Contact Population Debate*. Norman: University of Oklahoma.

Herrnstein, R. J., and C. Murray

    1994. *The Bell Curve: Intelligence and Class Structure in American Life.* New York: Free Press.

Hertzberg, Hazel W.

    1979. Nationality, anthropology, and Pan-Indianism in the life of Arthur C. Parker (Seneca). *Proceedings of the American Philosophical Society.* 123:47–72.

    1988. Indian Rights Movement, 1887-1973. *In* Wilcomb E. Washburn, ed., *Handbook of North American Indians,* Vol. 4: *History of Indian-White Relations,* pp. 305–323. Washington DC: Smithsonian Institution Press.

Hinsley, Curtis M.

    1981. *The Smithsonian and the American Indian: Making a Moral Anthropology in Victorian America.* Washington D.C.: Smithsonian Institution Press.

    1992. Collecting cultures and cultures of collecting: The lure of the American Southwest, 1880-1915. *Museum Anthropology.* 16(1):12–20.

Hinsley, Curtis M., and David R. Wilcox (eds.).

    1996. *The Southwest in the American Imagination.* Tucson: University of Arizona Press.

Hoig, Stan

    1961. *The Sand Creek Massacre.* Norman: University of Oklahoma Press.

Hooton, Earnest Albert

    1930. *The Indians of Pecos Pueblo: A Study of Their Skeletal Remains.* New Haven: Yale University Press.

Horsman, Reginald

    1988. United States Indian policy. *In* Wilcomb E. Washburn, ed., *Handbook of North American Indians, vol. 4: History of Indian-White Relations,* pp. 29–39. Washington DC: Smithsonian Institution Press.

Howard, E. B.

    1936. Early Man in America with particular reference to the southwestern United States. *American Naturalist.* 70:313–323.

Hoxie, Frederick E.

    1984. *The Final Promise: The Campaign to Assimilate the Indians, 1880-1920.* Lincoln: University of Nebraska.

    1988. The curious story of reformers and American Indians. *In* Frederick E. Hoxie, ed., *Indians in American History,* pp. 205–230. Arlington Heights, IL: Harlan Davidson.

    1992. Exploring a cultural borderland: Native American journeys of discovery in the early twentieth century. *The American Journal of History.* 79(3):969–995.

Hoxie, Frederick E. (ed.)

    1988. *Indians in American History.* Arlington Heights, IL: Harlan Davidson, Inc.

Hrdlička, Aleš

    1901. An Eskimo brain. *American Anthropologist.* 1926.The race and antiquity of the American Indian. *Scientific American.* July, pp. 7–9.

    1942.T he problem of man's antiquity in America. *Proceedings of the Eighth American Scientific Congress,* pp. 53–55.

Hughte, Phil

    1994. *A Zuni Artist Looks at Frank Hamilton Cushing.* Zuni, NM: Pueblo of Zuni Arts & Crafts. A:shiwi A:Wan Museum and Heritage Center.

Jarcho, S.

    1959. Origin of the American Indian as suggested by Fray Joseph de Acosta (1598). *Isis.* 50:430–438.

Jefferson, Thomas

    1954 [1787]. *Notes on the State of Virginia,* William Peden, ed. London: John Stockdale (reprinted Chapel Hill: University of North Carolina Press).

Jennings, Francis
1984.The discovery of America. *William and Mary Quarterly.* (July):441.

Johansen, Bruce E.
1999. Kennewick Man: The "great 'white' hope"? Paper presented at the Conference on American Indian Origins, National Museum of the American Indian, October 26–27.

Johnson, George
1996. Efforts of archeologists are stymied by Indian creation myths. *The New York Times,* October 22.

Johnson, Paul
1997. *A History of the American People.* New York: Harper Collins Publishers.

Johnson, Troy R.
1996. *The Occupation of Alcatraz Island.* Urbana: University of Illinois Press.

Johnson, Troy R. (ed.)
1999. *Contemporary Native American Political Issues.* Walnut Creek, CA: AltaMira Press.

Johnson, Troy R., Joane Nagel, and Duane Champagne (eds.)
1997. *American Indian Activism: Alcatraz to the Longest Walk.* Urbana: University of Illinois Press.

Josephy, Alvin M., Jr.
1961. *Patriot Chiefs.* New York: Viking Penguin Inc.
1992. *America in 1492: The World of the Indian Peoples Before the Arrival of Columbus.* New York: Alfred A. Knopf.

Kaplan, F.E.S., ed.
1994. *The Role of Objects in National Identity.* New York: St. Martin's Press.

Keegan, William F.
1989. Creating the Guanahatabey (Ciboney): the modern genesis of an extinct culture. *Antiquity.* 63:373–379.
1992. *The People Who Discovered Columbus: The Prehistory of the Bahamas.* Gainesville: University Press of Florida.
1996. West Indian archaeology. 2. After Columbus. *Journal of Archaeological Research.* 4(4):265–294.

Kehoe, Alice Beck
1998. *The Land of Prehistory: A Critical History of American Archaeology.* New York: Routledge.

Kennedy, John Michael
1968. Philanthropy and Science in New York City: The American Museum of Natural History. Unpublished doctoral dissertation. Ann Arbor: University of Michigan.

Kennedy, Roger G.
1994. *Hidden Cities: The Discovery and Loss of Ancient North American Civilization.* New York: The Free Press.

Kessler, A. F.
1968. How we found Ishi. *Pacific Historian.* XII:22–29.

Kidder, Alfred V.
1927. Early Man in America. *The Masterkey.* 1(5):5–13.

Killion, Thomas, William Sturtevant, Dennis Stanford, and David Hunt
1999. The facts about Ishi's brain. *Anthropology News,* September.

Kimball, Solon T., and James B. Watson (eds.)
1972. *Crossing Cultural Boundaries.* San Francisco: Chandler.

King, Thomas F.

  1998. *Cultural Resource Laws & Practice: An Introductory Guide*. Walnut Creek, CA: AltaMira Press.

Knickerbocker. B.

  1996. Bones of contention: Clues to the first American. *Christian Science Monitor.* November 12.

Kolata, Gina

  1987. Are the horrors of cannibalism fact—or fiction? *Smithsonian.* 17(12): 150-170.

Korsmo, Fae L.

  1999. Claiming memory in British Columbia: Aboriginal rights and the state. *In* Troy R. Johnson, ed., *Contemporary Native American Political Issues*, pp. 119–134. Walnut Creek, CA: AltaMira Press.

Kroeber, Alfred L.

  1899. The Eskimo of Smith Sound. *Bulletin of the American Museum of Natural History.* 12(21).

  1917. Zuñi kin and clan. *Anthropological Papers of the American Museum of Natural History.* 18(2):39–204.

Kroeber, Theodora

  1964. *Ishi in Two Worlds: A Biography of the Last Wild Indian in North America*. Berkeley: University of California Press.

  1970. *Alfred Kroeber: A Personal Configuration*. Berkeley: University of California Press.

Kurin, Richard

  1997. *Reflections of a Culture Broker: A View from the Smithsonian*. Washington D.C.: Smithsonian University Press.

Kuznar, Lawrence A.

  1997. *Reclaiming a Scientific Anthropology*. Walnut Creek, CA: AltaMira Press.

Ladd, Edmund J.

  1995. Frank Hamilton Cushing at Zuni: One Hundred Years Later. Paper presented at the American Anthropological Association annual meeting, November, Washington, DC.

Larsen, Clark Spencer

  1997. *Bioarchaeology: Interpreting Behavior from the Human Skeleton*. Cambridge: Cambridge University Press.

Lasswell, Mark

  1999. The 9,400 year old man; The White House keeps trying to bury him; Scientists are furious. *Wall Street Journal.* January 8.

Lawson, Michael L.

  1994. *Dammed Indians: The Pick-Sloan Plan and the Missouri River Sioux, 1944-1980.* Norman: University of Oklahoma Press.

Leeming, David, and Jake Page

  1998. *The Mythology of Native North America*. Norman: University of Oklahoma Press.

Leeming, David, and Margaret Leeming

  1994. *A Dictionary of Creation Myths*. New York: Oxford University Press.

Lehmann-Hartleben, K.

  1943. Thomas Jefferson, archaeologist. *American Journal of Archaeology.* 47(2):161–163.

Lekson, Stephen H.

  1988. The idea of the kiva in Anasazi archaeology. *The Kiva.* 53(3):213–234.

Lesser, Alexander

  1981. Franz Boas. *In* Sydel Silverman, ed., *Totems and Teachers: Perspectives on the History of*

Anthropology, pp. 1–34. New York: Columbia University Press.

Liberty, Margot

1976. Native American "Informants: The contributions of Francis La Flesche. *In* John V. Murra, ed., *American Anthropology: The Early Years*, pp. 99–110. 1974 Proceedings of the American Ethnological Society: St. Paul: West Publishing Company.

1978. Francis La Flesche: The Osage Odyssey. *In* Margot Liberty, ed., *American Indian Intellectuals*, pp. 45-59. 1976 Proceedings of the American Ethnological Society: St. Paul: West Publishing Company.

Limerick, Patricia Nelson

1987. *The Legacy of Conquest: The Unbroken Past of the American West*. New York. W. W. Norton & Company.

Lowie, Robert H.

1913. Review of *The Omaha Tribe* by Alice Fletcher and Francis La Flesche. *Science* 37: 910–915, 912.

1915. Oral tradition and history. *American Anthropologist* 17: 597–599.

1917. Oral tradition and history. *The Journal of American Folk-Lore*. XXX (CXVI):161–167.

Lurie, Nancy Oestreich

1966a. The Lady from Boston and the Omaha Indians. *The American West*. 3(4):31–33, 80–85.

1966b. Women in early American anthropology: Ethnographer on the Northwest Coast. *In* June Helm, ed., *Pioneers of American Anthropology: The Uses of Biography*, pp. 29–84. Seattle: University of Washington Press.

1998. Selective recollections on anthropology and Indians. *Current Anthropology*. 39(4):572–574.

Lyon, Edwin A.

1996. *A New Deal for Southeastern Archaeology*. Tuscaloosa: University of Alabama Press.

Lyons, Chief Oren, and John Mohawk

1992. *Exiled in the Land of the Free: Democracy, Indian Nations, and the U.S. Constitution*. Santa Fe: Clear Light Publishers.

Malone, Dumas

1951. *Jefferson and the Rights of Man*, Volume 2 of *Jefferson and his Time*. Boston: Little, Brown and Company

Mark, Joan

1980. *Four Anthropologists: An American Science in Its Early Years*. New York: Science History Publications.

Marks, Jonathan

1995. *Human Biodiversity: Genes, Race and History*. New York: Aldine de Gruyter.

1998. Replaying the race card. *Anthropology Newsletter*. 39(5):1, 4.

Martin, Debra L.

1998. Owning the sins of the past: Historical trends, missed opportunities, and new directions in the study of human remains. *In* Alan H. Goodman and Thomas L. Leatherman, eds., *Building a New Biocultural Synthesis: Political-Economic Perspectives on Human Biology*, pp. 171–190. Ann Arbor: University of Michigan Press.

McGee, W J, W. Holmes, F. Powell, A. Fletcher, W. Mathews, S. Cullin.

1900. Frank Hamilton Cushing. *American Anthropologist* (New Series) 2: 354-404.

McGuire, Randall H.

1992. Archeology and the first American. *American Anthropologist*. 94(4):816–836.

1997. Why have archaeologists thought the real Indians were dead and what can we do about it. *In* Thomas Biolsi and Larry J. Zimmerman, eds., *Indians and Anthropologists*, pp. 63–92. Tucson: University of Arizona Press.

McLaughlin, Robert H.

1998a. The Antiquities Act of 1906: politics and the framing of an American anthropology & archaeology. *Oklahoma City University Law Review*. 25(1&2): 61–91.

1998b. The American archaeological record: authority to dig, power to interpret. *International Journal of Cultural Property*. 7(2):342–375.

Mead, Margaret

1932. *The Changing Culture of an Indian Tribe*. New York: Columbia University Press.

1972. *Blackberry Winter: My Earlier Years*. New York: Simon and Schuster.

Means, Russell, with Marvin J. Wolf

1995. *Where White Men Fear to Tread*. New York: St. Martin's Griffin.

Meighan, Clement

1985. Archaeology and anthropological ethics. *Anthropology Newsletter*. 26(9):20.

1994. Burying American archaeology. *Archaeology*. 47:6, 64–68.

Meltzer, David

1983. The antiquity of man and the development of American archaeology. *Advances in Archaeological Method and Theory*, 6:1–51.

1991. Review of *Monte Verde, vol. 1* by Tom D. Dillehay. *Archaeology*. 93(3):739.

1993. *Search for the First Americans*. Washington, DC: Smithsonian Institution Press.

1997.Monte Verde and Pleistocene peopling of the Americas. *Science*. 276:754–755.

1998.Introduction.*In* Ephraim G. Squier and Edwin H. Davis, *Ancient Monuments of the Mississippi Valley*, pp. 1–96. Washington D.C.: Smithsonian Institution Press.

Meltzer, David J., Donald K. Grayson, Gerardo Ardila, Alex W. Barker, Dena F. Dincauze, C. Vance Haynes, Francisco Mena, Lautaro Nuñez, and Dennis J. Stanford

1997.On the Pleistocene antiquity of Monte Verde, southern Chile. *American Antiquity*. 62(4):659–663.

Michener, James A.

1989. *Caribbean*. New York: Fawcett Crest.

Mihesuah, Devon A.

1996a. Repatriation: An interdisciplinary dialogue. *American Indian Quarterly*. 20(2):153-307.

1996b. American Indians, anthropologists, pothunters, and repatriation: ethical, religious, and political differences. *American Indian Quarterly*. 20(2):229–237

Miller, John J.

1997. Bones of contention. *Reason*. 39(5):52–54.

Minthorn, Armand

1996. Human remains should be reburied. Confederated Tribes of the Umatilla Indian Reservation (www.umatilla.nsn.us/kennmn.html).

Moffitt, John F., and Santiago Sebastián

1996. *Brave New People: The European Invention of the American Indian*. Albuquerque: University of New Mexico Press.

Momaday, N. Scott

1996. Disturbing the spirits: Indian bones must stay in the ground. *The New York Times*. November 2.

Moodie, D. Wayne, A. J. Catchpole, and Kerry Abel

1992.Northern Athapaskan oral traditions and the White River volcano. *Ethnohistory*. 39(2):148–171.

Morell, Virginia
    1998. Kennewick Man: More bones to pick. *Science*. 279:25–26.
Morgan, Lewis Henry
    1851. *League of the Ho-de-no-sau-nee, or Iroquois*. Rochester: Sage and Broa.
    1870. *Systems of Consanguinity and Affinity of the Human Family*. Washington: Smithsonian
    Institution .
    1876. The hue and cry against the Indians. *The Nation*. July 20.
    1877. *Ancient Society*. New York: World Publishing.
Morison, Samuel Eliot
    1974. *The European Discovery of America: The Southern Voyages, 1492-1616*. New York: Ox-
    ford University Press.
Moses, L. G.
    1996. *Wild West Shows and the Images of American Indians 1888-1993*. Albuquerque: Uni-
    versity of New Mexico Press.
Moses, Yolanda
    1997. An idea whose time has come again: Anthropology reclaims "race." *Anthropol-
    ogy Newsletter*. 38(7):1, 4.
    1999. Race, higher education, and American society. *Journal of Anthropological Research*.
    55(2):265–278.
Nabokov, Peter (ed.)
    1991.*Native American Testimony: A Chronicle of Indian-White Relations from Prophecy to the Pre-
    sent*. New York: Penguin Books.
Nelson, Nels
    1919.Human culture. *Natural History*. 19(2):131–187.
    1933.The antiquity of man in American in the light of archaeology. *In* Diamond Jen-
    ness, ed., *The American Aborigines, Their Origin and Antiquity*, pp. 87-130. Victoria,
    Canada: University of Toronto Press.
Nichols, George P. and Thomas D. Andrews (eds.)
    1997. *At a Crossroads: Archaeology and First Peoples in Canada*. Burnaby, B.C.: Archaeology
    Press, Simon Fraser University.
O'Harra, Doug
    1998. Cave of the Sea Traveler. *Anchorage Daily News*.
Oakley, Kenneth P.
    1964. The problem of man's antiquity: an historical survey. *Bulletin of the British Mu-
    seum, Geology*. 9(5):83–155.
Oxendine, Joseph B.,
    1995. *American Indian Sports Heritage*. Lincoln: University of Nebraska Press.
Pääbo, Svante
    1993. Ancient DNA. *Scientific American*. November, 269(5): 87-92.
Pandey, Triloki Nath
    1972. Anthropologists at Zuni. *Proceedings of the American Philosophical Society*.
    116:321–37
Paquette, Robert L., and Stanley L. Engerman (eds.)
    1996. *The Lesser Antilles in the Age of European Expansion*. Gainesville: University Presses
    of Florida.
Parker, Dorothy R.
    1992. *Singing an Indian Song: A Biography of D'Arcy McNickle*. Lincoln: University of Ne-
    braska Press.

Patterson, Thomas C.
  1995. *Toward a Social History of Archaeology in the United States*. Ft. Worth: Harcourt Brace.
Pearce, Susan M.
  1992. *Museums, Objects, and Collections: A Cultural Study*. Washington D.C.: Smithsonian University Press.
Peden, William
  1954. Introduction. *In* Thomas Jefferson, *Notes on the State of Virginia*, William Peden, ed., Chapel Hill: University of North Carolina Press.
Petit, Charles W.
  1998. Rediscovering America: The New World may be 20,000 years older than experts thought. *U. S. News & World Report*. 125(4): 56–64.
Pevar, Stephen
  1992. *The Rights of Indians and Tribes: A Basic ACLU Guide to Indian and Tribal rights*. 2nd ed. Carbondale: Southern Illinois University Press.
Philp, Kenneth R.
  1999. *Termination Revisited: American Indians on the Trail to Self-determination, 1933-1953*. Lincoln: University of Nebraska.
Pope, Saxton T.
  1920. The medical history of Ishi. *University of California Publications in American Archaeology and Ethnography*. 13(5):175–214.
Preston, Douglas J.
  1986. *Dinosaurs in the Attic*. New York: St. Martin's Press.
  1989. Skeletons in the closet. *Harpers Magazine*, 278(1665): 66-75.
  1997a. Fossils and the Folsom cowboy. *Natural History* 106(1):16.
  1997b. The Lost Man. *The New Yorker*, 73(16): 70–81.
  1998. Skin & bones. *The New Yorker*, 73(46):52.
Protzman, Ferdinand
  1998. Justice delayed. *ARTnews*. December, pp.134-138.
Prucha, Francis Paul
  1984. *The Great Father: The United States Government and the American Indians*, Vols. I and II. Lincoln: University of Nebraska Press.
Raymond, Chris
  1990. Reburial of Indian remains stimulates studies, friction among scholars. *Chronicle of Higher Education*. (October 3), A13.
  1989. Some scholars upset by Stanford's decision to return American Indian remains for re-burial by tribe. *Chronicle of Higher Education*. (July 5), A4.
Rensberger, Boyce
  1997. Skeletons suggest Caucasoid Early American. *Washington Post*. April 15.
Richards, Horace G.
  1939. Reconsideration of the dating of the Abbott Farm Site at Trenton, New Jersey. *American Journal of Science*. 237(5):345–354.
Riding In, James
  1992. Six Pawnee crania: Historical and contemporary issues associated with the massacre and decapitation of Pawnee Indians in 1869. *Special Edition: Repatriation of American Indian Remains. American Indian Culture and Research Journal*. 16(2):101–120.
Ridington, Robin
  1992. A sacred object as text. *American Indian Quarterly*. 17(1):83–99.

Ridington, Robin, and Dennis Hastings
    1997. *Blessing for a Long Time: The Sacred Pole of the Omaha Tribe.* Lincoln: University of Nebraska Press.
Robbins, Catherine C.
    1999. Pueblo Indians receive remains of ancestors. *The New York Times.* May 23.
Roberts, David
    1996. *In Search of the Old Ones: Exploring the Anasazi World of the Southwest.* New York: Simon & Schuster.
Rockafeller, Nancy, and Orin Starn
    1999. Ishi's brain. *Current Anthropology.* 40(4):413–415.
Rohner, Ronald P.
    1966. Franz Boas: Ethnographer on the Northwest Coast. *In* June Helm, ed., *Pioneers of American Anthropology: The Uses of Biography,* pp. 149–212. Seattle: University of Washington Press.
Roosevelt, Theodore
    1887. *Winning of the West,* vol. 1. New York: G. P. Putnam's Sons.
Rosenstiel, Annette
    1983. *Red & White: Indians Views of the White Man.* New York: Universe Books.
Rydell, Robert W.
    1984. *All the World's A Fair: Visions of Empire at American International Expositions 1876–1916.* Chicago: University of Chicago Press.
Sagan, Carl
    1996. *The Demon-haunted World.* New York: Ballantine Books.
Sampson, Donald
    1997. Science has no compelling need to destroy part of the skeleton of Kennewick Man. *Insight.* December 22, p. 26.
Schlesinger, Arthur M., Jr.
    1992. *The Disuniting of America: Reflections on a Multicultural Society.* New York: W. W. Norton & Company.
    1998. *The Disuniting of America: Reflections on a Multicultural Society.* Revised and enlarged edition. New York: W. W. Norton & Company.
Schneider, Alan L.
    1998. Kennewick Man update. *Anthropology Newsletter.* September, pp. 22–24.
    1999. Kennewick Man myths. *Anthropology Newsletter.* April, pp. 21–22.
Sellers, Charles Coleman
    1980. *Mr. Peale's Museum.* New York: W. W. Norton. Shanachie Entertainment Group
    1994. *Ishi: The Last Yahi.* The American Experience.
Shanklin, E.
    1994. *Anthropology and Race.* Belmont, CA: Wadsworth Publishing.
Sheehan, Bernard
    1974. *Seeds of Extinction: Jeffersonian Philanthropy and the American Indian.* New York: W. W. Norton.
Sheffield, Gail K.
    1997. *The Arbitrary Indian: The Indian Arts & Crafts Act of 1990.* Norman: University of Oklahoma.
Silberman, Neil A.
    1998. Invisible no more. *Archaeology.* Nov/Dec: 68–72
Silverberg, Robert
    1968. *Mound Builders of Ancient America: The Archaeology of a Myth.* Greenwich, CT: New

York Graphic Society, Ltd.

Simmons, Marc
1979. History of the Pueblos since 1821. *In* Ortiz, Alfonso Wilcomb, ed., *Handbook of North American Indians*, Vol. 9:206–223. Washington DC: Smithsonian Institution Press.

Slayman, Andrew L.
1997. A battle over bones. *Archaeology*. Jan/Feb:16–23.

Smith, Paul Chaat, and Robert Allen Warrior
1996. *Like a Hurricane: Red Power from Alcatraz to Wounded Knee*. New York: The New Press.

Smiley, B.
1999. Sand Creek massacre. *Archaeology* Nov./Dec: 22.

Stanford, Dennis
1997. Interview. http://www.nmnh.si.edu/arctic.

Stannard, David E.
1992. *American Holocaust: Columbus and the Conquest of the New World*. New York: Oxford University Press.

Stanton, William
1960. *The Leopard's Spots*. Chicago: University of Chicago Press.

Starkey, Armstrong
1998. *European and Native American Warfare 1675-1815*. Norman: University of Oklahoma Press.

Steiner, Stan
1987. *The Vanishing White Man*. Norman: University of Oklahoma Press.

Stocking, George
1983. Anthropologists and historians as historians of anthropology. *In* George Stocking, ed. *Observers Observed: Essays on Anthropological Fieldwork*. Madison: University of Wisconsin Press.

Stocking, George W., Jr. (ed.)
1968. *Race, Culture, and Evolution: Essays in the History of Anthropology*. New York: Free Press.
1974. *The Shaping of American Anthropology: 1883-1911: A Franz Boas Reader*. New York: Basic Books, Inc.
1985. *Objects and Others*. Madison: University of Wisconsin Press.
1988. *Bones, Bodies, Behavior: Essays on Biological Anthropology*. Madison: University of Wisconsin Press.
1989. *Romantic Motives*. Madison: University of Wisconsin Press.

Stone, Anne C., and Mark Stoneking
1993. Ancient DNA from a Pre-Columbian Amerind population. *American Journal of Physical Anthropology* 92: 463–471.

Strickland, Rennard
1997. *Tonto's Revenge*. Albuquerque: University of New Mexico Press.

Sturtevant, William C.
1983. Tribe and state in the sixteenth and twentieth centuries. *In* Elisabeth Tooker, ed., *The Development of Political Organization in Native America: 1979 Proceedings of the American Ethnological Society*, pp. 3-16. Washington D.C.: The American Ethnological Society.

Swann, Brian, and Arnold Krupat, eds.
1987. *Recovering the Word: Essays on Native American Literature*. Berkeley: University of

California Press.

Swanton, J. R. and Dixon, R. B.
1914. Primitive American history. *American Anthropologist.* 16:383.

Swidler, Nina, Kurt E. Dongoske, Roger Anyon, and Alan S. Downer
1997. *Native Americans and Archaeologists: Stepping Stones to Common Ground.* Walnut Creek, CA: AltaMira Press.

Swisher, Karen
1989. Skeletons in the closet. *The Washington Post,* October 3.

Szathmary, Emoke J. E.
1993. Genetics of aboriginal North Americas. *Evolutionary Anthropology.* 1(6):202-220.

Thomas, David Hurst
1998. *Archaeology,* third edition. Fort Worth, TX: Harcourt Brace.

Thomas, David Hurst, Jay Miller, Richard White, Peter Nabokov, and Philip J. Deloria
1993. *The Native Americans.* Atlanta: Turner Publishing Company.

Thomas, W. Stephen
1955. Arthur Caswell Parker: 1881-1955. *Rochester History.* 17(3):1–30.

Thornton, Russell
1987. *American Indian Holocaust and Survival: A Population History Since 1492.* Norman: University of Oklahoma Press.
1990. *The Cherokees: A Population History.* Lincoln: University of Nebraska.

Tieri, Michael Two Horse
1997. What kind of beef are we talking here? *Red Ink.* 5(2):18–21.

Trachtenberg, Alan
1982. *The Incorporation of America: Culture and Society in the Gilded Age.* New York: Hill and Wang.

Trigger, Bruce
1980. Archaeology and the image of the American Indian. *American Antiquity* 45(4):662–676.
1984. Alternative archaeologies: nationalist, colonialist, and imperialistic. *Man.* 19:355–370.
1985. The past as power: anthropology and the North American Indian. *In* Isabel McBryde, ed., *Who Owns the Past?* pp. 49–74. Oxford: Oxford University Press.
1986. Prehistoric archaeology and American society. *In* Meltzer, David J., Don D. Fowler, and Jeremy A. Sabloff, *American Archaeology Past and Future: A Celebration of the Society for American Archaeology,* pp. 187–216. Washington D.C.: Smithsonian Institution Press.
1989. *A History of Archaeological Thought.* Cambridge: Cambridge University Press.

Turner, Christy
1986. What is lost with skeletal reburial. *Quarterly Review of Archaeology.* 7(1):1.

Turner, Frederick W., III
1971. *I Have Spoken: American History through the Voices of Indians.* Athens, OH: Swallow Press.

Tyler, S. Lyman (ed.)
1988. *Two Worlds: The Indian Encounters with the European, 1492-1509.* Salt Lake City: University of Utah Press.

Ubelaker, Douglas, and Lauryn Guttenplan Grant
1989. Human skeletal remains: Preservation or reburial? *1989 Yearbook of Physical Anthropology* 32: 249-287.

Vickers, Scott B.
  1998. *Native American Identities: From Stereotype to Archetype in Art and Literature*. Albuquerque: University of New Mexico Press.
Vitalianao, Dorothy
  1973. *Legends of the Earth*. Bloomington: Indiana University Press.
Vizenor, Gerald (ed.)
  1989. *Narrative Chance: Postmodern Discourse on Native American Literature*. Albuquerque: University of New Mexico Press.
  1990. *Crossbloods*. Minneapolis: University of Minneapolis Press.
Walker, Deward E.
  1990. Anthropologists must allow American Indians to bury their dead. *Chronicle of Higher Education* (12 September); also letters to the editor on same subject, October 10.
Walker, Phillip L.
  1999. Bioarchaeological ethics: A historical perspective on the value of human remains. [in press]
Washburn, Wilcomb E.
  1994. *Red Man's Land, White Man's Law*, 2nd ed. Norman: University of Oklahoma Press.
Weaver, Jace
  1997. Indian presence with no Indians present: NAGPRA and its discontents. *Wicazo Sa Review*. 12(2):13–30.
Weisman, George, et al. (eds.)
  1981. *Buffalo Bill and the Wild West*. Pittsburgh: University of Pittsburgh.
Welch, John R.
  1997. White eyes' lies and the battle for DZH NCHAA SI'AN. *American Indian Quarterly*. 21(1):75–109.
West, Frederick Hadleigh (ed.)
  1996. *American Beginnings: The Prehistory and Paleoecology of Beringia*. Chicago: University of Chicago Press.
West, W. Richard, Jr., and Kevin Gover
  1988. The Struggle for Indian Civil Rights. *In* Frederick E. Hoxie, ed., *Indians in American History*, pp. 275–293. Arlington Heights, IL: Harlan Davidson.
White Deer, Gary
  1997. Return of the sacred. *In* Nina Swidler, Kurt E. Dongoske, Roger Anyon, and Alan S. Downer, eds., *Native Americans and Archaeologists: Stepping Stones to Common Ground*, pp. 37–43. Walnut Creek, CA: AltaMira Press.
White, Leslie A.
  1973. The anthropologist and the American Indian. *Newsletter of the American Anthropological Association*, 14(6):2.
White, Richard
  1991. *The Middle Ground: Indians, Empires, and Republics in the Great Lakes Region, 1650-1815*. New York: Cambridge University Press.
Wilford, John Noble
  1991. *The Mysterious History of Columbus: An Exploration of the Man, the Myth, the Legacy*. New York: Alfred A. Knopf.
  1997. Excavation in Chile pushes back date of human habitation of Americas. *New York Times*.

1999. New answers to an old question: Who got here first? *The New York Times*, November 9.

Willey, Gordon R., and Jeremy A. Sabloff
1993. *A History of American Archaeology*, third edition. San Francisco, CA: W. H. Freeman.

Wilson, Samuel M. (ed.)
1997. *The Indigenous People of the Caribbean*. Gainesville: University of Press of Florida.

Winsor, Justin
1995 [1884]. *Native American Antiquities and Linguistics*, edited by Anne Paolucci and Henry Paolucci. Jamaica, NY: St. Johns Press.

Wolf, Eric R.
1981. Alfred L. Kroeber. *In* Sydel Silverman, ed., *Totems and Teachers: Perspectives on the History of Anthropology*, pp. 35–66. New York: Columbia University Press.
1994. Perilous ideas: race, culture, people. *Current Anthropology.* 35(1):1–11.

Wolpoff, Milford, and Rachel Caspari
1997. *Race and Human Evolution*. New York: Simon & Schuster.

Woodard, Charles L.
1989. *Ancestral Voice: Conversations with N. Scott Momaday*. Lincoln: University of Nebraska Press.

Zimmerman, Larry J.
1989a. Made radical by my own: an archaeologist learns to accept reburial. *In* R. Layton, ed., *Conflict in the Archaeology of Living Traditions*, pp. 60–67. London: Routledge.
1989b. Human bones as symbols of power: aboriginal American belief systems toward bones and 'grave-robbing' archaeologists. *In* R. Layson, ed., *Conflict in the Archaeology of Living Traditions*, pp. 211–216. London: Routledge.

INDEX